Communication and Simulation: From Two Fields to One Theme

INTERCOMMUNICATION SERIES

INTERCOMMUNICATION 4
Series Editors: Howard Giles and Cheris Kramarae

Communication and Simulation: From Two Fields to One Theme

Edited by

David Crookall and Danny Saunders

MULTILINGUAL MATTERS LTD
Clevedon · Philadelphia

Lovingly dedicated to our close relatives who have helped us in more ways than we can tell

Rebecca, Hilde and Robert, Jean and Michel
and
Gail and Oliver, Gene and Islagh, Simon

Library of Congress Cataloging-in-Publication Data

Communication and simulation.
(Intercommunication ; 4)
Bibliography: p.
Includes index.
1. Communication—Simulation methods.
I. Crookall, David. II. Saunders, Danny.
III. Series: Intercommunication (Clevedon, England) ; 4.
P93.6.C66 1988 001.51 88-5279

British Library Cataloguing in Publication Data

Communication and simulation : from two fields to one theme—(Intercommunication; 4).
1. Communication. Analysis. Use of simulation games
I. Crookall, David II. Saunders, Danny
III. Series
001.51

ISBN 0-905028-85-6
ISBN 0-905028-84-8 Pbk

Multilingual Matters Ltd

Bank House, 8a Hill Road
Clevedon, Avon BS21 7HH
England

&

242 Cherry Street
Philadelphia, PA 19106–1906
U.S.A.

Typeset by Mathematical Composition Setters Ltd, Salisbury
Printed and bound in Great Britain by WBC Print, Bristol

Contents

Preface ix

SECTION ONE: INTRODUCTION

1 Towards an Integration of Communication and Simulation
David Crookall and Danny Saunders 3

SECTION TWO: MEANINGS AND REALITIES

2 Gaming/Simulation: A Gestalt Communications Form
Richard D. Duke 33

3 Game Identities and Activities: Some Ethnomethodological Observations
David Francis 53

4 Discourse Rehearsal: Interaction Simulating Interaction
Stuart J. Sigman and Anne Donnellon 69

5 Computerised Simulation as Mediator of Language
Edward B. Versluis, Danny Saunders and David Crookall 82

6 Our Multicultural Global Village: Foreign Languages, Simulations and Network Gaming
David Crookall, Rebecca Oxford, Danny Saunders and Roberta LaVine 91

SECTION THREE: SOCIAL RELATIONS

7 Knowing Oneself: A Symbolic Interactionist View of Simulation
Charles F. Petranek 109

8 Problem-solving and Decision-making Skills in Deaf and Partially Hearing-impaired Groups
James J. Fernandes and Martin Noretsky 117

9 Simulation as a Basis for Consciousness Raising: Some Encouraging Signs for Conflict Resolution
Dennis J. D. Sandole 127

10 Transcending Role Constraints through Simulation
Marvin D. Jensen 141

11 Simulation as a Preparation for Communication in Counsellor Training
Anne B. Pedersen and Paul B. Pedersen 147

12 Culture, Prejudice and Simulation/Gaming in Theory and Practice
Jenny Noesjirwan and Klaas Bruin 155

13 Intergroup Communication and Simulation in Low- and High-context Cultures
Stella Ting-Toomey 169

14 Individual and Organisational Communication and Destructive Competition
John F. Lobuts and Carol L. Pennewill 177

SECTION FOUR: ORGANISATIONS AND INSTITUTIONS

15 Simulations for Learning about Communication
Stewart Marshall 191

16 Business Games: From Business Schools to Business Firms
James M. Freeman and Philippe Dumas 201

17 Understanding Organisational Communication Processes: The Use of Simulation Techniques
Alan Coote and Laurie McMahon 214

18 Simulation and Communication in Women's Networks: Power and Corporate Culture
Barbara B. Stern 226

19 Policy Formation through Simulation and Communication
Jan Klabbers and Jeff Hearn 236

20 The Manipulation of Information in Urban Planning and Simulation
Hubert Law-Yone 247

21 Media Simulations
Danny Saunders, Tim O'Sullivan and David Crookall 256

SECTION FIVE: DISCUSSION

22 Extending the Range of Experience
Cathy Stein Greenblat 269

References 284

Associations and Periodicals 323

Contributors 325

Index 327

Preface

This book was prompted by our concern for the present state of teaching and learning practices. Having experienced 'good' practices (either through attendance at various simulation conferences or through witnessing eagerness and interest in our own students) we wished to ask why such practices were not as widespread as we think they should be. Whenever terms like 'good' or 'should' are mentioned there must be some degree of bias, and we freely admit such a bias towards alternatives to the talk-and-chalk tradition still all too common in many schools, colleges and training units. We hope that this book will contribute to the current moves towards educational modes which also involve learning by doing, rather than those which exclusively require people to sit passively in front of pedagogic dinosaurs.

It is not that experiential learning is anything new; primary school teachers have been doing it for years. It seems somewhat ironic, though, that children so often find learning enjoyable and actually look forward to school, whcrcas many older students dread the next class. In further and higher education, the dominance of the word 'lecture', and the existence of a profession of 'lecturers', underlies this hidden agenda. In recent years the establishment of academic and practical debates about communication, and the emergence of entire courses on it (e.g. Communication Studies) have inevitably highlighted questions about what is and should be happening between *people* (rather than students and teachers). These questions are not recent either; the quotations which follow were written, respectively, over 25 years and nearly 20 years ago. But they are almost as relevant today as they were when they were first published. There has been a shift over the last few years, and the ideas expressed are more familiar and widely accepted; had they been written today, the following quotations would probably have sounded less urgent and more optimistic—or would they? That, however, is a question more appropriately answered individually by readers of this book.

> In our junior schools, particularly, we have learned the value of making poems, stories, plays, figures, models, music, dance. ... But

> the major limitation now built into this kind of teaching is that it is regarded as a form of *play*. This means that at a certain age it can be safely dropped, and put away with other childish things. ...
>
> But these creative activities are also forms of work: for many adults, the work to which they give their whole lives. It is only the prejudice of a very narrow and early industrial society that the value of these activities is seen as a sort of harmless and indifferent play or therapy. From these activities comes much of man's real society, and they should be given that kind of respect throughout education (Williams, 1962; emphasis in original).

> There is no way to help a learner to be disciplined, active and thoroughly engaged unless he perceives a problem to be a problem or whatever is to be learned as worth learning, and unless he plays an active role in determining the process of solution. That is the plain unvarnished truth, and if it sounds like warmed-over 'progressive education', it is none the less true for it. ...
>
> We have largely trapped ourselves in our schools into expending almost all of our energies and resources in the direction of preserving patterns and procedures that make no sense *even in their own terms*. They simply do not produce the results that are claimed as their justification in the first place—quite the contrary.
>
> The new education can be achieved in a number of ways. ... Although the word 'game' has connotations that are not usually associated with intellectual growth, there are few concepts or skills that could not be learned with a rare degree of understanding and durability through an educational game approach. In fact, a 'game approach' permits the development of a learning environment that is much more congruent to what we know about learning than any other approach now used in schools (Postman & Weingartner, 1969; emphasis in original).

Our interests are in simulations which recognise (rather than take for granted) the importance of communication dimensions and perspectives. The chapters in this volume can be considered as collectively constituting a new, if not radical, discussion on both communication and simulation. In bringing together such a diverse set of points of view, we hope that the reader will gain an insight into the multi-faceted dimensions of both the role of communication in simulation and the contribution that simulation may make to communication.

The contents of this book have been organised so as to allow a broad coverage of viewpoints and dimensions. The five sections in the book cover a wide range of issues and perspectives. Section One contains just one chapter (by David Crookall and Danny Saunders), which discusses the nature of each field (communication and simulation) taken separately, and then attempts an outline unification.

Sections Two, Three and Four move from micro to macro considerations, while the last section provides a summing up. Section Two, 'Realities and Meanings', contains six chapters. Both communication and simulation essentially depend on the realities of creating, negotiating and interpreting meanings and on the meaning of realities. Chapter 2, by Richard Duke, discusses various communication modes, and shows how simulation may be conceived as a particularly powerful communication form, which can, far more effectively than language, encourage understanding of complexity and convey holistic insight. Chapters 3 and 4 employ the tools of ethnomethodology to analyse aspects of communication within simulation and of communication as simulation. David Francis introduces, in Chapter 3, the notion of 'double-settingedness' which accounts for the ways in which participants create identities, embedded in communicative activities in a business game, by drawing upon common-sense knowledge and ordinary communicative competencies. Stuart Sigman and Anne Donnellon, employing a more dramaturgical orientation, discuss in Chapter 4 how people plan for and practise future communicative events. They show how such discourse rehearsal is a form of natural simulation, but also how such rehearsal may itself take place within a formal setting; we thus have simulation of communication within simulation. Chapters 5 and 6 examine how simulation may encourage the development of first language and foreign language skills. In Chapter 5, Edward Versluis, David Crookall and Danny Saunders briefly review ways in which first language communication patterns are shaped by the configuration of computerised simulations, ranging from communication between participants to communication between machine and participant. Chapter 6, by Rebecca Oxford, Roberta LaVine, David Crookall and Danny Saunders, outlines how the growth in multilingual communication and the increasing communicative emphasis of foreign language instruction have lead to greater use of simulation for the development of foreign language communication skills.

Section Three, 'Social Relations', covers two of the most studied areas of interest to simulation theorists and designers: interpersonal and intergroup communication. Chapter 7, by Charles Petranek, links one of the more powerful sociological theories dealing with play—symbolic interactionism—to simulation, and shows how, through communication, simulations offer the potential of better knowing one's social self. In Chapter 8,

James Fernandes and Martin Noretsky discuss how, in a college for deaf students, the use of simulation develops two interrelated communication processes: language and social skills (in English and American Sign Language), and the breaking down of barriers between groups of different fluency. Issues of co-operation and conflict are addressed by Dennis Sandole in Chapter 9. Provided that we are aware of the potential negative effects of conflict, simulations can encourage co-operative communication, especially when futile zero-sum situations are discussed. Chapter 10, by Marvin Jensen, discusses the playing of multiple roles in simulation, and how this may be therapeutic for those exposed to situations where contradictory communications produce personal stress. Anne and Paul Pedersen continue the theme of therapy and self-discovery in Chapter 11, but focus on how simulation can help develop certain critical communication skills needed in counselling contexts. Prejudice and discrimination, and ingroups and outgroups, are discussed by Jenny Noesjirwan and Klaas Bruin in Chapter 12. The authors emphasise the potential of simulation as a communication aid in the exposing and then the reducing of prejudice and discrimination. Chapter 13, by Stella Ting-Toomey, presents aspects of low- and high-context cultures that are characterised by different communication styles, norms and expectations. Simulation proves to be a useful device for illustrating different perspectives on culturally-bound communications. Finally, John Lobuts and Carol Pennewill discuss, in Chapter 14, the very important aspect of the destructive and competitive communication patterns in simulation, especially in zero-sum situations. Many 'successful' simulations subtly communicate deep-grained competitive values to participants, and we should be aware of these pitfalls.

Section Four moves on to concerns more closely associated with institutions and organisations. In Chapter 15, Stewart Marshall traces the institutional development of various strands in Communications Studies courses, and shows, through examples, how simulation may contribute to a greater integration of theory and practice in such courses. In Chapter 16, James Freeman and Philippe Dumas show how the use of simulation can provide students with a bridge between, as well as alter the communication patterns in, business education and training. Moving on from here, in Chapter 17, Alan Coote and Laurie McMahon walk us through a series of simulations designed to highlight certain types of communication process in organisations, and show how simulation may help in communicating about organisational communication. In Chapter 18, Barbara Stern shows how simulation can be used to help women understand corporate culture and increase the effectiveness of women's networks both internally and as a means for achieving greater power within corporations. Chapter 19, by Jan

Klabbers and Jeff Hearn, deals with the problems and importance of communication processes in simulations of policy-making and planning systems within the frameworks of incrementalism and decrementalism, and with how simulation may help us analyse communications in such systems. A specific instance of this interest is discussed, in Chapter 20, by Hubert Law-Yone. He tackles problems of communication and information control in urban phenomena and in simulations thereof and makes the important point that, if the communication processes in the system are not clearly mapped out, then any simulation of that system is likely to result in spurious outcomes. Chapter 21, by Tim O'Sullivan, Danny Saunders and David Crookall, deals with mass communication, and in particular with how simulation may help in understanding media processes, and how media simulation may help in analysing interactional processes.

Section Five, like the first, contains just one chapter, by Cathy Greenblat. This concluding discussion ties together some of the major issues raised in the book, outlines some future research themes that might be based on the preceding chapters, cautions us about allowing our enthusiasm to portray too rosy a picture of our endeavours, and finally emphasises 'the enormous power of simulation/communication tools to expand the range of experience of participants'.

Both communication and simulation are essentially practical pursuits, but they can be subjected to close analytical and theoretical scrutiny. Books on communication generally contain theoretical interpretations of practical events, processes and productions; many books on simulation tend to have a more practical bent, in that they present ready-to-use or adaptable exercises—sometimes accompanied by some background discussion. This volume does not contain any ready-to-use exercises (although many are referenced). It is a multi-perspective and interdisciplinary discussion on the connections between the two fields of communication and simulation, and presents a more theoretical and analytical, even philosophical, view of the interconnections between the two fields. But through such an examination, the contributors to this book unearth the assumptions underlying the practitioner's resources employed and deployed in the activities of communication and simulation. An examination of communication and simulation as one theme thus holds some interest for the practitioner, too, in that it renders more visible that upon which s/he relies for the successful achievement of the more practical communication and simulation matters. It is our view that practitioners, as well as theorists, will ignore the points made throughout these chapters at their and, crucially, their students' peril; and researchers, too, may need to reassess their paradigms in the light of many of the points made.

All the chapters in this book, including our own, have gone through many revisions. However, all the contributors have responded with understanding and unflinching enthusiasm to our often incessant demands, and over the last two-and-a-half years the various chapters have gradually taken shape. We believe not only that each one now constitutes a unique contribution to the separate literatures on communication and on simulation, but also that collectively they form the first attempt at unifying two extremely fluid fields. We have few illusions about this attempt at unification; it will suffer the inevitable fate of being proven faulty in many ways. 'What [we] are hoping for is that it will be found to contain a shadowy pattern of truth' (Koestler, 1964).

Our sincere thanks, therefore, go to the contributors; without them this volume would not have been written; and without any one contributor this book would be incomplete. Cathy Greenblat deserves special thanks for accepting the difficult task of writing the discussant chapter. Rod Watson has taken a close interest in this volume, and did much to encourage us during difficult times. A great many colleagues and friends have inspired or helped us in numerous ways, and we cannot name them all here. But, we particularly wish to acknowledge: Jon Wilkenfeld and Dick Brecht (University of Maryland, USA), Don Thatcher and June Robinson (Solent Simulations, UK), Alan Coote (Polytechnic of Wales, UK); also Chris Higley and Henry Thompson (University College Cardiff Computer Centre) and Ray Kingdom and David Morgan (Polytechnic of Wales Computing Centre) for their help in solving our electronic mailing problems; and our copy editors Richard Leigh (UK) and MaryAnn Zima (USA). Finally, we express gratitude to Mike Grover, the Publisher, and the *Intercommunication* Series Editors, Howard Giles and Cheris Kramarae, for their patience, encouragement, and critical acumen during the gestation period of this book.

David Crookall, Le Pradet, France
Danny Saunders, Dinas Powys, Wales
December 1987

SECTION ONE: Introduction

1 Towards an integration of communication and simulation

DAVID CROOKALL
The Pennsylvania State University, U.S.A.
and
DANNY SAUNDERS
The Polytechnic of Wales, UK.

> The time will come when the Universal Declaration of Human Rights will have to encompass a more extensive right than man's right to information, first laid down 21 years ago in Article 19. This is the right to communicate (D'Arcy, 1969).
>
> As the world's favourite airline, British Airways has always recognised the importance of good communication with its passengers (from *HighLife Magazine*, May 1987).

The above quotations emphasise two aspects of communication: the right to communicate and the importance of good communication. This book is about communication and about a particular methodology called 'simulation'. But it is more than that: its underlying aim is to unify these two fields into one theme. To achieve this aim, our authors explore the reasons why and the ways in which communication and simulation may be seen as mutually interdependent. Various aspects of this relationship are analysed on a number of levels, and from a variety of perspectives and disciplinary standpoints.

New themes of study often emerge from a bringing together of previously disparate disciplines. For example, social psychology 'joined' with language studies to create the social psychology of language. We do not expect this book to give birth to a new discipline of, say, 'communicative simulation' or 'simulative communication'. However, there exist a sufficient number of powerful reasons to consider communication and simulation as one theme.

The linkages between communication and simulation are not always easy to establish, because the two fields are separated by convention and even by established academic philosophy. Communication has become an area of study, whereas simulation (while also the object of much study) is conventionally viewed as a technique, technology, or methodology. Each field has developed important and well-established academic agendas, rich with theory, research, and practical applications. But this, if anything, also tends to mask their potential interdependence.

The underlying interrelatedness between communication and simulation, however, is becoming increasingly apparent, can be found at different levels, and is of several types. One set of direct connections is to be found in the way the two fields already make use of each other, in the way other fields make use of both communication and simulation, and in the isomorphism of their respective features. Simulation is proving to be an extremely powerful means of studying communicational processes. Communication researchers have made frequent use of simulation for observation and analysis of communication patterns and training in communication skills, largely because communication plays such a vital role in simulation performance. Such applications serve to illustrate how many common subject areas are addressed by both communication and simulation. Moreover (and consequently), many of the subject areas in which communication is important are also the ones which tend to make most use of simulation.

The two fields of communication and simulation are both by their very natures essentially interdisciplinary. Communication has long been recognised as such, bringing together such diverse disciplines as psychology, sociology and linguistics. By contrast, simulation has only recently enjoyed the academic limelight, and is now rapidly moving from a somewhat fragmented and 'nomadic' multi-disciplinary status towards unified interdisciplinarity.

We emphasise that both communication and simulation depend on rules, symbols and codes—the very basis of language. Both involve models, representations, realities, and negotiated meanings. Later on in our introduction, these and other complementary features will be discussed in a little more detail. Such characteristics of communication and simulation are examined throughout the chapters of this book from several perspectives (including, among others, practical, theoretical, positivist and interpretivist), as well as through the eyes of different disciplines or specialisms (e.g. foreign language learning, media, urban planning, and ethnomethodology). In so doing, the volume also explores how simulation may be used to study communicational processes and phenomena (whether it be for education, training or research), while at the same time demonstrating how we may benefit from paying greater attention to communicational aspects of simulation.

Our aim, in this introductory chapter, is largely of an orientational kind; so, rather than outline each paper individually we shall confine ourselves to a more general commentary. We first discuss the nature of each field (communication and simulation) taken separately, and then attempt an outline unification of the two fields by further discussing the above similarities. Finally, we mention how these are organised within the volume.

Communication

Communication has, in recent years, become a popular theme for eclectic discussions that cannot easily be contained within any one conventionally defined discipline, and has attracted scholars from many areas. Communication is now widely recognised as a vital resource on many fronts. This is reflected, for example, by the heated debates going on in various international forums on the right to communicate, by the UN proclamation of 1983 as World Communications Year, by the rapidly expanding field of Communication Studies and, above all, by the heightened awareness of the central importance of communication in many other related disciplines, such as sociology, social psychology, sociolinguistics, social psychology of language, foreign language learning, management studies, economics, politics, international relations, media studies, urban planning, policy-making, education and computing. Here we present a definition of communication, outline its scope, summarise factors leading to a general increase in communication, touch on the concept of communication as a basic human right, and mention some barriers to communication.

Scope and nature of communication

As Fisher (1982) succinctly puts it, 'Life depends on communication'. It is thus crucial to the continuation of the human race, so before discussing definitions, we wish to highlight the importance and ubiquity of communication. These are captured in the following extract from the well-known

MacBride Report (MacBride *et al.*, 1980):

> Communication maintains and animates life. It is also the motor and expression of social activity and civilization ... it creates a common pool of ideas, strengthens the feeling of togetherness through exchange of messages and translates thought into action, reflecting every emotion and need from the humblest tasks of human survival to supreme manifestations of creativity—or destruction. Communication integrates knowledge, organization and power and runs as a thread linking the earliest memory of man to his noblest aspirations ... Self-reliance, cultural identity, freedom, independence, respect for human dignity, mutual aid, participation in the reshaping of the environment—these are some of the non-material aspirations which all seek through communication. But higher productivity, better crops, enhanced efficiency and competition, improved health, appropriate marketing conditions, proper use of irrigation facilities are also objectives—among many others—which cannot be achieved without adequate communication.

This quotation also embodies assumptions about what communication is. Any general term attracts a multitude of definitions, and 'communication' is no exception. One of the most dominant, yet unsatisfactory, sets of definitions centres on the concept of information flow, and on the sending of signals. Consequently, catchphrases and key queries emerged, such as 'Social interaction through messages' (Lundberg, 1939), and 'Who says what in which channel to whom with what effect' (Lasswell, 1948). At the base of such theorising there lay assumptions about channels, senders and receivers, and above all about *transmission*. For years, the most popular model was Shannon & Weaver's (1949) mathematical formulation of communication as a linear, one-way process. This suited those disciplines which were interested in, and even trying to emulate, science and technology. After all, information theory has much appeal to a researcher who values a perspective based on making accurate and quantitative measurements of systems and their components. DeFleur's (1970) development of the Shannon & Weaver model attempts the ultimate in such mechanistic reductionism by drawing a circular diagram to represent a fundamentally linear framework. This is like attempting, as it were, to fit a square peg into a round hole. Frustrations with information perspectives gradually emerged. Somehow, the 'heart' of communication was missing while discussion of such phenomena as feedback, entropy, redundancy and noise abounded—usually with a preference for putting communication into little ethereal boxes. We are brought back to earth by Cheery's (1957) reminder that 'communication is essentially a social affair', which recognises the priority of conversation and language. These involve human participants rather than inanimate senders and receivers pumping information along channels; to put it another way, communication is more than two robots on the telephone.

In the wake of this reductionist view, a new school emerged that saw communication as the dynamic creation, interpretation, negotiation and exchange of patterns, processes and meanings by individuals and social groups (Fiske, 1982; O'Sullivan *et al.*, 1983). The major interest now focuses on aspects of negotiation and interpretation between parties who are actively involved with the social situation, and who may construct a variety of meanings that are rooted in cultures, media and society. The concept of message is now replaced by *text*, something which can be read (and even 'deconstructed'). There is no longer an exclusive interest in whether a 'message' is 'received'. Instead, there is analysis of institutions and agencies which construct texts according to power relations within society, and of the ways in which dominant readings of these texts prevail. Of course, the concept of 'text' includes much more than the printed word; it also refers to television, radio, cinema and computer productions. But problems appear when the concept of text is applied to *people*.

The emerging tradition in Communications Studies has thus addressed two major corner-stones: media and culture. Occasionally authors have overstated their case; witness McLuhan's (1964) famed assertion that 'the medium is the message'. Despite such overexcitement, what emerges from a negotiated meaning perspective on communication is a valuable focus on codes, signification and their contexts. Any recognition of agreed systems for signs and symbols puts language at the centre of communication. Moreover, sign systems are constantly being modified and may even be radically restructured; communication is therefore viewed as a qualitative dynamic process rather than as a quantitative static entity.

The is not the place for a detailed historical review of communication research.[1] What should be emphasised, though, is that both schools of communication prevail today, and are associated with the chapters contained within this volume. Although something of an overgeneralisation, it may be said that the first school of information transmission tends to be associated with American theorising, traditional psychology, and management science, while the second school of meaning negotiation is more closely linked with European thinking, sociology, language, and English studies. Having said this, we should also recognise the actual and potential overlaps between the two schools, their terminologies (e.g. one talks about the 'receiver', while the other discusses 'audience') and research interests (e.g. the effects of new technology in society).

The expansion of communication

But why or how has communication come to be considered as so important in recent times, and not just by academics? As a consequence of technological innovation, the world is becoming smaller, and is doing so at an ever-increasing rate. When this recognition is combined with a general increase in population and with a growing imbalance in access to ever scarcer resources, then interests in communication become paramount, and not simply for esoteric reasons.

It is difficult to differentiate between the causes and effects of increased communication; it seems to be a chicken-and-egg question. For example, has communication led to greater international trade, or has trade resulted in more communication? The relationship is more spiral-like than circular. Certain types of increased communication, especially international communication, can be traced to technological advances over the last half-century, such as in air travel, radio, cars, TV, satellites and, of course, military hardware. Some of these advances have enabled trade to increase, which in turn has required even faster and denser communications, which have led to increased trade. Thus, more trade entails more communication, which enables (or, indeed, engenders) more trade.

> One of man's earliest preoccupations has been to increase the impact, diversity and intelligibility of his messages, while simultaneously developing his capacity to intercept and decipher them (MacBride *et al.*, 1980).

Apart from communications technology itself, the exponential increase in communication generally and at all levels of human activity, can be seen in many areas. Whether these are causes, effects or symptoms is beyond our present discussion; but we may mention the following, among others: population movements of various kinds and for a variety of motives; the growing self-awareness of ethnic groups and, often, their desire for independence from nation states; the ever increasing complexity of politics both within and among nations; the increase in travel; the explosion in media (telephones, television, satellites, networks, etc.); the proliferation of publications of all kinds, the never ending depletion of natural resources (such as the Amazon forest); and, last but not least, the wars waged in many corners of the world.

To illustrate the dominant attitude towards new communications developments as well as the widespread failure to realise how fast things are moving, we should like to quote at length from the keynote address, given by the distinguished engineer and writer, Arthur C. Clarke, at the UN on

World Telecommunications Day, 17 May 1983. Clarke had already shown in 1945 that communications and broadcast satellites were perfectly feasible, some 20 years before the first one was launched. The importance of a new invention is not always easy to assess, as Clarke (1983) points out:

> When news of A. G. Bell's invention reached the U.K. the chief engineer of the British Post Office failed to be impressed. 'The Americans', he said loftily, 'have needed the telephone, but we do not. We have plenty of messenger boys.' ... In contrast to the British engineer, the mayor of a certain American city was wildly enthusiastic. He thought the telephone was a marvellous device and ventured this stunning prediction: 'I can see the time', he said solemnly, 'when every city will have one'.
>
> Miracles of electronics that would have been beyond belief 20 years ago, the symbols that cross those digital displays, now merely give time and date. When the zeros flash up at the end of the century they will do far more than that. They will give you direct access to most of the human race, to the invisible networks girdling our planet. The long-heralded global village is almost upon us, but it will last for only a flickering moment in the history of mankind. Before we even realize that it has come, it'll be superseded by the global family.

The same might be said, *mutatis mutandis*, of simulation.

The right to communicate

These phenomena have given a new impetus to a long-standing debate on communication as a basic human right. Given the factors described above, communication is now recognised as a vital and ubiquitous resource for the world as a whole, and there is greater awareness of the importance and scope of communication as a moral entitlement rather than as a privilege.

> Communication is the basic human process not only in each local community but also in the emerging world community. The human communication process flows back and forth through every social institution and is essential to many aspects of human development. Consequently, the realization grows that everyone must have the right to communicate (Harms & Richstad, 1977).

However, defining something as a right does not automatically guarantee that it is possible to exercise it without impediment. The details are too long to relate here, but the debate covers such notions as what is to be defined as the right to communicate and what is to be done about the imbalance between the rich and the poor. Nevertheless, this debate can also be seen as an indicator or warning of impending problems, and the urgency with which they must be tackled.

Problems in communication

Despite the growth in communications of all types, and the increased awareness of the right to communicate, there may also be barriers and objections to such communication. The increase in communication has brought with it a multiplicity of problems. These include complexity (e.g. international relations), speed (e.g. satellite transmission), change, multilingualism, and the assertion of social and cultural identities. Indeed some of the factors which have lead to an increase in communication have also turned out to be doubled-edged swords; they have also put up communication barriers.

> As the world has advanced, the task of communication has become ever more complex and subtle—to contribute to the liberation of mankind from want, oppression and fear and to unite it in community and communion, solidarity and understanding. However, unless some basic structural changes are introduced, the potential benefits of technological and communication development will hardly be put at the disposal of the majority of mankind (MacBride *et al.* 1980).

A historical illustration might be the growth of the British Empire through military and economic conquest. As suggested by Billig (1982), domination of one society by another may be openly accomplished through force, and may also be achieved in a more closed fashion, through imperialism based on economic and cultural control. It is, therefore, strategically useful for an expanding society, should military invasion prove impossible, to establish communication links with another community possessing valuable resources. Although tempting offers might be made through what appears to be altruism and co-operative motives, in the long run there may be a loss of identity, language and even culture for the dominated side. Such possibilities have been explored by Tajfel (1982), Husband (1982), and Lawrence (1982) with reference to intergroup behaviour and racism in contemporary Britain, which can easily be traced back to a colonial past. It is thus important to recognise that cynical motives do arise for establishing and promoting communication, and to recognise the likely victims.

Barriers of whatever kind tend to generate a need to develop learning methods, which not only help people to learn about communication, but also help them learn to learn. The need to understand the nature of communication in all its interlocking facets, as well as the obstacles which impede communication, is thus more urgent than ever. One avenue of research into and study of communication which has proved to be increasingly fruitful and powerful is simulation. It is this to which we now turn.

Simulation

We have discussed various aspects of communication as a backdrop to our discussion on simulation. Here we will emphasise the potential interdisciplinarity of simulation, touch on the concept of simulation as a language for education, training and research, and analyse aspects of simulation as both representation and reality.[2]

In a similar way to communication, simulation has become a major area of activity and analysis that cannot be exclusively located within any one context. Simulation has come to be widely recognised as constituting a dynamic and powerful tool in the study of a whole range of phenomena and fields such as conflict, decision-making, language behaviour, intergroup relations, and cultural values. We emphasise that communication forms an integral feature of all these areas, indeed it is essential to most areas in which simulation is used.

Simulation, like communication, is thus characterised by its interdisciplinary potential. There has been widespread recognition, in a great many fields, of the powerful features of simulation as a tool of research, as an experiential study aid, and as a professional training instrument. The result is that in recent years simulation has witnessed a spectacular development for those purposes, as well as becoming a legitimate object of study in its own right.

Simulation as a language for learning

Duke (1974) has called simulation a language. Both simulation and language have their own vocabularies, syntax, meaning systems and analytic tools. We learn about the world in learning a language, and likewise the activity called 'simulating' is also learning about the world. Three ways of learning correspond to three main areas of simulation application: education, training and research. While the reasons for using simulation may differ from area to area, underlying them is a common belief (for any methodology ultimately requires an act of faith) that simulation can achieve certain objectives and accomplish certain things that other techniques cannot. These are often referred to as the 'advantages' of simulation. In education and training, three interrelated reasons are often cited. Simulation is much more motivating and more fun, it is more congruent with the learning process, and it is more like the 'real' world, than traditional classroom procedures. It is thus considered to result in more active participation, improved performance, greater retention, and better understanding of complexity. In research, simulations may be used, for instance, to generate data (e.g. for statistical analysis), as objects of study in themselves (learning about what happens in them), as measuring instruments (to test students), and as predictors (exploring how people perform in a given situation, or to gain insight into possible futures).

Representation and reality

There are two main ways of viewing simulations. One perspective sees them as merely *representations* of some other 'real worldly' system, and has been called the representational viewpoint. However, another, less commonly held view sees simulations as *operating realities* in their own right, i.e. as not necessarily having direct or explicit representational power or value. This may be termed the 'simulation-as-reality-in-its-own-right' viewpoint or the 'reality' perspective. Both these views are expressed, sometimes implicitly, across the chapters in this volume.

The usual assertion is that simulation somehow represents some (aspect of a) 'real' system, that it is a symbol with a referent, and thereby that it draws its essential meaning from that referent. However, participants do not necessarily see things in this way while they are participating. For them simulation is a very real experience, it is its own reality, which *might* also have relevance to some other world or system. In this lies the essential nature of the 'reality' perspective. Simulation is often defined as real by participants, and it may thus be conceived as a real world in its own right.

The two perspectives are not necessarily incompatible. Neither is sufficient to explain the phenomenon of simulation; both are necessary for a full understanding of what constitutes simulation. Debriefing is seen as an essential link between the two perspectives, allowing parallels to be drawn between the reality of the simulation performance and that of the 'real' (non-simulation) world.

The representational perspective

Within the 'representational' perspective we find such keywords as 'system', 'model', 'rule', 'simulation', 'game', 'role-play'—concepts which require elaboration. In brief, simulation is taken as a general category, which may contain elements of games and/or role-play. Games in the strict sense are seen to be the converse of simulation, though (perhaps paradoxically) simulation is able to incorporate game elements. Role-play is seen as simply one aspect of simulation; simulation may not always incorporate role-play, but a role-play is always a simulation. The concepts of role-play and game conjure up images of theatre or fantasy or competitions, where acting or playing rather than participating predominates. However, they are usually inspired by some kind of other external reality, so that actors or players can see some relevance to their actions. It is because of this underlying representational property that role-plays and games popularly form a sub-category of simulation. Having said this, we will shortly argue that games can (or should) technically be considered as the converse of simulation.

It is often said that a simulation is a special kind of model, representing a 'real' system. However, the essential nature of this 'specialness' is often glossed over. The difference between model and simulation hinges on two fundamental concepts: those of *rules* and *strategies*. The rules contained in the model determine the specific pattern of the simulation, while the strategic selection of moves made during the performance allows a simulation to evolve. Only rules may be represented in a model, whereas both rules and strategies operate in a simulation.

A simulation is like a map; indeed, the process of building a simulation is sometimes called 'mapping'. The two main uses of simulations are (a) to represent a so-called 'real world' system, and thereby (b) to reduce the cost of error for that system. These two features (representivity and error cost) are fundamental, and need to be examined in a little more detail.

Representation is achieved through at least two processes: abstraction and symbolisation. A simulation *abstracts* from the real system by way of conceptualisation, selection and simplification. The features abstracted from the system are mapped into the simulation by means of *symbols*. A simulation is a symbolic abstraction, or a metaphor, of a system; it is a kind of language.

The second characteristic of simulation is the relatively low *cost* of an error in the model, compared to that of a similar error in the 'real' system. One of the purposes of a simulation is to broaden and deepen participants' perceptions and interpretations of the 'real' world, while another is to refine their skills; both cases constitute learning. The drawback of performing for real is that the learner is prone to making mistakes which may be costly for the system (including the learner him/herself). So we replace the system with a replica.

Simulation thus protects people from otherwise severe consequences of their mistakes, and yet in so doing allows these mistakes to be examined. It provides learners with a relatively safe (or non-threatening) learning environment. The mistakes are made in the simulation, not in the outside world. However, a learner does not lose all fear of making a mistake just because s/he is in a simulation, for a simulation can become a totally real situation for participants (as we shall see later).

Games and role-play

The fact that the term 'play' is often associated with games highlights the relationship between games and the rehearsal functions of play in animal and human development. For present purposes, it is useful to reserve the term 'play' for particular types of enjoyable behaviour which, it should be remembered, are found both in everyday life and in games and simulations. Indeed, there is far more than just a passing resemblance between play behaviour in simulation and gaming and that to be found in ordinary life (Bruner *et al.*, 1976; Raabe, 1980). The term 'game' is often used to refer to simulation, but not always the other way about; and many instances of use require no distinction to be made—in which case the term 'gaming' is often used. There are two interpretations of the term 'gaming': a broad, everyday one (where 'game' is equated with 'simulation'), and a strict, technical one (where they are different but complementary concepts).

The fundamental difference between some game forms (in the strict technical sense) and simulations lies in the two major features discussed above—representivity and negligible error consequence. In terms of representivity and error cost, games show almost the contrary effects to simulations. In contrast to a simulation, a game (in our technical sense) is not always intended to represent any 'real-world' system (although it may have been inspired by one), and costs of game errors can be high for the 'real' world (as, for example, in losing money at poker). Both are related; consequences arise precisely because a game is not a representation. The cost of an error in a game is not *always* high, but the point is that it carries a potentially high penalty. This is readily admitted by all who play or watch games; a classic example is the nationalist fervour generated by the Olympic

Games, which is expressed, not only by those actually taking part, but well beyond the games themselves, by fans, sponsors and the like.

A game in the strictest sense, therefore, does not purport to represent any part of another system; it has no 'real-life' referent, and it is a 'real-world' system in its own right. A game is formally constructed as a kind of mini-system, which takes place or 'happens' along with other social (sub-)systems, whereas a simulation is a bracket, a hiatus, within the ongoing 'real-world' (sub-)systems. A game is a formalised system in its own right, while a simulation is a formalised representation of another system; a game is a 'real' system, and a simulation a meta-system, but both are separated from the 'other external reality' by what Goffman (1972) terms a 'membrane'. Despite this technical distinction, some activities often referred to as 'games' actually simulate processes, and their substantive area is relatively unimportant, e.g. decisions are made in many types of context. Thus, some games aim to mirror various social processes; this is the usual sense of the term, not the technical one. General usage allows the terms 'urban gaming' and 'business game' but these should strictly be regarded as simulation.

It seems, then, that some types of game are, strictly, to be linked with 'reality', rather than with representation. However, if a game takes on representational value it should properly be regarded as simulation. Indeed, the kinds of game referred to in this volume tend to be those that mirror or parallel some part of a conceptualised 'real' system. This is the general meaning, and such games are to be equated with simulation. Debates about the differences between simulation and game continue, and the major journals within this field reflect a healthy willingness to compromise: *Simulation/Games for Learning* and *Simulation and Games*. Although the distinction is not crucial, it needs to be pointed out, and readers of this volume are invited to make up their own minds. For the time being, we accept the inherent ambiguity that arises from these terms, especially as they tend to be used interchangeably throughout the volume, as indeed they are in much of the literature on this topic. Rather than detracting from a fruitful discussion on simulation/gaming, such fluidity may even contribute to the debate by keeping doors open.

Concerning 'role-play', it is useful to consider this as a component embedded within simulation, rather than as a totally separate (albeit similar) type of activity. A role-play is always a simulation, but a simulation need not necessarily involve any significant role-playing. Role-play is usually defined as a social or human activity in which participants 'take on' and 'act out' specified 'roles', often within a predefined social framework or situational blueprint (a 'scenario'). This view, however, does not explicitly express the simulation aspect of role-play, and sees role-play as the generic category, rather than as a particular aspect of a more general activity—that of simulation.

In our view a role-play is always a simulation. The participant in a role-play performance is representing and possibly experiencing some character or stereotype known in everyday life. The interaction between participants in the role-playing performance is a simulation of a social situation. The distinction between role-play simulation and 'straight' non-role-play simulation is a question of degree, not of kind.

The reality perspective

Simulation is a model 'brought to life' by participants. In being activated, however, it gains autonomy and takes on a reality of its own, thereby leaving the domain of 'pure' representivity. During a simulation the notion or feeling of representivity becomes distilled, or is even lost. It is only within a simulation, as opposed to a model, that risks can be taken and errors experienced.

Thomas's (1951) well-known assertion that 'if men define situations as real, they are real in their consequences' implies that social behaviour proceeds from what participants decide is going on around them, and from the meanings attributable to that behaviour.[3] If participants define a simulation session as real, their behaviour and the meanings attached to it will be taken as real for all practical purposes. Because participants define the simulation activity as real, the consequences of that activity are experienced as real. Moreover, 'human beings respond to others, not according to external, structural causes, but according to their understandings, that is to their definition of the situation. People react to a "situation" or to a social object, *as they see it*' (Lee, 1987; emphasis in original). Thus, participants in a simulation will respond not merely to its objective features, but mainly to the meanings the simulation experience has for them. And as Keats (1819) said, 'Nothing ever becomes real till it is experienced'. It is through the experience furnished by a simulation that it becomes real. One might broaden Thomas's assertion to say that a situation is defined as real if you are involved with it. The value of simulation lies in its potential for allowing participants to create their own realities, and to experience the consequences of behaviours in those realities. These very real consequences, though, remain largely within the bounds of the simulation activity. Participants are able to experiment (test hypotheses) in the simulation without the fear that any errors will have the same consequences as they would in the 'real' (non-simulation) world—yet at the same time they are able to experience, as well as examine, those consequences.

A simulation, like any social situation, is socially constructed and thus open to varying interpretation through negotiation. A real situation, whether simulation or any other, is one in which participants are personally involved, and in which they may 'live through' its dynamics—its social relations, issues, problems. Indeed, during a performance, participants may not be explicitly aware of 'simulating'; they do not continually ask themselves 'what does this represent?' in terms of the 'real' world. This is precisely because they get involved, and the performance becomes very real in its own terms; it is the paramount, taken-for-granted reality. Just as in the 'real' world, simulation participants define their own simulation meanings, and meanings form the bedrock of socially negotiated realities. If simulation is regarded and treated as a 'reality' taken for granted in its own right, then the experiences of participants become 'real', and they are able to live through and live out one of the fundamental aspects of social life—that of the reality-defining process.

Indeed, much of what happens in a simulation is a result of what participants 'import' from the 'real' world by virtue of the fact that most simulations, being social situations, powerfully mobilise participants' common-sense cultural understandings and competencies as ordinary society members. The participants themselves both make the situation real and respond to that reality. This is because, as social actors, we are all individually and collectively both producers and products of our socially defined and negotiated realities, whether this be in 'society' or in those short episodes we call 'simulation'.

Linking the two perspectives

Debriefing is the process in which participants and organiser together critically appraise simulation activities and behaviours. It is in the debriefing that 'ex-participants' can reflect on and examine what happened in the simulation. During simulation, participants may at times be aware of the other (non-simulation) world, but essentially they will be, as it were, locked into the reality mode; their situation will be the paramount reality. On leaving the simulation reality, one of the purposes of debriefing is to allow simulation-bound mistakes to be discussed openly and dispassionately, and thus to encourage lasting positive consequences in the 'real' world, rather than negative costs.

Debriefing allows parallels to be drawn between simulation realities and 'real' realities; it allows realities to be examined in a new, more 'realistic' light. Participants can then export the learning and insights gained to their other 'real' (non-simulation) world. In the debriefing, however, participants will consider the experience from both the representational and the reality perspectives, and thus attempt to tie the two together in a creative and insightful appraisal of both realities: that of the simulation and that of the 'real' world. Many consider debriefing to be the most important part of the simulation methodology—yet it is the least discussed in the literature.

In some areas of social science, the achievement of internal validity (where the exercise is taken seriously and matches the investigator's aims) resembles the reality dimension or mode we have evoked. We can also shift into external validity (where the exercise has clear relevance to the mundane world), which reflects the representational perspective. Indeed, although they are not usually referred to as such, many social psychological experiments[4] can easily be regarded as simulation, in which both the representational and reality perspectives can be seen to be working. They were not naturally occurring events, but situations set up expressly for the purposes of research, to produce data. As such they were situations considered as valid, albeit sometimes oversimplified, reflections of similar naturally occurring situations (previous events, dilemmas, and the like). In other words, if the experimenters are to be believed, the experimental situations were characterised by external validity, and thus were considered to represent or simulate the natural situations. However, for their data to be considered as valid, the researchers necessarily assumed that the experimental situation constituted a real experience for the subjects—that it had internal validity—otherwise the subjects' actions could not be counted as reliable or congruent. Many experimental situations are indeed simulations, albeit relatively tightly controlled ones, and they should show both external and internal validity; in other words they are both representative and very real events for the subjects or participants. We should also note, however, frequent criticisms of some laboratory-based experiments because of a failure to achieve both internal and external validity, a disregard for ethical considerations, or a rushed and even non-existent debriefing (for further discussion see Harré, 1979; Aronson, 1984). In sum, representation (i.e. recognition of the parallel between the experimental situation and the naturally occurring one) and reality (i.e. experience of the experiment as a real situation) are very strongly linked in many simulations and experiments, and so organisers and researchers need to go through, if not fairly elaborate, certainly often extended, debriefing sessions.

Interdependence and aims

Having discussed communication and simulation separately, we would now like to outline their mutual interdependence and highlight some of the ways in which they may be conceived as forming a single theme. We then summarise how we have attempted to do this in the way the book is organised.

Interrelations and connections

Both fields of communication and simulation are essentially interdisciplinary; communication has more clearly recognised this, while it has yet to be made explicit for simulation. Such double interdisciplinarity, as well as the similarity of disciplines covered by the two fields, highlights their potential interrelatedness. It should, therefore, prove fruitful, both for interdisciplinary pursuits *per se* and for the two fields themselves, to treat them as one theme. This volume explores the interdisciplinary nature of both fields, their interrelatedness and growing interdependence, while integrating them into one theme on a number of complementary levels and from a multi-perspective standpoint.

Our own interests developed out of two complementary realisations: first, that communication is central to any understanding of simulation, whether theoretical or in terms of the participants' experience; and second, that simulation itself can contribute to our understanding of commercial processes, whether they be in practical educational contexts or in more theoretical research. One cannot ultimately use or study simulation without attending to the communications of participation. From the moment simulation is envisaged, a whole series of communicational issues are raised. Even in the simpler experimental situations, such as in the PRISONER'S DILEMMA game,[5] many questions related to the form and content of communication arise (for a review see Eiser, 1980).

One major criticism that can be levelled at much simulation literature, especially that produced during the 1960s and 1970s, is its failure to address some of the fundamental issues associated with social interaction in simulation contexts. This has generally resulted in fragmentary discussions, all too often limited by the 'splendid isolation' of positivist rationality. No firm link between the various issues has so far been established, nor yet based on any unifying criteria. By contrast, communication has become a reasonably integrated domain and has produced a plethora of analyses by authors from a variety of backgrounds. In essence, communication already claims a measure of *inter*disciplinarity, whereas simulation has tended to remain *multi*-disciplinary, and is keenly looking round for a unifying framework. We believe, therefore, that the linking of communication and simulation within one volume will do two things: it should further increase the scope of communication analysis, and perhaps more importantly, it should break new ground in the search for theoretical unity in the 'world' of simulation.

Thus two related aspects of communication and simulation which provide strong links are the inherent interdisciplinarity of each field and the vast range of common subject areas. Moreover, many of these subject areas are common to both fields; subject areas in which communication is important are the ones which tend to make most use of simulation (e.g. sociology, planning, language learning, social psychology, decision-making, policy formation, media studies). However, they are also becoming increasingly interdependent in two other respects, which have already been touched upon. The vital role of communication in simulation is becoming apparent, and this is related to the increasing importance being attached to communicational phenomena in a great many subject areas (such as those mentioned above). We have also begun to see the usefulness of simulation in exploring communicational processes, to realise that simulation is uniquely suited to exploring many aspects of communication involved in a wide variety of areas, especially those in which various forms of social interaction play an important role. This has resulted in two further developments. First, gamers (or 'simulators') are becoming more aware of the need to examine the communication patterns that evolve during simulation. Second, the introduction of simulation into courses on whatever subject-matter inevitably increases the types, complexity and importance of communication patterns during the course.

These connections in turn reveal a number of further links, some of which we shall briefly mention. Simulations offer much for the two schools of communication discussed previously. If information flow and transmission channels are discussed, then simulation packages offer a wealth of data for subsequent analysis. If negotiated meaning perspectives are preferred, then participants' viewpoints and identities become paramount, as do content analysis of simulation texts, and the interpretation of power relations within simulation groups. Ironically, the wealth of material generated by simulations has increased dramatically in recent years, not least because of greater access to audio-visual equipment, itself a feature of communications technology. Both communication and simulation involve the use of sign and symbol systems, e.g. language. Indeed, simulation has been conceived of as a language (Duke, 1974), while communication makes use of various languages. Language, and to a lesser extent other sign systems, form the bricks and mortar of both simulation and communication; both depend upon language for their operation. Communication between people (and between people and technology) consists largely, though not exclusively, of language behaviour. As we have seen in the previous section, simulation is often considered as modelling, while communication has been the object of model-building. Indeed, communication is made possible only because the communicating entities operate with implicitly or even ostensibly similar models, and a simulation is often used to help learners understand these structural relations by providing them with a model. However, we should be wary of an exclusive concern with models and modelling; this has recently become the object of some serious misgivings (see, for example, Anderson, 1987; Berlinski, 1976).

We have been at pains to demonstrate that simulation is both representation and reality. It is not at all far fetched to consider communication from these perspectives either. Simulation, as we have mentioned, has traditionally been considered as being essentially a representation with a referent. Many forms of communication can indeed be seen as prime examples of representations, the most pressing of these being language. De Saussure's (1916) terms 'signifier' and 'signified' could easily be used in the simulation literature. Mass media is another example of a communication form simulating or representing a world beyond the message. Taking the complementary perspective of reality construction, there are close parallels between simulation and communication, as both can be considered as forms of reality construction. Communication is a central component in the construction of realities; only by being able to communicate are people able to construct their social realities. It is indeed through communicative behaviour that participants, during simulation, construct their game realities. Both communication and simulation involve representations and create realities. One of the most distinctively human characteristics is the capacity to communicate verbally; language is the principal medium by which humans negotiate and interpret meaning, represent and attribute meaning to the world, interact socially, and create social realities. It is not fortuitous that language is the key pillar in Berger & Luckmann's (1966) well-known *The Social Construction of Reality* (where they show that language has both representational and reality-producing power), nor that language and communication are high on the agenda of many disciplines interested in social realities. Simulation performance also involves the negotiation of meanings, while communication is often defined as such. Simulation performance depends on communication, and communication can be simulated. Certain communication forms can be considered as simulations, while simulation as a form of language can be thought of as a means of communication. In many ways the ultimate conclusion of such theorising is that communication is simulation is communication. Some of the above ideas are neatly and insightfully summed up and linked to experience, the primary purpose of simulation, by MacBride *et al.* (1980): 'Meaning is in fact created by the receiver in the light of the experience which he already possesses. Experiences and language are thus the pre-conditions of all acts of communication.'

Communication is also important in another aspect of simulation: design. Simulation design is a complex process, and has attracted much attention (see, for example, Greenblat, 1987c; Jones, 1986). An understanding, not only of the nature of simulation, but also of communication, is important to any design endeavour. Indeed, as Hubert Law-Yone (Chapter 20) clearly emphasises, unless the communication patterns in the referent system have been carefully and accurately modelled, any simulation based upon that model is likely to lead to spurious outcomes. Another concern is communication between gamers on the design process (see Crookall *et al.*, 1987), but of particular importance for the simulation/gaming endeavour is communicating to non-gamers about the design process. Simulation design is sometimes regarded by certain sections of academia as not constituting valid research or academic activity. The design process, on the contrary, may involve research that is often more complex and difficult than 'ordinary' research. (See Greenblat, 1987b, for an excellent discussion on these issues.) Thus an understanding of how communication and simulation interrelate should help in the design process.

Obstacles

Because of these and other links discussed in the subsequent chapters of this volume, the growing interdependence of communication and simulation is becoming increasingly apparent. However, there are major hurdles which confront scholars who seek such interdependence. We have noted that communication has gained interdisciplinary ground, while simulation has tended to remain more multi-disciplinary. One reason for this is that whenever methodologies are examined, the diverse applications tend to be concerned with their own fields and see little interest in pursuing fields seemingly unrelated to theirs. Moreover, as in our case of simulation, the sheer variety of applications tends to obscure any search for cohesion and unity, especially in its early development. One other reason for this inter- versus multi-disciplinarity is that simulation has generally been viewed as merely a methodology, whereas communication enjoys greater variety of interpretation and legitimacy. A field, such as communication, which has been imbued with greater social and political acceptability will more easily gain recognition (mainly through, and in the form of, resources), and thus the means to acquire interdisciplinarity. This contrasts with simulation, which has not enjoyed the attention it deserves (particularly in communication literature), for reasons which we now outline.

A serious objection to any 'merger' between communication and simulation might stem from Communication Studies (sometimes called the 'modern sociology') because of its tendency to distrust particular uses of simulation by other 'dominant discourses', e.g. by such authorities and disciplines as the police and mainstream psychology, which may be seen as legitimatised and legitimating institutions. In essence, if simulation is viewed as a powerful tool for maintaining control and power structures, it will be seen as a formidable weapon at the personal and social, even international, levels. There are clear reasons for such suspicion. After all, simulations are often used to find and test a winning strategy within competitive situations, or even as a means to rehearse methods to cope with threats to, and so-called breakdowns in, the social order. Some communication theorists may criticise and even condemn simulations because their findings justify, maintain or perpetuate social inequalities. Examples of simulations which have proved useful for powerful authorities and nations include Sherif's (1966a; 1966b) and Deutsch's (1973) research on de-escalating conflict between groups. As noted by Horowitz (1970) and Billig (1976), conclusions about trust and communication derived from games of conflict and strategy (especially wargames) may even provide scientific justification for an aggressive nation's entire foreign policy.

How does simulation/gaming reply to this type of objection? One possibility is to separate the above genre of wargames from mainstream simulation, but, as we have previously argued, the distinction between games and simulations is fraught with philosophical and conceptual problems. Moreover, it is not even the term 'game' which is problematic, 'war' being the operational word here. A second, and pessimistic, possibility involves total rejection of simulation activity because it offers potentially threatening information. We argue that this would be something of a paranoid reaction, which only leads to dogmatism and isolationism within Communication Studies, which should, on the contrary, be aware of paying too much attention to media sensation about certain high-profile laboratory simulations, if any discipline should; after all, it is in the communication literature that moral panics are most often discussed. Moreover, such engrained mistrust or even defiance is liable to turn any viable values system on its head, for there are other far more dangerous things that need to be eradicated—nuclear weapons and hunger, to mention but two examples. Looked at optimistically, we would even say that simulation, rather than doing any harm, may contribute in some small way to educating about these issues.[6] Some elements of the educational, academic and research communities have yet to recognise the full potential of simulation as it is practised by the majority of gamers, i.e. by people who genuinely wish to see changes for the better, and who are fully aware of the pitfalls. Potential threat can be seen in almost any new methodology or technology (see the quotation above from Clarke about the telephone). And any tool can be viewed as a potential weapon; imagine confiscating the mechanic's spanner because it might one day be used to bolt the gates in a lock-out. Instead, the focus should be as much on the underlying rationale, and even on the production of academic research, as on the methods employed.

A third and more optimistic stance takes the view that the rehearsal of communication through simulation encourages awareness of the futility of zero-sum strategies and outcomes. Consequently, and as noted by Schelling (1966), simulations may have much value in preventing conflict, rather than in encouraging it. Furthermore, constructive solutions emerge more frequently from simulations than do destructive consequences, although we should be aware of the destructive potential that is inevitably there (as emphasised by Lobuts & Pennewill in Chapter 14). Finally, social abuse does not miraculously appear because of a research method or educational technique; once appropriate channels for funding research and education have been opened, political and even military influences tend to emerge in almost every methodology. It is unfortunate that simulations which resulted in less than positive outcomes have received so much publicity at the expense of other aspects of simulation activities and research, and especially when these other areas are diametrically opposed to the promotion of conflict and aggression. But then one does not often expect to see the good news hit the headlines.

Organisation of contents

Within the general theme of communication *and* simulation, at least six interrelated and overlapping sub-themes both highlight this interdependence and summarise some of the points made above: simulation *for* communication; communication *through* simulation; simulation *via* communication; communication *in* simulation; simulation *of* communication; communication *about* simulation. The underlying aim of this volume is thus to show how we may integrate the two fields of simulation and communication into one theme. This implies four further objectives. One is that of fostering interdisciplinary discussion of simulation through emphasising issues of communication that have already been extensively discussed within a range of social sciences. The second, and complementary, major objective is that of extending the interdisciplinarity of communication through the experience and concepts of simulation. A third objective is to explore how simulation may be used to study communicational processes and phenomena, whether it be for education, training or research. Reciprocally, and at the same time, the fourth objective is to demonstrate how we may benefit from paying greater attention to communicational aspects of simulation performance. In essence, these objectives should create a gestalt effect wherein the whole is more than the sum of the parts.

Five major sections have been selected for organising the chapters in this book. At this point we must recognise an inherent problem associated with any work that aims for interdisciplinarity: organisation of material. If there is more than one way of looking at something or writing about it, then there is likely to be a number of acceptable permutations of perspectives, subject-matter, methodologies, and so on. There are doubtless alternative plans that would have been suited to the volume's broad aim of integrating our two fields, but the plan chosen at least has the advantage of being relatively simple, and conceptually the three central sections move from the micro to the macro.

Sections One and Five each contain just one chapter. The chapter in *Section One* is a general introduction to the connections between communication and simulation, while the chapter in *Section Five* provides a discussion based on the other chapters and ties together the various threads running through them.

Section Two, on 'Meanings and Realities', is fundamental. Because both communication and simulations essentially depend on the realities of creating, negotiating and interpreting meanings and on the meaning of realities, this area appears as the most obvious introductory section for the book. Such issues form the basis of discussions on simulation as a form of language and communication, on analyses of communication patterns within simulations, on communication behaviours that appear as simulations for rehearsing future situations, and on using simulation to encourage communicative language work. Obviously, there are limitations to what can be done here, for this area alone would probably warrant a whole book in itself.

Section Three covers a whole range of 'Social Relations', from individual, through interpersonal, to intergroup communication. This second section reflects the popular, if simplistic, definition of communication as 'social interaction through messages'. Simulation research has examined issues such as prejudice, social skills, role-playing and leadership, all of which involve communication processes. However, such relevance is rarely made explicit in the literature. Furthermore, simulation research within this area remains unsatisfactory on a number of counts, yet such criticism remains relatively scarce. One objective of this section is therefore to integrate simulation research and practice with theories of social interaction. Here, chapters look at such issues as social identities, destructive competition, conflict, multiple roles, counsellor training, prejudice and discrimination, and intergroup communication.

Section Four concentrates on 'Organisations and Institutions'. Relevant subject areas for discussion include Communications Studies in educational institutions; business gaming as a means of moving from educational institutions to business organisations; types of organisational communication; a specific area of organisational communication, that of women's networks; the wider problems of communication in policy formation; the control of communication by institutions involved in urban planning; and finally, the media institutions. Again, such discussion is essentially interdisciplinary: at one end of the continuum it concentrates on the study of the social status of the individual whilst at the other it accounts for aspects of social structure and ownership of control.

So, to recap, the overall objective of the volume is to move towards an integration of the two fields of communication and simulation into one theme. This means concentrating as much on process as on product or outcome. It also means tackling the theme from both fields. From one field, a new synthesis shows how simulation contributes to our understanding of communication. From the other, the synthesis shows how a keener awareness of communicational phenomena helps our understanding of simulation. Moreover, the interdisciplinary natures of both fields complement each other on many levels, and greater interdisciplinarity is achieved by bringing both fields closer together. We contend that this kind of interdisciplinary endeavour is probably more powerful than looking at just one field in terms of the other. Both communication and simulation have much to contribute to each other if they can be combined together to form a new whole.

The importance of interdisciplinarity is not always recognised, either by gamers ('simulationists') or by communications scholars. Neither has the interrelatedness of communication and simulation yet become an important focus for discussion. The linkages between communication and simulation are, nevertheless, fast becoming a central issue in both fields. Scholars and practitioners are becoming increasingly aware that studying communicational phenomena and simulation techniques from a single perspective is at best only scratching the surface of the richness and complexity of the processes and issues involved. Unifying these two interdisciplinary fields into one theme and dealing with them from an integrated multi-perspective standpoint should go some way towards generating new ideas that are the offspring of interdisciplinary endeavour.

Concluding remarks

Taken together, the chapters in this volume offer a provocative and intriguing set of ideas, and highlight a variety of perspectives on a whole host of questions. One major question for the future is whether these varied perspectives and analytic paradigms are incompatible or irreconcilable, each leading to views and even developments which cannot be contemplated together, except during moments of creative leaps. Although certain perspectives may be seen as mutually incompatible, e.g. 'Lee (1987) and Sharrock & Anderson (1987) suggest [that] the establishment of a relationship between conversational analysis and linguistics is highly problematic' (Button & Lee, 1987), a range of 'frameworks', even if divergent, is necessary to understand our two fields of communication and simulation, as well as to draw out the interconnections between them. We believe that the different approaches represented in the chapters in this book complement each other in ways that are essential to a complete picture of the wealth offered and sought by the communication and simulation/gaming endeavour.

The need to understand and to accept other cultures is more urgent than at any time in the history of humankind. These cultures may be ethnic or national, but cultures have also built up around academic and practical pursuits (see, for example, Snow, 1959). Simulation has a culture of its own, and so does communication as a field of study, if only in their use of jargon. As Jorgensen (1983) reminds us: 'Communication is to understand and to be understood'. Both simulation and communication need to understand each other in better and more varied ways; moreover, each can help us provide a better understanding of the other—communication enables us to understand simulation, and simulation does much to help us understand communication. Communication between the two fields should help us to draw them together as one theme.

The chapters in this volume, both individually and collectively, integrate communication and simulation. We are concerned about the paucity of published material that specifically addresses the theme of communication and simulation. The volume demonstrates how contrasting perspectives, especially when dealing with two complementary and interdisciplinary fields as a unified theme, can produce a fruitful cross-fertilisation of ideas, push forward our current thinking in these two fields, and advance our understanding of such polymorphous concepts.

Notes to Chapter 1

1. The reader interested in detailed discussions on the various theories of communication is referred to: Corner & Hawthorn (1985); Curran *et al.* (1977); Fiske (1982); Gumperz & Hymes (1972); McQuail & Windahl (1981); O'Sullivan *et al.* (1983); Saville-Troike (1982); Williams (1958; 1981).
2. This part of this chapter is a considerably condensed and slightly modified version of a much longer paper that originally appeared elsewhere, and the reader is referred to that paper (Crookall *et al.*, 1987) for a more detailed discussion of the issues raised. Extracts from that paper are reprinted by kind permission of SAGSET (see the section 'Sources and Resources' at the end of the book). Many people have inevitably had a considerable influence on the thinking outlined here. It is not possible to list all the authors whose work has helped to shape these ideas, but some of them should be acknowledged here: Bob Anderson, Peter Berger, Alan Coote, Richard Duke, Dave Francis, Howard Giles, Cathy Greenblat, Ken Jones, Arthur Koestler, David Kolb, Thomas Luckman, Neil Postman & Charles Weingartner, Alfred Schutz, Wes Sharrock, Henri Tajfel, Don Thatcher, Ludwig von Bertalanfy, and Rod Watson. (References to some of these people's works are given in the bibliography.)
3. Although formulated within the context of his discussion on the attribution of moral responsibility, Goffman's (1971) cautionary remarks are relevant here:

   > On the other hand, it is just as apparent that when all parties to an action agree as to its cause, they can, in terms of their own culture's selection practices, be wrong. Believing something is true makes it true (W. I. Thomas notwithstanding) if this belief so fits with other practices for assessing fact in the society that no contrary evidence would be possible in that society.

4. Examples of experiments that can be considered as simulations (for the purposes of research) include the following. Of particular note, especially because of their 'naturalistic' setting, are Sherif's summer camp experiments (Sherif *et al.*, 1961; Sherif, 1966a; 1966b; Sherif & Sherif, 1953). The series of experiments on intergroup relations by Tajfel and his colleagues, triggered by the famous minimal group discrimination experiments (Tajfel *et al.*, 1971; Billig & Tajfel, 1973), constitute more 'controlled' simulations. Zimbardo's controversial Stanford prison experiment (Haney *et al.* 1973; Zimbardo, 1969) is recognised by the researchers themselves as a simulation. A fourth example is of particular interest from a simulation perspective. This is Milgram's (1974) well-known studies on (simulations of) obedience to authority. In simulation research a number of

studies have specifically addressed media issues by way of replicating conditions associated with media processes (see also Chapter 21). Yet at no point has an attempt been made to link such simulation research with the more extensive literature on communication research. This is somewhat surprising when we consider the intriguing possibility of all media material being perceived as simulation by audiences. This, however, is a theme for future research. But to return to Milgram: his experiments/simulations were the inspiration of an excellent French film, entitled *I comme Icar*, directed by Henri Verneuil, with Yves Montand in the lead role. Taking our above speculation that a film may itself be considered or perceived as a simulation, we have here a situation in which a simulation (the experiment) is simulated by another (the film). The film simulation aims to communicate to the public at large something about the experiments, themselves a means for communicating to researchers something about authority.

5. Oppenheimer & Winer (1988) have designed an excellent computerised simulation, called COOPERATION AND CONFLICT, which may be set up to include experimental PRISONER'S DILEMMA situations in which communication patterns can be varied.
6. A few examples from just one area of urgent concern will illustrate our point: the AID COMMITTEE GAME provides insight into the processes of deciding priorities in giving aid; CAPJEFOS highlights substantive issues of rural development facing African and other nations; the DEVELOPMENT GAME examines development problems in underdeveloped areas; the GRAIN DRAIN brings home some of the truths about the trading and commercial relationships of the world's rich and poor countries; GUNS OR BUTTER deals with the problems of balancing national security and social and economic welfare; HUNGER ON SPACESHIP EARTH helps participants understand some of the inequities in the world social and economic situation and some of the feelings of helplessness and frustration they cause. And, of course, the chapters in this volume amply demonstrate that 'mainstream' simulation is dedicated to making our world a better place in which to live.

SECTION TWO: Meanings and realities

2 Gaming/simulation: A gestalt communications form

RICHARD D. DUKE
University of Michigan, U.S.A.

Introduction

An extensive literature exists in the related fields of simulation and gaming. Usage of these two terms has not been consistent over time or among the various professionals using these techniques. This lack of precision in terminology has been troublesome in many ways; there is little prospect of clear, consistent, international use of these terms in the near future. To some professionals, 'simulation' means a highly quantified computer technique; to others it means 'gaming'. Gaming, in much of the literature, seems to mean a great variety of things!

In response to this confusion, Duke (1974) combined the two terms (as 'gaming/simulation') as the most reasonable description of the phenomena as seen from perspective of that work. A definition of this new term and of related terms was then presented. A few of these definitions are reproduced here to clarify the use of the terms in this chapter.

> *Gaming/simulation*—A gestalt communications mode which contains a game-specific language, appropriate communication technologies, and the multilogue interaction pattern.
>
> *Gestalt*—A structure or configuration of physical, biological, or psychological phenomena so integrated as to constitute a functional unit with properties not derivable from its parts in summation.
>
> *Communication mode*—A form of communication composed of a language, a pattern of interaction, and a communication technology.

Game-specific language—A symbol set and its conventions of use, unique to a given game.

Communication technology—Device for encoding, transmitting, and decoding a message.

Multilogue—Multiple, simultaneous dialogues organised by a 'pulse'.

Pattern of interaction—The relationship between parties engaged in communication.

Communication

Communication defined

For the purposes of this chapter, any given mode of communication

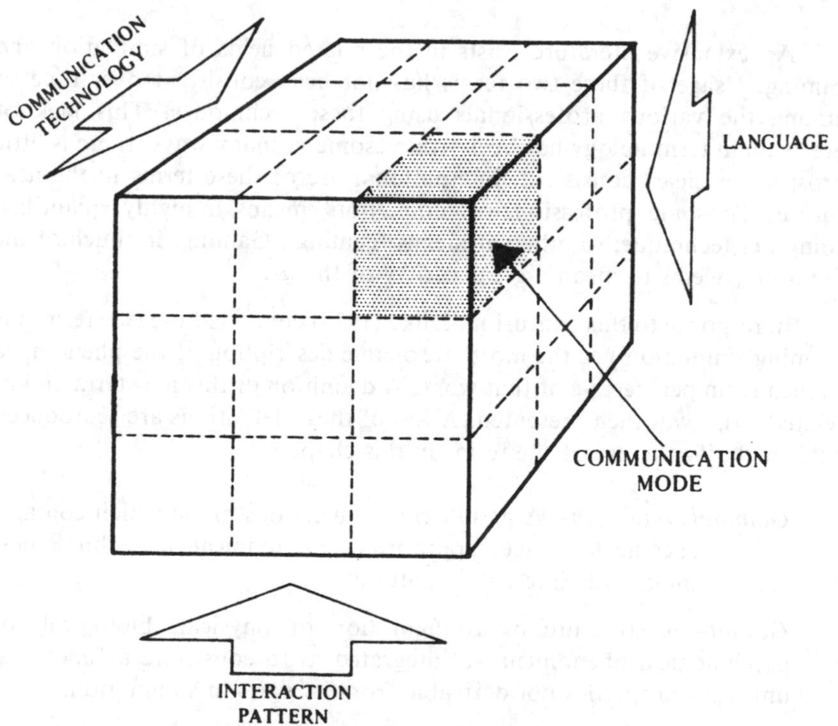

FIGURE 2.1 *Patterns of interaction*

is defined as being composed of three components: language, pattern of interaction among the respondents, and the communication technologies employed (Figure 2.1). Although communication technology has advanced rapidly in recent years, the pattern of interaction is still archaic for most modes of message transmission. Messages are still sent in highly sequential, static, one-way and non-interactive modes which inevitably hinder any effort towards depth of communication where the receiver is viewed as an active participant in the process. The most sophisticated film possible today still acts on, rather than with, the recipient, stereophonic sound and holography notwithstanding. Interactive video techniques, now emergent, hold promise but remain essentially sequential; though they do, at least, provide the participant with the opportunity partially to control the sequence of the experience (the participant can choose a path, but cannot create one).

Why has modern communications science limited its attention to the one-way sender-receiver mode of communications? Certainly this mode is well suited to propaganda purposes (advertising, for example); but can an 'in-depth' confrontation of any significant modern issue be effective it if is always one-sided? If the commentator is presumed to be the 'expert', and the receiver the 'dummy', will any communication of depth occur?

Communication and learning

Moore & Anderson (1975) identify four characteristics that are central to any learning environment; these also appear to be central to any environment where true communication is to occur. These four principles are paraphrased below, as they address the communication environment:

1. The sender must succeed in motivating the receiver before information is transmitted.
2. The receiver must be an active rather than a passive participant in the process.
3. The communication flow (information) must be individualised so that the pace for the receiver is correct.
4. The receiver must have prompt feedback in the dialogue so that messages can be challenged and differing opinions expressed.

Gaming/simulation and communication

Modern communications are, for the most part, technology-driven; technology, for the most part, is highly sequential. The response to this limitation has been the spontaneous creation of serious game/simulations as a new interactive mode of communication. These are increasingly found in use where any semblance of depth of understanding of the subject-matter can only be achieved through an exchange of views, a building of consensus, among or between interested and knowledgeable members of a group. The historic term for this exchange was 'dialogue'. A more modern concept would be 'multilogue', the simultaneous dialogue of multiple actors in pursuit of a greater understanding of the topic at hand.

These new instruments often employ exotic technology, but it is subjugated to the needs of the message environment. Talking 'at' is replaced by talking 'with'. The four conditions of Moore & Anderson (1975) govern the communications environment, and an 'in-depth' discussion takes on new meaning since it is achieved by the group within its own resources rather than being 'painted' on by some outside force.

Changing times mean changing communication needs

Gaming/simulation as a hybrid communication technology is essential to modern society because of the complex nature of policy issues, both public and private. It is essential that these multi-dimensional issues be addressed in their totality; or as a 'gestalt' phenomenon.

The need for conveying holistic thought, or gestalt, is urgent. A trenchant statement on this need has been made by Rhyne (1972). While describing the need for holistic communication, he states: 'There is a macro-problem, an interweaving of adverse conditions that is more extensive, more richly structured by interior lines of interaction, and more threatening than any circumstance faced before by all mankind.' Rhyne's article was formulated 'to stimulate exploration of the means whereby appreciations of complex wholes may be more quickly and more reliably told to others'. He rejects our ancestral language forms as inadequate to the task and argues that new forms must be invented. Arguing that decision is a gestalt event and not a logically determinable process, he believes that the citizen, the policy researcher or other decision-makers must first comprehend the whole, the entirety, the gestalt, the system, before the particulars can be dealt with. Rhyne suggests a variety of approaches to this problem and alludes to gaming/simulation as having a particular potential.

Changing needs create new forms of communication

The central thesis of Duke (1974) is that gaming/simulation, in and of itself, is a language; a new form of communication emerging suddenly and with great impact across many lands and in many disciplines and problem situations. This new form of communication represents the first effort by man to formulate a language which is orientated to the future. This future will in all certainty differ dramatically from the past, and the languages which have passed to us from antiquity will no longer suffice. The problems which must be faced differ because of their relative complexity, the rapidity of their occurrence, the newness of their character, and the systemic origin of the basic problems involved. As with every language in its infancy, the 'grammar', i.e. the structure, has not yet been rationalised (most people who use a language do so without understanding the inherent rules or structure of that language!). The technique of gaming/simulation, now in widespread use, urgently needs thoughtful attention to this phenomenon.

It is now apparent that we must deal not with a future but with *many* futures. Increasingly, society is seeking consensus on policy questions; this must be developed by groups in interactive (as contrasted with traditional hierarchical) processes. The languages historically available to us leave much to be desired.

Communication means language

Language has as its strongest component the use of analogy, because through analogy we are able to modify associations derived from past phenomena. Mankind must now develop analogies which are pure conjecture, but which can be used by co-operative, interactive groups, to formulate hypotheses about the future. In short, those holding the responsibility for setting policy must learn to reminisce about the future, thoughtfully, carefully and in realistic detail if we are to select that future which best serves society.

Virtually all our language forms have come from antiquity and have sufficed for planning purposes, in spite of their sequentiality, because they rely heavily on analogy. The analogies employed were predicated on historic circumstance not expected to change, except by minor adjustment through time. Changes in society since World War II (Figure 2.2) imply a future situation far more involved, particularly in the dimensions of complexity, future orientation, number of alternatives, and interlocking systems. Necessity is the mother of invention, and the post-war period has produced

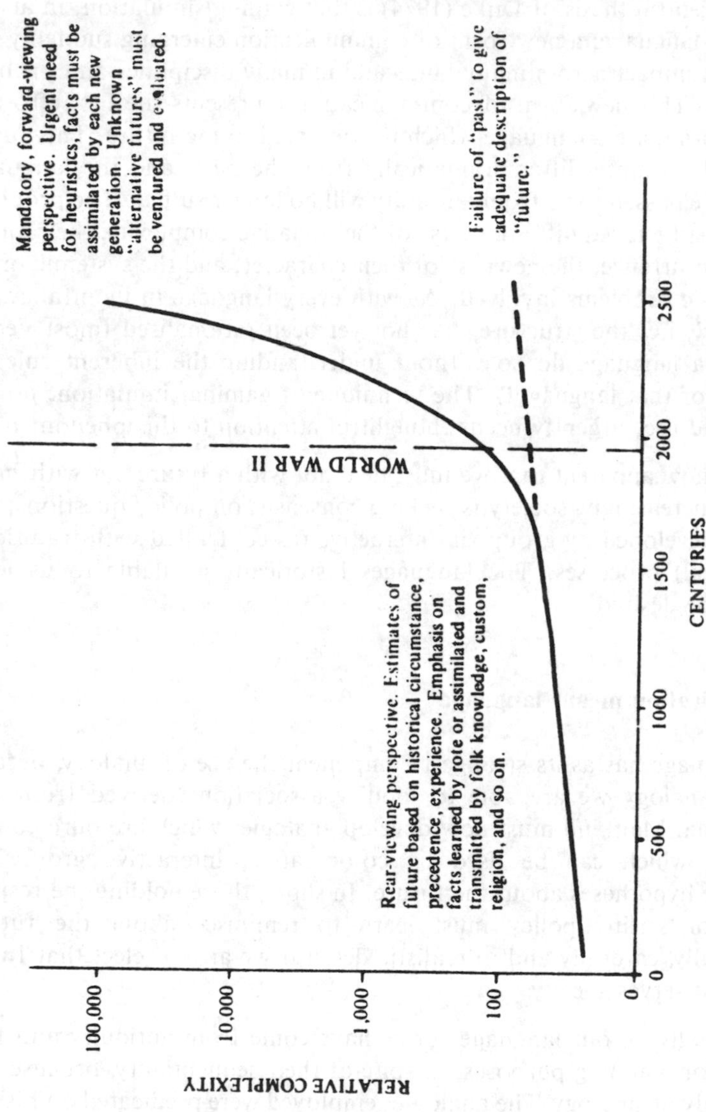

FIGURE 2.2 *Increasing complexity*

many innovations in communication which attempt to deal with this increased complexity. Each reflects an attempt to convey gestalt, or at least to escape from the harsh burden of the strict sequentiality of written and spoken language.

Communication is situation-specific

The various modes of communication currently in use rest along a continuum ranging from primitive to sophisticated; we can divide these into four major categories: primitive; advanced; integrated-simulated; and integrated-real. In a sense, the two extremes of the continuum can be viewed as being linked, in that two parties fully sharing a reality need no overt communication or can suffice with primitive modes. The greater the communications gap and the more involved the reality to be confronted, the more elaborate and sophisticated the language must become.

A quick review of the various communication forms is called for (Table 2.1). Primitive forms can be divided into informal (grunts and hand signals) and formal (semaphore or light signals). In situations which are simple and transitory, the former will suffice; but as the communications need becomes more important, more involved, or more consistent, these have been formalised. Both forms are characterised by spontaneity, limited message content, and immediacy to experience. They are generally used in face-to-face contact. For example, a cry of warning is almost universally understood by people of all cultures. Its function is to alert someone to a danger; it is effective only in so far as the person warned shares the other's perception of current reality, i.e. he is in the same place at the same time and is knowledgeable about his environment. Similarly, the standardised international traffic signals are an example of the primitive-formal category.

Advanced forms of communication include spoken languages, written languages, emotional forms (art, acting, role-playing) and technical forms (pictures, mathematical notation, musical notation, schematic diagrams, etc.), which are often used as supplements to other advanced forms. It is quite common, of course, to use these in some combination (for example, slides with a lecture), and such uses can be viewed as rudimentary forms of the integrated languages suggested by the final two categories. Of these, integrated-simulated, is characterised by deliberate combinations of media (film and television) or by hybrids (gaming/simulation) which employ all prior forms in any combination which best enhances the transmission of some reality.

TABLE 2.1 *The Communications Continuum*

(Examples of each form of communication)	*Primitive*		*Advanced*				*Integrated*			
							Simulated		*Real*	
	Informal	*Formal*	*Spoken*	*Written*	*Emotional*	*Technical*	*Multi-media*	*Hybrid*	*Experience*	*Reality*
Characteristics	Grunts Hand signals	Semaphore Lights Flags	Conversation Lecture Seminar Radio	Telegraph Manu-script Books Text	Acting Art Role-playing	Maths notation Musical nota-tion Schematics Diagrams	Film Television	Gaming/simula-tion	Apprentice Job train-ing	Any shared real time percep tion
SEQUENTIAL-GESTALT (degree to which the form is constrained)	Most constrained because of sequential nature		Basic character is sequential but various devices employed to ease constraint				Highest gestalt ability short of reality		Fully gestalt because actual reality	
SPECIFICITY-UNIVERSALITY (degree of flexibility of use)	Employed for all situa-tions but limited in material conveyed		Standard (universal) modes selectively employed to meet specific communication need				Mode specifically tailored to commu-nication need		Specific (it is the reality encountered)	

SPONTANEITY OF USE (user resistance, skill required, 'dryness' of form)	Natural, easy, convenient	Special skills required. Sophistication often accompanied by dryness, artificiality of use inherent	Special effort to initiate; then spontaneous in use	Natural 'life' form, skill limit involvement
CHARACTER OF CONVENTIONS EMPLOYED (formality, complexity)	Relatively few, simple, informal	Formal and informal, simple and complex, highly structured, many	Many, unique to each situation, fairly complex	Many, informal, complex
CHARACTER OF CODING AND DECODING (inherent)	None required or simple effort	Essential; may be elaborate and highly specialized	Elaborate coding to initiate simple effort by user	None required
CHARACTER OF THE MESSAGE THAT CAN BE CONVEYED (complexity, analogy, qualitative or quantative thought, subtlety, permanence, precision, intangibles, time constrained, system characteristics)	Only rudimentary message	Sophisticated messages	Gestalt substitute for reality	Reality

The final category, integrated-real, does not attempt this in an artificial manner, but rather this level of communication inherently demonstrates the circular nature of the communications process, and consequently extracts from reality itself. One illustration of this would be apprenticeship programmes where the learner (the party receiving the message) is placed in a situation of reality but buffered from the consequences of full participation. As he gains 'experience' (better perception of reality) these buffers are systematically removed until he becomes fully part of reality.

Characteristics of language

Six major characteristics are associated with the various language forms:

1. Sequential-gestalt constraints—the inherent ability of the language form to convey gestalt.
2. Specificity-universality constraints—the degree of flexibility inherent to the language form in adapting to new substantive material.
3. Spontaneity of use—the ease or relative freedom encountered by the user.
4. Character of conventions employed—the degree of consistency, the extent of complexity, the relative formality and their general or special use in a given communications attempt.
5. Coding-decoding—the extent to which the message must be artificially coded by the initiator and reconstructed by the receiver.
6. Character of the message that can be conveyed—the success with which a number of message characteristics can be conveyed, including but not limited to complexity, analogy, qualitative thought, quantitative thought, subtlety, permanency (ability to re-establish), precision, intangibles, time constraints, and systems characteristics.

These are illustrated in Table 2.1 as a communications continuum. All along the continuum the transmission of perceptions of reality remains the purpose of communication. But as the perception to be conveyed becomes more comprehensive, a price is always paid. When coding becomes more complex and specific to the situation, use of the communication technique is less spontaneous and application less universal. Primitive forms can close only small perceptual gaps; integrated forms can close wide gaps in perception of reality. In exchange for this capacity, integrated forms first simulate reality, and then structure it, until the continuum approaches reality itself.

At this point, when 'sender' and 'receiver' simultaneously share experience (reality), and the gap between perceived realities closes, the purpose of communication disappears because shared reality is total communication. The communications continuum has come full circle; it has returned to the point where any communication required by a short gap in experience can be satisfied with a primitive mode of communication.

Gestalt communication

Gestalt or holistic communication differs significantly from sequential communication. Gestalt communication implies a less rigid transmission of facts or specifics with a focus, instead, on ideas which emphasise a heuristic understanding of some complex reality. This permits the receiver a greater flexibility in addressing facets of complexity than could be obtained from a sequential presentation. A sequential presentation is burdensome and exhausting, but, more importantly, complex reality is a system which can never be comprehended by the exclusive examination of the individual components.

What are the major stylistic differences in transmitting comprehension of an environment of 'complex reality' through traditional sequential communication and through gaming/simulation?

Dialogue

In a typical lecture or conference situation there are several impediments to the discussion of a serious topic, stemming both from the problems of perceiving and transmitting complexity and from the mechanical aspects of engaging a group of people in dialogue. In the first instance, a complex topic must be abstracted to a manageable level and committed to some trial statement (usually written) which serves as a basis for discussion.

Figure 2.3 starts with a complex reality that is all one fabric, although its pattern is partially obscure; none the less, the process of abstracting and organising inevitably results in a segmented presentation to the receivers. The choice of the term 'complex reality' deliberately suggests a problem whose dimensions cannot readily be grasped in their entirety by human faculties.

Whatever reality may be, there are always barriers to its perception; and the perceived reality which filters through these barriers becomes the

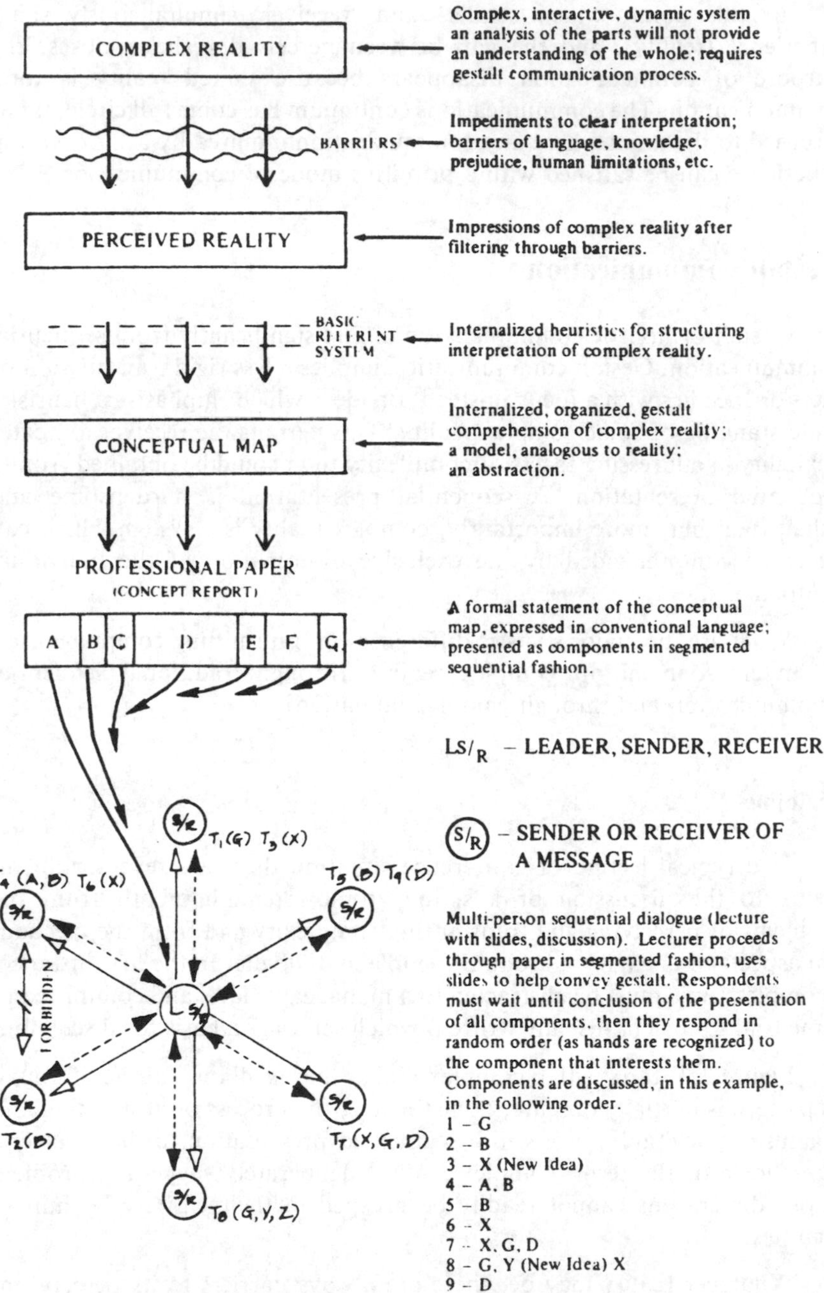
COMPLEX REALITY
Complex, interactive, dynamic system an analysis of the parts will not provide an understanding of the whole; requires gestalt communication process.
BARRIERS
Impediments to clear interpretation; barriers of language, knowledge, prejudice, human limitations, etc.
PERCEIVED REALITY
Impressions of complex reality after filtering through barriers.
BASIC REFERENT SYSTEM
Internalized heuristics for structuring interpretation of complex reality.
CONCEPTUAL MAP
Internalized, organized, gestalt comprehension of complex reality; a model, analogous to reality; an abstraction.
PROFESSIONAL PAPER
(CONCEPT REPORT)
A B C D E F G
A formal statement of the conceptual map, expressed in conventional language; presented as components in segmented sequential fashion.
LS/R – LEADER, SENDER, RECEIVER
S/R – SENDER OR RECEIVER OF A MESSAGE
T1(G) T3(X)
T4(A,B) T6(X)
T5(B) T9(D)
FORBIDDEN
T2(B)
T7(X,G,D)
T8(G,Y,Z)
Multi-person sequential dialogue (lecture with slides, discussion). Lecturer proceeds through paper in segmented fashion, uses slides to help convey gestalt. Respondents must wait until conclusion of the presentation of all components, then they respond in random order (as hands are recognized) to the component that interests them. Components are discussed, in this example, in the following order.
1 – G
2 – B
3 – X (New Idea)
4 – A, B
5 – B
6 – X
7 – X, G, D
8 – G, Y (New Idea) X
9 – D

FIGURE 2.3 *Multi-person sequential dialogue*

basis for discussion. Barriers to a complete and unambiguous understanding of reality include real limitations of understanding the subject in its particulars (lack of empirical or theoretical base) as well as human limitations in interpreting what is known (e.g. it was obvious for a long time that the sun circled the earth every 24 hours—the empirical evidence clearly supported this—those who challenged the obvious (perceived reality) were in considerable jeopardy). Different social groups will develop biased perceptions of reality, prompting the need for sophisticated message exchange concerning the problem.

Different people will organise their perceptions in various formats, even though they refer to the same reality. Each individual has some basic referent system (frame of references; patterned approach to perceiving and transmitting a problem) which serves as an internalised heuristic for structuring personal interpretation of complex reality. (For example, if you were to request a statement from a sociologist, economist, geographer, political scientist, engineer, and urban planner concerning the problems of a major urban community, the structure of their response would vary considerably, both in emphasis and organisational mode; there is one reality, but there are many styles of perceiving and organising abstractions of it.)

The result of this personal process of sorting an impression of some complex idea into an organised and manageable scheme—a form capable of transmission—can be called a conceptual 'map'. This is viewed as the internalised, organised, abstracted gestalt comprehension of complex reality that the author chooses to transmit or discuss. In some sense it is a model, analogous to reality. This conceptual map may or may not be committed to a formal written document.

Typically, this abstracted model of reality will appear as a professional paper (for gaming/simulation purposes, the term 'concept report' is used—see Figure 2.3). Because of the limitations of written communication, the original reality will now appear in segmented form; each chapter or section will analyse a logical component as though it truly existed in isolation. Normally, special devices will be employed to emphasise the integrity of the reality; various graphics and/or statements indicating the linkage between components will be employed to suggest the actual dynamic.

Communicating complexity

Having achieved an organised statement of complexity designed to serve as a starting point for discussion, we now encounter a problem of logistics. The report will be presented verbally to a group of potential respondents who may or may not have had prior access to the written statement. Upon completion of the presentation, discussion ensues. Respondents are selected in the order in which they seek recognition, or, more commonly, in the case where multiple respondents wish to speak, in some random pattern. To avoid chaos, conventions are employed which govern these 'discussions'. Respondents are discouraged or prohibited from private exchanges, and all voices must be recognised by the chair and a response given. Courtesy demands that the chair recognise those wishing to comment according to temporal equity, rather than according to the logical content of the proposed comment (the chair has no way to fathom who will address what aspect of the topic). Time constraints force limits to a given exchange to 'allow time for other comment'; but, unfortunately, the other comment may prove to be less, or more, relevant. Potentially interesting 'tangential' ideas must be stifled to ensure a fair airing of the author's views (e.g. 'the chair regrets the necessity of moving on ... certainly your speculation that the earth spins around the sun is very provocative, but we must stay with the central theme').

Multilogue

Figure 2.4 is concerned with establishing communication about the same kinds of complexity as in the previous illustration, but in this instance the communication mode is gaming/simulation. The process of perceiving, abstracting, and organizing the problem is much the same as the process employed in preparing for a lecture, but the device employed to facilitate communication about the topic is quite different. Because of the complexity involved, both abstraction and organization are required, and our internalized heuristics guide us in formulating a model of reality. This internalized model or conceptual map, whether or not independently committed to paper, becomes the basis for the construction of the game/simulation. If the process is successful, the product is in some sense analogous to reality.

Gaming/simulation

In gaming/simulation, the conceptual map, an internalised, organised overall comprehension of complex reality, serves as a mental blueprint to help convey complex systems. The conceptual map classifies, sorts and stores information: it provides a heuristic language to be used as a common symbolic structure for discussing a given complex system. Data conveyed

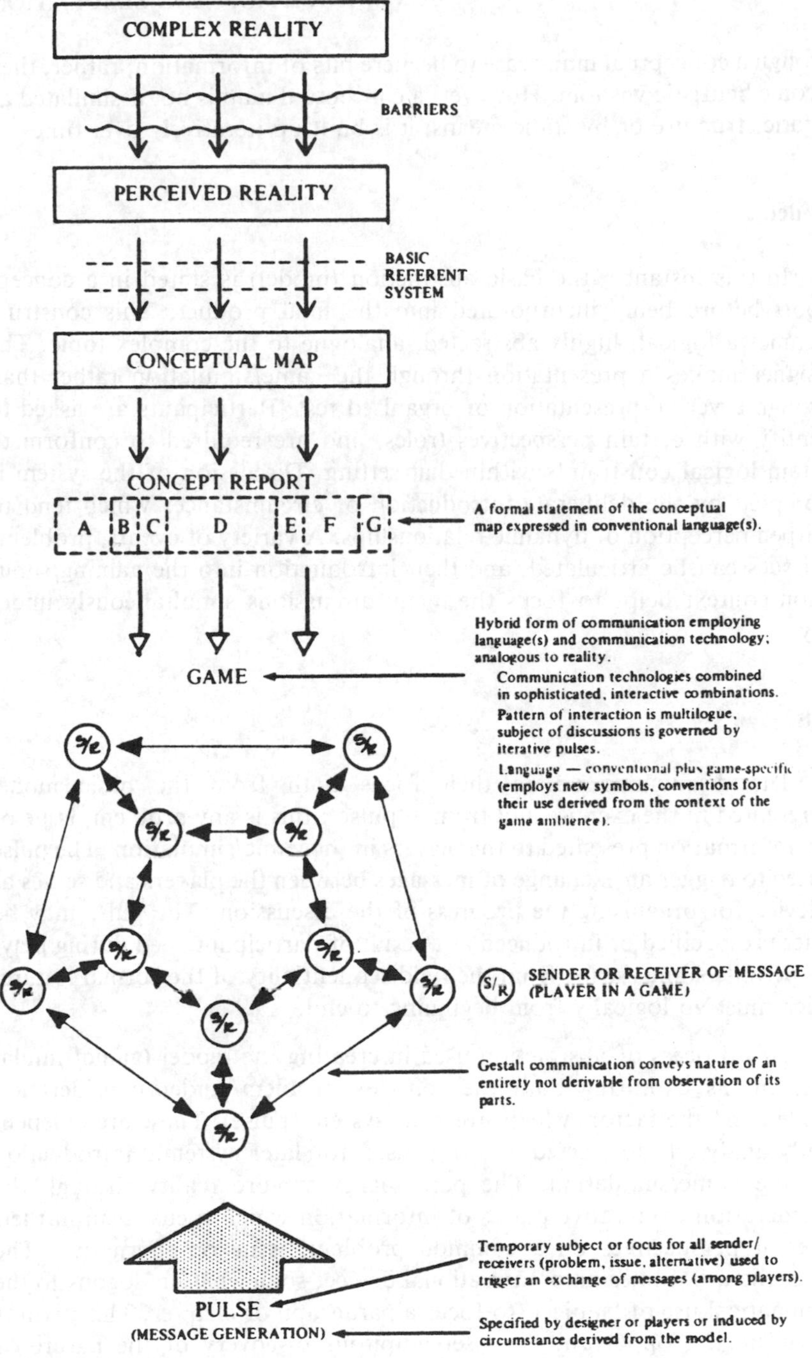
COMPLEX REALITY
BARRIERS
PERCEIVED REALITY
BASIC
REFERENT
SYSTEM
CONCEPTUAL MAP
CONCEPT REPORT
A
B
C
D
E
F
G
A formal statement of the conceptual map expressed in conventional language(s).
Hybrid form of communication employing language(s) and communication technology; analogous to reality.
GAME
Communication technologies combined in sophisticated, interactive combinations.
Pattern of interaction is multilogue, subject of discussions is governed by iterative pulses.
Language — conventional plus game-specific (employs new symbols, conventions for their use derived from the context of the game ambience).
S/R
SENDER OR RECEIVER OF MESSAGE (PLAYER IN A GAME)
Gestalt communication conveys nature of an entirety not derivable from observation of its parts.
Temporary subject or focus for all sender/receivers (problem, issue, alternative) used to trigger an exchange of messages (among players).
PULSE
(MESSAGE GENERATION)
Specified by designer or players or induced by circumstance derived from the model.

FIGURE 2.4 *Multilogue*

through a conceptual map cease to be mere bits of information; rather, they become heuristic wisdom. However, a conceptual map is not assimilated as a static structure or by static means; it is built up iteratively over time.

Model

In this instance, the basic abstraction (model) is stated in a concept report before being incorporated into the final product. This construct becomes a logical, highly abstracted, analogue to the complex topic. The designer makes a presentation through the game/simulation rather than through a verbal presentation or organised test. Participants are asked to identify with certain perspectives (roles) and are required to conform to certain logical constraints within that setting. Discussion of the system is prompted by the deliberate introduction of circumstances which tend to sharpen perception of dynamic relationships. A variety of events, problems or issues can be articulated, and their introduction into the gaming/simulation context helps to focus the many discussions simultaneously under way.

Pulse

The discussions obtain their focus both from the basic model represented in the exercise and from a 'pulse'; this is any problem, issue or new information presented to the players in the game/simulation. The pulse is used to trigger an exchange of messages between the players and serves as a device for organising the progress of the discussion. The pulse may be either prespecified or introduced as a result of participant need during play; this permits some escape from the rigid sequentiality of the formal lecture, which must go logically from beginning to end.

This process of abstraction used in creating the model (game/simulation) entails capturing both the complex problem under consideration (model) and the factors which stress the system (pulse). These are independently analysed, abstracted and organised for later systemic introduction into the game/simulation. The participants explore reality through the consideration of iterative pulses of information which focus them in their different perspectives on a common problem, issue or alternative. The pulse, then, becomes an organisational device, somewhat analogous to the grammatical use of 'subject' to focus a paragraph or chapter. This permits the group the opportunity for serendipitous discovery of the nature of complexity.

The construct is all of one piece and, once under way, has no logical entry or exit point *per se*. This permits the individual to enter into the multilogue from his/her own frame of reference or point of perspective. It permits and encourages a tumbling, ongoing discussion among changing and unstable coalitions who come together as their ideas coincide, and quickly break away to form new conversational units. (All of those whispered sessions at the back of the room that the chair has continuously to suppress are encouraged to form and pursue their productive course.)

Because the respondents are roaming freely within a logical construct, they discern its shape and characteristics by a series of vignettes of their own making. They are free to explore in a sequence that appears logical to them rather than constrained to an arbitrary and preordained path of inquiry. In reviewing this model it is important to differentiate between multilogue and many dialogues being conducted simultaneously. Multilogue is the organised simultaneous inquiry into some complex topic; contrast this with a cocktail party which is characterised by many simultaneous dialogues covering a broad array of disjointed subject-matter.

Communication through gaming/simulation

Multilogue occurs quite naturally in some small group situations. It is frequently deliberately contrived as counterpoint to a lecture in a formal conference session (following a presentation, those present are split up into small 'discussion groups', typically of five to seven persons, and subsequently returned to the original conference format). The multilogue interaction pattern is central to the simulation's ability to convey gestalt. Figure 2.5 explores the dynamics of communication within such an exercise. Complex reality is represented in the diagram as a hexagon, with the various nodes representing decision points, and all lines connecting these points representing potential information flows.

Several items of significance must be emphasised. First, the players are assumed to be engaged in different roles requiring differing perceptions of the modelled reality. Because they are simultaneously engaged in the process, the message-interchange pattern contains many concurrent dimensions and the term 'dialogue' is insufficient to describe the process. Rather, it should be thought of as many parallel and simultaneous dialogues (multilogue), all pertaining to some aspect of a complex phenomenon. Serendipitous occurrence, both during the play of the exercise and in the organised critique which follows, will heighten the significance of these message exchanges in terms of what they convey to the player about the

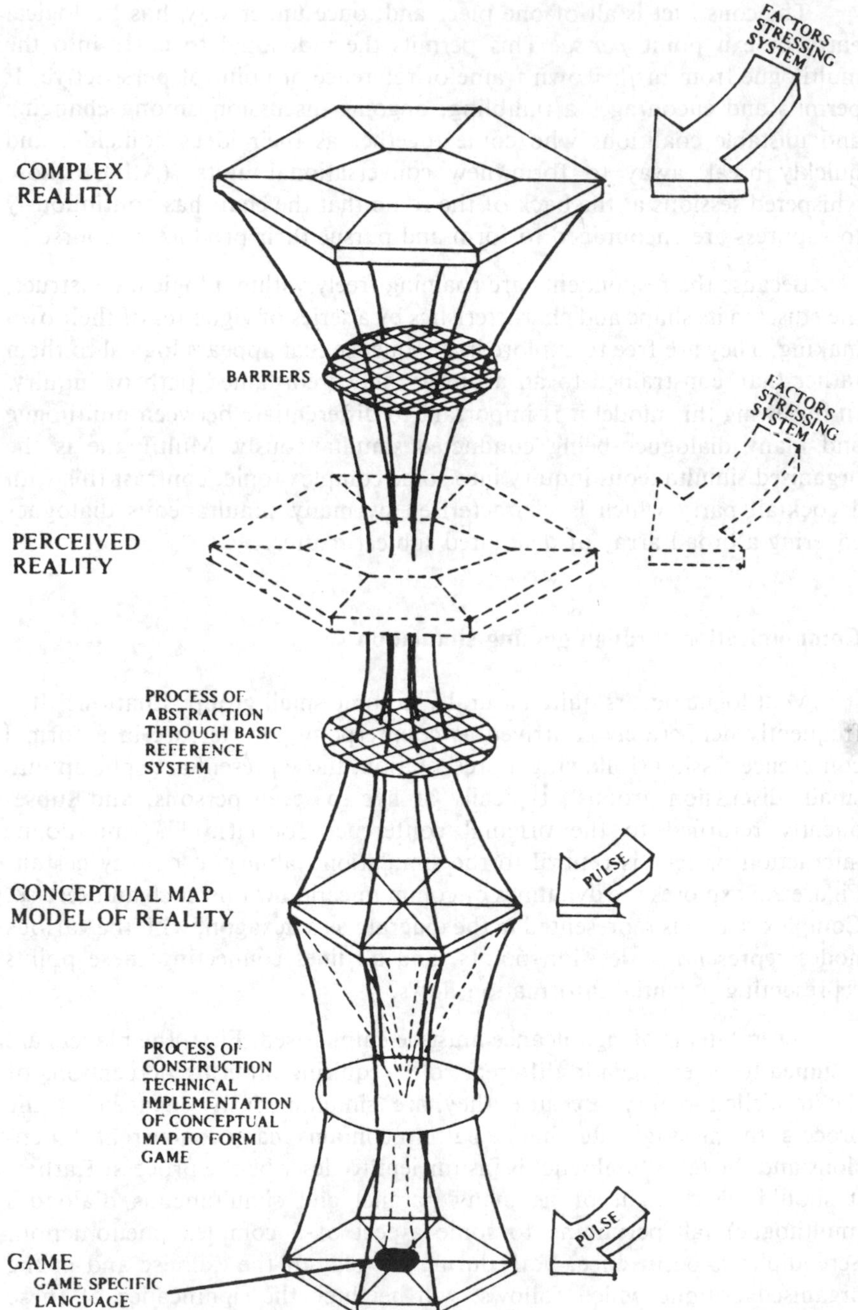

FIGURE 2.5 *Communicating through gaming/simulation*

nature of the complex reality. The basis for achieving greater depth of communication through this approach derives from two basic characteristics: first, these constructs serve as an environment for self-instruction, permitting *n*-dimensional entry (and, therefore, simultaneous multiple sensing from different perspectives in a safe environment), and convey heuristics (general and structural learning) in a responsive environment; and second, their iterative character permits enlarged perception and logical mental closure with each iteration, permitting an emphasis on gestalt or overview, the establishment of context, as perceived to be relevant to the player, and supplemented by reality testing through formal critiques.

Problem-specific language

The multilogue model, when functioning during the event of a game/simulation, creates a problem-specific 'language'. The jargon employed to describe components of reality becomes the symbols which are unique to the problem being explored. The behaviour of the participants creates a set of conventions governing the use of the symbols employed in the exercise. The symbols used in the game/simulation acquire specific meaning for the participants through their experiences in the exercise. This problem-specific language may be deliberately designed or inadvertently created by the players as jargon. The problem-specific language must be sufficiently complex to improve discussion, but simple enough to be readily learned.

Summary

In gaming/simulation, the 'conceptual map' serves as a mental blueprint to help convey complex systems. The conceptual map classifies, sorts and stores information; it serves as a heuristic model of reality. This model, in turn, provides a referent for a common symbolic structure used to discuss a given complex system. Data conveyed through a conceptual map cease to be mere bits of information; rather, they become heuristic wisdom.

Properly designed gaming/simulations represent abstract symbolic maps of multi-dimensional phenomena. We are better able to communicate through these exercises because they serve as basic reference systems for tucking away the bits and pieces of detail associated with any complex problem. They assist in the formulation of inquiry from a variety of perspectives which can only be transmitted through an *n*-dimensional, abstract, symbolic mapping procedure.

Before World War II the need for pragmatic information and fact, learned by rote, was imperative. In today's world there is urgent need for the acquisition of heuristics, a flexible set of highly abstract conceptual tools which will let the participant view new and emerging situations, having no precedent, in a way that permits comprehension and in-depth discussion with others. We learn through gaming/simulation because it provides a relatively safe environment which permits the exploration of any perspective chosen by the individual, expressed in the jargon of the individual, and subject to a prompt feedback.

Language in antiquity performed basically one of two purposes: it was either a pragmatic means for the common man to transmit to his neighbour the essentials of day-to-day life or it was a mode of communication among a sophisticated elite used to maintain their position in society. We now need to find a vehicle of communication which permits us better to comprehend the future, and which permits more intelligent dialogue about complexity by larger groups.

Gaming/simulation is a hybrid communication form. It is new, not well understood, poorly used, and in its infancy. None the less, there is convincing evidence that, when it is treated with the same precision and understanding as traditional forms of communication, it will prove to be very useful. The technique has the ability accurately to convey sophisticated information with greater perception of the interrelationships involved than possible through simple language forms.

3 Game identities and activities: Some ethnomethodological observations[1]

DAVID FRANCIS
Manchester Polytechnic, U.K.

In this chapter I aim to open up simulation/gaming to ethnomethodological analysis. The findings presented are initial and exploratory. They in no way represent a systematic or thorough analysis of simulation/gaming from an ethnomethodological point of view. At this stage of my investigations, I do not know what systematicity might consist in. I wish only to show that there are some constitutive features of simulation/gaming as an interactional, communicative activity that can be elucidated by ethnomethodological analysis.

Ethnomethodology and simulation/gaming

It should be stressed at the outset that the concerns of this chapter are quite different from those which characterise 'professional' analyses of simulation/gaming (e.g. Gray & Waitt, 1982). Such analyses are fundamentally 'use-orientated'. Their concerns are practical and critical. By contrast, ethnomethodology's distinctive concern is to treat the practical organisation of social activities as a phenomenon of analytic attention in its own right (see Heritage, 1984; Sharrock & Anderson, 1986). Therefore, in bringing this attention to bear upon simulation/gaming, I shall not attempt to provide criticisms, correctives or remedies, either of simulation/gaming in general or of the particular game from which the data are drawn. Instead, using transcribed excerpts from a business negotiation game in progress, this chapter attempts to describe what simulation/gaming actually consists in as a concerted, communicative activity. What are the behavioural characteristics that can be noticed? What are the oriented-on features of simulation/gaming which provide participants with a sense of the 'reality' and uniqueness of a game? These are the sorts of question an ethnomethodological approach leads one to raise.

In taking an ethnomethodological approach to simulation/gaming, this chapter seeks to explore the possibilities opened up by conceiving of a game as a locally managed interactional order (Garfinkel 1986). By contrast with other approaches to social behaviour, ethnomethodology conceives the properties of interactional settings and communicative activities as produced 'from within'. It rejects any reduction of interactional competencies and communicative understandings to sets of fixed, standardised 'expectations' or 'dispositions'. Rather, it views the intelligibility and orderliness that a setting or activity has for its participants as the methodical product of situated 'work' of practical reasoning. In seeking to describe this practical reasoning, ethnomethodological analysis pays attention to two massively observable but taken-for-granted features of social behaviour. These are the contingency of interaction and its locally oriented character.

Social actors routinely have to conduct real-world interaction under circumstances in which they know neither what will happen next nor how a course of action will ultimately turn out. As involved participants, social actors cannot wait until they possess 'perfect knowledge' of relevant circumstances before acting, even assuming that such knowledge might in principle be attainable. But this does not mean that social actors treat their own or others' behaviour as random or senseless. Rules, norms and expectations are revisable as to their meaning and relevance for the situation at hand. Only by monitoring an unfolding course of events can social actors decide that they are doing or have done 'the right thing'. Such judgements are always open to revision in the light of later happenings. Furthermore, the reality of a setting or activity does not consist simply in its being recognisable as an instance of this or that general type. Social actors have to deal, not with this *type* of event, but with *this* event, here and now. They may have experienced other situations like this one, but whether they have or not they must respond to the particular circumstances which obtain *this time*. To say that interaction is 'locally oriented' does not mean that social actors treat as circumstantially relevant only that information which has been gleaned from personal experience or those objects which are amenable to direct manipulation. On the contrary, as Schutz & Luckmann (1973) were at pains to emphasise, it is a taken-for-granted fact of practical daily life that there are matters which the individual can only know indirectly and which are beyond his/her ability to influence. Interaction is locally oriented because as an involved participant a social actor's first and overwhelming necessity is to *act*, to respond to his/her immediate situation.

A further feature of ethnomethodological analysis is that it seeks to ground its analytic descriptions in the phenomena it investigates in a strong and detailed way. Instead of deriving its analytic categories from a given theory, ethnomethodology is committed to the principle of formulating its categories in the closest possible consultation with the actual conduct to which those categories refer. Therefore it rejects the notion that real-worldly social events should be 'simplified', in order to provide idealised phenomena more readily amenable to analytic description and explanation. It favours techniques of investigation which as far as possible preserve the naturally occurring content of communicative interaction. Thus there is a strong preference for the use of audio- and video-taped data in ethnomethodological studies. These forms of data have the dual advantages, first, that they make it possible to examine closely the fine detail of communicative interaction, and second, that they can be reproduced for disinterested perusal, so that the reader can have available the actual data on which an analysis is based. Audio- and video-tapes are notorious among sociological researchers for providing 'too much data'. They confront conventional forms of analysis with the problem of being swamped by detail. Ethnomethodology, by eschewing the synoptic aims of conventional approaches, turns this feature of audio- and video-taped data to analytic advantage. It aims to locate the constitutive features of social settings and activities in the detail of communicative exchanges.

These methodological principles have been most fully and successfully realised in the study of everyday conversation. Conversation analysis (C.A.) has painstakingly built up an impressive body of findings concerning the sequential and interactional organisation of conversation. It has been demonstrated that the structures of conversational organisation operate at the finest levels of detail in talk. It has also been shown that the findings of C.A. have relevance for the analysis of activities other than ordinary conversation. A series of studies have shown that activities such as courtroom proceedings (Atkinson & Drew, 1979), classroom lessons (Mehan, 1979) and labour–management negotiations (Francis, 1986) are conducted in and through talk in ways which involve systematic modification of the interactional structures of ordinary conversation. The same issue can be posed in relation to simulation/gaming. Since so much simulation/gaming involves talk, one can ask how the interactional and communicative tasks which simulation/gaming imposes upon participants are managed via the modified application of conversational structures. The analysis to be presented below does not pretend to offer a fully worked-out answer to this question. However, it will show that conversation-analytic methods can make available the detailed communicative work through which participants accomplish a simulation/game.

Playing a business negotiation game

The analysis of simulation/gaming in this chapter is based upon a video-tape, recorded by myself, of a business negotiation game in progress. The game being played was CHEMICAL CONSTRUCTION COMPANY. It was being played as part of a three-day course in business negotiation, organised by the Department of Business Studies at a large institution of higher education in the U.K. The eleven participants in the course were all sales personnel in the advertising department of a large national newspaper. The course was run by two tutors in Business Studies and the training officer of the newspaper. The business negotiation game was one of a variety of activities that made up the programme of the course. Playing the game took up the morning and most of the afternoon of the second day.

CHEMICAL CONSTRUCTION COMPANY involves three teams of players, representing executives of a multinational petrochemical corporation, 'Ajax Chemicals', executives of a large civil engineering construction company, 'Chemical Construction', and officials of a trade union, the 'Civil and Constructional Engineering Union'. The course participants had already been divided into three teams for a previous activity and these teams were retained for the negotiation game. Each participant was given two sets of written instructions. All were given one set of notes describing the game situation, the identities of the parties, the titles of the members of each team and other 'general information'. In addition, each team was given a separate, shorter set of notes containing information about its own circumstances and other details unknown to the other two teams. After these documents had been distributed the course leader gave a brief introductory talk about the game. He outlined the game situation and its background. He then allocated each team a room as its 'headquarters'. It was emphasised that teams could and should communicate with one another in a variety of ways: by telephone and letter as well as in face-to-face meetings. He also indicated a timetable for the game. The course programme required that the game be completed by mid-afternoon. He suggested that each half hour, by clock time, should be taken to represent one day of negotiations by game time.

The framework of the game, as described by the course leader to the participants, is as follows. Chemical Construction (CC) is engaged in the construction of a refinery and associated facilities for Ajax Petrochemicals in a rapidly developing Third World country. The estimate of costs originally submitted by CC was US $48 million, which was $8 million more than the Ajax management had forecast. Despite this difference in estimates, Ajax's pressing need for the facility and the fact that other cost estimates were even higher led the Ajax board to request CC to commence construction work immediately. CC was asked to submit a more detailed cost breakdown, on the basis of which a final, fixed price contract would be agreed.

'At this moment' work has been in progress for eight months, but Ajax and CC have been unable to agree a final price for the project. Therefore CC have suspended all work at the site pending the outcome of negotiations. This has created a number of problems between CC and the Civil and Constructional Engineering Union ('the union'), which represents the entire work-force at the site, both the expatriate workers (mainly engineers and technicians) and locally recruited employees (mainly skilled manual workers). The union have a wage claim outstanding. In addition, a competitor of CC, 'Global Construction', are beginning work on another large civil engineering project nearby and are seeking to recruit workers. The course leader stressed that while the interests of the parties were not identical, all three had much to gain in reaching agreement with one another. The game began with each team retiring to its room to discuss the presented information and consider its courses of action.

In line with the methodological remarks earlier in the chapter, there are several reasons why I am not going to attempt a case-study analysis of this particular game. The first is that the video-tape I made is not a complete record of what occurred. Not all the meetings of the teams were recorded or observed. The taping was done in a fairly unsystematic way, the researcher moving from room to room in order to record some of the discussions of each team and some of the meetings between the teams. But also, even if I were in possession of a longer, fuller tape, I would still be at a loss to know what a comprehensive, case-study analysis of the game might usefully consist in. It is not simply that the game was long and complex (even the selective recording fills a three-hour video-tape). I see no good reason to assume that one set of categories will adequately describe 'everything' that occurred. Neither is there anything to be gained by assuming that some overall pattern must exist in the game. Rather such matters can be investigated as features of the practical activities of participants.

In playing the game, participants have to distribute tasks, manage contingencies and decide strategies. In tackling these and other game-provided tasks they treat the game as an unfolding reality. They continually interpret how it is 'progressing' and what 'pattern' is emerging in the developing relationships between the parties. Constitutive features of the game setting can be and *are* treated as facts to which actions must be adjusted. In the ways in which they fit their actions to these facts, participants produce the game as an orderly, intelligible, manageable course of events. It is in this *production work* that the application of interactional and conversational structures can be observed.

Game identities and activities

The remainder of the chapter will focus upon just one aspect of the local production of a simulation/game: the management of identities. The participants in a game communicate and collaborate with one another on the basis of social identities they possess. The courses of action they engage in are made relevant by and are intelligible in terms of these identities. The game setting is distinctive in that it involves two layers of identities. On the one hand, there is a set of identities provided by the game instructions. These can be called the *identities within the game*. Distribution of these identities, in the form of parties or titles, is a prerequisite for a particular play of the game. Typically this is done, as in this case, prior to the commencement of play. It forms part of the pre-play activity to set up the game. On the other hand, there are the set of identities constituted by the organisational and/or educational context of the game 'this time'. These can be called the *game-context identities*. A basic distinction is between 'organisers' and 'players'. The distribution of this pair of categories is governed by the organisational/educational context. CHEMICAL CONSTRUCTION COMPANY, forming as it did part of a business training course, involved congruent distribution of the identity sets 'organisers/players' and 'course tutors/course participants'. However, as we shall see, the relationship between these identities and the distribution of activities was not rigid or absolute. The existence of these two layers of identity in the game setting means that the participants have two normative frameworks to which they are required to orient. Crudely, they are required to enact their role *within* the game while at the same time paying attention to the organisational/educational context *of* the game. I refer to this dual orientation as the 'double-settinged' character of simulation/gaming. It can be hypothesised that this double-settingedness may create specific problems of interactional and communicative adjustment for participants. What forms might such problems take and how might participants handle them?

One class of game incidents in which the double-settingedness of simulation/gaming is observable is generated by the requirement for *game realism*. An omni-relevant condition of game play is that it should reflect the kind of situation indicated by the game instructions. Participants interpret and apply these instructions on the basis of their common-sense understandings of the kind of situation the game is intended to be. They do not treat the game instructions as self-evident rules of conduct, to be followed mechanically or uncritically. Nor do they treat as relevant knowledge only the information contained in the instructions. Participants routinely fill out the information in the instructions in various ways both before, during and after the play, on the basis of 'what anyone knows' about situations 'of this kind'. They are able to identify and resolve specific problems of how to play. They are also able to *improvise* courses of action and introduce new elements into the game in an *ad hoc* fashion. As a construct of common-sense knowledge, the game situation constitutes an open set of relevancies in terms of which the meaningfulness, appropriateness and effectiveness of specific game actions can be interpreted and judged by both players and organisers. The identities within the game provide participants with interpretative resources by which to realise the common-sense game situation in the play. They can invoke 'what we all know' about such identities to organise the ongoing course of play. They can trade upon common-sense ties between identities and activities (see Sacks, 1974) on the assumption that other participants will recognise their local meaning and significance.

In the CHEMICAL CONSTRUCTION COMPANY game, participants repeatedly invoked common-sense properties of 'business life' to structure the play. By treating business life as a common-sense interactional order, they were able to improvise game activities and relationships in ways which served to realise their roles as putative members of business organisations. Two sets of circumstances in which such improvisation was most evident were, first, in allocating activities among the members of a team, and second, in managing the relationship between one's own team and another. I will present some conversational extracts to illustrate these points.[2] In Extract 1, from a meeting of the Chemical Construction team, Alistair, the 'chairman' of CC, announces to the rest of his team that he is going to telephone the chairman of Ajax. The cheque he refers to is the stage payment CC are seeking for the work already done. The two chairmen have already discussed this payment at a prior face-to-face meeting.

(1)

Alistair: Well now mmm (.) I'm goin' to phone their chairman jus' to get (.) to ask them to send that cheque round (.) so that we've got that cheque in our hands

John: That's right an' [we can-
Alistair: [One (.) two one is it?
((Alistair rises from table and moves to the telephone))
Maggie: ((Looks towards Anna)) Two five four
((Alistair picks up telephone and begins to dial))
Alistair: ((To Maggie)) You'll have to ask (.) say you-you're speaking on behalf of the chairman (.) you've got a call for (.) their chairman
((Alistair hands the phone to Maggie))
Alistair: (You might) get the same old biddy you spoke to ( )
((Laughter))
(5.0)
Maggie: This is Chem-Chemical Construction speaking, could we have your-speak to your-er chairman please (.) we have a call for him
Alistair: ((Whispers)) From our chairman
Maggie: From our chair-yes, it's from our chairman
(8.0)
Alistair: ((Quietly)) He's in the bar
(1.0)
Maggie: Erm-I've got a call for you ((Maggie hands telephone to Alistair))
Alistair: Hel_lo_, oh Tim old boy, terrific, nice to talk to you again (.) er-Tim (.) absolutely (top hole) old boy
((Laughter))

It can be seen in this extract that these participants are able to treat 'business life' as a known-in-common organisation of identities and activities. One aspect of this organisation is that the distribution of business activities is associated with status differences between identities. Sacks (1974) speaks of activities which are commonsensically tied with identity categories as 'category-bound activities'. Social actors treat these common-sense ties as adequate grounds for inference and action. Thus the perceived performance of certain actions can serve to identify who or what the persons concerned 'must be'. Identities can be routinely read off from activities, while knowing 'who' someone is can establish 'what' is being done. Such common-sense ties are drawn upon by these game participants to simulate business life.

In Extract 1 members of the CC team structure the emerging course of action in accordance with the common-sense properties of the identities 'chairman' and 'secretary' so as to produce 'business communication'.

Alistair and Maggie's simulations of chairman and secretary are *for the sake of the game*. As such, they need only be realised in actions which count, that is, actions which are observable and accountable as 'moves in the game'. But assembling the simulation requires interactional work among the members of the team. It is noticeable how economically the work of simulation assembly is co-ordinated with the game move of making the telephone call. For example, Alistair makes use of the time it takes to dial and the response time involved in answering the call to organise Maggie's 'secretarial' course of action. The result is a call which has the game appearance of a business communication.

Extract 1 demonstrates that game realism is a practical, contextual phenomenon. Participants do not seek literally to reproduce a real-world situation. The game is 'just a game'. As an educational/professional activity it should be taken seriously. But identities within the game should not be given improper precedence over relevant game context identities. This can constitute taking the game *too* seriously, so that interactional problems that might be marked by embarrassment, disagreement or annoyance can be occasioned by overseriousness. Alternatively, overplaying of identities within the game can provide the basis for humour. In Extract 1 Alistair's 'exaggerated' impersonation of a company chairman occasions laughter from the other members of his team. Extract 2 contains a more extravagant example of a similar phenomenon. It comes from a later meeting of the same team. Present are the four members of the team (Alistair, Maggie, Anna and John) and three others (Dianne, Louise and Alan). CC are still awaiting the stage payment from Ajax. They have set a deadline for it, after which if it is not received they will 'withdraw from the project and seek recompense through the courts'.

(2)

Alistair:	They've messed us around for over a week now, haven't they
John:	Yeah ((Telephone rings))
John:	That (could be them) =
Alistair:	= Tim?
Dianne:	((Picks up telephone)) Chemical Construction, good afternoon
Dianne:	I'm very sorry, he's actually in a board meeting at the moment. Can I take a message for you? ((Anna and Maggie exchange smiles)) (12.0)
Dianne:	Well er I'm afraid actually he's not available but can I send a runner round to collect it for you?

	(5.0)
	((Alistair imitates running movements with his arms, causing quiet laughter))
Dianne:	It-it's perfectly okay it's no trouble at all from our point of view we can a messenger round straight away
	(2.0)
Alan:	((Quietly to Alistair)) How do you want the cheque?
Alistair:	( )
Dianne:	((Puts her hand over the mouthpiece)) They've got 'til quarter to (.) 'Oh (we've got) the cheque but we want to talk to the chairman'
Alistair:	We want the cheque now
	(1.0)
Alan:	((Looks at his watch)) We're running out of-what's the time?
Alistair:	( )
John:	We need the money now
	(1.0)
Alan:	(Stewed) long enough I think =
John:	= We've made all the running up 'til now, so-
Alan:	I know what you're doing
Louise:	( )
	(1.0)
Alan:	They should come around actually
	(2.0)
Dianne:	((Into telephone)) In that case will you possibly send somebody over here with it (.) er-I'm sure the chairman could probably pop out of the board meeting for a moment
	(5.0)
Alistair:	(Not in the-)
Dianne:	In that case I'm <u>very</u> sorry I don't think I can help you an' you-
	(2.0)
Dianne:	Thank you very much indeed I'll pass your message on
	(1.0)
Dianne:	((Holds telephone away from her face and looks at it)) Snotty bugger! ((Replaces telephone))
	((Wild, raucous laughter from the others. This goes on for approx. 15 seconds, during which several remarks are made, inaudible except for))
John:	Very well done there

Alistair: (Superb that was)
Louise: (She's) taking it personally
Maggie: Oh God

This extract illustrates that participants in the CHEMICAL CONSTRUCTION COMPANY game did not treat identities as fixed and rigid determinants of 'who does what'. Both in their discussions prior to play and in the play itself, members of the teams elaborated, modified and sometimes even abandoned identities given in the game instructions, replacing them with others which would make the play 'more realistic'. Also, the distribution of game activities was an occasioned matter, related to the local interactional circumstances that obtained when a particular game action needed to be taken. This flexibility applied not just to identities within the game but also to the game-context distinction between players and organisers. As the game went on, the organisers became increasingly involved in the play. Much of this involvement took the form of activities designed to monitor and evaluate the progress of the game. Thus, for example, after a meeting between the chairmen of CC and Ajax, the course leader, Alan, took Alistair on one side to discuss how the meeting had gone and to question him about the strategy the CC team were adopting in their dealings with Ajax.

Here and elsewhere, the organisers were careful to exercise their right to monitor the play in ways which did not interrupt the flow of the game. But in addition to organisers' activities such as these, they at times participated in the play itself. Thus, in Extract 2, Dianne, one of the course tutors, answers the telephone, and trading upon the known-in-common situational relevance of 'secretarial action', acts as a spontaneous member of the CC team. It is this *double simulation*, perhaps, which stimulates the exchange of smiles between Anna and Maggie, two bona-fide members of the team. Dianne then improvises a course of action which recognisably is grounded in the strategy that the CC team have adopted in their dealings with Ajax. She displays her understanding of that strategy by spontaneously refusing the Ajax request to speak with the CC chairman, and offering to send a messenger to collect the cheque.

Dianne's actions thus have something of the formal characteristics of a stage performance. Like a stage actor, her actions are *dually directed*. They are addressed to her Ajax caller, but also are produced for the others present in the room, in particular the members of the CC team. In acting spontaneously on behalf of the team, Dianne invites judgement of her improvised actions, both in terms of their 'game effectiveness' and as an impersonation of a player. The seriousness with which she enacts her assumed 'false' identity within the game is highlighted by the exclamation 'Snotty bugger!' It is, perhaps, the ironic *overseriousness* of this remark, produced by an organiser acting as a player simulating a secretary, which occasions the raucous, extended laughter. The remarks produced during this laughter include comments upon the overseriousness ('She's taking it personally') as well as congratulations to Dianne for her performance ('Very well done there').

Extract 2 shows that the intertwining of identities within the game and game-context identities can be complex and subtle. One final extract from the CHEMICAL CONSTRUCTION COMPANY game illustrates such complexities in a different way. In Extract 3 the setting is again the CC team's room.

(3)

Alistair:	We've been messed around for so long, haven't we
	(1.0)
John:	You know who I think Global is
	(1.5)
John:	Ajax Corporation
	(2.0)
Maggie:	[[((Quietly)) Yeah
John:	[[Under a different name
Dianne:	Sorry?
John:	I think Global is Ajax Corporation under a different name, talking to the unions =
Louise:	((Quietly)) No::
John:	= You don't think so?
Louise:	No
John:	Just to put the cat among the pigeons?
?:	((Quietly)) No:::
John:	It would make a lot of sense
Dianne:	We::ll
	(1.5)
Louise:	Well
	((laughter))
John:	[[It would make a lot of sense if that was the case
Anna:	[[(made) a deal
Alistair:	It's a red herring John
Anna:	It is, yeah, I can =
John:	= It certainly would
Dianne:	[[( ) I'm sure of that
Louise:	[[Well Global-no-no Global exists

John: No it exists, sure [but I -
Louise: [Well I don't think (.) I don't think they'd put any ( ) agreement
Alistair: [[It's a red-
John: [[It's an opportunity, I would have thought, for somebody like Ajax [to put-
Alistair: [It's a red herring
John: M::m?
Dianne: ( )
Anna: Completely
John: M::::m?
Alistair: ((To Dianne)) Sorry?
Dianne: The whole thing
Alistair: It's a red herring, I don't see it as (anything else) because er- (.) we don't know who they are, we don't know anything about what work they've got, no one is [saying ( )
Louise: [This is Global?
Anna: Global
Maggie: [[( )
Alistair: [[An (.) well, if the work was so terrific =
John: = Why didn't they-
Alistair: An' it was available now, the workforce would be over there

In this extract a good deal of subtle interactional manoeuvring is performed, on the basis of the distinction between players and organisers. I have already noted that organisers have limited rights to intrude in the playing of the game. Participants *negotiate* their rights between players and organisers. They know that the two identities involve different responsibilities for and knowledge about the game. The proper concerns of organisers are defined by the educational/professional objectives which inform the game. The organisers have chosen (or constructed) the game *for a purpose*. It is their responsibility to monitor the play, on the basis of some kind of expert knowledge that they alone possess, to judge how well they play 'this time' meets the objectives for which the game is being conducted. Organisers can be presumed to hold secrets, to know what these objectives are and how the game relates to them. Therefore organisers legitimately can be asked, by players and others, for their perceptions and assessments.

Organisers' responsibilities for the objectives of the game also give them the right to manage the play in certain respects, in order that their educational/professional goals are more effectively realised. This management can take different forms, but a common one in negotiation games like CHEMICAL CONSTRUCTION COMPANY is for the organisers to introduce new information into the play which substantially changes the situation of one or all of the parties. For example, at one point in this game the course leader, Alan, took the chairman of Ajax, Tim, on one side and presented himself as a representative of the Nigerian government. He brought news of a new grant that the government were prepared to make in order to help resolve the problems with the refinery project. Tim then reported this news back to his team.

However, normative entitlements find expression in interaction in many different ways. Being exercised by those who 'possess' such rights is only one of them (see Sharrock, 1974). For example, organisers' rights to manage the game can occasion queries from players about 'what is happening'. Knowing that game information is under the control of the organisers and *can* be changed in the course of the game, players can speculate about whether ambiguities or inconsistencies may have been intentionally created. Also, players may exercise *their* right to play the game 'to the best of their ability' to challenge any arbitrary manipulation of the game.

If such a challenge is explicit, it is likely to generate interactional difficulties and strain the relationship between players and organisers. Therefore players may look for ways of raising such matters indirectly or implicitly. It is this sort of delicate communicative work that is going on in Extract 3. There is an imbalance of knowledge between players and organisers in the CHEMICAL CONSTRUCTION COMPANY game. The organisers are in possession of all the game information, while the three teams each have only part of it. Therefore, it is open to players to speculate about 'what we do not know' and about how such information may bear upon their game decisions and actions. Such speculation is legitimate action within the game. Indeed, it might be taken to constitute thoughtful and imaginative play. Since the organisers are the authoritative source for this information, players might seek to make such speculations in their presence. Such speculation by a player in co-presence with an organiser might be seen as both an attempt to extract information and a display of the player's (or the team's) involvement in the game.

However, for the reasons outlined above, players might seek ways of making such speculations that do not have the effect of directly challenging organisers. It is noticeable in Extract 3 that John does not directly ask Louise or Dianne whether Global *is* Ajax Corporation under a different name. The enquiry is put together in a roundabout way. He produces it in the form of an opinion, which enables him then to ask others whether they agree. In this way, the two organisers are not faced with having directly to confirm or deny the speculation. John's enquiry enables them to respond in kind, as though they are giving their opinion. However, the fact that they *are* organisers means that anything Louise or Dianne say *can* be taken as imparting 'organiser's information'. It is this, perhaps, which explains their evident hesitancy ('We::ll') and the laughter which follows it.

Louise and Dianne's identity perhaps also has relevance for Alistair's remarks. In a subtle way, Alistair constructs an argument within the framework of the team's game knowledge to reject John's speculation. He does this by formulating things that the team *does not know*. But unlike John's remarks, the unknown identity of Global is here presented as indicating its irrelevance for the team's conduct of the game. Thus, in a neat manner, Alistair uses the state of the team's knowledge within the game to nullify the potential challenge to the organisers contained in John's remarks.

Conclusion

I hope the brief and exploratory analysis presented in this chapter has shown that simulation/gaming is a complex and interesting interactional phenomenon. If so, it has also indicated why any attempt to lay out a *theory* of gaming behaviour is premature and ill-conceived at this stage. We need to know much more about what simulation/gaming *consists in* as communicative behaviour before we try to construct generalisations. There is very little point in trying to explain why simulation/games happen as they do, or why they do not always happen as those who design and run games would like them to, until we have much more detailed knowledge of *what* happens in a game. The task at this stage is one of description rather than explanation. The professional and practical concerns of simulation/game designers and players are ill-served by analytic approaches which purport to delineate the 'skills' involved in simulation/gaming without coming to terms in any way with its interactional complexities. In particular, it remains wholly unclear in such approaches precisely how game players are able to improvise and create *game action*, action which is 'for the sake of the game' yet which is recognisably realistic. It is clear that in doing so participants draw upon common-sense knowledge and communicative competencies they possess as everyday social actors, and that game play thus *trades upon* everyday social life. Equally clearly, simulation/gaming is a distinctive activity and is treated as such by participants. The interweaving and interdependence of these two dimensions is displayed in the detail of game behaviour. Ethnomethodology points us towards this behaviour.

Notes to Chapter 3

1. I would like to thank my friend and colleague, Rod Watson, for his help in the early stages of the work which led to this chapter.
2. The following transcription symbols, adopted from the conventions created by Gail Jefferson for conversation analysis (see Sharrock & Anderson, 1986: 77–79), have been used in this chapter:

[[	Double brackets indicate that two utterances start simultaneously.
[	Single bracket indicates the point at which one utterance overlaps another.
=	Equals signs indicate no interval between end of one utterance and start of next.
(1.0)	Numbers in parentheses indicate elapsed time in seconds.
(.)	Dot in parentheses indicates a very brief silence (less than 1.0 second).
( )	Single parentheses indicate that transcriber is not sure about words contained therein. Empty parentheses indicate nothing could be made of the sounds.
(( ))	Double parentheses indicate descriptions of the talk or non-verbal actions.
:	Colons indicate that prior sound is prolonged. The more colons, the longer the sound.
-	Dash indicates cut-off or 'hitch'.
_	Underscoring indicates stress through pitch or amplitude.

4 Discourse rehearsal: Interaction simulating interaction

STUART J. SIGMAN
State University of New York, Albany, U.S.A.
and
ANNE DONNELLON
Harvard University, U.S.A.

A dramaturgical or theatrical model of social behaviour has been advanced by a variety of investigators (Goffman, 1959; Harré, 1979; Lyman & Scott, 1975). One aspect of the threatre metaphor that has not been systematically developed concerns the rehearsal processes (or phases) of face-to-face interaction. In this chapter, we discuss the processes by which social actors establish rules and routines for interaction with other actor groups by planning for and simulating future interaction events. We label these processes *discourse rehearsal*. Our goal is to discuss both the processes and functions of discourse rehearsal, and to relate this phenomenon to the study of simulation. A case study employing data from an organisational dynamics simulation is also presented.

Structures of face-to-face interaction

Previous investigators have advocated one of several approaches to the study of social interaction. These various approaches can be placed on a continuum: at one extreme are studies which conceptualise interaction events as preprogrammed, i.e. as adhering to a socially dictated structure (e.g. Birdwhistell, 1970; Kendon, 1977; Leeds-Hurwitz, 1985; Sigman, 1983); at the other extreme are studies which consider an emergent and negotiated quality to interaction (e.g. Erickson, 1982; McDermott *et al.*,

1978; Sacks *et al.*, 1974). Both extremes of this continuum are discussed and critiqued in this section, and the need for an alternative perspective combining structural and negotiational approaches is developed.

Scheflen (1968; 1974) has been the most ardent proponent of the a priori structural approach to interaction. Scheflen suggests that interaction is guided by culturally delineated 'programs'[1] or sets of rules for participants' contributions to particular scenes and/or activities. A program statement developed by an investigator to account for the organisation of a particular event describes: the units of observable behaviour; the expected relations among units, e.g. sequentiality, simultaneity; the social context(s) in which each relationship is found; and the degree of normative force behind the actors' performance of each unit and unit relationship (see Sigman, 1985).

Scheflen (1968) notes that the application of a program is context-determined and that a program contains alternative branches which are appropriately employed under specific contextual and/or contingency conditions. A program contains a number of 'fixed' alternatives, whereby the momentary selection and performance of one unit from the behavioural repertoire serves to invoke or specify additional behaviours for subsequent performance and to exclude others. The emergent nature of any particular interaction event results from the actual selections made by the interactants and the behavioural entailments performed on that occasion.

Scheflen's (1968; 1974) work represents an extreme form of cultural determinism. Scheflen (1974) seems to suggest that the appearance of presumedly 'novel' actions and episodes represents faulty observation on the part of the investigator:

> An observer's notion that a form of speech or gesture is idiosyncratic usually reflects his ignorance of other cultures and subcultures. Actually, it is highly unlikely that a variant has been invented *de novo* by an individual and is limited to his repertoire alone.

Such a framework leads to the conclusion that moment-by-moment rule negotiation is the result of actors' selections from a larger (albeit limited) behavioural repertoire, and that rule creation is itself an interaction process regulated by a program or programs (Sigman, 1980).

A significant shortcoming in this structural approach is that it leaves no room for researchers to study the possibilities of participants' strategic application of behavioural alternatives, and that it views social situations in general as prior to, rather than products of, the participants' behaviour. It seems possible for individuals to create new programs for their interaction events, albeit by borrowing and modifying existing behavioural forms, and to define the scope of new interaction events. Much as new lexical items enter a language while adhering to prior morphophonemic and syntactic rules, so too can new programs be instituted by conforming to prior cultural expectations for behaviour.

The approaches to interaction study at the opposite end of the continuum, perhaps best represented by the ethnomethodological perspective first articulated by Garfinkel (1967), emphasise the creative capacities of human actors, suggesting that communication skills extend beyond the ability to select between alternative but pre-existing codes of conduct. Commenting on research undertaken by Garfinkel, in which students were asked to bargain with shopkeepers rather than accept posted prices, Handel (1982) writes: 'It is clear that people are able to respond flexibly and extemporaneously to situations. People are able to successfully improvise a line of conduct and coordinate their activities with others without prior instruction or experience.'

Garfinkel (1967) coined the term 'ethnomethodology' to refer to the subject-matter of his sociological investigations—the practical, everyday reasoning processes by which people jointly produce orderly social action despite a lack of explicit rules. Among the *ad hoc* procedures Garfinkel discovered interactants using for interpretation and action in social settings are: the tendency to 'let pass' (or ignore) ambiguous behaviours; the adoption of a 'wait and see' attitude toward such behaviours which anticipates that subsequent behaviours will clarify the meaning of earlier ones; and the frequent 'formulation' or display of one's interpretation of the ongoing action for one's co-participants.

Within the ethnomethodological framework, the role of context in guiding contributions to interaction, as both resource and constraint, has been most clearly and comprehensively articulated by the conversational analysts Sacks *et al.* (1974). They offer a model which, though it recognises the necessity of some 'context-free' organising principles, maintains that the most influential contexts in the production of interaction are those behaviours which are most 'immediate' to (i.e. occurring just prior to, immediately following, or simultaneous with) the interactants. Thus conversational patterns are specified in terms of sequentially relevant behaviours (e.g. question–answer sequences), and interactants are said to orientate to these behavioural guides to the extent that even minor variability is sufficient to create a new context and, consequently, to alter the behavioural stream under production. Sacks *et al.* (1974) refer to such situatedness of behaviour as the 'local management' and 'recipient design' of interactions.

In an attempt to avoid the extremes of both cultural determinism and radical contextualism, Erickson (1982) conceptualises interaction as the product of structural programs and negotiation. He suggests that discourse results from moment-by-moment display and co-ordination of behaviour by co-participants, and that 'local production' is made possible by the existence and display of a priori behavioural patterns. Unlike the structural approach discussed above, however, the interaction episode as a whole is not considered to be preprogrammed. Erickson (1982) writes: 'Interactional partners must have means available for establishing and maintaining interdependence in their collective action. These means appear to be patterns of timing and sequencing in the performance of verbal and nonverbal behavior.' These patterns function to signal to one's interactants which behavioural sequence is being performed at a given moment and to delimit the range of acceptable responses. Unlike the discourse contributions described by Sigman (1983) which served to call into play a particular agenda for the overall interaction activities of the task group studied, the statements described by Erickson do not structure entire events, but only immediately subsequent utterances.

Erickson (1982) writes that the focus of his investigations into classroom discourse stands 'at a midpoint on the continuum between highly ritualized, formulaic speech events, in which all functional slots and their formal contents are prespecified, and highly spontaneous speech events, in which neither the successive slots nor their content is prespecified'. Classrooms involve participants in a number of activities that are structured by shared cultural norms, but are also open to chance occurrences, and are best thought of as constructed through improvisation. Rather than view 'performance' as an incomplete version of underlying 'competence', Erickson suggests that performers improvise, adapting the culturally delineated template for ideal behaviour in order to remain true to the underlying spirit and functions of that model in the face of moment-by-moment contingencies.

An alternative approach to the two extremes, and a variation on Erickson's (1982) improvisational perspective, is proposed in the remainder of this chapter. What is called for is an approach to interaction study which recognises that: some interaction events are prestructured, and, indeed, planned for; prestructuring can represent more than a passive adherence by actors to an a priori cultural program for such event(s); and participants can be observed generating and rehearsing a 'vocabulary' for action in preparation for real-time upcoming interaction events.

Discourse rehearsal

Gergen's (1982) critique of the social sciences is directed in part at the notion that human behavioural patterns are fixed and unchanging. To the contrary, he notes:

> In addition to reflexive capacities theorists frequently endow the human with capacities for the *autonomous envisioning of alternatives* ... One need not accept the given as immutable, but may autonomously develop (1) alternative means for achieving a given end, (2) alternative ends that may be reached through any given means, and (3) entirely novel means-ends composites (emphasis in original).

The notion of discourse rehearsal acknowledges such insights, suggesting that there are moments in interaction when social actors are confronted by a range of alternative behaviours, or on their own invoke the possibility of a range of alternative behaviours, and that selections from such repertoires are explicitly made and rehearsed by the actors prior to exhibition to some 'audience' (Goffman, 1959).

If one sees the semiotic codes out of which communication interactions are constructed as containing numerous branches and strategic options (see Duncan, 1972), then it is certainly the case that all of continuous behaviour involves option selections, most of which differentially entail responses and differentially constrain subsequent behavioural selections by all participants. However, discourse rehearsals are different from these everyday occurrences in that thcy have a *projective quality* to them: they project the current interaction episode (particularly the moment or moments of rule selections) onto some future episode. The upcoming event represents the planned-for moment of performance and invocation of previously chosen behaviours. Thus, discourse rehearsals, as we define thcm, are not merely 'ends' in themselves, but rather are interaction events in which 'ends' are negotiated, alternative 'means' are generated, and the scene is set for 'novel means-ends composites' to evolve. We argue therefore that discourse rehearsals are interactions simulating interaction.

There are two vantage points from which discourse rehearsal can be conceptualised. The first considers discourse rehearsal to be an event, an interaction episode of a particular type. The second considers discourse rehearsal to be a function or outcome of interaction, and thus as a continuous process comprised of intermittent 'active' contributions over time. Our perspective integrates these views. It recognises that the 'event' perspective facilitates the analysis of particular occasions of interpersonal and intergroup communication for purposes of both training and research.

The 'process' view allows for the analysis of social behaviour in general, without regard for episode boundaries and, additionally, illuminates aspects of the relationship between communication and simulation (see the discussion in the final section of this chapter).

When discourse rehearsal is considered as an event, a distinction is implied between the discourse rehearsal moment and the projected performance. The two interactions are sequentially located in time and, given the meaning structures that the discourse rehearsal projects onto the subsequent performance, they are 'semantically' related as well. That is to say, the rehearsal creates expectations for the structure, content, goals, and participants of the upcoming performance. During the rehearsal, interactants can be observed planning 'what will be done', 'by whom', and 'how' (see below).

Additionally, there is a difference in the 'frame' (Goffman, 1974) surrounding the two interaction events. For example, there may be a difference between the rehearsal and the performance with regard to expectations for feedback. Whereas the commentary on rehearsals is likely to concern the selected rules and their entailments (consequences), the expected feedback from the audience of a performance is some substantive content. The sense or substance of the rehearsal is the selection of rules; for performances, the rules are usually in the background. Whereas the latter can be seen to *proceed along* a 'main story line' (Goffman, 1974), the former can be said to be *about* a 'story line'.

Nevertheless, it is wrong to make too concrete a distinction here since rehearsals are also performances, and must be treated as situationally bound and rule-governed interaction events in themselves. Although discourse rehearsals occur at moments at which there are behavioural options available for selection, and actual option selections are taking place, the accomplishment of the rehearsal interaction implicates particular behavioural rules and routines. A five-part structure is described below.

From the process perspective, the rehearsal frame links the behaviour of interactants across multiple interaction episodes. Interactants can be observed selecting behavioural options and generating new rules for the selection and application of subsequent behaviour. The subsequent behaviour is interpretable in light of its position in the overall rehearsal-performance process. For example, one manager's (A) asking another (B) about how a new secretary is working out may be interpreted as a preliminary step to making a request for help, if this goal was established in prior rehearsal in manager A's group. Otherwise, the question might be interpreted as small talk or an expression of personal concern. The rehearsal need not have occurred during a single interaction event, however. Several weeks of secretarial shortage and seeking assistance might have precipitated the one request noted here.

A brief description of the development of the notion of discourse rehearsal may help elucidate some further features. Sigman (1983) observed the meetings of a task-orientated group in a health-care institution whose function was to discuss and evaluate admissions applications. During the course of several months of observation, Sigman noted a similarity in the set of discourse contributions allowed participants across meetings. There seemed to be an agenda or program for the sequential activities of the group. The program was composed of alternative choice nodes, and depending on the initiating remark(s) by the group leader, different subprograms were followed. In this case, it appeared that some overarching program, which contained a number of subprograms or subroutines, governed the sequential organisation of the event.

Our subsequent naturalistic observations and video-recordings of group interaction in other settings led us to suggest that individuals seem to draw on a generalised repertoire of behaviour for prestructuring upcoming interaction events. Unlike the overarching programs whose existence and potential application were related to specific episodes of interaction, there did not seem to be a clear spatial and temporal delimitation of the 'negotiated' rules we were then seeing. While it was clear that interactants established the *when* and *where* of the rule applications, the rule negotiations themselves preceded a variety of types of interaction. In addition, these negotiations did not only concern the sequential placement and appropriateness of the participants' verbal contributions to the group's process. Rather, they seemed to be concerned with the entire contents of the future communication event(s), including (but not limited to) ostensible goals, co-interactants to be included, strategic locations, etc. In a sense, the participants seemed to develop and project an ethnography of communication description (see Hymes, 1974) of the upcoming event(s).

Our conceptualisation of discourse rehearsal considers the following: the discourse rehearsal process; its functions; and its contribution to the understanding of the relationship between communication and simulation. These concepts are explained further below through illustrative examples from a case study of interaction which simulated interaction, all within the context of a simulation.

Case study of a simulation

The data used for these illustrations are drawn from video-recorded conversations of college students simulating an organisation as part of a course in organisational theory. The organisation is minimally prescribed by published instructions (Miles & Randolph, 1979) which specify four departments (labelled Green, Blue, Yellow and Red), each of which is further subdivided into groups. With the exception of group leaders, no management personnel are specified or required. Successful performance of the organisation requires members to establish procedures for managing employees, purchasing raw materials, producing output, and managing environmental exigencies.

The organisational simulation ran for seven class sessions of approximately one hour each. Each group session was video-taped with the knowledge and permission of participants. We believe that the continuous filming over multiple sessions, and the force of regular performance evaluations, served to dissipate the effects of participants' self-monitoring over time. Evidence of this change is observable in the decreasing number of references to the camera during the course of the seven weeks.

Several interactions occurring within this simulation were interpretable as discourse rehearsals; we will focus on one particular incident which provides rich illustrative detail. Members of the personnel group received a message indicating that a resource cutback due to a takeover of the company necessitated the temporary layoff of eight people. The personnel group decided to use this situation as an opportunity to seize control of the organisation by laying off leaders of the other groups and subsequently installing themselves in the leader positions.

The following interaction sequences, occurring after the cutback message had been received, demonstrate the process of discourse rehearsal.[2]

1 **J**: No, now it's time to fire so//meone.

...

2 **D**: Here's what we can do, we can take over//

...

3 **D**: //the group leaders. OK at least a couple. The money goes to the group leaders doesn't it? So we'll have control over all the money//

...

4 **?**: We have to rehire them.

5 **?**: (   ) we'd have central control.

6 **D**: We can still produce without them.

...

7 **T**: Look, hey hey here's something to think about.

8 **T**: We can go in there and talk//very sweet

...

9 **J**: Let's decide what we're gonna do.

10 **T**: This is what we should do. When we come in to t-t-tell the group what's going on or take over the group leader or whatever. We got to say, look, you know, tell them the story, what happened. And say we had to put these people, we picked them out of a hat and these people came down as//as temporarily idle.

11 **M**: Should we tell them the story though?

12 **T**: We'll make up a story. They are going to be temporarily idle and they're going to be brought back on the next time so it doesn't hurt the performance level indicators. Actually it makes a lot of sense.

...

13 **T**: Yeah, and then we could bring them back and it would cost less, right?

14 **D**: How many do we have to lay off?

15 **S**: Eight.

...

16 **J**: Let me have that, wait I'm going to have to read it to, a, the groups.

17 **M**: What should we tell them?

18 **J**: The truth =

19 **M**: Should we tell them the truth?

20 **J**: We have to.

...

21 **M**: Hey now wait a minute, should we tell them the whole thing =

22 **J**: Yeah.

23 **M**: Or should we make up a story that we don't have enough base wage tickets? The permanent wage tickets are gone. =

24 **T**: They are gone. =

25 **M**: Okay, but don't tell them about the company.

26 **S**: But that's what, that's the truth, just tell them the base wage tickets are gone.

27 **M**: Don't tell them about the takeover or anything.

...

28 **T**: Everybody expects it anyway. Say we have a special event and a =

29 **D**: They're not gonna know.

30 **S**: And just say you picked these names out of hat and these are the people that are going =

31 **S**: I wouldn't even tell them till next session. I wouldn't even ( ), I don't think you should tell right now.

...

32 **D**: Listen, nothing leaves this room, okay?

Later, J enters the office of Green Department:

101 **J**: I got something to read to you. ((Reads message about the takeover and resource cutback.)) So that means that eight people every round are going to have to be idle. So what we did we went down the list and we took people = we didn't take any controllers cause we fig = because they were necessary to stay in here = you know to get the tickets//

102 **H**: //Heh, heh, heh//

103 **J**: //and we threw some people = we just went down and took some random names and = next round, there'll be eight more people on idle, so they won't become permanently idle.

At this point in our research, based on analysis of the above interactions and others, we have developed the following five-part idealisation of the discourse rehearsal process:

1. Recognition (or establishment) of the upcoming event.
2. Rule establishment, which includes interactants' selections from the repertoire of culturally allowable rules, as well as the justification of these selections, given ostensible goals which are themselves accountable.
3. Simulation or rehearsal of interactions which make use of the selected rules.
4. Critique and revision of the previously rehearsed rules.
5. The actual implementation of the rules.

It must be recognised that, as an idealisation, the five units of the sequence can be seen on particular occasions to be elided in a single speaker's utterance or turn, that the order may be reversed in some events, that the prominence (or absence) of one or more units is possible, and that the sequence, and the units, are recursive. Steps two and three, for example, are governed by a rule of alternation in which either or both units may appear; and within step two, a selection may be explicitly made or merely implicated by some justificatory utterance.

We will now flesh out each of the five steps through reference to the interaction fragments quoted above. First, at some point in an interaction, participants recognise, require or prescribe impending contact with other social actors. In the organisational simulation, the students experienced this anticipation as they considered the implications of the message about the takeover and cutback, as turn 1 depicts. Almost immediately, behavioural options for response are proposed (turn 2), during which the precipitating event is interpreted as an opportunity to seize control of the organisation. Turns 3, 5, and 6 are interpretable as justifications for that strategy selection, necessitated by the critiques implied in turns 4 and 6, respectively, that such behaviour could entail both direct and out-of-pocket costs to the organisation.

After the goals for the impending interaction have been established, the rehearsal sequence proceeds with interactants projecting ('trying out') options for the slots of the prospective performance; i.e. actors are suggested for key roles, various scenes are considered, etc. In turns 8 and 10, T displays one of the clearest examples of performance simulation, specifying actors, lines of dialogue, and even the key or manner ('very sweet') in which the performance should be conducted. In an extended critique of the core of the simulation (turns 11, 17, 19, 21, 23, and 25), M proposes a revision to the script which is not accepted by the group. In turn 31, S proposes a revision in the timing of the performance.

Having established through this simulation the 'motivation' informing the performance, other performance details and even lines to be used (e.g. 'picked ... out of a hat' from turns 12 and 30), the group members tacitly recognise the right of their group leader (J) to enact the preferred role which has been jointly created. From the video-tapes, it is noticeable that all comments regarding the proposed performance are kinesically directed towards J, no other actor proposes to play the role, and when, in turn 16, J expresses the intention to initiate the performance by reading the message about the takeover, no one challenges this assumption.

In turns 101–103, we observe the beginning of the implementation of the rehearsed discourse. Following the script outlined earlier, J begins his performance for the Green Department by reading the message received from the environment. His later references to 'random names' and going 'down the list' are linguistic choices consistent with the impression of impartiality which the rehearsed line 'out of a hat' would have conveyed.

Although we do not have the space to elaborate further here, the remainder of J's performance in this interaction similarly conforms to the rehearsal. However, this is not to say that rehearsals automatically entail performances. To the contrary, our data suggest that occasionally performances deviate from the rehearsal, and sometimes they do not occur at all, despite the simulation.

The discourse rehearsal thus functions to guide individuals' contributions to interaction, and even to provide a template for interactants to interpret one another's behaviour. The latter function can be observed in the discussions about what story to tell. It is clear that M understands (as does T) that the group is creating a 'story' for the others, but it is not until turn 25 that he expresses his concern about how much of the truth can be used to create a compelling story.

Discourse rehearsal fulfils several other functions as well. As demonstrated in the case above, such simulation of future behaviour allows a group to clarify its goals by providing an opportunity for objections to possible actions and outcomes to be voiced in advance. It thus also provides the occasion for enhancing group cohesiveness. The paralinguistic and kinesic data from our video-tapes in which the members of Blue Department seemed to 'lose' themselves in the frenzy can be interpreted as displaying such developments and functions.

Discourse rehearsal can also result in a defining function or style of group interaction. As a mid-range account of social behaviour in face-to-face interaction, discourse rehearsal depicts the rule generation and application processes as guided by strategic selections from a repertoire of options, rather than regulated by social programs or emerging from the immediate interactional context. In the simulation and performance of these options, new social forms (styles) can be created by the participants.

Finally, the discourse rehearsal perspective on interpersonal communication suggests that simulation, usually considered as an artificial enterprise, is actually a natural and important part of everyday events. In this manner, it can be deliberately selected from various behavioural options as a pedagogical or experimental technique. The organisational simulation examined here was conducted to provide college students with an opportunity to learn about concepts such as organisational behaviour, design, change, and development in an experiential manner (Miles & Randolph, 1979). The simulation has also been used by researchers to investigate social phenomena such as conflict, power, and group development (Donnellon *et al.*, 1986). The key issue to be noted here is that interaction simulating interaction is a ubiquitous feature of everyday social behaviour.

Notes to Chapter 4

1. Scheflen's use of the term 'program' is not to be confused with the terminology of computer programming. Rather than the fully explicit steps which intentionally govern the operations of a computer, Scheflen's (1973: 212) 'programs

provide for performance of standard, recognizable behavior units, integrated hierarchically and programmed to be performed successively in steps'. Though members of society regularly perform such programs with considerable predictability, thus displaying their 'knowledge' of the routines, these need never be explicitly described in the culture, nor be articulable in the sense that computer programs must be, in order to be properly executed.

2. Transcription conventions for these interactions include the following:

=	immediate speech, no pause
...	points where utterances have been deleted
( )	unintelligible utterance
//	overlapping speech begins.
(( ))	descriptions of the talk or non-verbal actions.

5 Computerised simulation as mediator of language

EDWARD B. VERSLUIS
Southern Oregon State College, U.S.A.
DANNY SAUNDERS
The Polytechnic of Wales, U.K.
and
DAVID CROOKALL
The Pennsylvania State University, U.S.A.

The future promise of computerised simulation is hinted at by Kay's (1984) description of the computer itself:

> The protean nature of the computer is such that it can act like a machine or like a language to be shaped and exploited. It is a medium that can dynamically simulate the details of any other medium, including media that cannot exist physically. It is not a tool, although it can act like many tools. It is the first metamedium, and as such it has degrees of freedom for representation and expression never before encountered and as yet barely investigated. Even more important, it is fun, and therefore intrinsically worth doing.

For our present purposes, one major emphasis is that a computer simulation can serve as a language-rich task master, evoking for students communication challenges from the real world. The computer's role, in evoking those challenges, is a complex and fascinating subject.

We wish here to touch on some issues related to communication and interaction in contexts which include the use of computerised simulation. This is closely linked with the analysis of interaction through media simulations (Chapter 21), and we can distinguish two broad types: first, where the focus is more on the individual's relations with the machine; and second, where emphasis is placed on communication between people.

The contexts in which computers are used, e.g. office, home, education, simulation, will determine to some extent the roles it can be expected to play. The context that concerns us here is, of course, simulation, but we wish to restrict this further to computerised simulation for educational purposes. Although simulation is an extremely flexible tool, as the various chapters in this book show, and the roles that computers can play in simulation are almost as equally varied, we wish here to highlight three of them.

The computer as communication network

Sometimes the most sophisticated students can benefit from the computer's most transparent role, that of a communication vehicle relaying messages to far-flung audiences. The best example is ICONS, discussed in Chapter 6. But however complex such a simulation and the roles it offers its human participants, the computer's role is rather restricted. Essentially the entire simulation relies on the computer's function as a word-processor-wire-service, instantly transmitting the carefully worded communications between the simulation participants. We can characterise the computer in this role as an international spider's web, filled with danger and opportunity. But that characterisation is in actuality based upon an ironic circumstance—that the computer, directly in the path between any two teams, is virtually invisible. It only reaches international players, whose communications in response to the demands of the simulation create our awareness of a fabric of interwoven messages.

The computer as catalyst for communication

Yet another way in which the computerised simulation can inspire communication is in two of its most common roles: as a resource (or data base) and as a calculator (number cruncher). A common example is seen in computer simulations for the least sophisticated users—schoolchildren. In this role the computer facilitates communication by serving as a focus of attention, the place where the group encounters problems and the place where the group tries out its solutions. Several commercially available computer simulations work this way. One, MARY ROSE, a simulation of locating and excavating the underwater site of King Henry VIII's flagship, aims

> to provide children with the opportunity to find the ship themselves, to carry out dives on the wreck, to participate in the processes of excavation and research which are the tools of archaeological and

> historical investigation, and to share in the exciting business of bringing to life our past (Holmes *et al.*, 1982).

Since MARY ROSE is a complex simulation, the activities listed in that description depend partially upon taking notes with pencil and paper on what has been and what has yet to be done. There is a lot to keep track of.

> During the dives there is a screen display of current position, duration of dive, depth and air supply, all of which are continually updated. This information will be used at each stage by the children to determine their moves and make group decisions about strategy (Holmes *et al.*, 1982).

The social interaction is rather involved, too. The class is divided into small groups which can proceed separately or exchange supervisory roles. The computer's role, then, is as a catalyst and guide for small-group communication.

Using the computer in a simulation primarily as a tool to reach other people, or as a source of information to be discussed, clearly promotes communication skills. But the computer can be used as more than a passive mediator of information. THE PENGUINS OF DEATH is a computer simulation where the problem to be solved is explicitly a communication problem. Here pairs of children in their early teens face a computer screen and try different approaches to achieving paragraph coherence. The task is simply to reassemble ten sentences into the two well-ordered paragraphs that existed before somebody ran a lawn-mower over a letter to Mother. Grouping and ordering sentences are communication skills (albeit humble ones) which require the two students to negotiate with each other very quickly what each step will be. A significant complicating factor has been added. Not only must the students communicate, but now the subject of their communication is communication itself. This new factor can be exploited to the limit of the simulation writer's knowledge of what elements constitute a communication.

Similar communication skills are developed in MANEDES, where participants become part of a new microcomputer company, and are required to reach group decisions that enhance production, sales and marketing for each three-month period of game time. In addition to the final decision that has to be agreed by all participants, the players are sub-divided into departments that are responsible for specific decisions about production, sales, finance and personnel. Consequently, each department has the task of communicating its own analysis of the situation to other departments. It is only when all players reach an overall conclusion about the predicaments faced and strategies reached by all departments that their final decisions are then processed by computer. Share prices and profits are subsequently announced, and the simulation moves on to the next financial period. MANEDES emphasises that access to the computer is severely restricted, with the major objective being that of group negotiations in a business context as opposed to a computerised one. This advice is based on the fundamental recognition of the frequent detachment of a computing department (and associated profession) from the rest of a company or organisation. Difficulties then emerge when highly technical computer-based information has to be disseminated to people who are unfamiliar with computer language (some would say 'jargon') and who may even have a certain amount of resistance to such high-technology mediation.

To conclude this section, it is worthwhile mentioning some of the positive arguments proposed by Greenfield (1984), who suggests that computer-aided interaction within the classroom actually encourages and fosters communication through group membership, interpersonal involvement, and co-operation. By drawing on examples of secondary or high-school classroom contexts, she notes how word processing affects communication by developing friendship, as observed in relation to one teacher's class project which involved the writing and production of an entire book:

> The computer also encouraged co-operation among the children in the writing project. According to their teacher, this class had had some troublc getting along with one another, but the computer drew them together. There were always three or four children standing around the computer working together on the book. This theme that computers foster co-operation is one that we have met before. But when each child has a computer to write with, they become so involved in writing itself that this sort of co-operative activity does not take place. It seems to be the need to share computers that prompts children to work together (Greenfield, 1984).

The clear advice here is for computer-*aided* interaction as opposed to computer-*centred* activity. The above quote paints a rosy picture of computers within the classroom, but it should be remembered that such a set-up can easily develop into group conflict when there is limited access to consul and/or VDUs, and where there are divided group friendships, loyalties and interests. However, there are patterns of communication between participant and computer that are worth exploring and that hold much in store for the future.

The computer as participant

The next step, of course, is to cast the computer in the role of a participant in the message exchange itself. At this stage, what is being communicated can be composed of whatever people want to discuss. How it is being communicated is by interaction with the machine. In what sense can we be said to communicate with a machine? Actually there are two senses. Telephoning another person is communicating with (i.e. using) a machine. And there is another more problematic sense. Information can be put into a computer in anticipation of producing a human response from the machine. Of course, this second sense is only illusory. The telephone mediates an instant human response. The computer mediates (or rather 'triggers') a delayed human response. That delayed human response was deposited in the computer program at an earlier date. Hence it is a mild illusion to speak of 'communicating with a machine'.

Operator–machine relations may even adopt an *interactive* property, especially when the computer or word processor is ascribed *personality* characteristics of one sort or another. Indeed, the entire notion of user friendliness conjures up images of the consul or terminal as a person-substitute that engages in what some theorists have called 'para-social interaction' (Horton & Wohl, 1956; Rubin *et al.*, 1985). By way of illustration, ELIZA is a computerised program that tries to simulate elementary conversation between operator and machine. This is well summarised by Frude (1983):

Eliza: Hi, I'm Eliza, what's your problem?
Neil: I feel tired.
Eliza: Tell me more about such feelings.
Neil: I'm not alert.
Eliza: Did you come to me because you're not alert?
Neil: Yes.
Eliza: Are you sure?
Neil: Maybe I have other problems too.
Eliza: You don't seem quite certain.
Neil: Sorry.
Eliza: Please don't apologize.

This type of language simulation has some potential within such areas as counselling, as developed by the PLATO program based on a form of therapy called 'dilemma counselling'. PLATO provides a series of alternative courses of action for selected dilemmas or crises encountered in everyday life, and simply asks the operator to choose: each choice leads on to other dilemmas within a complex set of routines and sub-programs that make up the PLATO package. In some computerised simulations, both patterns will operate side by side.

Both of the above-mentioned encounters with what Frude (1983) calls the 'inanimate' involve simulations of communication within psychotherapy and counselling contexts. They are simulations rather than 'the real thing' because both are clearly described by their authors as experimental and simplistic games with language that involve person–machine communication. It is emphasised that they are currently limited in their scope and complexity when it comes to sophisticated language analysis, although we should recognise that eventually there may well be the possibility of the inanimate medium being more effective than 'the live other' within certain forms of interaction that prove too stressful or demanding for the person seeking advice or company. Indeed Weizenbaum (1976) himself turned against his creation and argued that there is a very real danger of machines simulating people, to the extent of some operators developing a preference for such para-social interaction as opposed to the 'real' company of people. However, provided participants do not delude themselves and see the illusion for what it is, much valuable exploration of communication can be encouraged by this form of computerised simulation.

The illusion of an immediate human–machine communication is exploited in a couple of computer simulations. AUNT SADIE'S GIFT was designed to teach audience analysis. Generally the task is to compose an acceptable letter thanking your Aunt Sadie for an unusual Christmas present (a frozen six-foot rattlesnake, now thawing back to life). That means the student or user must address two entities with quite different origins. The first obvious audience is Aunt Sadie. The student or user (now assuming the role of Sadie's nephew, Waldo Lungtrout, alias 'Bubby') reads her letter and some additional notes about her warm past relationship with him. Then Aunt Sadie is to be communicated with via a letter composed of sentences the student or user selects from groups of two or three possibilities offered as the simulation progresses. The end result is one of over a hundred acceptable (if not wonderful) thank-you letters.

Is the student's letter communication? None of the sentences are actually invented by the student. Aunt Sadie does not actually exist as a real human being and, real or simulated, is not going to respond. On the other hand, no communication is made up of elements totally invented fresh for that instance. The alphabet, words, phrases, even whole sentences are drawn from a person's repertoire to be bound together into a message. And people daily write off to fictional entities addressed with the names of offices, companies or government agencies. One objection is that there are real people behind those fictional names; there are even real non-human entities. Government agencies do, we must often soberly admit, have very substantial existences. And those real people within those real entities can respond to a letter in a way that fictional Aunt Sadie cannot.

There is, to be sure, a significant difference between Aunt Sadie as a target of communication and any real-world human or collection of humans. She cannot respond, and, if a real or potential response is required to satisfy your notion of communication, then communication in this simulation is impossible. There are just two little problems with that conclusion. First, there are frequent instances of human messages that require audiences, but preclude response. 'This end up' on a box is an example. Or one remembers those words posthumously attributed to the Spartan heroes at Thermopylae. We do not respond to the writers of printed instructions or epitaphs. Yet both are instances of writing with considerable concern for communication. The simulated Aunt Sadie would seem, at least, to be a simulated audience. Conceiving of hypothetical audiences is a practice that is implicit in the very idea of rhetoric. 'How would such a one respond?' is the key question for an ancient Roman orator or a modern letter writer. It is just a short step from imagining a response to incorporating an imagined response into a communication simulation.

Secondly, and more interestingly, it is not strictly true to say of the AUNT SADIE'S GIFT simulation that there is no response to the student or user's letter. As a matter of fact, there is constant response stemming from two sources. The first source of response is, of course, the simulation writer who has written a comment for each of the sentences the student or user chooses. As the choice is entered, a comment appears, evaluating the choice and how it contributes to or detracts from the letter as it has taken shape up to that point. That is what the student or user sees, an evaluation by the simulation writer, waiting to be triggered by a particular selection from among a group of sentences.

But this is a computer simulation. So the simulation writer can hide behind a persona, a fictional character who waits to comment on the student or user's choices. At the simulation writer's call is a half-formed creature, implicit in computer programs themselves. Whenever someone uses a computer program, little prompts (messages explaining how to manipulate the machine toward a given end) appear on the screen. Prompts are the computer programmer's way of guiding the user in performing machine operations during the course of a program. Since the sum of the user's experience of these prompts tends to be a sensed human presence, some care must usually be taken to make them 'friendly' (i.e. to make the sensed human presence warm rather than intimidating).

In a simulation like AUNT SADIE'S GIFT, where reconsidering the choice of a sentence requires a machine operation, the simulation writer's fictional persona and the implied human presence of the prompts begin to merge. The result opens up some interesting opportunities for computer simulation design. The full range of what this synthesised fictional persona expresses can be called 'computer commentary'. Computer commentary covers the entire relationship of the student or user to the machine and to the simulation. Since the response to any student or user's action is immediate (instant feedback is one of the computer's chief assets as an instructional device), something like human communication is produced. Once the sources of the computer commentary are traced back to human writers and programmers, it can be seen that this really is a remote cousin of the instant transparent conveyance of messages found in ICONS.

THE EXCAVATION OF OBJECT C-9, an advanced-level computer simulation currently under development, has the student or user prepare a number of reports and memos while assessing the technical and human elements in a complex operation—the salvaging of part of an archaeological site on an unstable planet in the Andromeda galaxy. The human elements involved are the tangled clash between inter-agency jealousy and scientific curiosity. The knowledge of writing involved ranges from the general principles of audience analysis to the specific requirements of particular report formats. That is, throughout the simulation, language tasks are cast in terms of problem-solving, whether it be the complaint and request kind of technical writing assignments or the more abstract use of graphics to analyse problems. Since THE EXCAVATION OF OBJECT C-9 is a suite of computer programs, it is quantitatively richer with communications opportunities than is AUNT SADIE'S GIFT. However, of more relevance to this discussion is the extension of the idea of the persona projected by the computer commentary. In AUNT SADIE'S GIFT the language tasks required comments that inevitably produced a persona whose knowledge of writing was markedly greater than the student's or user's. In THE EXCAVATION OF OBJECT C-9 problem-solving of a wider variety is being added to the language tasks. And the intention is to produce a persona whose implied knowledge will only occasionally be superior to the student's or user's (more like a sidekick).

The benefits of widening the range of tasks and reducing the persona's authority are fairly obvious. Real-world writing challenges often appear in the context of largely political or mechanical problem-solving situations.

Reducing the persona's authority encourages the student or user to be more independent.

Even though AUNT SADIE'S GIFT is an example of a computer simulation where all of the activity is confined to the interaction between the student or user and the program in the machine, it would be misleading to confine the value of that program to what can be derived from that transaction alone. As with any instructional aid, the primary responsibility for pointing out implications and suggesting applications still rests squarely on the teacher. In fact AUNT SADIE'S GIFT is only one of three letter-writing programs. BUCCANEER BILLY'S BAD BARGAIN, a complaint-letter simulation, and MORTAL REMAINS, a request-letter simulation, offer alternative letter-writing experiences. Buccaneer Billy has written a furious (and somewhat incoherent) complaint letter to the Acme Cannon Co. The student or user must analyse Billy's complaint and then write a more effective letter to Acme. MORTAL REMAINS involves writing to the widow of a famous public figure to request the return of a personal article (a school cap in the family for three generations) which he had borrowed just prior to his death. One computer program accommodates these and other letter-writing simulations. To draw out and reinforce generalisations about communication from those particular experiences is still the teacher's work. THE EXCAVATION OF OBJECT C-9's individual simulations will be spread out over so great a portion of the school term that supplying or reinforcing continuity may be an added requirement. Some logistical problems are still to be surmounted.

Conclusion

The conclusion to be drawn from this quick survey of what roles can be assigned to the computer to assist and encourage communication is that the potential variety is considerable. From simulated telephone to simulated sidekick, the computer as a mediator of language can excel in those roles. How each of those roles can be extended to the greatest benefit of students of communication is the province of enlightened and imaginative teachers.

6 Our multicultural global village: Foreign languages, simulations and network gaming

DAVID CROOKALL
The Pennsylvania State University, U.S.A.
REBECCA OXFORD
Annenberg/CPB Project, U.S.A.
DANNY SAUNDERS
The Polytechnic of Wales, U.K.
and
ROBERTA LAVINE
University of Maryland, U.S.A.

Introduction

The need to understand and deal with other cultures in today's global village is more urgent than at any time in the history of humanity, and underlies the rising prominence of multilingual communication round the world. The sense of our planet as a global village and increased multilingual communications have grown together. About 60% of the world's population today is multilingual, and the mastering of foreign languages as a means of cross-cultural communication has become crucial to the survival of the world. The urgency for effective international communication raises a key question: how well does present-day language-teaching methodology meet the need?

We begin this chapter by outlining a number of reasons for the general growth in multilingual communication. We then summarise shifts in foreign language instructional methodology and attempt to show why simulation is an excellent way to learn certain communication skills in a foreign language (henceforth abbreviated to 'FL'). The more recent and more communicatively orientated FL teaching methodologies have advocated, if only implicitly, greater use of simulation as an important language-learning technique. This parallels the increase in simulation use in a wide range of other disciplines, particularly in those which recognise communication as essential to their full understanding and practice. Finally, we describe some examples of simulations used in FL classrooms, including a computerised, international, multilingual simulation, which illustrates how FLs may be integrated with other disciplines.

Multilingual communication

When we speak of communication between cultures we necessarily speak of using a variety of languages, some of which may be foreign to at least one of the parties to the communicative act. The mastery of FLs has thus come to the forefront of educational activity and international concerns, and there is no reason to suppose that the importance of multicultural communication and of FLs will decrease. It is useful to look at some of the reasons, for they highlight the necessity of being able to communicate in a FL, and they help focus attention on the methods we use to learn a FL.

One major reason for increased world-wide multilingual communication is modern technology, especially the so-called 'new technologies' —media, computers, telecommunications. For example, computerised systems using satellites and fibre optics have led to the creation of dense international communications networks of a kind that would hardly have been dreamt of a few decades ago. Such systems allow us, for example, to chat with a friend on the other side of the globe, make our credit cards work internationally, link stock exchanges round the world, and give us access to sophisticated navigation aids. Computer chips made in Far East form the heart of our Western 'home-grown' personal computers; and it takes multilingual communication to bring all the components together. Thus, new technologies both arise from, and give rise to, the need for multilingual communications.

This brings us to our second factor in increased multilingual communication: trade and economic interdependence. Japanese factories spring up in rural America and Europe; American and British firms compete for corporate clients round the world; international meetings, such as those held by the IMF or GATT, are followed closely by the world community. Related to technology and economics is a third factor, internationalisation of the media. This has profoundly influenced many walks of life, including entertainment, publishing and broadcasting. Newspapers have become increasingly international; books and periodicals circulate round the world; and international broadcasting is evolving rapidly (short-wave radio is more popular than ever, and European TV channels are springing up fast).

A fourth contributor to greater multilingual communication is international politics, whether this be seen as 'collaboration' (e.g. organisations such as the UN or the EEC), or as competition and intervention (e.g. the nuclear arms race and continuing wars). Related to political upheavals, as well as to economic disparities, are two other international phenomena, both influential in multilingual communication. These are population movements and minority cultures. Reasons for movements are economic immigration (e.g. Mexicans going to the United States), the flight of political refugees from their homelands (e.g. the Vietnamese), and pleasure travel (as seen in hugely increased international air traffic). Related to this is the rise of minority cultures. In the United Kingdom, for example, Pakistani and Indian minority groups have their own cultural identities, as do Blacks, Hispanics, and South-East Asians in the United States. Greater political and economic power and a heightened consciousness of minority identities result in a general pluralisation of cultures and in more multilingual communication.[1]

For these reasons (technology, economics and trade, media, politics, the movement of people, the rise of minority cultures) and, no doubt, others, multilingual and multicultural communication has become a critical area of concern high on the educational agenda of many nations. Communication is now a vital and ubiquitous resource for the world as a whole, and there is greater awareness of the scope of the right to communicate, which is now conceived as encompassing many other more specific rights (MacBride *et al.*, 1980). One of these sub-rights must inevitably be the specific one of the right to learn a FL. Indeed, natural languages are not only mankind's most important sign system (Berger & Luckmann, 1966) but are *ipso facto* the major means of communication across the world. Just as our world would not exist without communication, much communication would hardly be possible without language. However, it is another question as to whether FL teaching and learning techniques are as effective as they should be in achieving their objective of making multilingual communication possible.

Communication in FL instruction

A brief overview of the changes in FL instruction over the centuries will show how the concern with communication has influenced instructional developments. Our summary focuses on the communicative aspects of FL instruction, and will thus provide a conceptual backdrop to the use of simulation in FL teaching.[2]

Up to the fifteenth century, Latin was the primary spoken and written language of commerce, religion, government and education in the Western world. However, political changes in the sixteenth century allowed French (and later Italian and English) to eclipse Latin's importance as an international linguistic form. The teaching of Latin then lost its practical purpose, and became a rigorous intellectual exercise, emphasising grammar and rhetoric, and ignoring communication skills. This later evolved into the rigid Grammar-Translation Method (GTM), which dominated FL teaching in Europe from the 1840s until the 1940s. Based in part on 'faculty psychology', which proclaimed that the mind is a muscle requiring vigorous exercise, it emphasised reading comprehension, while natural communication in the FL had no role, instruction being conducted in the student's native tongue. Students learned to translate written passages with the utmost precision, but many of the sentences were unlikely to be found in authentic text, and were almost devoid of meaning. Despite Labov's (1970) warning that 'It is questionable whether sentences that communicate nothing to anyone are part of language', the GTM is still popular among some elements of academia because of its supposed mental discipline, its emphasis on literature rather than on language use, its lack of demands on classroom organisation skills by the teacher, and its easily 'testable' skills. However, it is disliked by many students, who feel cheated when they realise they are generally unable, even after years of study, to utter more than a few phrases, let alone communicate, in the FL.

In the last half of the nineteenth century, reformists began introducing new methods which attempted to address the question of communication. One of these was the Direct Method (DM), which was adopted by many private language schools. The DM emphasised oral communication solely in the target language, without translation. However, it was very unstructured, and often resulted in a 'glib but inaccurate fluency' (Rivers, 1981). For these and other reasons, the DM was never popular in state schools, although modified forms of the method are still used in many institutions. Another reform movement was dubbed Situational Language Teaching (SLT), also known as the Oral Approach. This arose from British structural linguistic theories and was influential from the 1930s until the 1960s in the teaching of English as a FL. SLT assumed that language could be predicted on the basis of situational events; it stressed communication in the FL but used such carefully controlled grammar and vocabulary that the resulting talk often bore little resemblance to natural social interchange. In the 1950s the Audiolingual Method (ALM) emerged from the work of American structural linguistics, contrastive analysis, and behavioural (stimulus-response) psychology. The ALM focused on drilling a variety of FL dialogues and patterns until they became an automatic habit for the learner, but these were often memorised without the student's even knowing their meaning, nor their appropriateness in a given social context. The method waned when consumers realised that the skills it taught were restricted and did not transfer to authentic communication situations. Nevertheless, the ALM continues to be used in some classrooms throughout the world.

Dissatisfaction with previous methods led to the development of the eclectic but powerful Communicative Language Teaching Approach (CLTA) in Britain and elsewhere in the 1970s. In this approach, communication of meaning in the FL is the most important element. Emphasis is placed on the nature of meanings, on the functions played by utterances in real discourse, and on their appropriateness to specific contexts. Learning activities are directed toward the communication of meaning; language learning is defined as learning to communicate. The use of standard dialogues, drills, translation, and the student's native language is allowable, but only in the service of developing skills to communicate meaning in the target language. This perspective led to the development of a number of more specific types of methods, all of which emphasised the ability to communicate.[3]

Pioneered in Canada since the late 1960s, and more recently introduced in the United States, FL immersion programmes have proved extremely successful, especially in the development of skills to communicate meaning. In true immersion programmes, all school subjects are taught using the FL as the primary *medium* of communication (rather than the FL being an object of instruction), while in partial immersion selected subjects only are taught in the FL. The results of these programmes, especially in regard to developing communicative competence and altering language attitudes, have been both impressive and consistent.[4]

A controversial method, called the Natural Approach (NA), was developed relatively recently in the United States. It emphasised the communication of meaningful messages and emotional factors. Although some of the NA's tenets and practices, especially the distinction between acquisition and learning, have been criticised, the method has been influential and is used in many institutions. Other recent methods also stress communication and affective factors in mastering a FL. Community Language Learning (CLL) is based on psychological counselling principles; Suggestopedia uses music, breathing exercises, and special classroom arrangements in order to relax students; Total Physical Response (TPR) involves language learning through game-like physical actions; in the Silent Way (SW) students learn the language through 'discovery learning' techniques using coloured rods and charts.[5]

Communication is a major goal in most of the recent methods, although they do vary in the relative explicitness with which they aim to achieve communicative competence. In addition, most of these methods recognise that an individual's motivational level and emotional state strongly affect language learning.[6] Communication itself is an important element of motivation. A student who can see no (communicative) value in what is learned will probably not be particularly interested in learning with that method, especially if he/she needs to be able to communicate with others. The communicative aspect of FL teaching methods has waxed and waned over the centuries and is now at a high water mark. A spate of books and articles has recently been published about communicative FL teaching and its close relative, proficiency-orientated instruction. However, the theoretical popularity of communication and proficiency begs the question of what is actually going on in the FL classroom. As we have noted, in many institutions, some of the older methods linger on; and observations of real classroom behaviour (e.g. Seliger & Long, 1983) show that communicative language teaching is sometimes more an ideal than a reality, even for teachers who are aware of communication as a major goal. But, even when teachers have accepted the general idea of communicative language instruction, they do not always know what it is or how to implement it.

Encouraging communication among students in the classroom requires a rather radical shift in roles and classroom organisation. 'It is now inconceivable to regard the teacher as sole arbiter and controller of what goes on in language classrooms' (Maley, 1984). Communicative FL instruction changes the essential role of the teacher from that of a classroom conductor to that of a resource person and facilitator of learning. Many teachers find this change to be a threat, especially when it necessitates letting go of cherished ideas and familiar habits inherited from their own teachers or encouraged by their employers. Despite these problems, there are many language classrooms around the world in which FL communication is not only encouraged, but also effectively taught. The basic strategy behind a communicative FL classroom is to put students in social situations and give them interesting activities, which, by allowing them to interact, 'create' in them a desire to communicate. But thinking of such situations and activities is not such an easy task, so the more enlightened FL teachers are beginning to look elsewhere than to FL instructional theory and applied linguistics for ways of creating a communicative climate in the classroom. Such sources of ideas and materials include the social sciences, business training, and cross-cultural orientation. These areas already use some rather creative and interesting exercises, which capture students' interest and imagination, and which therefore encourage them to interact. Examples of such activities used in FL instruction include problem-solving activities, debates, trips, and celebration of festivals and special events typical of the FL country. But one of the most promising and increasingly popular techniques for encouraging communication in the FL classroom has proved to be that of simulation/gaming.

Enhancing FL communication through simulation

An intriguing suggestion has been made that all types of FL classroom activity can be thought of as simulations of actual language behaviour. Extremely artificial language-learning situations, such as those that require memorising word lists or drilling dialogues, 'can be viewed as instances of low level simulation of language activity' (Gardner & Lalonde, 1989). Role-playing, dramatic techniques, and similar exercises, however, 'exemplify simulation strategies that foster language development' of a more natural, authentic kind (Gardner & Lalonde, 1989). In this chapter we shall be discussing this latter interpretation.

The advantages of simulation for communicative FL instruction are many, and we shall only have space here to touch on a few,[7] but they are related in some way to the basic aim of creating an environment which encourages social interaction and communication. Simulations are much more than a Friday afternoon respite from more tedious exercises. Indeed, these techniques are an extremely powerful FL learning tool, to be used as a standard feature in FL learning situations. It is somewhat unfortunate that early applications of simulation by inexperienced teachers resulted in the inappropriate criticism of simulation as a time-killer that required little thought and skill. On the contrary, simulation has been perceived as a means of overcoming certain limitations of the classroom as a learning environment, or as Sharrock & Watson (1985) express it, for 'declassrooming the classroom'. In so doing, simulation extends the range of experiences normally made available to FL learners. One of these experiences is precisely that of encouraging students to use the FL communicatively, i.e. in a self-initiated and purposeful way. Simulation allows FL learners to create their own communication realities, rather than being entirely dependent upon the teacher for providing a model.[8]

The language used in simulations is more authentic and richer than that usually found in a typical teacher-directed classroom, which means the problems of 'real' communication can be explored. In a simulation, communication may proceed uninterrupted by teacher intervention, just as it does in most other situations, allowing participants to grasp and convey meaning in a more natural, free-flowing way. Simulations thus generally provide large quantities of FL input. But as Scarcella & Crookall (1989) and Long (1983) point out, input is not enough to produce communicative proficiency in the target language; students may be exposed to a lot of input and not pay attention to it. Active involvement in communication is therefore essential; simulation is intrinsically involving because it provides learners with an appealing and relevant context in which, collectively, they make decisions, solve problems, negotiate agreements, and the like. Moreover, apart from the tasks and problems in the simulation at hand, freer interaction is itself motivating, and allows students to practise a variety of communication strategies (Oxford, 1989). There are those strategies which are useful when the learner lacks sufficient vocabulary or structure for a given purpose (using, for example, synonyms, circumlocution, gestures and mime). Then there are those more closely related to the management of talk, such as turn-taking, which are almost impossible to practise in teacher-controlled discourse (Cunningsworth & Horner, 1985; Sharrock & Watson, 1985).

One important characteristic of simulation is its low error consequence for the 'real' system; in other words, the system being represented will not be greatly affected if errors are made in the simulation. When this principle is applied to a FL simulation, it means that FL communication gaffes made during the simulation, while real and meaningful in the simulation itself, will not have any serious effects on the 'outside' world, which allows the FL learner to make mistakes in the simulation that would be less acceptable elsewhere. As a result, the anxiety level is often lower in a simulation than it is elsewhere (including in teacher-directed classrooms). Simulation reduces anxiety in several other ways, as well. Participants are under less pressure to produce complex language than they may be in other situations, and Jones (1982) notes that anxiety is reduced in simulations because the teacher's role is reduced. In addition, as the focus of comparison is on peers, simulation 'reduce[s] anxiety associated with communicating in a second language ... creates a sense of self-confidence ... [and] permits the development of the non-verbal component' (Gardner & Lalonde, 1989). Harper (1985) emphasises the advantage of simulation in helping FL students to build a positive self-image. Reduced anxiety encourages the simulation participant to communicate more, and more spontaneously, although some tension can help in FL learning (Brown, 1987). We should also be cautious about universal and inevitable reduction of anxiety and inhibition in simulations, especially when students already work in a competitive atmosphere or hostile environment, particularly if it is created within a simulation such as STARPOWER.

Another aspect of simulation that is especially pertinent to FL teaching is its ability to reflect the culture of the target language (Dubin, 1985; Sawyer-Laucanno, 1987). Human communication is culture-bound; that is, membership in a particular culture determines the ways in which we communicate. At the same time, culture is defined and learned through communication, so there is a reciprocal relationship between culture and communication (Ruben & Lederman, 1989). Although some simulations are culture-generic, a FL simulation often embodies elements of the specific culture surrounding the target language. Simulation, because of its participatory quality and because it not only simulates reality but also constitutes a reality in itself, allows the learner to communicate as a member of the temporary simulation culture. 'Simulation and game designs familiarise participants with the cultural and social significance of a second language' (Saunders & Crookall, 1985). Related to this, finally, is the role of play in learning (Bruner *et al.*, 1978; Raabe, 1980); 'simulation ... encourages adolescents and adults to once again play with symbols and enjoy themselves while learning—in much the same way as we learned our first language' (Saunders & Crookall, 1985).

Underlying the above advantages of using simulation in FL classrooms is the general principle of providing students with a relatively safe learning environment in which they may practise and develop communication skills. These can then be transferred more easily to the 'real' or 'outside' world than they can from the traditional classroom situation. Cunningsworth & Horner (1985) show how simulation helps the FL learner to move from the classroom to the 'real' world.

There are, of course, drawbacks, and it might be suggested that certain features make simulations unrealistic—among them the fact that we must live with our errors and cope with consequent anxiety in the real world. The counterargument is that simulation is a stepping-stone. If, in the classroom, there is little significant learning of FL communication skills because of anxiety and punishment of errors, then there is little chance that the longer-term effects of such anxiety or punishment will miraculously disappear outside; and even if they do, the learner will anyway be left with few of the necessary FL communication skills. The value of simulation is in 'gently' introducing participants to many of the demanding aspects of FL communication and cultural plurality. It is generally acknowledged that students learn more efficiently when the FL learning experience is made real, when it is taken out of its more usual, purely academic setting, and when the student must actually function in the FL. Let us now turn to specific examples of FL simulations.

Examples of simulations used in FL learning

There are many types of simulation used in FL instruction, and we can only discuss a few here.[9] Many exercises have been designed specifically for the FL classroom, but many simulations designed for other purposes (such as business or politics) can be used effectively and with little modification in the FL classroom. Very simple games such as foreign language SCRABBLE are very useful for practising certain language items in the FL classroom. Other more socially orientated games are, however, more effective both for the practice of structures and for fostering communication, e.g. 20 QUESTIONS, CHARADES, HOTEL RECEPTIONIST (where students try to communicate a message to a dumb hotel receptionist, who can therefore only communicate through gestures), ALIBI (where several students are interviewed separately, with the aim of finding discrepancies between their individual versions of the same story), and PICTURE STORIES (where groups of students use picture cards to make up a story, which they then tell to other groups). Such activities can be carried out with very little or no material. Small vignettes requiring the simplest of materials are also very useful (Barrows & Zorn, 1983; 1989).

More complex simulations often require materials development, with a more elaborate design stage. Two achetypal situations are the job interview and the board or public meeting, where participants represent specific, sometimes conflicting, positions. In OIL THREAT TO RADLEIGH, for example, participants take on roles such as ‘oil company’, ‘townspeople’, ‘environmentalists’, and have to communicate their opinions in deciding how to tackle the oil-pollution question as it concerns their town. An excellent series is Ken Jones’s (1986) nine graded simulations, which were originally produced for secondary school pupils, but have proved very popular and successful in the FL classroom; in RADIO COVINGHAM, for example, editors produce a news and views programme; a campaign followed by a public inquiry into the building of a new airport is played out in AIRPORT CONTROVERSY. Another series, by Leo Jones (1983), specifically designed for FL learning, covers such topics as news broadcasts and urban planning. Many longer simulations of greater complexity, originally designed for purposes other than FL instruction, are ideally suited to languages for specific purposes, such as business or international relations. SURVIVAL GAME, for instance, deals with unemployment, WINE LAKE is concerned with EEC agricultural policies, while THE ALPHA CRISIS GAME explores the origins of World War I.[10]

Simulation has been associated with computers ever since the latter appeared on the scene, but the use of computerised simulation (CS) poses special problems when the objective is communication among humans. Although the emphasis in FL simulation is on communication, there is still a need for students to develop accuracy. TERRI is an excellent CS for the teaching of accuracy within a communicative context. The simulation requires that students type in accurate and communicatively appropriate commands to order the computer to move objects around until a preselected arrangement is accomplished. One type of CS which has been used with great success in promoting communication between FL learners is where decisions are made by students for a given period and entered into the computer, which then calculates the results for the end of the period before moving on to the next. An interesting account of the use of a simple simulation of this type is provided by Jones (1986), who shows that CSs 'provide an excellent source of speaking practice'. During one exercise, YELLOW RIVER KINGDOM, participants have to talk to one another in order to make various collective decisions (how much rice to plant, how many people to work in fields or maintain dykes). More sophisticated types of CS abound. The topic areas range from environmental crises to shop management, the classic one being the business game. One of these, especially adapted to increase communication among participants, is MANEDES. In order to market their product and make a profit, company executives make a whole range of decisions (on such matters as the amount of raw materials to buy, salary levels and advertising). When used for FL instruction, learners have to deal not only with the usual problems of communication, but with specialised vocabulary.[11]

In all the above simulations, the participants work in the same room (or suite of rooms), and the entire exercise lasts from a few minutes to several days. We shall now examine a simulation which lasts for a whole month, and in which participants are situated in different parts of the world. The basic principle, however, remains the same: only by communicating with each other can participants hope to tackle the problems involved and make decisions. As in the real world, communication forms the bedrock of human activity, and the use of simulation allows this to happen in a foreign language.

Large-scale simulation for intercultural communication

We noted earlier how computer technology has been combined with simulation to encourage communication. The same technology has been used as one of the main communication channels of a particular type of simulation, known as network gaming.[12] This unites three elements into a new methodology: intercultural communication, simulation and computer technologies. The basic principles underlying this type of simulation are not dissimilar to those that have inspired the use of smaller-scale ones, such as those described above. However, we shall outline here those aspects and issues that are essential to understanding the potential of this type of simulation in the promotion of FL communication. We should also like to examine some related communication patterns to be found in such institutional simulations.

The particular simulation we shall dwell on here is called 'International Communication and Negotiation Simulation' (ICONS), in which some 20 university teams around the world each represent a different nation in a month-long international relations simulation. A certain number of teams represent their own country, e.g. a team of French students in Toulon (France) represents France. Other countries are represented by non-nationals, e.g. teams based in the United States represent the Soviet Union and the People's Republic of China. Typically, some 250,000 words will be exchanged among over 500 participants during a five-week exercise. Currently, seven languages are used (English, French, German, Hebrew, Japanese, Russian and Spanish), some of which emanate from culturally authentic sources, e.g. Spanish messages that are written in, and transmitted from, Argentina. ICONS may thus be considered as a kind of partial immersion context.

The basic FL communication process involves each team sending its outgoing messages in the language of the country it represents, and therefore receiving incoming messages from the other teams in a FL. For example, French nationals in the France country-team read the incoming messages directly in FLs and write their outgoing messages in French. As all team members are directly and intensively concerned with every incoming message, reading for fluency (communication) and for accuracy (grammar) are integrated in a natural way. In ICONS a FL is no longer an abstract system devoid of meaning or consequence; it becomes a purposeful, authentic and communicative activity, a means for negotiating realities. The state of the world depends upon a full understanding of messages in several languages.

The multicultural context itself is also an important motivating factor. One reason is the fact that participants know that real and meaningful multicultural communication takes place; for example, students in France know that messages sent by the Argentina country-team were written by 'real' Argentinians. Teams representing their own countries provide a culturally authentic perspective, while those representing other than their own countries are forced to see the world in a new cultural light. The social-psychological aspects of FL learning are again relevant here; it has been shown, for example, that negative attitudes towards FLs discourage learning.[13] ICONS helps to neutralise these negative effects. First, as students begin to realise that they are living in a multilingual world, they begin to see the relativity of their own native tongue and culture. Second, students realise that their own native language is indeed an important FL for their colleagues abroad, which in turn encourages them to be more receptive to the FL of their colleagues. Students from different countries thus help each other to learn a variety of FLs.

ICONS is also a medium for the study and practice of various communication disciplines in a complex arena of international relations. Participants explore and tackle foreign policy and diplomatic issues in a wide range of areas, such as superpower relations, human rights, trade and business, European integration, the Middle East conflicts, and North–South relations. Students are confronted by practical, real and urgent international issues in a communication-rich context which provides an authenticity of experience unobtainable elsewhere. The vital skills developed include analysis and understanding of complex situations, diplomacy, policy implementation, articulation of ideas, and decision-making, all of which require various types of communication skill.

We should like here to outline briefly a number of interlocking levels of communication networks. The first level is telecommunications which operate via packet switching systems and satellites; these are the same as the ones used by institutions all over the world (e.g. banks, news agencies and governments) to communicate with each other. The second level is team-to-team international communication, touched on above. The composition and organisation of individual teams vary greatly; probably the most educationally valuable type of communication is that which takes place between various groups and individuals within teams. Many teams are divided into sub-groupings (sometimes termed 'commissions' or 'ministries'). Various types of meeting are held frequently in each team, ranging from plenary or cabinet sessions through commission and *ad hoc* inter-commission meetings, to meetings of two or three students. This will also involve student–teacher communications, thus helping to break down the traditional student–teacher communication barriers so common in higher educational institutions. In addition, participants from different disciplines (e.g. politics, economics, FLs) are brought into contact.

To sum up, ICONS provides a natural multilingual laboratory both for the development of language as a vital instrument of communication, and for the exploration of culturally defined (often divisive) issues. It provides a relatively structured 'multi-communication' learning environment, where computing, international studies, FLs, and a variety of skills are experienced as being mutually supportive and interdependent. ICONS can be conceived of almost purely as a series of interlocking communication networks of various kinds; the very essence of ICONS, as indeed of many simulations, is communication.

Concluding remarks

To conclude this chapter, we would like to return to some of our previous themes, including technology and our multicultural world. The need for people to be communicatively proficient in at least one language other than their mother tongue is increasing. Certain sections of the language-teaching community have realised the importance of multilingualism and are seeking ways (methods and techniques) of enabling learners to acquire communicative proficiency in a FL with greater ease. Just as simulation promotes the learning of communication skills within other disciplines, it is becoming a standard feature in many enlightened FL classrooms, and is proving to be an effective means for enhancing FL communication.

Of particular relevance to many of the larger-scale simulations is technology, especially computing and telecommunications. In many cases, such technology can contribute to the power of simulation to foster communication. In other cases, computer networks themselves constitute a communications system which actually makes a simulation possible. Technology has allowed multicultural and multilingual communication to take place at an even faster rate than before, and in so doing has increased the need for greater multilingual competence and multicultural understanding.

In FL instruction, the fields of communication and simulation are drawn together, while technology also helps to unite them into one theme. Without communication, many simulations would hardly exist except as a concept. Only communication can bring simulation to life; simulation is communication. In a simulation such as ICONS, the reality of our multicultural global village is brought into classrooms around the world.

Notes to Chapter 6

1. For further discussions on multicultural and multilingual issues see, among others, Asuncion-Lande (1978); Baetens Beardsmore (1982); Foster & Stockley (1984); Luce & Smith (1986) Megary *et al.* (1981); Shapson & D'Oyley (1984); Sitaram & Cogdell (1976); Skutnabb-Kangas (1984); Smith (1981); Twitchin & Demuth (1985); Verma & Modgil (1985). An influential and extremely informative journal to be recommended is the *Journal of Multilingual and Multicultural Development*, published by Multilingual Matters, Bank House, 8a Hill Rd, Clevedon, Avon BS21 7HH, England.
2. Fuller accounts of changes in FL instruction will be found in: Bowen *et al.* (1985); Howatt (1984); Kelly (1969); Stern (1983).
3. For discussions on the Communicative Language Teaching Approach, see Brumfit & Johnson (1979); Canale & Swain (1980); Candlin, (1981); Finocchiaro & Brumfit (1983); Johnson (1982); Littlewood (1981; 1984); Munby (1978); Omaggio (1986); Rivers (1983); Savignon (1983); Valdes (1986); Widdowson (1978; 1983); Wilkins (1976).
4. Immersion programmes have been described in Anderson & Rhodes (1984); Cohen (1974); Gardner (1985); Gardner *et al.* (1977; 1979); Lambert & Tucker (1972); Swain & Lapkin (1982); Tucker *et al.* (1976).
5. On NA, see Krashen & Terrell (1983); and, for criticism of this, Ellis (1984); Omaggio (1986). On CCL, see Curran (1976); LaForge (1983). On Suggestopedia, see Bancroft (1978); Lozanov (1978). On TPR see Asher (1982). On SW see Gattegno (1972). General surveys of these methods will be found in Larsen-Freeman (1986); and Richards & Rogers (1986).
6. The importance of the social-psychological dimension, especially the affective and motivational aspects, of FL learning, has been studied and emphasised in much research; see Ball *et al.* (1984); Gardner (1979; 1982); Gardner & Lambert (1975); Gardner *et al.* (1987); Giles & Berne (1982); Giles *et al.* (1980; 1983). The best single exposition of this whole area is by Gardner (1985). An excellent journal, which carries articles on these and related aspects of language, is the *Journal of Language and Social Psychology*, published by Multilingual Matters, Bank House, 8a Hill Rd, Clevedon, Avon BS21 7HH, England.
7. Various advantages of simulation for FL learning relate to communication. On its uses in learning a few foreign phrases for travel purposes or in achieving native-level proficiency, see Hare & McAleese (1985); and Raz (1985). On its suitability for languages for specific purposes (LSP), such as science, technology and business, see McGinley (1985); Hutchinson & Sawyer-Laucanno (1989); and Brammer & Sawyer-Laucanno (1988). Fernandes *et al.* (1989) deal with its uses in learner training. On its uses in conducting research in FL acquisition, see Stevens (1985; 1987). Finally, Littlejohn (1989) and Evans *et al.* (1987) treat its uses in FL testing.
8. Ethnomethodological analyses have shown, *inter alia*, how such 'realities' are sustained by FL learners and teachers in simulated contexts, and provide important insights into how learners grapple with a FL in the less restrictive context of simulation. See Sharrock & Watson (1985); Watson & Sharrock (1987; 1989). Chapters 3 and 4 in this volume provide ethnomethodological analyses of simulation work. For background reading the following are highly recommended: Anderson *et al.* (1985); Atkinson & Heritage (1984); Button & Lee (1987); Sharrock & Anderson (1986).

9. For recent bibliographies and resource lists of references and games related to FL education, see Crookall (1986); Lonergan (1986).
10. Other sources of simulation material designed especially for the FL classroom include Byrne & Rixon (1979); Clark & McDonough (1982); Herbert & Sturtridge (1979); Klippel (1984); Livinstone (1983); Omaggio (1979); Paulston *et al*. (1975); Porter Ladousse (1987); Rogers (1986); Ur (1981); Watcyn-Jones (1978).
11. Increasing use of computerised simulations of various kinds is being made in many areas. For a range of uses and views, see Crookall (1988a,b). For a discussion on communication and interaction patterns in CSs see Crookall *et al*. (1986). For a full discussion on MANEDES see Coote *et al*. (1985, 1987), and for an ethnomethodological analysis of its use in a FL teacher training workshop, see Sharrock & Watson (1987). For other examples of, and discussions on, the use of CS for FL instruction, see Coleman (1987, 1988); Crookall *et al*. (1989); Diadori (1987); Higgins & Morgenstern (1989); Matheidesz (1987, 1988); Morgenstern (1987).
12. There exist two large-scale network games in the world; one of these, known as ICS (Interactive Communication Simulations), is run by the University of Michigan, U.S.A. and the other, ICONS (International Communication and Negotiation Simulation), by the University of Maryland, U.S.A. Some features are common to both (e.g. computers and satellite telecommunications technologies to transmit messages between teams, and international relations). However, there are two major interrelated differences: ICS participants are drawn mainly from the United States, whereas ICONS participants are to be found in a number of countries around the world; and ICS does not use FLs, but runs entirely in English, whereas one of the main components of ICONS is the use of FLs and intercultural communication. Our major focus here is therefore on ICONS, although it should be noted that ICS has much potential in FL education. Full descriptions of ICS can be found in Taylor & Goodman (1987); Wolf (1987). More detailed descriptions of, and background discussions on, ICONS and network gaming can be found in Brecht *et al*. (1984); Crookall & Wilkenfeld (1985; 1987); Noel (1979); Noel *et al*. (1987); Wilkenfeld (1983). Useful discussions on general aspects of international relations simulations are Clarke (1978); Guetzkow & Valdez (1981); Ward (1985).
13. See note 6.

SECTION THREE:
Social relations

7 Knowing oneself: A symbolic interactionist view of simulation

CHARLES F. PETRANĚK
University of Southern Indiana, U.S.A.

Would it not be fascinating to have fun and learn at the same time? Would not recapturing the childhood excitement of learning be appealing? Would not learning more about oneself be impressive? Simulations offer these intriguing qualities. When applying symbolic interactionist ideas of early socialisation to simulations, there are several similarities between the two which help to elucidate the rich learning experience of simulations. From the communication patterns of debriefing and journal writing, participants know more about themselves. People learn within simulations because they experience a miniaturised version of early socialisation.

The symbolic interactionist viewpoint

Symbolic interactionists consider the main concepts in socialisation to be: self, I and Me, three stages of development, generalises other, and self-communications. According to this theory (Mead, 1934a), the development of self happens in stages and the child's social world is both defined for him and by him. The self has two states of consciousness: the I and the Me. The I develops first and is the active, spontaneous, immediate and impulsive state of the person (Hewitt, 1979). Meltzer (1964) points out that the I offers the potential for new, creative activity but is unorganised and undirected. For example, as one is walking along, this active I might spontaneously desire to run to the beach and enjoy its beauty. The objective state of the self is the Me and has the ability to think of itself as an actor. The Me takes the role of others and embodies other people's attitudes, values and expectations. Meltzer (1964) emphasises that the Me regulates and disposes the person to goal activity and conformity. For example, if a person wants to run to the beach, the Me would detail the potential consequences of losing a job, the physical distance of the beach, and the awkwardness of running downtown in a suit. Symbolic interactionists with their I and Me concepts are capturing those aspects of human conduct that are novel as well as routine, innovative as well as conforming (Hewitt, 1979). Kolb (1944) takes Mead to task about the I being a residual category with a vague definition. Meltzer (1964) counters that the concept is still useful because it avoids pure determinism of human conduct.

It is argued that the genesis of the self for a child passes through three stages: preparation, play and game (Meltzer, 1964). The preparation stage, which is implied by Mead, is associated with the imitation of significant others by copying action and repeating sounds—eventually they are connected to particular symbols. As language is developed, there is progression into the play stage where different roles are rehearsed: for example, the child plays mummy, daddy, fireman, nurse or doctor. Spontaneity dominates action, but there is some realisation about the consequence of action. Meltzer (1964) stresses the importance of play-acting because the child is placed in a position to act back towards himself. The self originates from taking the role of others, even though there is no unified concept of self but several discrete objects of self. According to Denzin (1975) play and games that are 'fun' activities that socialise a child by guiding discovery of when and where he fits into the social structure. According to Charon (1979) the continual free-floating imagination in role-playing is not isolated daydreaming, but a self-instructional time of how the self is related to others. Stone (1970) believes that play is the essence by which young people's lives are made meaningful because the self is made an object and placed in relationship to other objects in the world. The child learns from communicating with others and communicating within himself.

In the game stage reality is viewed from various perspectives simultaneously and a response to several people's expectations emerges (Meltzer, 1964). Consequences of an action from others' viewpoints, parents or teachers or friends, are realised. Mead's (1934b) illustration of these processes is a baseball game because each player has to visualise the expectations and actions of all the other players. Organised rules affect the individual in the game stage, whereas spontaneity is more characteristic of the earlier stages. Impulses are controlled through rules. Stone (1970) stresses that the self is integrated through team games because one envisions several people's expectations and adapts one's own behaviour to the generalised expectations of the entire team.

Mead (1934b) states that the rule-bound character of a game helps a child develop ideas of the generalised other. For Mead the generalised other is the person's internalised idea of society which is the perception of 'most people' or the collective 'they'. The generalised other imposes limits on the spontaneous ideas of a child, outlines consequences, and encourages others' expectations to be taken into account. For example, in the game of checkers the player has to anticipate several future moves of his opponent and calculate his own reactions. The ability to take the role of the other implies a 'better' player. Moreover, there is the essential discovery of pleasure associated with a rule-bound setting. The young child learns to control the spontaneous and hedonistic self which might want to throw the checker-board in the air, but realises the need for balance between the I and the Me. In the game stage a person can view himself in a unified manner—as a whole. Meltzer (1964) lists three consequences of this development of self: the individual may engage in interaction with himself and view himself in a new way; he will have a mental life by making himself and others objects; and he will be able to control his impulses and direct his behaviour.

Mills (1963) expands on Mead's notion of the generalised other by viewing the self-communication between the person and the generalised other as thinking. For Mills the generalised other is the person's internal audience which allows the person to carry on a conversation with himself. This self-communication leads to means of testing reality by taking others into account before action is taken. Such internal communication develops into self-knowledge and a person's position in the social structure (Turner, 1975). Meltzer (1964) summarises from the standpoint of the generalised other, the individual has a universe of discourse and a system of common symbols and meanings to communicate with himself. Manis & Meltzer (1972) emphasise that an individual is an active creator of his social world. A human being interprets, creates, and moulds his social and physical world from interactions and decision-making. Thus, the self matures with more self-communication, and negotiates meanings associated with the many symbols of language and of socialisation.

Simulations and symbolic interaction theory

Further development of the I and Me happens as a person matures and this process can be accelerated by participating in a simulation. The spontaneous and restrictive nature of the I and Me, the three stages of socialisation, the generalized other, the new social reality and emotional learning are all present in a miniaturised form within the simulation. The simulation player experiences all the main symbolic interactionist processes quickly and concisely. The active and interactive character forces a person to perform and then to think about that action. The public manner urges the individual to make sense out of his activities. The make-believe nature allows and encourages innovative behaviour. The emotional aspect imprints the interaction on the person's mind. The debriefing quality promotes communication with others and self. Simulations present the possibility of an intense consolidation of the socialisation process.

Simulations possess the polarities of experimentation and rules, spontaneity and controls, impulse and institution (Turner, 1976), innovation and conformity, and the I and the Me. An example of this I and Me consciousness happens in the SIMSOC simulation. SIMSOC is an elaborate simulation with 18–80 players which runs from eight to 20 hours. It is a simulated society with four regions that have varying degrees of wealth and power. There are industries, news media, political leaders, workers, travel agencies, subsistence leaders, poor people and rich people. While playing the simulation a student might want to be a political leader because he wants to explore some utopian, socialist ideas. After one round he conceives of a society in which all people would be provided for and all wealth would be equally shared by all. For three more rounds he is able to convince people that his idea is a good one. During the fourth round some industrial leaders want to arrest people and take their money. The utopian student's instant response is to yell and scream at them for disturbing his plan. He realises that his screaming would only lead to more trouble. Instead he calmly sits down and discusses the issues with the other leaders. He is able to persuade them to sign an agreement not to arrest anyone and agrees that any excess money in the society will be used for a party. The utopian leader writes in his journal that at the moment of signing he feels like Henry Kissinger negotiating world peace. This simulation offers a chance for experimentation in a limited atmosphere. The consciousness of the I and Me, spontaneous and restrictive, are continually intertwined in a simulation.

The symbolic interactionist suggests that a person develops through stages to achieve a unified idea of self. Often in a simulation a player passes through the three socialisation stages of preparation, play and game. The individual experiences imitation, then play-acting, and finally response to several people's expectations. An example of these stages takes place in PLEA BARGAINING. The simulation has six to ten criminal cases that are brought before a judge. There are public defenders, prosecuting attorneys and defendants. Some defendants are guilty and others are innocent. Each defendant wants to plea bargain for the lowest sentence possible or even to have the charges dismissed. A student, who is not sure she wants to be a judge, is assigned the task of being the judge. At first she copies the instructions on how she should act as a judge. Then she plays the role of judge as she has observed on television. As she hears more cases she starts to experiment with the role and varies the sentences. She tries to synthesise many people's opinions to arrive at a unified view of the courtroom. She realises that action in one case affects her interaction in subsequent cases with the same lawyers. She feels herself developing a particular manner as a judge. She writes in her journal that she is learning more in PLEA BARGAINING than any other simulation because she has more power and has developed her own style of being behind the bench. The simulation offers her a chance to progress through each of the three stages of socialisation.

In the third stage the generalised other is important to developing a unified idea of self. In simulations the participants learn quickly the consequences of their actions and the expectations of others. SIMSOC provides an example of being aware of the consequences of one's actions. A business leader in a rich region has the confidence of all the people in two of the four regions. A leader from the second region convinces seven out of the eight people in the rich region to have a certain person arrested. The business leader is against it because it is contrary to the philosophy that he is advocating. He knows that even though it is not his idea to arrest, everyone will blame him because of his speeches and leadership abilities. He sees his power base crumbling. For over an hour he resists, but then gives in to the relentless group pressure. After the arrest 'most' people think that he is behind the devious arrest because the arrest comes from his region. 'They' do not allow him to be their leader. The simulation provides a rich learning experience about generalised others and group pressure.

Just as a child discovers social reality by interacting with others, a participant in a simulation discovers the official rules and unofficial norms by playing. Although the rules of a specific simulation remain the same, each group develops its own informal norms and expectations. It is interesting to listen to students from different years discuss the same simulation. Each student believes that the social reality which developed when they played was the 'natural' or 'right' or 'best' one. This sense of correct social reality happens continually in one simulation, BAFA BAFA. It is about two different cultures. One is friendly and traditional while the other is competitive and impersonal. The participants are randomly assigned to the various cultures. They learn their culture, perform their roles, and have a brief chance to visit the other culture. After two hours of play they are asked which culture they prefer. It is amazing that 80% pick their assigned culture. They emphasise the good points of 'their' culture, discount the negative aspects and accept the new social reality. Simulations provide a relatively safe avenue to explore different social realities.

Learning is not just intellectual activity, it can also be associated with emotional involvement with a specific context or event. In simulations there is a wide range of emotions from joy and excitement to sadness and depression. Whenever there is emotion, learning within a simulation leads to a lasting memory for participants years later. The emotions and ambiguous situations create tension and stress within the self, along with the desire to resolve such stress. A person searches for answers and explanations by discussing things with others and himself. Simulations motivate an individual to reflect about himself because of their excitement, public nature, spontaneity and restrictiveness. Simulations are miniaturisations of early socialisation processes.

Knowing oneself through communication

Learning about oneself occurs in many forms. The first form ensues from an individual participating in the simulation because he learns about the formal and informal norms of the simulation and his reaction to them. Many things happen to him, and he has to make sense out of all the activity. The activity forces the individual into thinking about the context for social interactions and the emotional excitement. Symbolic interactionism emphasises that we learn much about self because of feedback from others within social encounters. Indeed, the concept of the looking-glass self as developed by Cooley (1902) encourages notions of social reflections that constantly inform us about other people's perception of our selves.

In order to gain deeper insight into the social structure and one's own life, a second form for learning is necessary—debriefing. Most simulations recommend some form of debriefing or discussion after the simulation is completed. This activity is indispensable to gain an overall view of the simulation and to discover other people's reactions to certain situations. At first during the debriefing there is a discussion of actual things that occurred. This sharing of activities is important because often everyone is not aware of their taking place. Participants are also encouraged to describe their feelings, emotions and reactions to different activities. A person can learn by discussing some of his feelings and then in turn by listening to others' reactions to the same event. Very often people have different feelings about the same event and debriefing helps to sort out the reasons for some of these differences. This revelation of sensitivities is a major advantage over other learning devices because of the insight into others' lives. Obviously, this phase of debriefing can be very sensitive and the debriefer has to be aware of potential problems.

At another level of debriefing the participants discuss any similarities or dissimilarities between the simulation and real life. Participants utilise their personal experiences to substantiate the different activities. The director of the simulation often points out the aspects of the simulation that are exaggerated to emphasise a particular point. At an even higher level, theories are applied to the simulation to help explain some of the behavioural reactions and to link our simulation experience with that of others. These theories from social psychology, business, psychology, sociology, organisations, political science, economics and education can be utilised to account for individual behaviour and feelings, interpersonal actions, and organised movement. The debriefing is a valuable tool because the learning can happen on several levels about oneself and others. The main insights come from listening to people describe their feelings and emotions to a situation and discovering that they have very different experiences. A common example of this happens almost every time BAFA BAFA is played. In this simulation there are two different cultures in which players visit the other culture and sometimes violate the norms. Often the visitor is kicked out of the group and baffled by the experience because he is not sure why it happens. During the debriefing the cultural group explains the serious violation of males talking to females without permission. The visitor pleads that he knows nothing of this law and feels hurt and rejected. The cultural group responds that their action of removal was not personal, but the visitor finds it difficult to believe. Everyone learns from the discussion about cultural norms, personal feelings, deviance, intentions and interpretations of actions.

The third form of learning is the writing of journals. This technique is usually not mentioned in the literature but can prove to be very meritorious (Petranek, 1981). It involves an original and enjoyable process of communication through writing rather than speaking. After the playing of the simulation and the debriefing, a participant starts with a brief description of the actual occurrences and then discusses his reactions and feelings about these events. As with the debriefing, in order to develop deeper insight the writer has to form analogies to real-life situations and finally search for explanations by applying theories to the interactions. The writing helps the person focus his attention and organise his experiences. The most valuable aspect of authorship is the application of theoretical concepts to explain behaviour. For example, in a simulation like GHETTO, a student is often frustrated because he is being hustled and loses points. Since he cannot achieve his goals, he retaliates by hustling and hurting other people. In his journal he analyses behaviour in relation to frustration-aggression theory and discovers that his retaliation is a common response after being frustrated. The self-communication of the journal and theory leads to a deeper understanding of his life. Another example is when a student is placed in a group for the HUMANUS simulation, and she detests a particular person. After the interacting and planning with him, the student writes that he is not as bad as she originally thought. This idea surprises the student until she reads about the jigsaw classroom technique of Aronson (1984). The student discovers that Aronson has students learn about subjects from other students. Each student presents a segment of information. If one of these students is a minority child and despised, the others are dependent on him for material and have to interact with the minority child. This interdependence reduces the prejudicial attitudes. This same phenomenon occurs in simulations when participants are dependent on each other. The self-communication from the journal writing encourages thinking and self-knowledge.

In conclusion, the symbolic interactionist viewpoint envisions that participants in simulations know themselves and others from their communications during and after the simulation. The excitement of simulations emerges because the early socialisation processes are recaptured. The main concepts of the I and Me, stages of development, generalized other, social reality and self-communication are all present. The simulations stimulate communication.

The miniaturised socialisation offers people the opportunity to learn about themselves and others in a consolidated manner. Simulations are intriguing ways of communicating as a learning tool: they provide appeal and excitement. From the communication techniques of debriefing and journal writing people discover themselves quickly and concisely.

8 Problem-solving and decision-making skills in deaf and partially hearing-impaired groups

JAMES J. FERNANDES
and
MARTIN NORETSKY
Gallaudet University, Washington, DC, U.S.A.

In recent years the use of simulations for on-the-job training applications in the private sector has become more widespread. The use of simulations to teach the content of college courses is also becoming more prevalent. Business and engineering departments were among the first to employ simulations (Wales & Stager, 1977). Today there is probably no academic field left in which the literature does not describe at least one incidence of using simulations as a teaching strategy.

One such academic application is to be found at Gallaudet University, which includes a liberal arts college for the deaf, where the Department of Communication Arts uses a print simulation to teach students to solve problems by following a systematic decision-making process. This application of simulation to education for hearing-impaired groups illustrates the utility of simulation in learning about communication processes in general and about the impact of hearing impairment on communication in particular.

A brief background on deafness

The hearing-impaired population is usually viewed erroneously by the larger normally-hearing world as a homogeneous group. There is in fact great diversity within the hearing-impaired population. The degree and age of onset of hearing loss account for much of the diversity and, coupled with variations in communication training and educational approach, can lead to linguistic and cultural differences among hearing-impaired people.

Hearing impairment can profoundly affect how and how well language is acquired. We all rely on language, in our case English, which we use to satisfy the majority of our communication needs. We learned our language easily, relying on our hearing to internalise its rules and to mimic its sounds. Hearing-impaired persons who lose their hearing after approximately the age of five or who maintain enough residual hearing to benefit from hearing aids can also learn English in this fashion. However, without sufficient hearing, prelingually deafened children must be 'taught' the rules of English. The difficulty of learning language under these circumstances is evidenced in the large numbers of hearing-impaired people with demonstrated English language deficiencies.

In addition to the degree and age of onset of hearing impairment, there is another major factor which affects language mastery. We learned English because it was the language of our parents and the language of people in the place we lived. Hearing-impaired people (at least in the United States) do not always learn English as their first language. A sizeable number of hearing-impaired people (about half a million American and Canadian citizens) learn their first language from deaf parents, relatives and friends. This language is signed, not spoken, and is called American Sign Language (ASL). In the last two decades linguists examining ASL have found that it has its own linguistic rules as well as other features which enable it to meet the criteria of a language (Baker & Cokely, 1980). Those ASL users who learn English are therefore learning it as a second language.

However, many hearing-impaired people understand neither English nor ASL fluently, and therefore communicate by borrowing parts they understand from each system. In addition to linguistic differences among the hearing-impaired, there are cultural differences to consider. Many of our cultural similarities emerge through gradual assimilation of norms and rules associated with socialisation, by which we value and conform to particular behaviours. Hearing-impaired people differ in their desire to assimilate. Most hearing-impaired people would probably be interested in assimilating into the hearing world to some degree; however, those who have hearing parents and relatives, and who live and were educated among hearing people, are likely to prefer a *greater* degree of assimilation.

Those who have deaf parents and relatives, and who live and were educated among deaf people, prefer a lesser degree of assimilation. They are more likely to have strong affiliations with the 'deaf community' and prefer to use ASL as their native language, having learned it from their parents or from their peers in residential schools for the deaf. As adults they socialise in clubs and churches and in local and national organisations of the deaf. They read publications of a deaf press whose roots go back some 150 years.[1]

American deaf people are justly proud of their shared language and heritage and in many ways take on the characteristics of an *ethnic* group or cultural minority. Regardless of the degree of audiologically measured hearing loss, they identify themselves as deaf, i.e. members of the deaf community. Professionals working in deafness-related fields use the term 'hearing-impaired' to encompass the full range of hearing loss, from audiologically deaf (profound loss) to hard-of-hearing. However, members of the deaf community tend to distinguish between 'deaf' (i.e. culturally deaf) and 'hearing-impaired' (which signifies a person who does not identify with the deaf community, regardless of his or her severity of hearing loss).

Hearing-impaired people often assess each other on the basis of their degree of cultural deafness. At one end of the continuum are people who communicate orally (not gesturally and visually) and who wish to affiliate within the culture of the hearing world only. At the other end of the continuum are those who have substantial hearing losses (or believe they do), communicate predominantly in ASL, and wish to socialise exclusively within the deaf community. There are numerous hearing-impaired people who fall all along this continuum, sharing characteristics of each of the extremes described.

In summary, hearing-impaired people do not view themselves as a homogeneous group. They vary primarily by the degree to which they wish to identify with the hearing world or with the deaf community. Yet most hearing-impaired people are not easily categorised into two dichotomous groups, but reflect to different degrees the desire to identify solely with the deaf community and to assimilate into the hearing world.

The communication environment at a college for the deaf

Given the varied communication characteristics of deaf and hearing-impaired people, the study of communication at a college for the deaf is an important aspect of the undergraduate curriculum. As part of their general education requirements, all Gallaudet undergraduates take an introductory freshman-level course entitled 'Communication Processes and the Hearing-Impaired'. After completing this course, they select either a group discussion or public speaking class. The objectives of the Communication Processes course include providing students with a basic understanding of the communication process, the audiological aspects of hearing impairment, the languages and modes of communication used by hearing-impaired people and each student's own communication skills.

Affective learning is also an objective of the first course, in an effort to help dismantle some of the communication barriers experienced by this population. Often attitudinal in nature and the result of differences in background and training, such barriers exist not only between deaf and hearing people but among deaf and hearing-impaired people themselves. Currently, about half of Gallaudet students come from residential schools for the deaf, which have traditionally emphasised sign language as a mode of instruction. These students are generally fluent in ASL and use it as their preferred means of communication. Most other students come from 'mainstream' education, where they have been taught in the same classes as their hearing peers (with the possible assistance of a sign-language interpreter, note-taker or tutor) or in special classes within regular public (i.e. free, state-supported) schools. A few have attended private (i.e. privately owned, tuition-charging) 'oral' schools, which emphasise speech and auditory training and minimise the use of sign language. The non-residential students tend to be less fluent signers and less acquainted with ASL than their residential school counterparts. Rather, they depend more on residual hearing, with amplification through hearing aids, and on lip reading and speech.

In the college the mode of communication generally employed is the Simultaneous Method, which entails speaking or mouthing English while simultaneously using signs (mostly borrowed from ASL) and finger-spelling in English word order. From a linguistic point of view, the result of using the Simultaneous Method is Pidgin Sign English (PSE), a kind of hybrid of English and ASL. PSE is thus the *lingua franca* on campus.

As might be expected, their differing communication backgrounds and preferences tend to divide students. Native ASL signers may look down on their peers who can only sign PSE and scorn those who are completely new to sign language. Orally orientated students (and even some whose first language is ASL) may be under the mistaken impression that ASL is 'broken' English or at most an inferior language rather than the complex and sophisticated language linguists have proven it to be. Hence, an important goal of the Communication Processes and the Hearing-Impaired course is to correct misconceptions that students may have about methods of communication, and to encourage more open attitudes and greater acceptance of different communication preferences. As Fernandes (1983a: 117) states, a major purpose of teaching hearing-impaired undergraduates about the communication process as it relates to deafness 'is not only to open these students to an awareness of their unique communication heritage but to open them to each other'.

Simulations used to teach communication skills

With this goal in mind, a simulation activity has proven useful as a tool for helping Gallaudet students learn about the process of verbal communication and the nature of language while at the same time instilling in them a greater appreciation and tolerance for language and communication variations among hearing-impaired people. The simulation, which involves the creation of new 'languages' by small groups of students, has been described in detail elsewhere (Fernandes, 1983a; 1983b; Fernandes *et al.*, 1988), so will only be alluded to here.

MICROLANGUAGE requires each group to view itself as a cultural microcosm and develop, during two or three class sessions, a basic lexicon and grammar for its own 'language'. In the process of struggling to invent a new language and in subsequent 'debriefing' discussions, students become aware of basic concepts such as the arbitrary but conventional nature of language, and the Sapir–Whorf hypothesis (Whorf, 1956) that language influences perception. Because hearing-impaired students invent sign languages, they learn about the property of iconicity, whereby many signs bear a visual resemblance to their referents. Most importantly, they become aware of their own attitudes about language and the communication barriers that linguistic chauvinism can erect. As a result of the MICROLANGUAGE experience, students who had previously looked down on ASL as an inferior or truncated language develop new awareness and respect for its complexity and refinement. The process of negotiating in the group for the adoption of rules and vocabulary awakens students to the political implications of language. As the MICROLANGUAGE exercise engenders awareness of the impact of language on human thought and social interaction, students develop greater tolerance of the linguistic and cultural diversity among hearing-impaired people.

In the Group Discussion course at Gallaudet University, another simulation is used to help students learn about the group communication process itself—in this case, specifically about decision-making in groups. This structured practice in group decision-making is referred to here as GUIDED PROBLEM SOLVING (Fernandes & Noretsky, 1984). It is a variation on the 'guided design' approach which was developed and is being promoted by Wales & Stager (1977) and the Center for Guided Design at West Virginia University.

Briefly, guided design involves group work on solving simulated problems provided by the instructor. The problems may be general in nature, or in specific courses they might be designed to resemble particular 'real-life' situations. Thus, students can learn about chemistry, anthropology and even business administration by working on problems that professionals in these fields might actually encounter. Through this method students learn specific content and at the same time develop skills in gathering, evaluating and communicating information, using 'rational' thinking, and co-operating in a group.

To adapt the guided design approach for Gallaudet students and group discussion classes, it was applied to the Creative Problem-Solving Sequence (CPSS), a decision-making procedure developed by Alex Osborn, Sidney J. Parnes and their associates at the Creative Problem-Solving Institute (Brilhart, 1978). The steps derived from the CPSS are as follows: identify and state clearly the problem and goal; gather and share information and analyse the problem; generate possible solutions; identify criteria; evaluate possible solutions; and implement the chosen solution.

A decision-making simulation, THE CASE OF THE FALSE ALARMS, allows students to work through the CPSS in order to solve the problem of repeated false fire alarms in a college dormitory (Fernandes & Noretsky, 1984). Each group's progress is monitored by the instructor in class, and as one step is satisfactorily completed, the group receives written feedback describing how a model group would have handled that step, and written instructions explaining what the group must do next. Basically, the instructor's role is that of a facilitator, providing feedback and helping the group, when necessary, to come up with an acceptable response to each instruction sheet. The instructor decides whether or not the group's response is acceptable before handing out the printed feedback and next instruction. The printed feedback models acceptable responses to a given instruction, but there is often more than one right answer.

THE CASE OF THE FALSE ALARMS begins with a description of the problem situation or setting and the first instruction: to state the problem and goal. The correct problem and goal statements are often simpler than many groups expect: the problem is simply that there have been too many false alarms, and the goal is to reduce or prevent them.

The second step involves gathering data and analysing the problem. The groups are asked to consider what sources would provide information about the extent and causes of the problem and about previously attempted solutions. Then each group member is given an information sheet from a different source (for example, the fire department, the Dean of Students) and is instructed to share that information with the group during analysis of the problem. After comparing their analyses with the printed feedback, the groups move on to brainstorming for possible solutions. Feedback for this step consists of a list of possible approaches to solving the problem.

Before evaluating their ideas and choosing a solution the groups are required to establish their criteria for acceptable solutions. The instructor may need to prime the discussion at this stage by pointing out that for many problem situations, budgetary and time constraints are common examples of criteria. Feedback for this step is guided by a list of criteria.

The final instruction asks the group to evaluate their possible solutions according to their criteria and then to reach a consensus decision on the best solution or a ranking of acceptable choices. The last feedback sheet provides one version of this process and includes a discussion of how a group would proceed to plan implementation of a chosen solution. The simulation itself, however, does not require students to discuss implementation.

When the groups have completed the activity, they can share the results of their deliberations with each other in a class discussion. The instructor may ask the groups to report their responses and have the class discuss why responses varied but were still acceptable.

The interplay between simulation and communication

We have argued elsewhere (Fernandes & Noretsky, 1984) that the guided problem-solving approach and the CASE OF THE FALSE ALARMS simulation are effective in promoting the learning of a rational group problem-solving sequence. Of particular relevance here is the relationship between the use of a simulation and the learning of group communication skills by hearing-impaired students. There are six ways in which using this group simulation seems to foster learning about the communication process.

In the first place, the simulation thrusts a group of students together and forces them to communicate with one another in a psychologically 'safe' environment. Because they are taking on roles and playing a part, students approach the group task with a playful attitude. Defences can be relaxed and new behaviours experimented with in the context of a simulation. Thus a simulation activity can give students more freedom to communicate with each other than when confronting a 'real' task. This, 'ice-breaking' quality of simulations helps account for their prominence in communication training generally.

Second, and more specific to the Gallaudet population, a group's success with the CASE OF THE FALSE ALARMS simulation demands input from all group members. For example, analysis of the problem requires the pooling of different pieces of information given to each member. Likewise, the emphasis on creativity and quantity of solutions mandated by brainstorming calls for contributions from everyone (Coon, 1957). The need for full participation posed by this simulation in turn motivates efforts to overcome communication barriers. Given the kind of barriers described above, barriers which separate hearing-impaired people from one another, this is a particularly important outcome of using the simulation.

Third, the structured nature of the CASE OF THE FALSE ALARMS simulation addresses the problem of ambiguity—a communication difficulty shared by hearing-impaired persons and others who must communicate in a less familiar language. As discussed earlier in this chapter, many hearing-impaired people learn English as a second language. This being the case, they, like many second language speakers, are prone to literal interpretations of instructions and examples. Our experience has shown that the behaviour modelled in the simulation needed to be precisely that which we wanted our students to emulate. Earlier use of a more ambiguous simulation, Wales & Stager's FISHING TRIP, had confused our students.[2]

A fourth and related aspect of the impact of the CASE OF THE FALSE ALARMS simulation on social interaction is simply that the use of printed instructions and feedback reinforces acquisition of English language skills. In the group context, students do not simply read the printed information; they must work through that information by discussing, interpreting and drawing inferences from it. While the discussion itself may occur in PSE or even ASL, it is written English which is being clarified, understood and responded to. Thus the simulation encourages the acquisition of literary English as a means of communication. Since deafness, from the point of view of the larger society, is fundamentally a communication handicap, this is an important feature of the simulation. Literary skill is therefore being encouraged, as well as oral and visual-gestural communication.

A fifth interrelationship between communication and the use of this simulation is that THE CASE OF THE FALSE ALARMS models and reinforces positive group communication norms. Because the group activity is divided into a series of steps with intermediate goals or checkpoints and directed by an instructor, the group cannot persist for long in counterproductive communication. In addition, the printed feedback exemplifies productive communication norms such as active listening, tactful criticism of ideas, focusing discussion on the group goal, and building cohesiveness through the use of group-centred language. In effect, the simulation is both a means and a model for learning effective communication skills.

Finally, we would argue that the primary purpose of the simulation (to enhance the learning of a group decision-making procedure) focuses directly on the communication process as it occurs in groups. What is group decision-making if not the process and product of communication? The length of time a group requires to arrive at a decision and the quality of that decision largely depend on how efficiently and effectively the group was able to communicate. A rational decision-making procedure, such as the CPSS, is simply a tool for structuring and guiding group communication. Hence, when students use a simulation to learn a group decision-making procedure, they are acquiring a tool of effective communication.

In sum, the relevance of simulations to learning about the communication process may be no more apparent than in the group communication classroom. When group communication students happen to be hearing-impaired, the relationship between communication and simulation provides additional educational benefits. The experience at Gallaudet University confirms the conclusion that simulations provide an effective means for communication training and are particularly useful in addressing the communication needs of hearing-impaired students. Likewise, the study of communication helps further the field of simulation to the extent that a learning simulation (particularly a group simulation) is itself a communication event. Our experience has shown that in the process of discussion and mediating the learning which occurs through simulation many of the insights and observations relate to the dynamics of communication among participants. Hence, the more instructors and students know about the communication process and the better they are able to communicate about the learning acquired through simulations, the more profound will be the learning experience. We conclude that there is indeed a synergistic relationship between communication and simulation.

Notes to chapter 8

1. In 1837, the *Radii*, a weekly newspaper published in Canajoharie, NY, became the first American newspaper to be edited by a deaf person. It included a column of interest to deaf people and by 1844 was being mailed to deaf citizens throughout New York state. This was followed in 1860 by the *Gallaudet Guide and Deaf-Mute's Companion*, a monthly magazine which was the first periodical aimed exclusively at deaf people. Perhaps the best-known contemporary periodicals are the *Deaf American*, a monthly magazine published by the National Association of the Deaf, and the *Silent News*, a monthly newspaper. For a more detailed account, see Gannon (1981).
2. FISHING TRIP is a group problem-solving simulation which involves a fishing party faced with the threat of dehydration while stranded on a desert island. The printed feedback of the simulation includes illustrative errors made by the imaginary feedback group (for example, focusing on solutions before clarifying the problem). Our hearing-impaired students were prone to interpret the erroneous behaviour as that which they were supposed to practice. The broad lesson to be learned here is that simulations themselves communicate messages. Hence, simulation creators need to be mindful of how those messages will be interpreted by simulation users. This last point illustrates how simulations become the property of the group and are open to negotiation as group members consider how to proceed. It also underlines the importance of instructor-mediated follow-up discussions to clarify and promote assimilation of the learning experience triggered by the simulation.

9 Simulation as a basis for consciousness raising: Some encouraging signs for conflict resolution

DENNIS J. D. SANDOLE
George Mason University, VA, U.S.A.

There appears to be a new 'fashion' sweeping the globe these days. The conventional, popular term applied to the phenomenon is 'terrorism'. For many people, the term has a simple definition—the use of indiscriminate violence by small groups against innocent people for the purpose of achieving some psychological and/or political objective. For many people, only certain groups fall into the category of 'terrorist', such as the Palestinian Liberation Organisation (PLO), the Red Brigade, the Red Army Faction, the Irish Republican Army (IRA) and others. With few exceptions (e.g. Stohl & Lopez, 1986), the actions of nation-state governments are never defined as terrorist, except to the extent that they are in support of the smaller groups (Iran, Libya and Syria are among those cited). And for many people, the typical—indeed, the *only*—response to the violence of terrorism is the violence of what could be called counter-terrorism: 'fight fire with fire'.

For many people in the United States, Israel, South Africa, and elsewhere, this view of terrorism is compatible with prevailing notions of common sense. But there are others for whom this is not the case. For them, terrorism includes not only the violent actions of some Palestinians, Shiites, Irish, Italians, Germans, and Basques, plus the states that support them, including the Soviet Union, but also some of the actions of South Africa, Israel, the United States and others.

The first of these views of terrorism is the narrower of the two and, far from facilitating a victory over terrorism (Netanyahu, 1986), leads, I believe, to further frustrations on the part of those who tend to be defined as terrorists. When a nation-state government uses force, its behaviour can be legitimised under international law, including the United Nations Charter, as self-defence.[1] If a non-governmental or non-state actor attempts the same thing, however, it is terrorism. This not only shows up some of the absurdities inherent in the present state system but, via some frustration-aggression, self-fulfilling dynamic (Sandole, 1986), may be counterproductive, leading to protracted conflict (Azar & Burton, 1986).

Merton (1968) has suggested an apt term in this context: 'moral alchemy'. According to the 'engagingly simple formula of moral alchemy ... the same behavior must be differently evaluated according to the person who exhibited it' (Merton, 1968). Hence, 'you are stingy but I am prudent', 'you are opportunistic but I am successful', etc. We could easily insert: 'you are a terrorist but I am a freedom fighter'. The 'in-group readily transmutes virtue into vice and vice into virtue, as the occasion may demand' (Merton, 1968). The American Secretary of State, George Shultz, seems to have engaged in a bit of this by declaring that terrorists are 'beasts' who murder innocent people, and that 'the idea that they are freedom fighters is a bunch of baloney' (cited in Goshko, 1986). Conceivably, the actions of the United States during World War II in Hiroshima and Nagasaki, where tens of thousands of innocent non-combatants were targetted with nuclear weapons, might be viewed as 'freedom fighting'.

Moral alchemy seems to be part of the ethnocentric tendencies which characterise humans in most, if not all, cultural settings: 'I am part of the *good* ingroup and you are a member of the *bad* (or at least, *not so good*) outgroup', etc. (LeVine & Campbell, 1972). Hence, it promises not to be an easily resolvable problem. And to complicate matters, it is part of another problem which also appears somewhat intractable. Aspects of this larger problem are touched on by attribution research conducted by Mark Snyder and his associates which indicates not only that ordinary people behave much like Thomas Kuhn's (1970) 'normal scientists', i.e. they are 'hypothesis testers' and approach hypotheses (about the self and other people) by 'preferentially gathering evidence whose presence would tend to confirm hypotheses under scrutiny'; but also, in self-fulfilling fashion, that their 'actions toward other people can elicit behavioral confirmation for [their] predictions' (Snyder & Gangestad, 1981). Alan Sillars's (1981) review of the literature and his own research also touch upon the problem, indicating that, from the interpersonal to international levels, conflicting parties 'tend to overattribute responsibility for conflict to the partner or adversary and underestimate the effects of their own behavior'. Hence, as I have argued elsewhere (Sandole, 1984; 1986; 1987), when conflicting parties are characterised by narrow, one-sided views, they tend to behave in ways which facilitate the development of self-fulfilling, self-maintaining conflict cycles, without ever seeing the causal role that they themselves play in such dramas.

These difficulties notwithstanding, is there not something that can be done? Quite clearly, when someone is in the process of attacking, or is about to attack us, we must act quickly, perhaps with violent measures of our own. But can we not go further than this; can we not do something of a longer-term nature which might cut down on the incidence of violent attacks, of self-perpetuating conflict cycles? And, for purposes of the present volume, can communication and simulation play a role in this?

Competitive versus co-operative processes of conflict resolution

Deutsch (1973), among others, distinguishes between two general orientations to conflict resolution: competitive processes, which may be associated with destructive outcomes, and co-operative processes, which can be associated with constructive outcomes. The first of these is implicit in the use of violence, whether 'terrorist', 'counter-terrorist', or otherwise. Competitive processes have a long history: they appear in the earliest recorded descriptions/prescriptions of what has come to be called political realism or *Realpolitik*, a political philosophy synonymous with a bleak and cynical view of human nature and an emphasis on the attainment, preservation and use of power. Thucydides, who lived in fifth-century BC Greece and chronicled the Peloponnesian War, and Kautilya, who lived in fourth-century BC India and advised political rulers, are but two examples.

The co-operative processes of conflict resolution, which may be linked to the opposite of *Realpolitik*, political idealism, also have a fairly long history, going back at least as far as Confucius, who lived in sixth–fifth-century BC China, with his emphasis on justice. Though the co-operative processes may be less 'viscerally tempting' to employ, particularly if one has been outraged or brutalised by some violent attack, they do exist as an option, and not just in principle (see, for example, Goldberg *et al.*, 1985; Sandole & Sandole-Staroste, 1987).

Jandt (1973a) tells us that 'the development and control of conflict is determined through communication'. This is compatible with John Burton's (1969) position that 'conflict occurs as a result of ineffective communication, and that its resolution, therefore, must involve processes by which communication can be made more effective'.[2] Folger & Poole (1984) argue that, although 'communication processes ... are rarely the sole source of conflicts ... [they] can worsen or improve conflict interaction, and they ... do play a critical role in defining issues'. Clearly, communication is, to various degrees, involved in conflicts and attempts to deal with them. The question is what kinds of communication styles are associated with co-operative and competitive processes.

Deutsch (1969; 1973; 1980; 1987) tells us that co-operative processes are characterised by open and honest communication, increased sensitivities to common interests, a perceived legitimacy of the interests of the other, a trusting and friendly attitude, limitations on the scope of conflicting interests and of the parties' emotional involvement in them, a reliance on the techniques of persuasion, and a recognition of the necessity for a problem-solving solution which satisfies the needs of both (all) parties. Competitive processes, on the other hand, are characterised by diminishing and misleading communication (and consequently, attempts by parties to obtain information about each other through indirect means such as espionage), increased sensitivities to differences and threats, minimisation of the legitimacy of the interests of the other, a suspicious and hostile attitude, expansion of the scope of conflicting interests and of the parties' emotional involvement in them, and a reliance on the techniques of coercion coupled with an emphasis on 'winning' at the expense of the other.

Of the two orientations, the competitive processes are clearly more likely to be associated with the use of violence, with the development of self-fulfilling, self-maintaining conflict spirals. This is not to suggest, however, that competitive processes, or elements thereof, lead *only* to destructive consequences and that co-operative processes, or aspects thereof, lead *only* to constructive outcomes. Billig (1976), for example, notes that 'It is possible for trust to be used strategically for ends which Deutsch would not consider constructive' (e.g. limited war). Contrariwise, Folger & Poole (1984) argue that 'Productive conflict interaction can be competitive at points; both parties must stand up for their own positions if a representative outcome is to be attained'. This is implicit in Pruitt's (1987) notion of 'firm but flexible and conciliatory'. 'Firm' certainly is an aspect of competitive processes, but coupled with 'flexible' and 'conciliatory', it is clearly part of an overall co-operative orientation which, as indicated above, is characterised in part by an emphasis on constructive ('win–win') outcomes. When 'firm' is accompanied by 'rigid and hostile', on the other hand, it is part of an overall competitive ('win–lose') orientation which can result in destructive ('lose–lose') outcomes, including violent conflict spirals. Assuming that such spirals are counterproductive, as indicated, for example, by events leading up to the outbreak of World War I (see, for example, Richardson, 1939; Holsti *et al.*, 1968) or by the strategic and 'intragalactic' arms race between the Soviet Union and United States, it is vital that we develop or otherwise discover ways to, as a minimum, complement competitive with co-operative approaches.

Cognitive dissonance: A light at the end of the tunnel?

Burton (1984) has argued that people will not undergo a shift from coercive to problem-solving approaches until they have experienced failure. Failure can be linked to Leon Festinger's (1962) notion of 'cognitive dissonance': a discordant relationship or breakdown between, for example, expectations and whether (and the degree to which) they are fulfilled. Cognitive dissonance is experienced as acute psychological discomfort (e.g. anxiety). People respond to it either by avoiding situations and information which could increase it or by changing one of the elements in the discordant relationship, in effect assimilating the problem which originally gave rise to the dissonance. For active users of competitive processes to be characterised by the second of these two possibilities, they may have to experience dissonance directly and vividly, in one or both of two possible ways: either by observing that competitive processes have led to the unintended consequence of counterproductive outcomes and/or that there are other ways to achieve 'stability', 'law and order', or 'peace'. For those who resort to competitive processes less often, an indirect experience of either form may suffice.

In either the direct or indirect case, however, dissonance may, depending upon the interplay of factors involved, lead to (a) no change, (b) strengthening, or (c) some change of attitudes regarding conflict management approaches. Though it may not be clear what kinds of dissonance lead to what effect (Weick, 1968; Jervis, 1976), there are some hints in the literature. For example, Aronson's (1980) review of dissonance research, including his own, indicates that the more our self-esteem is threatened or contradicted by our perceptions of our own 'stupid', harmful, or immoral behaviour, then the greater will be our experience of dissonance. The greater the dissonance, the more likely it is that we will attempt to justify the actions which led to it. The greater our commitment to, or self-involvement in, those actions and the smaller the external justification for them, the more powerful a subsequent attitude shift which reduces or eliminates the dissonance. We can combine this with Sillars's (1981) attribution research which 'suggests that other-directed blame leads to reciprocation and conflict escalation in response to distributive acts, whereas self-directed blame leads to de-escalation and conciliation'. Hence, dissonance resulting from threatened or contradicted self-esteem could complement, if not replace, other- with self-directed blame, and—depending upon whether any subsequent depression (Peterson & Seligman, 1984) permits—thereby move a conflict away from competitive/destructive towards co-operative/constructive processes. We must not forget, however, as Deutsch (1969), in his reference to cognitive dissonance, points out, that 'The result of ... pressure for self-consistency may lead to an unwitting involvement in and intensification of conflict as one's actions have to be justified to oneself and to others'.

For the active user of competitive processes, the real world would probably be the optimal context for experiencing dissonance. For the less active user, a cinema, TV lounge, or laboratory setting may suffice. It is in this sense that simulation *may* play a role in facilitating the shift from competitive to co-operative processes. But can simulation generate the experiences capable of threatening or contradicting self-esteem, leading to the kind of dissonance that may result in attitude change? Jandt (1973a) suggests an answer from the classroom use of his environmental conflict simulation, INTERACTIVE SYNECOLOGY:

> It is necessary to study student evaluation of any simulation. There is some suggestion in the evaluations of previous uses of [INTERACTIVE SYNECOLOGY] to support the instructors' feeling that during and immediately after the experience, participants feel highly uncomfortable. Weeks later, however, the instructors perceive the students expressing the feeling that the simulation was the 'highlight' of the course. As an 'uncomfortable' experience, perhaps the simulation takes on added value over time.

Simulation, therefore, may be relevant to generating, and to exploring the consequences of, dissonance.

Simulation: The impact of the 'unreal' on the real

Simulation involves the design of a model that replicates some aspects of a corresponding system, real or imaginary; a script in terms of which it can be played out, agents of operation (computers, humans, or some mix of the two), and then operation of the model in accordance with the script. Simulation is used because it may facilitate (a) training and teaching, (b) the development of alternatives, and (c) theory-building. Practitioners in many fields (such as business, diplomacy and the military) would be concerned with (a) and (b), while researchers/theorists would be concerned with (b) and (c). In my work in conflict and peace studies (CAPS), I have used one particular operation for all three reasons: the PRISONER'S DILEMMA SIMULATION (PDS) (Powell, 1969). As indicated elsewhere (Sandole, 1980b), PDS is a gaming/simulation: it employs primarily human beings but also some programmed elements. It is so called because it incorporates the structure of the paradox known in game theory as the 'prisoner's dilemma': a clash between individual and collective rationality, with collective loss the outcome of decisions based exclusively on individual self-interest (Rapoport, 1960). PDS incorporates the structure of this paradox by permitting participants to trade (collective rationality) or to arm (individual rationality), but *not* to do both with respect to the same target group at the same time. Hence, participants may often be confronted with conflicting interests: whether to trust the members of another group and trade with them or to distrust and arm against them. The consequences of the latter option may be a 'war' in which both groups are worse off. The paradox here would be that decisions based upon enhancing self-security would have had the inadvertent consequence of undermining that security.

Prior to the first round of the typical PDS operation, participants are divided into two nation-groups, each of which has decision-making and validation components. The determination of who goes where is based upon participants' responses to certain items on a questionnaire.[3] The decision-makers in each group decide whether to trade, arm, declare war or do nothing with regard to the other group and the validators decide whether to approve or disapprove of these decisions.

Addenda to a Basic Simulation Manual are administered periodically to the players in order to increase progressively the complexity of their environment. According to the first of these, the validators in each group can stage coups, split off from their parent group, and form a new group, thereby facilitating the transformation of the system from a two- into a multi-group 'world'. Thereafter, the role of validator is assumed by structured routines and all players then occupy decision-making roles, making decisions with regard to the 'United Nations' and alliances as well as to trading, arming (nuclear or conventional), and war.

My use of the PDS for theory-building involved an exploratory study of the influence of more than 20 potential explanatory variables on the conflict behaviour of groups in five PDS operations, each of which encompassed 26–30 hours of 'game time' over a 13–15 week period. One particularly interesting observation generated by this study was that as group/societal actors mature, 'environmentally stimulated conflict may come to be replaced by *self-stimulated* conflict, a phenomenon sustained in part by elements of *Realpolitik* belief-value systems' (Sandole, 1983).

In one case of my use of the PDS for teaching and alternatives generation, in a postgraduate seminar on international bargaining processes, I wanted to provide my students—who were members of the international business, diplomatic, and military communities in London, England—with a dynamic context in which they 'could experience and feel some of the concepts they read about and discussed in class' (Sandole, 1980a). I also wanted to explore the impact, if any, of my overall approach to teaching international relations, which included, in addition to the PDS, a perspective not unlike John Burton's 'cobweb model of World Society' (Burton, 1972), which is a challenge to *Realpolitik*:

> Realism tends to view states as the only actors in international relations [whereas for me] the subject matter ... is comprised of multiple actors, who may or may not represent state authorities (e.g. individuals, groups, organizations), and the interactions within and between them ... (Sandole, 1980a).

To ensure that the PDS experience was an integral part of the course, I ran it for one hour of each weekly three-hour class for 10 weeks.

In the context of their PDS 'world' the students entered into non-armament agreements, formulated and considered international wealth-sharing and integration strategies, and in general 'were determined to avoid "war"' (Sandole, 1980a). Anecdotally, one student, a retired American navy officer, commented that the PDS

> taught me to appreciate that even a simple, almost primitive framework, could serve to elicit the words and deeds that mattered in real negotiations. [It] taught me the stupidity of the concepts of victory and defeat when applied to true and lasting negotiations and compromises.

Less anecdotally, I had administered to the bargaining processes students pre- and post-course questionnaires comprised of various attitudinal scales, including one on personal cynicism. According to the developers of the four-item scale (Agger *et al.*, 1961), personal cynicism is a contemptuous distrust of people in general, a negative view of human nature.[4] As such, it is a major component of *Realpolitik*.

Questionnaires were also administered to students in other graduate courses in which simulation featured minimally or not at all (Sandole, 1980a). These were mostly American military personnel stationed in the Federal Republic of Germany. Looking at the *mean* score for each course,[5] the bargaining course students not only underwent a decline in personal cynicism over time, but were also characterised by the largest negative net difference (– 0.30) of the courses examined. Two courses in research methods had the next largest negative net differences (– 0.29 and – 0.20). One course in conflict analysis/peace research had the next highest negative net difference (– 0.12), followed by another course in conflict with no difference (0.00) and a third with a positive net difference (+ 0.14). All three conflict courses were involved in the same one-day PDS operation of 4–5 hours.

These findings suggest that PDS is associated with the full range of cognitive dissonance possibilities: no change, plus decreases and increases in one major component of *Realpolitik*, personal cynicism; also, that the major decreases are associated with a game time of at least 10 hours during an extended period, and with the bargaining course, while the minor decreases, no change and minor increases are associated with a game time of 4–5 hours during a compressed interval, and with the conflict course. These findings suggest further a positive non-linear relationship between time and personal cynicism: early on in the development of some inter-actor relationship, as time progresses, personal cynicism may increase; as time progresses further, there may be no change; and beyond some 'crucial threshold', further movement in time may be accompanied by decreases in personal cynicism. Hence, the more time one has for experiencing and dealing with whatever it is that (certain kinds of) simulation represent, and the more time one has for moving back and forth between classroom and simulation, perhaps thc less cynical one becomes. That the two research methods courses, which did not involve simulation, had the second largest negative net differences in personal cynicism means that there are ways besides simulation of generating experiences that may result in shifts such as those implied here.[6]

Ersatz simulation: Role-playing exercises

John Burton and I conducted a 75-minute role-play exercise in the context of a senior seminar for undergraduates specialising in international studies. The exercise was an opportunity for the students to experience, either as participants or observers, Burton's 'controlled communication'/problem-solving approach to conflict resolution (Burton, 1969; 1979). The scenario selected was American–Nicaraguan relations. Three students role-played American officials, three were Sandinistas, and three were Contras. Their assignment, quite simply, was to discuss their role-based perceptions of the situation. Burton and I were the third-party panel: it was our job to ensure, as much as possible, the 'accurate receipt and interpretation of what was intended should be conveyed' (Burton, 1969).

In addition to the nine participants, there were 33 observers: 42 students in all. Although the exercise was too brief to allow for pre- and post-operation attitude testing, I did ask for comments. For example, 23 (55%) of the students said that the exercise afforded them an opportunity to observe the different, zero-sum perceptions that parties to conflicts have, plus the power framework in which they tend to operate. Some specific comments were:

> at the beginning of the [exercise] none of the ... groups get into their real interests, instead they begin by stating artificial and less important matters.

> each group seemed to be rigid in their own perceptions of the issue and did not pay much attention to the views of the others unless it served to fuel their own fires.

Eighteen (43%) of the students commented on the value of third-party intervention in general, and of John Burton's approach in particular, in facilitating understanding and agreement among the parties to conflict. Some comments:

> The informal method used ... facilitated communication and eventually understanding between the actors.

> The technique draws the problem straight out of the clouds and then proceeds to clarify it.

> The importance of the mediator [is that he or she is the] one who helps the opposing sides cut through misperceptions and unnecessary rhetoric in order to get to the *real* issues.

Three (7%) commented on the value of the exercise as a means for experiencing empathy. Two were participants and one was an observer; the latter commented:

> the participants identified with their role ... to the point where they were enunciating many of the same projections that have taken hold of the real-life players. ... my belief was confirmed that people should be confronted with their projections as part of a conflict resolution process.

One of the participants seemed to agree, in part:

> By participating in the role-play one actually becomes that person and unconsciously at times reflects the same characteristics.

Summing up the value of the exercise in general, one student said:

> in the role-play, we have the opportunity to be observers and participants at the same time, to theorize and to practice.

Simulation versus other experiences: A tentative verdict

The role-play exercise was a very brief part of a course for American undergraduates in the Washington, DC, area, specialising in international studies. They were involved in the exercise primarily as observers of a specific technique that was new to them. The 10-hour PDS operation was a major part of a course involving American but also non-American postgraduate students who were members of the international business, diplomatic, and military communities in London, England. They were all MA students in international relations and were involved in the PDS as participants. The 4–5 hour PDS was part of a course for American MA students in international relations who were military personnel stationed in the Federal Republic of Germany. They were involved (along with students from other courses, relatives, and friends) in the PDS as participants. The students in the two research methods courses which did not involve simulation were also American military personnel pursuing the MA in international relations in West Germany.

Are there any potentially generalisable observations here? Whether we are looking at American military personnel or cross-national professionals, reduction in one apparent component of political realism, personal cynicism (perhaps preceded by cognitive dissonance), seems to be a possible effect of participation in an extended operation of a particular simulation. The same seems to be true for American military personnel taking a course with a particular approach to research methods. American military personnel who participate in the shorter version of the particular simulation may be associated with relatively minor decreases and increases, plus no change in personal cynicism. Finally, a brief but focused exposure to a specific technique may have an 'eye-opening' effect on some young Americans, but we cannot say whether this will be preceded by dissonance and include attitude shifts.

In the bargaining course which featured the 10-hour PDS operation, the simulation seems to have been the dominant part of the course. In the research methods courses which did not involve simulation, Kuhn (1970) was required reading before the students became involved with the various aspects of constructing and implementing research designs, etc. Most of the students initially found Kuhn to be an uncomfortable, but ultimately a rewarding experience: 'Kuhn forces you to question your assumptions'. Kuhn, along with the John Burton *Festschrift* (Banks, 1984), was required reading for the undergraduates in the course involving the role-play, where a questioning of assumptions was also a course objective. Perhaps the 10-hour PDS, through its generation of various experiences, had the same effect. Conceivably, the 4–5-hour PDS may not have allowed sufficient time for this self-questioning to occur. As Walster & Berscheid (1968) point out, 'The passage of a certain amount of time seems necessary before dissonance reduction or consistency increase occurs'. Again, with regard to the 75-minute role-play, we cannot say whether the apparent consciousness raising was preceded by cognitive dissonance and included attitude shifts.

Is it conceivable that a simple operation of short duration could generate dissonance and attitude change? Janis (1968) reports that a one-hour psychodramatic role-play operated by himself and Mann led to 'an extraordinarily disquieting experience for the subjects and produced a relatively high incidence of decisions to stop smoking compared with a control condition in which the same information was conveyed without any role-playing'. Eighteen months after that experience the subjects 'continued to report a significantly greater decrease in amount of smoking than the controls'. The 'disquieting' information was that the subjects, who were playing the role of patients 'suffering from the harmful effects of smoking', were told that they had 'cancer of the lung and required immediate surgery'. Conceivably, nothing this upsetting was conveyed to the participants and observers in the Burton–Sandole role-play. Nevertheless, the Janis study suggests that a very brief operation, involving a very focused 'personal experience', can generate not only cognitive dissonance and attitude change, but behavioural change as well. Alternatively, perhaps the combination of an international authority figure (John Burton) and an explicit demonstration of a novel technique associated with him, in the context of a course which is designed to encourage a questioning of assumptions, might be sufficient to stir a bit of dissonance and the development of the idea that the technique might have some value in certain situations.

Interesting though these findings may be, any research conducted with one's own students should be viewed as a prime candidate for the operation of contaminating effects. This may be less true, however, in those cases involving pre- and post-course measurement of personal cynicism (which, again, was one of a number of scales students were asked to respond to, in each case on two occasions which were four months apart). We have also not disentangled simulation from other potential sources of attitude change (such as readings and lectures). For these and other reasons, this study is similar to many others which have attempted to assess the pedagogical effectiveness of simulations (Greenblat, 1975; Rosenfeld, 1975). On the other hand, the findings presented here are not merely anecdotal (a major problem with much of the assessment literature); also, they are compatible with the findings produced by some of the other studies (such as Alger, 1963; Robinson, 1966).

Conclusion

Simulation and other 'unreal' exercises might be worse than useless for 'terrorists' as potential venues for the experience of dissonance and the shifting of orientations from competitive to co-operative processes. They may, however, be of great value for police officers who must know something about hostage negotiation if part of their anticipated work is to secure the safe release of hostages and the surrender of hostage takers in crisis situations. They may also be of great value for police officers who normally would view any kind of communication with terrorists as 'criminal appeasement', who believe that 'force is the only language these people understand', etc. Hence, hostage-negotiation exercises have become an integral part of training courses in law enforcement. The justification for this, quite simply, is that hostage negotiation seems to work (Hassel, 1987).

This raises an important point about the value of simulation and other exercises in facilitating an awareness of alternative conflict-management orientations and techniques. It is not simulation alone, but as part of a multi-dimensional course of study, that may turn the tide in training and consciousness raising.[7] Such courses exist, including the Master of Science in Conflict Management (MSCM) at George Mason University, which is comprised of traditional classroom work, fieldwork, and internship, as well as laboratory/simulation opportunities (Wedge & Sandole, 1982; Sandole, 1985).

Some 20 years ago James Robinson (1966) commented that, regarding simulation, 'we have grounds for confidently recommending further research and replication to help decide whether our vision of an effective technique is a reality or a mirage'. I agree, but I also have the kind of 'face validity' faith that scientists have in new paradigms (Kuhn, 1970), that simulation and focused role-playing exercises—as vehicles for facilitating a shift from competitive to co-operative processes—are more reality than mirage.

Notes to Chapter 9

1. According to former Japanese Education Minister Masayuki Fujio, for example, 'under international law, it is not murder to kill in time of war' (cited in Burgess, 1986).
2. Since his earlier work, Burton (see, for example, Burton 1984, Ch. 15) has observed that the sources of conflict at all systems levels are institutions that inhibit or deny the fulfilment of basic human needs such as security, recognition, distributive justice, and others. This later statement is compatible with his earlier view that effective communication involves the recognition of the existence of such needs, a determination of the costs involved in continuing to violate them, and an exploration of ways to fulfil them.
3. These items are rough indicators of need for achievement and need for power. Those who score relatively high on them are assigned to the decision-making components and those who score relatively low are assigned to the validation components (Powell, 1969).
4. The items comprising the Personal Cynicism Scale are:
   a. Barnum was wrong when he said there's a sucker born every minute.
   b. Generally speaking, men won't work very hard unless they are forced to do so.
   c. It is safest to assume that all people have a vicious streak and it will come out when they are given a chance.
   d. The biggest difference between most criminals and other people is that the criminals are stupid enough to get caught.

   The first of these is a negatively-worded item: disagreement with it means some degree of possession of the attribute being measured. The other items are positively worded.
5. Personal cynicism involved a five-point scale response scheme: 'The higher the score achieved by an individual on a given variable, the more he or she would be moving in the direction of possessing the attribute being measured by the variable' (Sandole, 1980a).
6. The six courses cited here were conducted by me for the University of Southern California, British and German programmes in International Relations. The course in bargaining (nine students, plus some friends to help run the PDS simulation), was one of my British courses. My German courses included the two courses on methods (6 and 10 students), plus the three courses on conflict (8, 9, and 13 students, plus friends, relatives, and other students for the one-day PDS operation). In the four courses involving simulation, debriefings were conducted prior to the administration of the post-questionnaire.

   The students in the German sample tended to be male American army officers, while those in the British sample were more of a mixture, but with males still outnumbering females; non-Americans as well as Americans, with the former sometimes outnumbering the latter; and civilian as well as military personnel, with the former always outnumbering the latter.

   None of the findings emerging from the study were statistically significant (as determined by the Wilcoxon Matched-Pairs, Signed-Rank Test).
7. This is in agreement with, for example, Alger's (1963) observation that: 'Three years of experimentation with the simulation in laboratory sessions of undergraduate courses has shown that its successful use requires careful integration of the simulation with course readings, papers, lectures, and seminars.'

10 Transcending role constraints through simulation

MARVIN D. JENSEN
University of Northern Iowa, U.S.A.

Stevenson (1963) said that human beings are 'greater than the social uses to which they can be put'. They are also greater than the roles by which they are described. Without this awareness of human complexity, people are diminished in their perceptions and behaviours, becoming limited to a narrow range of responses dictated by their social functions. The result can be interpersonal conflict and intrapersonal stress.

Interpersonal conflict arising from a clash of roles is well illustrated in Peter Shaffer's (1974) play *Equus*. In this psychological drama, psychiatrist Martin Dysart longs to befriend his troubled young patient, Alan Strang, and join in his intense experience of life. Alan is abnormally passionate about horses, but at least he 'gallops', and his enthusiasm is a striking reproach to the restricted lives of his inhibited elders. Ultimately, Dysart is trapped in his professional role which dictates that he return Alan to normality and silence the boy's pain and passion. The conflict between them is the more tragic in view of their similarity as troubled, struggling, yet often admirable human beings. Their roles as doctor and patient prevent them from meeting as people. Similar role conflicts occur frequently between parents and children, teachers and students, employers and employees.

Goffman (1959) described individuals who co-operate in sustaining an interaction routine as members of teams, who avoid 'discrepant roles' which would contradict their prescribed functions in the performance. He noted: 'One over-all objective of any team is to sustain the definition of the situation that its performance fosters. This will involve the over-communication of some facts and the under-communication of others

(Goffman 1959: 141). Blinded to their deeper human similarities, team players act in subservience to rules imposed by society. Berger & Luckmann (1966) described this as an institutionalisation of conduct in which the complex human self is replaced by a narrowly defined social self. This social self acts as a type, limited to the typical role behaviour of a doctor, teacher, parent, patient, student, son or daughter, etc., and bound by strict rules in interactions with other types. The resulting confrontations and communication breakdowns between different types cannot be excused with the cliché that people are only human; in fact, in these instances, people are not human enough. Role-players fail to communicate because they interact as social selves, using only segments of their personalities, and avoiding discrepant roles.

Limited role definitions can also lead to intrapersonal strain—a form of internal communication breakdown. In *Equus*, Martin Dysart's torment is self-destructive even as his behaviours toward Alan are other-destructive. He is trapped between his training as a psychiatrist and his judgement as a man; this places him in a double bind, a dilemma in which he perceives that he will be wrong whatever he does. Bateson (1972) related the double-bind concept to an earlier precept known as the theory of logical types, a theory based on formal logic which postulated a discrete division or discontinuity between a type and its larger class. Bateson saw that this mathematically based theory did not account for the complexity of a human life which is inevitably comprised of 'multiple types'. In human terms a part contains all elements of the whole (an idea more analogous to genetic biology than mathematical logic). Any effort to function on the basis of a single 'type' or role creates an internal conflict between interconnected dimensions of the human personality, and actions based solely on one part will be unsatisfactory to other parts of the psyche. Thus, a double bind arises which can produce internal tension leading to pathological behaviour and even schizophrenia. However, this behaviour results not from the presence of conflicting roles, but from the unreasonable, impossible attempt to be the right type when in fact life is an ambiguity of multiple types.

Perhaps the most valuable implication to be derived from the work of Bateson (1972) and Laing (1969) is the conclusion that double binds are inevitable but not necessarily pathological—that awareness of multiple role demands can allow a person to experience a higher level of intrapersonal and interpersonal communication, a level at which paradox is not only acknowledged but welcomed. At this level, the perceived polarity of roles is transcended in a way that corresponds to the Hegelian concept of synthesis emerging from a confrontation of thesis and antithesis. In human experience, the synthesis emerging from a clash of roles is a more encompassing level of perception and behaviour—what Schutz (1967) described as 'type transcendence'. Bateson (1972: 303) expressed it in the words of William Blake: 'Without contraries is no progression'. By taking on contrary roles in a simulation, a person can experience type transcendence, and move towards greater respect for the complexity of self and others—a perspective which is essential to healthy communication.

The simulation: role transcendence

The simulation described below is intended, at minimum, to address Piaget's (1926) concept of egocentrism which he explained as a general lack of awareness of others' perceptual and cognitive experience, resulting in monologue or soliloquy instead of genuine interpersonal communication. Although Piaget described egocentrism as a temporary stage in child development, many adults also speak in monologues and might be described as suffering from arrested development. Vygotsky (1956) believed that the egocentric speech of childhood 'goes underground' and becomes a kind of inner speech that relies heavily on presuppositions in the formation of perceptions. True interpersonal communication can only be experienced when a person goes beyond the egocentric perceptions which are preserved and reinforced by inner speech.

In addition to encouraging other-awareness and challenging presuppositions, this simulation may allow participants to glimpse the human similarities which surface when they dare to move beyond particular roles or 'social selves', and may help each participant recognise the multiple overlapping roles which comprise his/her own identity. A deepened understanding of another's complexity simultaneously expands the perception of self—but without thc debilitating exclusiveness of egocentrism.

The participants in ROLE TRANSCENDENCE are seated in a circle. The circle can be comprised of any number. Each participant is asked to assume that the person on the immediate right is his/her parent and the person on the immediate left is his/her son or daughter. Thus, each person in the circle is playing two potentially conflicting roles simultaneously. (Other possible role assignments could be counsellor/client, teacher/student, or employer/employee.) Each participant should write a short note at the top of a blank page addressed to his/her parent requesting that a specific family rule be changed (e.g. that access to the family car be increased or alcohol consumption be allowed at home). This request is then passed to the parent who writes a short reply on the same sheet, denying the request and giving a reason. The sheets are then passed silently back and forth as subsequent responses are added. A possible outcome of this exchange is that participants may break through their habitual interaction patterns as opposing team members. (Possibly a 'parent' in this simulation might lower defences and acknowledge that alcohol in the home is a threat to his/her own fragile sobriety.) The result is the beginning of real communication.

After ample time has passed for the participants to respond several times in both roles, a second message may be initiated by the son or daughter. This should be a more detailed letter disclosing an intense positive or negative emotional experience and asking the parent if he/she can understand this experience. Each parent is to respond by describing a personal occurrence which involved a similar intensity of emotions. Participants should be encouraged to draw on real experiences from their lives and again silently exchange responses several times, including questions to probe further into the other person's perception of the experience. Silent interchange preserves this as a private two-way dialogue regardless of the size of the circle. The implicit or explicit appeals for understanding (perhaps of the authority figure's fears or self-doubts) again can break through the superficial level of 'impression management' as discussed by Goffman (1959). This second part of the simulation draws on Maslow's (1964) concept of peak experiences, described by him as moments of emotional intensity which all people have in common. May (1969) has written that these remembered peaks are the basis of empathy, that people often have not had the same experiences, but all have had the same intensity of experience, and thus on a level beyond roles or particular life histories all people are more similar than different. Rogers (1961: 26) echoed this insight when he stated: 'what is most personal is most general'. The leader of this simulation could discuss the ideas of Maslow, May and Rogers as a means of summarising the experience and might follow up the exercise by introducing a case study as described below.

Implications and follow-up

By allowing a person to experience multiple roles simultaneously, ROLE TRANSCENDENCE encourages the transcendence of egocentrism and the beginning of empathy. In addition to these interpersonal results, the simulation should demonstrate at the intrapersonal level that paradox need not be paralysing. Contrary to the negative connotations contained in Watzlawick *et al.*'s (1967) description of a paradoxical *injunction*, Berne's (1961) analysis of ego-state *contamination*, and even Bateson's (1972) concept of double *bind*, this simulation is a reminder that roles do not have to be interpersonal barriers or intrapersonal traps. Bateson (1972: 204) recognised that 'the ability to handle the multiple types of signals is itself a learned skill and therefore a function of the multiple levels of learning'. Moreover, it is apparent that the mature mind can simultaneously handle multiple perspectives and send multiple signals—a capacity which is at once complex, paradoxical and (when embraced) healthy.

The paradox of overlapping roles may be further studied by examining introspective writings, which can serve as case studies to confirm the simulation experience. One example is Lance Morrow's *The Chief: A Memoir of Fathers and Sons* (1984). Morrow's reflections show him to be simultaneously a son and a father, at once a hurting child and a confident adult. He finds a card game with middle-aged friends painfully reminiscent of the camaraderie when his father taught him and his younger brother to play poker. Morrow relives the power and guilt of adolescent hunting when he sees his own son relishing a kill, and is transported back to childish helplessness in the panic of an adult heart attack. These merging perceptions and emotions are more than fleeting *déjà vu* experiences; they reveal that Morrow, like each of us, carries within him a complex identity which surpasses his immediate roles.

While Morrow's recognition of overlapping multiple selves seems to disturb him at times, the simulation ROLE TRANSCENDENCE encourages receptiveness towards this human complexity. At best, this simulation exemplifies Makedon's (1984) concept of playful gaming in which the rules of the game are secondary to the players' spontaneity. Moreover, this and other simulations of childhood experiences can cross time barriers as well as role barriers, enabling a participant to glimpse a whole personality which includes and surpasses its many parts. This recognition allows a perspective which is healthier if not easier—for it allows both empathy and self-respect derived from the knowledge that we are larger than any single definition.

Conclusion

Socrates once said he was more a mob than a man. This ancient insight is not an admission of schizophrenia, but an acknowledgement of the paradoxical complexity of the human personality. Goffman (1971) reached a similar conclusion when he rejected umbrella terms such as 'individual' or 'person' as misleading in their imprecision. Goffman observed that it is too easy to say merely that the individual plays different roles, when in fact the individual can be different things depending on the demands of different interactions. An awareness of the multiple persons within each single body can be fostered through the simulation described in this chapter. This awareness can ease interpersonal conflict by enabling a person to see others as more than their immediate, transitory roles. Simultaneously, intrapersonal stress can be reduced as a person recognises that multiple personas are natural and liberating, and understands that synthesis of these multiple facets leads to an enlarged identity. The goal of better communication is served when this and other simulations encourage increased respect for others arising out of deepened respect for self.

11 Simulation as a preparation for communication in counsellor training

ANNE B. PEDERSEN
and
PAUL B. PEDERSEN
Syracuse University, NY, U.S.A.

If 'interviewing' is defined as a method of information gathering and 'psychotherapy' is concerned with long-term reconstruction of personality, then 'counselling' is helping so-called healthy, normal persons solve serious problems in their lives. Counselling requires a specialised form of communication that is both persuasive and purposive. Counselling is purposive in focusing the communication on a particular task which may include helping someone else solve a problem or make a decision. Counselling is persuasive in structuring the communication roles so that one person is the helper and the other person is effectively receiving help. The counsellor must, therefore, become an expert in this special form of communication.

There are other areas of social interaction as well, where counselling takes place but where a 'counsellor' and a 'client' are not usually identified in those roles. Many of the microskills required for counselling are also important for any communication where one person is helping another. In employee-assistance programmes, firms frequently depend on counselling to manage problems of motivation, drug or alcohol abuse, marriage or family problems, and a wide variety of concerns which affect the employee's work effectiveness. In educational settings, teachers become skilled in 'advising' as well as teaching their students in a wide range of concerns which affect the student's ability to learn. Lawyers, doctors, and a great variety of other professionals are frequently called on to help healthy, normal persons solve serious problems through counselling skills. Not all of these people are aware of their role as counsellors, and some of them might be offended if they were so labelled. The fact remains, however, that they do apply many of the skills for which counsellors are especially trained.

Learning skills through simulation

Simulation provides a relatively safe way to learn expert counselling skills, without risk to people seeking counselling on real problems. Simulation also provides the opportunity for expanding counselling skills to new areas of expertise as a form of preparation for real-life situations. Communication and simulation are two fields with the same basic theme of preparing experts with maximum learning effectiveness and minimum danger to either the counsellor or the client.

Simulation is a widely used technique for teaching counselling skills. For example, role-played counselling interviews have been used extensively in most basic counsellor education courses (Ivey, 1983). One approach to the use of simulation is focused on 'microskills' for counselling. Ivey (1983) defines a hierarchy of microskills from basic attending skills, to influencing skills, to skill sequencing and integration. The presumption is that counselling is a composite of smaller or 'micro' skills which can be taught separately as components of 'expert' counselling. Among the microskills amenable to the simulation method of instruction are: asking questions, paraphrasing, reflecting, interpreting, giving directions and summarising. Similarly, Egan (1986) suggests skills of attending, being concrete rather than vague, being empathic, focusing on an immediate rather than indeterminate time frame, and confronting and defining an appropriate action in response to the situation. Brammer (1979) lists an additional 22 separate skills which are organised into seven clusters, including direct and indirect leading, focusing, mediating, associating, advising and informing.

Simulated counselling interviews provide a safe setting to make mistakes and learn 'recovery skills' for getting out of trouble after having said or done the wrong thing. It is assumed that the student counsellor is then better prepared, having practised the microskills under simulated counselling conditions. The counsellor is also less anxious about making mistakes, having already rehearsed a variety of recovery skills for getting out of trouble.

Each of the microskills in counselling has been defined in a cultural context. In order to apply the microskills to culturally different settings, it is important to adapt each skill to the assumptions associated with the new cultural context. Simulations provide an ideal means of identifying cultural assumptions in each cultural setting and facilitating the transfer of microskills from one culture to another. For example, in some social contexts one may ask direct questions, in another questions must be asked very indirectly, in still other situations one would gather information by observations and any kind of questioning would be inappropriate. It is, therefore, important to identify and analyse culturally learned assumptions before proceeding to apply counselling microskills to a somewhat different cultural setting.

The importance of assumptions in counselling communication

Identification of culturally learned assumptions is the foundation of expert counselling communication. These assumptions influence both how the message is *appropriately* sent and how that message is *appropriately* interpreted by the receiver. Unfortunately, in many cases, unexamined and dominant culturally-learned assumptions are allowed to distort counselling communication. We are becoming increasingly aware of the negative consequences of unexamined assumptions in counselling across cultures. Cultural awareness by counsellors is evident in the increased emphasis on cross-cultural dimensions in counsellor education, the requirement of cultural training for accreditation of counsellor education courses, and the definition of ethical guidelines by professional organisations. Cultural awareness is required not only because of an ethical obligation to minority cultural groups, but more importantly for clear and accurate counselling communication.

Our learned assumptions are so often best concealed from ourselves. If you want to know about your own assumptions, you might better ask your friends to tell you because they are more likely to be aware of your assumptions than you are yourself. In debriefing counsellors on their assumptions, it is important to provide a structure where the assumptions become more explicit and obvious—and therefore less likely to distort counselling communication by accident. A series of structured simulations provides the opportunity to confront one's own assumptions. This series of brief simulation exercises involves role-playing to represent specific decision points in counselling communication. Counsellors can be debriefed to confront their assumptions and identify ways that these assumptions might distort counselling communication.

The five exercises for cultural awareness described in this chapter are examples of how counsellors can learn about their own cultural assumptions. Each of these exercises has been tried in dozens of training workshops over the last ten years (Pedersen, 1986) and modified to increase its impact for learning. While precise data are not available on the effect of each exercise, the exercises have proven helpful in motivating counsellors to examine assumptions in their own counselling communication, both in terms of their *knowledge* about counselling and their *skill* in applying that knowledge. Cultural awareness provides an essential foundation for knowledge and skill in expert counselling communication.

Simulations for teaching cultural awareness

The present authors define a simulation as the act or process of copying or representing aspects of perceived reality. According to this definition, the following exercises will simulate the process of making a decision, or identifying an assumption, or interpreting the meaning of a message, as it might occur in counselling. Each of the following exercises simulates one or another aspect of the communication process, where culturally learned assumptions are likely to distort the message if they are left unexamined.

THE TRUTH STATEMENT

A 'truth statement' is generated by the facilitator which is so general that all of the group are likely to accept it. One example might be: 'Accurate counselling communications are usually more helpful than an inaccurate counselling communication'. Another example unrelated to counselling might be: 'Good is better than evil'. As an alternative, the facilitator might get the group to generate their own statement which they can all agree is truthful.

Each participant is asked *individually* to identify a second statement explaining why the first statement is true, and then a third and fourth statement explaining why each preceding statement in turn is true. By that time, most of the group will have reached the point where they will say, 'I don't know or even care why it is true! It's just true!' They have followed a 'common-sense' logical reasoning according to their own assumptions. Each person's chain of logical common sense will have led them in different directions, and they will have agreed on the original truth statement for very divergent reasons. The conclusions we draw are frequently less important than the common-sense logic which leads us to those conclusions.

Truth is based on fairly arbitrary, culturally learned assumptions for each of us and can ultimately be traced back to assumptions which require no evidence, but which are 'simply true' according to common sense. We believe in the same truths for different reasons. A better understanding of the assumptions by which we derive truth statements is helpful to counsellors communicating with persons who have different culturally learned perceptions of truth.

WHAT YOU SAID, FELT, AND MEANT

In counselling, it is easy to confuse messages about what the other person actually said, what they felt while they were saying it, and what they meant or intended by the statement. For example, an Asian client might describe giving up a promising future for the sake of his or her family. The counsellor might hear this as an example of exploitation, when it is intended to be an example of loyalty. The counsellor might interpret the client's feelings as anger for being made a victim, when the client's real feelings might be satisfaction for having made a necessary sacrifice. The counsellor might interpret the client's meaning as seeking ways to break free from family bonds, when the client's real intention is to live harmoniously within the constraints of the family.

By separating the functions of fact, feeling and meaning in a message being communicated, it is possible to identify culturally learned assumptions in our interpretation of what other persons tell us. What one person says and what the other person hears are frequently different.

Participants are organised into three-person, multi-cultural groups with one person identified as a 'speaker', the second person as a 'recorder', and the third person as an 'interpreter'. First, the speaker talks for one uninterrupted minute about himself or herself. Second, without taking notes, the recorder repeats back the *facts* of what was said in one minute without adding any new information or omitting any actual information. Third, the interpreter spends one minute drawing conclusions or *inferences* about the speaker's feelings and meaning in the statement. Fourth, all three persons discuss the accuracy of how the message was interpreted both in terms of the facts and the inferences.

This interaction emphasises the differences between fact and inference in cross-cultural communication by simulating three aspects of the communication process.

THE LABEL EXERCISE

Each person can be thought of as wearing a different label, which identifies that person with positive or negative characteristics and stereotypes in one or another group. The label each of us wears may be quite different from that which we intend or even prefer. Skill in counselling communication will depend on an ability to interpret accurately the feedback we receive from others indicating the label *they* perceive us to be wearing.

In simulating this process, gummed labels describing personality attributes are attached to the foreheads of each group member. Rather than risk the unfortunate possibility of *accurately* matching a negative adjective to a participant, only positive adjectives should be used in the labels. Each group member is then asked to circulate among the other members providing feedback to each other *as though* the label were accurate. Participants are instructed not to 'guess' their label, but simply to interact more or less normally according to one another's label. Each participant will know the labels on all other participants' foreheads, but not their own label.

After exchanging feedback with most other members of the group in a five- to ten-minute period, the individual participants are asked to first guess their own label, and then remove the label to see how accurately they were able to process feedback from the other members. Whether or not the label is 'accurate' is less important than accuracy in interpreting feedback about others' perception of the label.

This exercise simulates the real-life condition of our wearing culturally defined labels, which are evident to others but not always evident to ourselves. The emphasis is on the accurate processing of feedback from others to describe others' perceptions of oneself. The activity simulates the process by which we enact and decode images or labels that represent ourselves.

OUTSIDE EXPERT

Patterns of response which are obvious and consistent from the viewpoint of the host culture can seem inconsistent and even hostile to the outside expert who does not know a host culture's rules. The dilemma of an outside expert is simulated by dividing the participants into outside experts and host-culture respondents.

Approximately a quarter of the group is asked to leave the room while a 'host culture' is being generated. When the outside experts return, they are instructed to ask as many questions as possible of each of the host-culture respondents. To simplify the exercise, the outside experts are limited exclusively to closed yes/no questions. While the outside experts are absent, the host culture respondents are instructed to follow three rules: men may only respond to men and women to women in providing any response at all; all questions from persons of the same gender must be answered by a 'yes' or 'no' response; and if the expert is smiling when asking the question, the same-gender host-culture respondent will respond 'yes', but if the expert is not smiling, the host culture respondent will respond 'no'.

The outside experts are instructed to ask questions which can be answered by a 'yes' or 'no', but they are *not* informed of the other two rules of the host-culture respondents. After about ten minutes, the outside experts report back individually to the group at large on what they have learned. Typically, the experts generate elegant interpretations based on the responses they received. These interpretations are total artefacts of the expert's own behaviours, preconceptions and assumptions.

Debriefing may apply insights by both participants and leaders to ways that social conditioning has reinforced each person to develop and construct a particular psychological interpretation for each event. Participants can be taught the importance of understanding a host culture's rules, and that inconsistency may be in the expert, as well as in the host culture. Furthermore, non-verbal cues (such as gender or expression) may be perceived as important means of communication, and that negative judgement about a culture may be seen as a result of misunderstanding the host-culture respondent's intention.

DRAWING A HOUSE

The importance of culture is that it teaches *patterns* of behaviour. The assumptions behind different patterns of behaviour may facilitate or block communication between two persons. The simulated task of 'drawing a house' provides a safe context to identify and discuss the variety of culturally learned patterns in a group.

Participants are divided into two-person teams and each team is provided with one pen or pencil and a piece of paper. They are both instructed to grasp the same pen or pencil and 'co-operatively' to draw a house on the piece of paper. They are *not* allowed to talk during the task. After two or three minutes, the participants are asked to stop and discuss similarities and differences in their behaviour patterns for this task.

Houses which are clearly and precisely drawn might indicate that both persons' behaviours synchronised exactly, or that one person drew the house while the partner 'hitch-hiked' without exerting any influence. Houses which appear to be parts of two houses joined together might indicate that first one and then the other partner took control of the task in sequence, but that they each had a different perception of the task. Sometimes the drawing does not resemble a house at all, but becomes more of a tangle of lines. This might indicate that both partners were extremely co-operative or that they were extremely competitive. One British civil servant and a Pacific island chief actually tore the sheet in half and left the room during this exercise!

Culturally learned patterns of behaviour that emphasise *relationship* (helping one another) and/or *task* (drawing a good house) are discussed as they relate to this simulated exercise, as well as more complicated real-life interaction. Likewise, culturally learned preferences for *leading* (controlling the pen or pencil) or *following* (facilitating the partner) are discussed both as they relate to the simulated task, and as they relate to multicultural contact in real life.

Conclusion

In each of these examples, the emphasis has been to simulate activities which increase cultural self-awareness in participants by identifying culturally learned assumptions about their own behaviour. A message being communicated might be compared to a rocket where—however straight the flight trajectory—the destination will be determined by the *direction* or *starting point*. Culturally learned assumptions are the starting points of communication, and in that way determine the accuracy of communication, not only in counselling but in other interactions as well.

These brief simulations of aspects of counsellor decision-making have been used to enhance cultural awareness as the basis for increased knowledge and skill in cross-cultural communication (Pedersen & Pedersen, 1985). Each exercise depends on skilled preparation, debriefing, and discussion by an instructor who can relate the simulation to specific training goals, such as those described as microskills. By creating an appropriate instructional framework, the trainer facilitates learning among the participants as they discover the implicit patterns of culturally learned assumptions that support the communication process.

12 Culture, prejudice and simulation/gaming in theory and practice

JENNY NOESJIRWAN
Kuring-gai College of Advanced Education, Australia
KLAAS BRUIN
Ubbo Emmius Teacher Training Institute, The Netherlands

Recent world history has demonstrated yet again the apparent incapacity of human groups to communicate with each other with tolerance and understanding. Communication across cultural and ethnic lines is commonly distorted along two dimensions. The horizontal dimension relates to meaning: the meaning that is intended becomes distorted and reinterpreted by the receiver with sometimes disastrous results. The vertical dimension relates to power: the relatively more powerful group attempts to consolidate its own superiority through the processes of communication control and distortion, through prejudice and discrimination. Yet if we are to survive on this planet it is necessary to understand more clearly how those communication processes become distorted, and how those distortions can be reversed. Simulation promises much in this endeavour, both as a research tool and as an educational technique.

Starting with a brief description of the prevailing theories of culture and prejudice, in this chapter some of the conditions under which simulation may and may not facilitate intergroup and intercultural communication are explored and a number of concrete examples of simulation games briefly described.

Culture and communication

It is often hard to explain to people that the behaviour they experience and qualify as 'strange' in other people is in fact no more strange than their own taken-for-granted behaviour patterns. While all humans are subject to the same biological imperatives, the way these are organised and expressed is a function of socialisation within a particular culture. Socially constructed patterns of behaviour represent culturally defined ways of achieving common human ends. 'Culture' refers to the development of attitudes, rules and values within a coherent belief system that is shared by a group of people. Culture defines not only what we should do but also what our actions mean to others.

The concept of culture can be used to analyse the patterns of interaction that are typical of a specific group or community. Moreover, the analysis of culture is a useful means of identifying and understanding differences between typical patterns of interaction of different communities. These differences become particularly salient when a member of one culture moves into or interacts with members of another culture. Such a person is likely to experience 'culture shock', an experience marked by feelings of surprise, confusion, alienation, hostility and anxiety (Oberg, 1960; Taft, 1976). Culture shock represents a form of communication breakdown which can be traced to the particular disjunction between the meaning structures of the respective cultures (Brein & David, 1971).

Successful communication involves a transaction based on shared meanings, such that what is intended by the sender is understood in the same terms by the receiver. The meanings of actions are embedded in the culture; they are created within the 'socially constituted stock of knowledge' (Schutz, 1967) and provide a taken-for-granted reality for the cultural participants. These shared cultural meanings are, of course, coded in the verbal language. They are also coded in every socially structured action that has cultural significance. The meanings of actions are partly defined by the rules and values of the culture. Rules of social interaction are propositions that guide actions (Harré & Secord, 1972), and as such provide recipes for actions. They also provide grounds for a common set of expectations, knowing what to expect of others. While rules relate to specific recurring social situations, they are ordered and integrated by underlying principles of unity or cultural values (Barth, 1966). The rules and values together serve to define the dominant public culture (Goodenough, 1971).

But meaning structures are culture-specific. Different cultures adopt different rules for achieving the same task. The expectations for actions differ, as do the meanings attached to the same events, and the same action is evaluated differently (Noesjirwan, 1978). When persons cross a cultural boundary they take with them the taken-for-granted meaning structure of their home culture. They continue to choose actions consistent with it and to interpret the actions of others in terms of it. Thus, in a cross-cultural encounter the actions of each are generated in terms of the meaning structure of the actor's culture, but they are interpreted and evaluated in terms of the meaning structure of the perceiver's culture. This generates a cognitive conflict and distorted cultural perceptions.

Culture and the simulation/gaming approach

Over the last two decades a number of simulation/games have been designed which are essentially based on the theoretical reasoning given above. They include CULTURE CONTACT, BAFA BAFA, THE CULTURE GAME, and SUMAH. The object is to confront participants with the experience of culture shock, with the consequences of communication that breaks down because of differences between 'cultures'. This confrontation, however, takes place in a controlled learning environment, and *not* in real life. In real life the consequences of a breakdown of communication are often unpredictable, incomprehensible and possibly damaging. But by experiencing the differences of culture in an experimental, rather than abstract, setting the participant has the opportunity to develop insights which can help facilitate communication processes in similar situations in real life later on.

As an illustration a brief description is given of the 'cultural discovery' game called BAFA BAFA. First, a class or group of participants is divided into two groups or 'cultures'. Each group is given a set of rules to govern their behaviour as members of the new culture. The Alpha culture is relaxed and values personal contact and intimacy within a sexist and patriarchal structure. The Beta culture, on the other hand, is an aggressive, money-orientated culture, in which a member's value is measured by how well s/he performs in the marketplace. Once all of the members understand and feel comfortable with the rules of their new society (after about 30 minutes), observers are exchanged. After a fixed time, they return to their respective groups and report on what they saw. Based on the information provided, each group tries to develop hypotheses about the most effective way to interact with the other culture. After that, the cultures proceed as before except that each person takes a turn at trying to interact with the other culture. Once everyone has had a chance to interact, the game ends and a debriefing is held. The structure of BAFA BAFA represents a kind of cultural voyage of discovery, the objective of which is to demonstrate that comprehension of a foreign culture is difficult, takes time and requires an open mind.

Prejudice and communication

Prejudice represents a form of communication breakdown which is rather different from culture shock, though there are elements in common. The concept of 'prejudice' usually implies a strong negative evaluation of 'the other' and is typically marked by an attempt to establish unequal power relations between the 'we' and the 'other'. Prejudice constitutes a special consequence of the general human capacities of categorisation, inference and competition.

It is a general characteristic of human beings to order and categorise the stimuli that come from the environment. A clearly arranged outside world gives us feelings of control and safety. Without it we would be permanently overwhelmed by a multitude of undirected impressions. Category systems are the basis of the cultural meaning system acquired during socialisation. With the very first development of language a young child learns to arrange, to distinguish and to name the people and things around him/her according to the category systems that prevail in the immediate social environment. Moreover, the young child is infected with the emotions that are attached to the different categories. At later ages the category systems acquired in childhood are extended and refined, mostly in interaction with the specific social groups a person participates in. A consequence of the above for the study of communication processes when prejudices are involved is that, although stereotyped views of other persons and groups are learned and not inborn, their cognitive and emotional basis is acquired in early childhood (see Tajfel, 1981), which makes them very resistant to change.

An effect of categorisation in general is, first, that it influences people's view of reality. Tajfel (1981) has shown that, after different categories have been established, people are inclined to perceive and judge the stimuli that confront them in a distorted way. Differences between qualities of units within a certain category are likely to be diminished, whereas differences between qualities of units belonging to different categories tend to be increased. There are good reasons to assume (Tajfel, 1981; Milner 1983) that this deformation of perception is likely to occur in the case of social categorisation as well.

A second important consequence of categorisation can best be described by taking into account the two components of this phenomenon: identification and inference. An analysis of the two basic ways these aspects can be interrelated clarifies the nature of prejudices, and the way information is (mis)handled when they are present.

It is quite normal that perception of or experience with individual cases leads to a conclusion being reached about the qualities of a certain social category. Generally, such a conclusion will take the form of a statement involving probability. An example of a statement describing this conclusion reached by inductive inference (see Figure 12.1) might be: 'most Alphans are useless'.

However, when new members of the category Alpha are approached later on, solely on the basis of the conclusion drawn beforehand, we speak of deductive inference. New cases that are identified as members of the category are confronted with a prefabricated judgement, based on the properties ascribed to the social category as a whole. In this case the typical reasoning is (see Figure 12.2) 'Alphans are useless': this is an Alphan, so this Alphan is useless. In this case the conclusion is derived from categorical

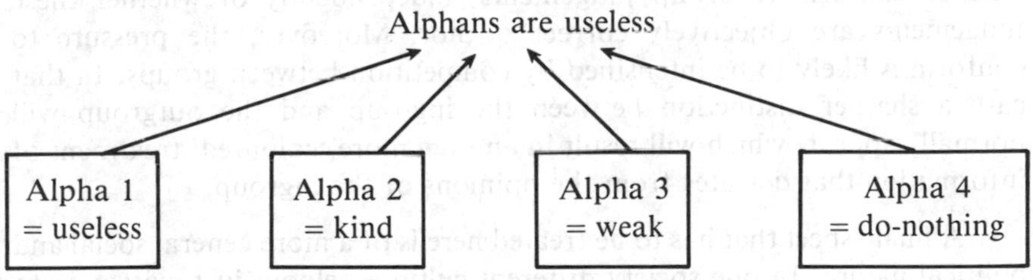

FIGURE 12.1 *Inductive Inference*

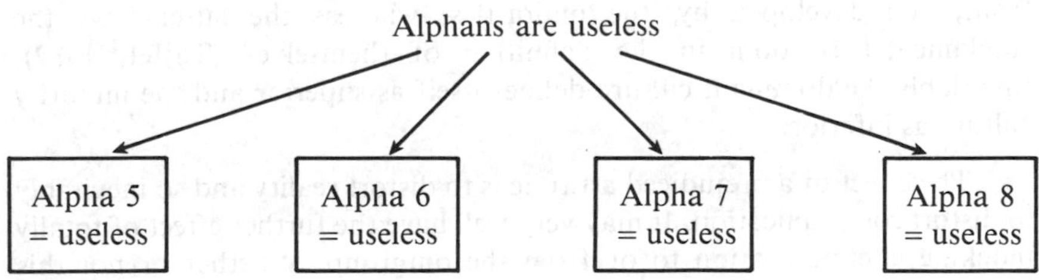

FIGURE 12.2 *Deductive Inference* (*Source*: Kok, 1979)

judgement: when individual qualities that contradict it are neglected, we speak of a prejudice.

Very often human beings perceive and value other people and social situations on the basis of pre-existing categorical frameworks. The reasoning given above has made clear that many people would rather persist in their own good–bad scheme than change it under the influence of new, alternative information. When contradictory information is presented, a rather typical reaction takes place: the facts are denied, distorted or called exceptional so that the basic prejudiced categorical framework remains intact. Essentially, prejudiced judgements are not based on facts. They include unverifiable allegations without proper indication of time and place. Sometimes the perception of or experience with one single case is generalised to a conclusion which comprises the qualities of the whole category. Finally, when contradictory, alternative information is presented, it is quite likely that the reliability of the source of this information is called into question.

There are two further aspects concerning prejudice that reinforce the distorting effects mentioned above. Social psychological research has shown (see Sherif & Sherif, 1953; Sherif, 1966a; 1966b) how members of a group tend to conform to group judgements, independently of whether these judgements are objectively correct or not. Moreover, the pressure to conform is likely to be intensified by competition between groups. In that case a sharper distinction between the ingroup and the outgroup will normally appear, which will result in an even more 'coloured' treatment of information that deviates from the opinions of the ingroup.

A final aspect that has to be treated here is of a more general social and political nature. In one society different cultures seldom just exist next to each other—we mostly observe the dominance of one culture over the other(s). Basically, this means that there is more to intercultural encounters than just differences of meaning structures encountered. The real problem is that 'minorities' are often defined on the basis of criteria originating from, and developed by, the majorities, whereas the latter have the fundamental freedom in the definition of themselves (Tajfel, 1982). Invariably the dominant culture defines itself as superior and the minority culture as inferior.

The effect of a prejudiced attitude is to distort reality and so inevitably to distort communication. It may very well have the further effect of totally blocking communication to or from the outgroup. Whether or not this happens depends on whether the *attitude* of prejudice is translated into the *behaviour* of discrimination.

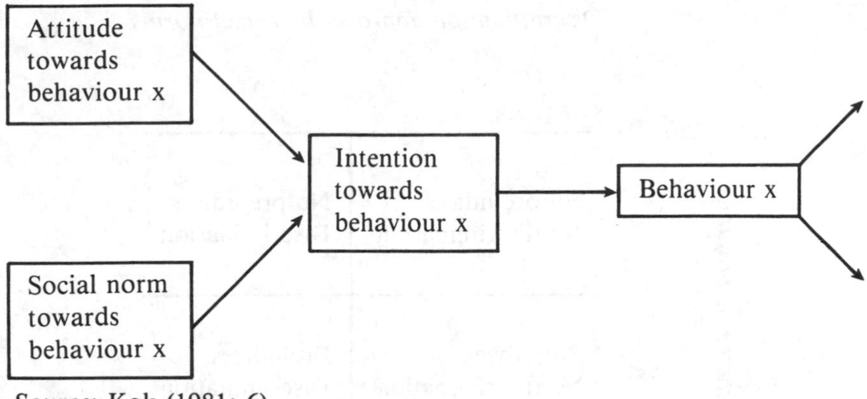

Source: Kok (1981: 6)

FIGURE 12.3 *Kok (1981) model of discrimination*

Behaviour does not automatically express an attitude. Behaviour is public and therefore subject to public scrutiny. The social environment can approve or disapprove specific behaviours and most people are inclined to take into account this public reaction in anticipation. Consequently, the social rules and norms of a group co-determine a member's ultimate behaviour. This is clarified in Figure 12.3.

Discrimination that is expressed in a specific social setting does not have to indicate that all group members actually possess prejudiced attitudes. On the other hand, however, the absence of discrimination, or even the disapproval of it, does not automatically mean that all group members are free from prejudices. Normally, the dominant opinions in a group, mostly put into words by its informal leaders, determine whether discrimination will be disapproved, tolerated, or possibly even demanded.

When the social norms that prevail approve discrimination, any counterinformation will result in opposition and rejection of the subject-matter and the source of information, and consequently, reinforcement of the discriminative norms themselves. Group members that are possibly tolerant will have to keep silent and will be pressed to conform. In this respect Robert K. Merton (see van den Berghe, 1978) has indicated the existence of the so-called 'prejudiced non-discriminator' and the 'non-prejudiced discriminator'. This theory is clarified in Figure 12.4.

However, a word of caution is needed. It is also true that for every phenomenon described above, the opposite occurs. While social categorisation occurs, so does the process of social particularisation (Billig, 1985).

Existence of prejudices		*Discrimination approval by social norms*	
		No	Yes
	No	No prejudices No discrimination	No prejudices Discrimination
	Yes	Prejudices No discrimination	Prejudices Discrimination

Source: Bruin (1986)

FIGURE 12.4 *Social norms, prejudices and discrimination*

While social conformity occurs, so does social differentiation (Moscovici, 1976). While group competition occurs, so does co-operation. Culture shock can lead to biculturalism. Where there is prejudice there is also tolerance. Perhaps, as Billig (1985) suggests, we should adopt a rhetorical or dialectical approach to prejudice.

Prejudice and the simulation/gaming approach

If prejudiced attitudes and discriminatory behaviours are learned, then it should be possible to design an educational programme about the processes by which prejudice occurs; a programme that reduces perceptual and communication distortion, and/or that reduces the likelihood that prejudiced attitudes will be translated into discriminatory behaviour.

Simulation/games can help facilitate communication processes in a number of different ways. In the following section a set of games will be described briefly that are each aimed at specific aspects of the phenomenon.

The contact hypothesis

It is possible for game participants from different backgrounds to make contact in a social situation that helps reduce their mutual stereotyped views. In this respect it is important to note that contact as such does not necessarily mean that prejudices are reduced. Research has shown that, depending on the circumstances, contact can result in change in the desired direction, no change at all, or even reinforcement of the prejudices. Among the factors that are shown to be relevant for reduction (Katz, 1979) are: equal status between the members of the groups; a favourable social climate for intergroup contact; intimate rather than casual contact; pleasant and rewarding contact; engagement in an activity with a mutual superordinate goal; equal numbers of the persons from the groups that have contact. In a research project cited by Weissbruch (see Katz, 1976), in which subjects from different backgrounds participated in a management game, at least five of the conditions mentioned were present. Operation in the game required intra-group co-operation for its success. The teams consisted of white and black females of approximately the same age. During the long sessions of the game there was a basis for fairly close contact, both in the game and during the breaks, which provided the (planned) opportunity for discussions on both race-related and personal topics.

The results of this study were both encouraging and disappointing. Compared with a control group, the experimental group of white females (who had been chosen because of their high scores on a racial prejudice test) showed a significantly greater favourable attitude toward their black colleagues in the game. On the other hand, these women had not significantly reduced their prejudices toward blacks in general.

This research project gives an indication that under specific conditions simulation/games can be used to bridge the communication gap between prejudiced majority members and persons of minority groups. It might even be possible in such a situation to open up communication on specific differential cultural elements.

Reversal of roles

One of the advantages of simulation/gaming is that roles that are normally performed in reality can easily be reversed. In the structured experience of a game the real-life discriminator can be put in a situation in which s/he is discriminated against. An example can be found in the A-B-Z GAME in which participants, after having been divided into two groups according to the trivial criterion of the first letter of their first name, are openly treated in an unequal way.

Other examples of role reversal leading to the experience of discrimination are found in the simulation/game MIJN MAAT IS MIJN MAAT (my mate has my size) which discriminates on the basis of shoe size, and the well-known STARPOWER game. There is at least some evidence (Katz, 1976) that the experience of being discriminated against may lead to an apparent decrease in prejudice and an increased willingness to interact with members of the other group, at least among children.

Differentiation between ingroups and outgroups

Teachers and group leaders know that it is very easy to create a conflict of 'us' against 'them' between different social groups. In this respect the experimental research done by Sherif and Sherif (1953; Sherif 1966a; 1966b) speaks for itself. A game that normally shows this effect very clearly, and can therefore help participants to become conscious of the risks of being a member of a group (in a sense become asocial) runs as follows.

Participants are first divided into five groups. Four of them are asked to invent a slogan on a subject they are familiar with (for a new club, or next year's conference). They are invited to be as creative as possible, but have to arrive at a single group slogan. The fifth group, however, gets a very different task that has nothing to do with the game—some valuable work for which they have to be rewarded later on. These persons are asked to leave the room altogether.

After some 20 minutes the first four groups are each invited to appoint a representative, who has to present the slogan created by his/her own group. The four representatives then have to sit around a square table, where they are given the simple task of deciding which of the four slogans produced is the best one. The other group members take seats just opposite their representative, so they can look him/her in the face. After a while they are allowed to send short messages to him/her. Normally in this situation the representatives seated in the middle fulfil their task very badly. They start mistrusting each other, defending their own slogan (although in many cases this is a very bad one), exercising power to win, and it usually takes a lot of time for them to reach a conclusion. It is the presence of those with whom they collaborated which prevents the representatives from reaching a new consensus.

The process becomes very clear to everyone when finally the fifth group is called in to perform the same task. They will normally start choosing some simple procedure, and finish the job within a few minutes. In a culture where competition between groups is a phenomenon implicitly recognised by anybody involved, the effect of this game is dramatic.

The simulation/gaming approach: Advantages and disadvantages

Research on the capacity of simulation/games to promote change has provided both positive and negative results (Bredemeier & Greenblat, 1981). Under certain circumstances and for some students simulation/gaming can be more effective than traditional methods of instruction in facilitating positive attitude change towards the subject and its purposes. The attitudinal effects of simulations/games that have been established include increasing empathy towards the subject involved, greater realism for the role that was played, and greater self-awareness. In all cases, how a game is run and who runs it appear to make a difference, and the debriefing is generally considered crucial to learning in any case.

Given the warnings indicated by the general literature on changing prejudiced attitudes, however, it seems safe to start from the rather pessimistic position that, normally, games will result in no change at all. They might be a useful tool in this respect when prejudiced attitudes are not yet completely developed (with young children: see Weissbruch in Katz, 1976) and possibly under very specific conditions (e.g. in a therapeutic situation) that can lead to some dramatic breakthrough.

At first glance the capacity for simulation/games to facilitate the development of social norms in a non-discriminative direction looks promising. Simulation/gaming is about social interaction. Its focus is on the dynamics of one group in interaction with another and how this all affects the individual. Moreover, it places the individual within a wider social context. Simulation/games represent some aspect of life in society and are an abstraction and a simplification that aim to grasp the fundamentals of social organisation.

When dealing with cultural differences, prejudices and discrimination, however, there are a number of specific problems and pitfalls that apply to simulation/gaming. First, we can imagine groups or participants where the communicative barriers caused by prejudiced opinions of foreign cultures are so intrusive that they refuse to participate in any game on the subject, even at an abstract level. Because their category system is constantly focused on the inferiority of other cultures, they will immediately recognise the proposed educational objectives, and dismiss them.

Resistance is all the more likely to happen when these strong opinions are embedded in the social climate of the class, with informal leadership that clearly approves discrimination, and when the source of counter-information (the game operator, the teacher) is considered unreliable. The prejudiced opinions can even be politically supported. Alternatively, it is possible that such a student group might actually *want* to play the game, but use it counterproductively, in relation to the original objectives. In most games social experiences are prominent. Most of the time the social climate of the participants is reflected in the decisions they make and the actions they attempt. It is up to them to decide and up to the game operator to stay neutral.

This means, however, that participants with prejudices are free to express *their* feelings as well. Logically we run the risk that either negative attitudes are expressed openly (which can result in reinforcement), or that discriminative actions occur in a social situation that is beyond the corrective influence of the teacher. Obviously, in the relation between gaming and prejudice/discrimination, the operation of social factors is confusing.

Normally, of course, the majority of participants will involve themselves in playing a game without the rather dangerous results described above. This does not necessarily mean, however, that social norms are changed permanently and automatically. Of special importance in this respect are the social norms and values that are present in other groups of which the participants in a game are members. When prejudiced judgements are contradicted and undermined only during and shortly after a gaming session in school, and reinforced the rest of the time in the peer group and at home, then any gaming attempt seems rather hopeless. Educational processes aimed at objectives such as learning what it is like to be discriminated against, and how easily mistakes are made when dealing with foreign cultures, must in some way be supported by the social environment of the learner. Otherwise the results will only be temporary and negligible in the long run.

When, during the post-game discussion, learning processes *are* actually started, and participants begin to understand how prejudices and discrimination are structured, there is a risk that the social norm in the group will adjust too fast in this new direction. An atmosphere may come into being in which persons outside the ingroup are considered the only victims of prejudice and in which no discussion at all can take place about the problems and the attitudes of the ingroup members themselves. A factor that complicates the picture even more is the fact that most participants in a game play different roles, occupy different positions, and consequently have different experiences (Greenblat 1981). Normally this will lead to differential learning effects.

Simulation as research tool

Simulation/gaming has an as yet largely unexplored potential for research. The great majority of studies dealing with simulation have examined the effect of the simulation experience. Few studies have used simulation/gaming as a research site. The reasons for this probably reside in the assumptions behind the design of most simulation/games, assumptions that do not rest comfortably with the epistemological basis adopted by positivist methodologies. Yet it is these same assumptions that render simulation/gaming a potentially rich arena for the study of human interaction in complex social organisation. The investigator is concerned not with isolated variables but with a gestalt. The parameters of the situation are specified but the variables within it are not. The players have an active rather than a passive role in producing the outcome. Causality is assumed to lie in the relationship between a network of events extending forward in time. The investigator is concerned to measure both individual variables and total holistic effects, to measure both overt behaviour and players' perceptions, to measure both process and outcome. Ultimately the investigator is concerned with constructing, within the simulation/game, a valid —albeit abstract and simplified—representation of some aspect of social organisation and to use the insights gained from the game to extend the understanding of the simulated phenomenon. Simulation may have a heuristic purpose in theory construction, or be a means of testing theories (Bell, 1975).

Recently Noesjirwan and Freestone (1979) designed THE CULTURE GAME in order systematically to explore the dimensions of culture shock. This followed a two-step process. The first step followed Bell's Model III, the basic premise of which is 'if the simulation/game rules (and the corresponding theory) are an adequate description of reality, then the behaviour occurring in the game should agree with the behaviour found in real life' (Bell, 1975: 281). The test of this was the degree to which the observed operation of the rules and values within the game is equivalent to the observed operation of the rules and values within the specific cultures in question. The second step followed Bell's Model I, the basic premise of which is that, if the theory proposed to explain the phenomenon in question (i.e. culture shock) is correct, then the resulting behaviour within the game should show characteristics known to be associated with the phenomenon. Such was the case. This kind of methodological approach could usefully be extended to a systematic study of prejudice and discrimination, perhaps to locate the conditions necessary for discrimination not to occur. To our knowledge this approach has not been used, although the early work of Sherif (1953) relied on an experimental method that was akin to simulation.

Conclusion

This chapter has explored some of the emerging issues in this fascinating topic, issues that emerge through the threading together of insights drawn from the theory of communication and the practice of simulation as applied to the fields of culture contact and prejudice. Clearly, this is the beginning and not the end of the exploration. While simulation may not provide the general educational solution we once hoped, it certainly can be a powerful training tool if used appropriately, and may very well prove an even more powerful research tool in the quest to unravel complex intergroup communication processes and their effects.

13 Intergroup communication and simulation in low- and high-context cultures

STELLA TING-TOOMEY
Arizona State University, Tempe, U.S.A.

Introduction

Intergroup communication entails the exchange of perceptions, impressions, evaluations, and the negotiation of verbal and non-verbal codes between members of two social and cultural collectives across temporal and spatial dimensions. Intergroup simulation involves members from two or more cultural groupings in a negotiation game of role re-definition and role re-learning processes. The purpose of this chapter is twofold: first, to point out the core cultural values that govern low-context culture (LCC) interaction and high-context culture (HCC) interaction; secondly, to apply the LCC–HCC framework in analysing intergroup simulations that engage both LCC and HCC participants in the learning environment.

Low-context cultures and high-context cultures

According to Hall (1976: 101), all human transactions can be divided into three communication systems:

> Any transactions can be characterized as high-, low-, or middle-context. HC (High Context) transactions feature preprogrammed information that is in the receiver and in the setting, with only

> minimal information in the transmitted message. LC (Low Context) transactions are the reverse. Most of the information must be in the transmitted message in order to make up for what is missing in the context.

Although no one culture exists exclusively at one extreme, in general, LCCs (with the United States as a prime example) value individualism, line logic, direct verbal interaction style, monochronic time rhythm, and maintain a horizontal societal structure. In contrast, HCCs (with Japan as the prime example) value collectivism, spiral logic, indirect verbal interaction style, polychronic time rhythm, and maintain a vertical societal structure. While the LCC and the HCC systems are not mutually exclusive, nevertheless they are governed by different sets of normative rules and values of interaction. Countless cross-cultural studies (Bond & Forgas, 1984; Gudykunst & Nishida, 1986; Hofstede, 1980; Hui & Triandis, 1986; Ting-Toomey, 1987; Triandis, 1986) have provided empirical evidence that the value orientations of individualism and collectivism are indeed reflective of the negotiation processes of the LCC and the HCC members. Individualistic cultures place a high emphasis on the attainment of individual goals over group goals in the negotiation process. Members of individualistic cultures are verbally more self-assertive and direct, and they are also more efficient with time management (monochronic-orientated) than members from collectivistic cultures. Conversely, collectivistic cultures place a high premium on the achievement of group goals over individual goals in the negotiation process. Members from collectivistic cultures are verbally more self-effusive and indirect, and they are also more relaxed with time management (polychronic-orientated) than members from individualistic cultures (Gudykunst & Kim, 1984; Hofstede, 1980; 1986; Okabe, 1983; Ting-Toomey, 1985). In fact, Hall (1983: 45–46) commented on cultures that differed along the dimension of monochronic time schedule (M-time) and polychronic time schedule (P-time):

> Like oil and water they don't mix. Each has its strengths as well as its weaknesses. I have termed doing many things at once: Polychronic, P-time. The North European system—doing one thing at a time—is Monochronic, M-time. P-time stresses involvement of people and completion of transactions rather than adherence to present schedules. Appointments are not taken as seriously and, as a consequence, are frequently broken. P-time is treated as less tangible than M-time.

While M-time members are more task-orientated in negotiation processes, P-time members are more socio-emotional-orientated. M-time members have a need for efficient time management in a task situation; P-time members have a need to develop a positive socio-emotional climate in the group before proceeding to task discussion. In sum, LCC systems and HCC systems differ on the dimensions of individualism–collectivism, direct verbal negotiation versus indirect verbal negotiation, and monochronic time schedule versus polychronic time schedule. Countless other cultures will probably draw upon some of the mixed values of LCC and HCC in their communication processes with one another. However, the intergroup negotiation process between two diametrically opposite cultures (with the United States culture as representing the extreme of the LCC system and the Japanese culture as representing the extreme of the HCC system) will be the primary focus of discussion in this chapter. It is also important to note that in a heterogeneous culture such as that of the United States, different ethnic cultures within the system will retain different elements of both LCC and HCC communication characteristics. In the context of this chapter, idea development is centred upon a comparison between white, middle-class culture in the United States and middle-class culture in Japan. The next section will apply the dimensions of LCC systems and HCC systems in the setting of intergroup simulations and learning.

Intergroup simulations and learning

Drawing upon the three dimensions of individualism—collectivism, direct verbal negotiation versus indirect verbal negotiation, and monochronic time schedule versus polychronic time schedule, this section of the chapter will address some of the potential problems and barriers that may exist in intergroup simulations that involve both LCC and HCC participants.

On a general level of analysis, an intergroup simulation game such as BAFA BAFA (which is designed to simulate two different cultures, Alpha and Beta, with different values and norms that guide verbal and non-verbal negotiation processes) has many advantages:

1. The game helps members to be more aware of intergroup attribution and stereotyping processes through the polarization of values between the Alpha culture and the Beta culture.
2. The game creates an experience-based learning situation in which both LCC members and HCC members can feel at ease in a low-threat environment.
3. The game provides a context of role-reversal situation in which both majority- and minority-group members can assume different group roles and adopt different norms of negotiation style.

4. The game presents an opportunity for both LCC members and HCC members to engage in constructive discussion during the debriefing period of the game, hence, members of both LCC and HCC systems can assume both insider and outsider roles of the Alpha and Beta cultures.
5. The game can increase the awareness and appreciation of value differences and communication differences of LCC and HCC members on both the cognitive level and the affective level in relation to behavioural practices.

Individualism–collectivism dimension

However, moving beyond the positive aspects of intergroup simulations and learning, trainers and teachers should also be aware of some of the potential problems that involve LCC and HCC participants in intergroup simulation/games such as BAFA BAFA. For example, members from individualistic cultures will emphasise:

1. individual winning over group winning, hence, a strong win–lose orientation in intergroup negotiation and also a strong win–lose attitude in within-group negotiation;
2. task outcome as more important than group interaction process;
3. individualistic stance rather than coalition stance in the bargaining process.

In turn, members from collectivistic cultures will stress:

1. group winning over individual winning, hence, a win–lose orientation in intergroup negotiation and a win–win orientation in within-group negotiation;
2. socio-emotional group process over task achievement;
3. coalition stance rather than individualistic stance in the bargaining process.

Hence, in an intergroup simulation game such as BAFA BAFA, extraordinary attention and effort have to be paid to mixed-value groups that play the roles of Alpha culture and Beta culture. The internal dynamics of negotiation between LCC members and HCC members within the respective cultures can be as interesting and as instructive as the intergroup negotiation processes between members of the Alpha culture and the Beta culture.

Furthermore, the learning-teaching style of both LCC and HCC systems can also pose some interesting problems. Hofstede (1986) argues succinctly that cross-cultural learning situations can be problematic in the following areas:

1. differences in the social positions of teachers and students in the two societies;
2. differences in the relevance of the curriculum (training content) for the two societies;
3. differences in profiles of cognitive abilities between populations from which teacher and student are drawn; and
4. differences in expected patterns of teacher–student and student–student interaction.

In particular, the last comment on 'expected patterns of teacher–student and student–student interaction' is a very important point in the context of using intergroup simulation exercises that involve both LCC and HCC participants. For LCC members who treasure individual value orientation, free forms of student–teacher and student–student interaction in the classroom, confrontation and testing of ideas, and a 'learning to learn' environment are posed as some of the classroom ideals (Hughes-Wiener, 1986). Conversely, for HCC members who prize collective value orientation and status hierarchy differences, restrictive forms of student–teacher and student–student interaction in the classroom, group harmony and a 'not standing out' interaction style, and a teacher-centred 'learning about' approach are posed as the educational ideals. Hence, depending on the cultural context in which intergroup simulations such as BAFA BAFA are conducted, trainers and teachers have to develop an extraordinary degree of sensitivity and awareness of both the instructional style and the anticipated learning style of teacher and student in that particular culture. While LCC members may be very comfortable with an experience-based approach to learning, HCC members may view an intergroup simulation exercise as highly threatening. While teachers in the LCC educational system may encourage the 'learning to learn' approach in the LCC classroom, HCC members may experience a strong sense of anxiety and uncertainty in an active, self-learning environment without the appropriate guidance from the trainers or the teachers.

Direct verbal negotiation and indirect verbal negotiation

Drawing upon the direct–indirect verbal negotiation style of both LCC and HCC systems, potential barriers can arise when LCC members (for example, from the American culture) attempt to:

1. spend too much time on task discussion to the neglect of socio-emotional discussion in within-group interaction;
2. be too direct concerning their intentions and motives during various negotiation sessions;
3. be too self-disclosive on private feelings and reactions during the debriefing period to the embarrassment of HCC members;
4. be too confrontative in conflict situations;
5. rely too heavily on verbal negotiation skills to the neglect of non-verbal nuances and tactics.

Conversely, potential misunderstandings and problems can arise when HCC members (for example, from the Japanese culture) try to:

1. spend too much time on structuring socio-emotional relationships and climate-building to the neglect of task accomplishments;
2. be too indirect and circumspective of their intentions and desires during bargaining sessions;
3. disclose too little of their private feelings and reactions during debriefing sessions;
4. be too ambiguous and compromising in conflict negotiation situations;
5. over-rely on and be over-sensitive to non-verbal cues and signals in the negotiation process to the neglect of using explicit, direct verbal negotiation tactics.

Intergroup simulation trainers and teachers in the LCC–HCC context have to pay special attention to both the verbal and non-verbal communication style differences of both LCC and HCC members. Teachers also have to develop a high sense of empathy for students who have difficulties in role-switching to different interaction roles that are diametrically opposite to their everyday cultural scripts and norms of behaviour.

Monochronic time schedule and polychronic time schedule

Finally, in drawing upon the temporal dimension of M-time and P-time of LCC and HCC systems, LCC members who tend to treasure monochronic time schedule (M-time) will have a greater tendency than HCC members to:

1. deal with one task at a time in the intergroup simulated game;

2. compartmentalise task activities and socio-emotional activities in the game;
3. end the negotiation process prematurely in the name of time efficiency and cost outcome;
4. make linear, cause–effect decisions;
5. equate task effectiveness with relational satisfaction.

Conversely, HCC members, who tend to value polychronic time schedule (P-time), will have a greater tendency than LCC members to:

1. deal with several tasks and problems at the same time;
2. integrate task activities and socio-emotional activities in the simulated game;
3. overprolong the negotiation process in intergroup situations;
4. make spiral, contextual decisions with non-clear-cut solutions and boundaries; and
5. view relational satisfaction above task effectiveness.

Hence, beyond familiarising themselves with the basic value orientations and the communication style differences between LCC and HCC participants, trainers and teachers in the intergroup simulation area need also to pay close attention to the temporal attitudes of members in different cultural collectives. The intergroup negotiation process, to a large extent, depends heavily on the timing, pacing, and rhythm of how two negotiators approach each other to accomplish what is hopefully a win–win solution for both parties.

Conclusion

In summary, this chapter has drawn upon the values of both low-context and high-context culture systems and applied them to our understanding of intergroup simulation exercises. Specifically, three value-communication dimensions serve as the focal points of idea development: individualism–collectivism, direct–indirect verbal negotiation style, and monochronic–polychronic time schedule. Potential problems and misunderstandings that involve both LCC and HCC members in intergroup simulation games were presented, and calls for empathy and understanding from trainers and teachers in the area of intergroup simulations in the classroom environment have been repeatedly emphasised.

In brief, it is by understanding the fundamental value differences between members of all cultures, the learning styles of students from all societies, and the negotiation styles of participants in different speech communities, that we can better understand how members from different cultures synchronise their worldviews and modify their communication patterns to adapt and adjust to one another on both the interpersonal level and the intergroup–intercultural communication level.

14 Individual and organisational communication and destructive competition

JOHN F. LOBUTS
The George Washington University, Washington, DC, U.S.A.
and
CAROL L. PENNEWILL
SMS Data Products Group Inc., VA, U.S.A.

Interpersonal communication

The word 'communication' is derived from the Latin word for 'commonness' while the prefix 'com-' suggests 'togetherness, joining, co-operation and mutuality'. Therefore, communication may be defined as a mutual exchange between two or more individuals which enhances co-operation and establishes commonality. Theory and reality, however, are often very distant.

We believe that attitudes, by influencing our perception of what is said, are by far the most important component of communication. Meanings of words, for example, are derived from individual and especially collective/social experience and do not (as is commonly believed) exist of and by themselves. Rather, they exist in the mind of both sender and receiver. 'Reality', then, is a rather ambiguous term, since it is something which is merely agreed upon by the majority of people. We all devise what Peck (1978) calls 'maps of reality' or what King *et al.* (1983) refer to as 'reality strategies'—responses and behaviours which have been developed as a result of our personal experiences. They are our unique adaptation to the world.

Often, we set up perceptual barriers which prevent us from establishing rapport with each other. This is particularly obvious when experts from various technical fields or people from different cultures attempt to communicate with one another. The authors believe that the perceptual 'bars' of destructive, competitive behaviour also influence the way we communicate with each other. Competition so dominates our culture and way of life that we are unaware of its power to distort our perception.

Perceptual distortion

Our perception of the world is, in essence, an outer projection of our inner world. The perceived world is so coloured by individual experience that distortion, exaggeration and minimisation of selected features are inevitable. We believe that fear associated with perceived threat is the primary factor in determining whether communication will be competitive or co-operative. Three manifestations of fear are frustration, anger and deceit.

Frustration

Frustration stems from feelings of helplessness, which, if sufficiently intense, can destroy an individual, physically and mentally. Sufficient intensity can also lead a group into making decisions that each, as an individual, may regret later. Harvey (1974) termed this type of group behaviour the 'Abilene Paradox', and it stems from the fear of not being accepted, not getting one's fair share, or losing something desired.

Anger

Anger, which is often associated with aggression, can be defined as an increase in psychological and physiological energy. This energy can be expressed in various ways, depending on the context of the cultural environment. The same physiological energy which may motivate one person to harm someone may also be experienced as extreme joy or the desire to jog around the block, depending on how the individual interprets the surge of adrenalin. Thus, anger can energise us and provide sources of power and strength, but we must first know how to harness it. Since our culture teaches us how to handle this energy, the potential for the escalation of destructive competition is indeed frightening. It can be argued that few media texts portray models of serenity and calmness, but instead teach their audiences to act out anger, to be aggressive. Orchestrated anger, in effect, sets the stage for destructive competition. Since the styles and contexts for anger are learned, constructive ways of expressing anger can also be learned.

To see how this works, one need only follow the success of Chrysler Corporation Chairman, Lee Iacocca. After assuming the directorship of the failing Chrysler Corporation, Iacocca (1979) reportedly said: 'I got mad, my colleagues within the corporation got mad and people throughout the Chrysler Corporation got mad ... we got together, talked about what was wrong and fixed it'. The Chrysler Corporation, under the direction of Iacocca, employed the technique of anger management. We argue that he took the neutral physiological energy of anger and used it *constructively*, making Chrysler the success story of the past decade. Remember, however, one must use this energy constructively, not destructively, as we have learned to do in most cases.

Deceit

The deliberate misleading and tricking of another party in order to secure personal profit and advantage is well established in the marketplace and in the international political arena. Deceit also involves skilled communication that requires bluff and counterbluff strategies. The best example is perhaps Hitler's deception of Chamberlain just before World War II. Many extol its virtues as just plain good business. However, there is a grave cost attached to the use of deceit and that is the loss of trust among friends, clients, co-workers and colleagues. Once you have lied and got caught, can anyone ever really trust you again? Not really.

Because of its nature, deception and the conflicts that arise from its use can never be justified. Deception merely ensures that all trust is gone. Business communities often fall victim to the employment of deception. For example, warranty agreements seem ideal in advertising, with their many promises which appear to remove all risk for the client or consumer. However, when individuals attempt to claim under these guarantees, many walk away angry and embittered. This effect merely boomerangs back to the corporation, resulting in a loss of reputation and long-term sales.

We would argue the contrary for the business environment. Deception is a totally unacceptable behaviour. The ramifications are simply too disastrous (see Lobuts & Pennewill, 1986).

Destructive competition

In an effort to resolve the competitive themes which now prevail in industrialised nations, much has been written recently about conflict resolution. It is clear that cultural attitudes that are negotiated within the family, education and media institutions encourage people to think in terms of competition rather than co-operation. This is seen and reflected everywhere in Western culture, from Little League baseball to being top of the class at school, from popular movies of the Clint Eastwood variety to best-selling books such as *Looking Out for Number One* (Ringer, 1978).

Healthy competition is much like stress. Not all stress is bad! On the contrary, some stress can be a great motivator for human achievement. It is distress which can be psychologically destructive. Competition has, in fact, been the foundation upon which industrialised societies base their way of life—a high quality of life in terms of material goods and technological progress. It is, however, destructive competitive environments we wish to address in this chapter, for destructive competition can destroy individuals, groups and nations.

What are the causes of destructive competition?

Beginning with Bandura's experiments in 1963, it has been fairly well established that much aggression is learned behaviour, pointing to certain cultural norms as the main culprit for the predominance of violence and aggressiveness in most industrialised societies. For example, Sanday (1981) carried out a cross-cultural study of rape, coding 156 societies as either rape-prone, rape-free or intermediate. If statistics on rape are to be believed, she found that 18% of these societies fell under the category of rape-prone, while 47% of the societies were designated as rape-free. Morokoff (1983) reports that this study generated two hypotheses. It was first proposed that rape occurs in societies which are prone to violence, both internally and externally, 'societies disposed to war, male toughness, interpersonal violence, and raiding of other groups for wives'. Second, it was suggested that rape occurs in societies which are male-dominated. (It is noteworthy that these descriptions clearly apply to American society as well as most Western societies.) Based on these hypotheses, 'Highly significant correlations between rape-prone status and existence of aggression and male domination were found. The rape-free societies were characterized by sexual equality' (Morokoff, 1983: 130).

This study suggests that aggression (against women) is at least partially learned behaviour (although the reliability and validity of such statistics have continually to be questioned here), reinforced by cultural norms and context. Also, since 47% of the societies studied were characterised as rape-free, it can be seen that aggression is *not* the norm because a large percentage of societies promote the norms of sexual equality and co-operation. It was found that 'where there is not an imbalance between environmental resources and population needs, where harmony with the environment exists, rape is rare. Where competition for resources prevails, the "male role is accorded greater prestige"' (Morokoff, 1983: 131). The key word here is 'competition'. As Morokoff (1983: 131) aptly explains: 'Our society would seem to fit well into Sanday's conceptualization. We are engaged in global conflict for diminishing resources. Male characteristics are valued, female devalued, and aggressive means of conflict resolution are glorified.' Social learning theory provides a lead into another major focus for communication: the influence of the media and role models on behaviour.

Media

It is obvious that the media, in the form of newspapers, radio, television, movies and advertisements, concentrates much of its attention on violence, coercion and using aggressive means to attain desired goals. Yet, the entertainment industries continue to deny that the portrayal of aggression and violence creates any ill effects. But what is the effect of viewing violence and aggression? Is it conclusive that film portrayals can teach aggression? We argue that the answer is an unqualified 'yes'. For example, 'Donnerstein and Hallam (1978) found a high level of aggression against men following a film portraying aggression against males (clips from *The Wild Bunch*)' (Morokoff, 1983) and numerous other experiments confirm these results. Morokoff (1983: 139) reports in her findings that 'Portrayals of rape and sexual violence in the mass media may be one mechanism by which aggression ... is taught'. Comstock (1983: 243) reports that 'The National Commission on the Causes and Prevention of Violence (1969) concluded that the evidence to date favored the view that television and film violence contributed to antisocial behavior'. The US National Institute of Mental Health Advisory Committee (Pearl *et al.*, 1982) found overwhelming evidence to support the theory that television violence has a negative impact on children. Additionally, two hearings which were held before the US Senate Commerce Committee in 1972 and 1974 upheld these views.

Role models also greatly influence behaviour. These include newscasters, teachers, professors, professional leaders, employers, as well as cultural 'heroes' such as actors and actresses. One of the primary ways a society negotiates values and ethics with its children is through social systems. We argue that competitive values have been inextricably woven into the fabric of Western culture. Two examples will illustrate this. First, Kohn (1986) discusses the effect of competition in the field of journalism. He argues that the frantic race for news sets reporters against one another. The end result of turning journalism into a competitive race is not better news coverage but less accurate information in the system. Second, grades teach students that those who follow the rules, i.e. conform and memorise, will be amply rewarded for their efforts and the rewards—status and prestige—are indeed inestimable. Those who do not conform often fall by the wayside and are relegated to second-class citizenship. The unstated value is that you must *compete* to get ahead and refrain from helping your 'competitors' along the way.

We argue that social systems impact the communications process. The impacts can promote a healthy competitive spirit or a destructive competitive environment. The systems, as discussed, are the media, the educational systems, and the entertainment industries.

Likewise, those who fill role model positions impact the communications of other people. Some of these role models include teachers, professors, parents, newscasters and cultural heroes.

We believe it behoves all concerned to understand what is intended to be communicated and what is actually being communicated. These are often one and the same. However, they are frequently two entirely different phenomena.

Therefore, it is an academic imperative that educators, teachers, professors, parents and trainers have some understanding of the impact and importance of communications in games and simulations.

Communication in games and simulations

Games and simulations

There are several reasons why the use of games and simulations has increased in recent years. First, they serve to close the gap between theory and practice by enabling the student or trainee to practise the methods which the instructor is teaching. This serves essentially the same purpose as an internship, by enabling the student to gain practical experience in the field. Second, technology and educational policy have made accessibility to games and simulations much easier. They can be produced faster and cheaper and computer terminals enhance their practical utilisation and reliability.

One of the greater myths about education is that learning is a direct result of teaching. An enormous amount of material is obtained without a teacher, parent or mentor. Wanting to learn is a primary ingredient, as well as readiness for the learning process. According to Hayakawa (1973):

> Learning is an extraordinarily active process. When you see the energy and enthusiasm with which young people acquire knowledge—especially about things you don't want them to learn—you cannot help being impressed by their learning ability. And little of what they learn is by the lecture method. ...
>
> The more freely students disagree among themselves, the more they have to know to back up their side of the dispute—and the more they read on their own, stimulated not by a teacher's requirements but by the demands of their peers before whom they must defend their position.

Simulation exercises can be used as a tool to activate learning in the classroom environment. If knowledge and truth are the goal of our modern-day classrooms, games and simulations take us a step beyond the lecture method to add the active ingredient. They can be used in a variety of situations and contexts, not only as teaching and training tools, but also for recreation. However, within the context of Western culture the writers believe that, either overtly or covertly, many games and simulations necessarily teach aggressive and competitive values. The most obvious examples are recreational games, such as MONOPOLY and DIPLOMACY, all of which are extremely competitive and often destructive. In fact, the harmful effect of two recreational games, DUNGEONS AND DRAGONS and ASSASSIN, has recently been reported in the American news media. It has even been claimed that college students and adolescents have been so caught up in role-playing the characters in these 'games' that some have either killed themselves or each other as a result.

But what about games which are employed as teaching and training tools? Are instructors also teaching destructive competition in public education and management training seminars? In most cases, games and simulations are designed with good intentions—i.e. to teach communication skills, practical skills and the importance of co-operation in groups.

Learning exercises, such as THE NICKEL AUCTION, PRISONER'S DILEMMA and LOST ON THE MOON, are designed to teach students the importance of trust, co-operation and the mutual exchange of knowledge for the benefit of the group. However, since communication is fundamentally concerned with how people know and comprehend their world, games and simulations may be said to replicate this life process. Interpersonal communication is concerned with the way people interact with each other and how they interpret the context of the communication. Thus, interpersonal games often deal with group dynamics, participation, leadership and power structures. Considering the exorbitant amount of social forces which reinforce competitive values, it is not surprising that many of these games teach competitive values. Let us first examine the communication process with regard to competition and then see how games and simulations can inadvertently teach destructive competition.

Win–win versus lose–lose

In our previous discussion of interpersonal communication, we stated that attitudes and perceptions greatly influence the effectiveness of communication and that three components of this process—anger, frustration and deceit—can generate destructive, competitive behaviour. The best way to examine this behaviour in communication is through the 'win–win' model developed by Filley (1974). The basic premise of this model is that there are three types of interaction between two parties: win–win; win–lose; and lose–lose. The goal for effective communication is the 'win–win' scenario, where both parties solve their conflict in such a way that both feel satisfied with the outcome. Destructive competition involves the opposite stance—that there is only one goal—to win, usually at the expense of the other party.

We believe that the perceptions of the individual determine how each will view the other, what the perceived gain or loss is and what the perceived 'rules' of the game are. Even though it is very easy to advise two conflicting parties that both stand to gain by employing a win–win stance, social influence is so strong that the perceptual 'lens' of competition is a great distorter.

Destructive competition in games and simulations

THE LEARNING GAME is a primary example of how a seemingly innocent game can inadvertently teach competition. Its purpose is to show

how learning is facilitated by patterning. Participants are given mimeographed booklets comprised of four pages, each with the numbers 1–60 scattered on the page. The first three pages are identical and the numbers are arranged so that all the odd numbers are on top and the even numbers are at the bottom. Within each half, the numbers are randomly distributed. On the fourth page, the odd numbers are on the left and the even numbers are on the right. In 45-second intervals, students must connect the numbers, beginning with 1, drawing a line to 2, etc. On a flip chart, the instructor records the last number reached by each participant. The process is repeated for the second page, after which the instructor informs his students of the pattern and scores are compared to the first two pages. The process is then repeated on the fourth page, where participants are not informed of the change of pattern. While the game seems very practical in terms of showing how patterns can facilitate learning, the game also reinforces prevalent competitive values. Viewed from this perspective, it involves learning a 'nonsensical' task in as short a period as possible. Since the scores are posted in front of the class, it can easily be seen who the 'quick' learners and 'slow' learners are and the situation has a subtle overtone of 'win–lose'.

INTERACT II is another example of a game which reinforces competitive values while seemingly teaching the importance of co-operation in groups. Participants are organised in five to 15 groups of five to ten members. The game can last either one or two semesters and it is the task of each group to prepare, produce and distribute a series of communication broadcasts or publications on predetermined topics. Periodically, these materials are distributed to the other participants who evaluate the products by assigning points and providing narrative feedback. Evaluation points are totalled and assigned to the group and these are divided among group members as they think appropriate. Members are also permitted to leave their group to work in another, start their own 'company' or work with the Executive Council, which oversees the simulation.

This simulation is excellent in terms of teaching the 'real world' of marketing and advertising, yet it appears to skirt the moral or ethical issue of what the product actually is. In other words, it demonstrates exactly the prevalent attitudes of consumerism, in the sense that it does not matter *what* you're selling, as long as you sell it. Students also learn a great deal about group dynamics, but again, competition comes into play because group members determine the distribution of points, and often the factor of dominance and aggressiveness comes into play more so than actual productivity.

To illustrate this, a discussion of the American motor-car industry's pricing game is appropriate here. In order to sell their product against strong competition from their Japanese counterparts—Honda, Nissan and Toyota—they have developed a sophisticated game of finance. In the autumn of 1986, the 'Big Three—Chrysler, Ford and General Motors—lowered their financing rates to a low of 2.9%. In order to be competitive, the American Motors Corporation offered financing rates at 0%. During the same period, the American banks were charging rates of up to 11% on motor-car loans.

This discussion would not be complete without including quality in the equation. Iacocca (1986) states that when he arrived at Chrysler the warranty programme was costing as much as $350 million a year. Could the quality of the product be a reason for the loss of market shares in the American motor-car industry to the Japanese counterparts? Pricing or quality, which game do we play? This is why Iacocca was so successful in saving his corporation. He realised that quality had to be raised if sales were to rise.

The motor-car industry has been caught in a pricing game in efforts to maintain its dominance. Prices produce short-term success. For the intermediate and long term, quality and service are the means to success. Quality and service are the way to recapture those market shares. The Japanese gained inroads to the American consumer through quality. The proof of how strong this force is can be viewed in the methods, communications and simulations developed and employed by Iacocca at Chrysler.

Conclusion

Anxiety and bewilderment prevail in a seemingly disorderly, dangerous, and ungovernable world. The United States is a nation which purports to trust and believe in God, yet it allows millions of people to die of starvation, torture, and other inhumane conditions. Poverty and malnourishment are not limited to Third World nations, however. Many citizens of the United States, for example, suffer from poverty because they are not able to partake of even a small portion of the national wealth.

With the constant threat of nuclear war, Americans are realising that their capacity to understand themselves and to deal with their problems is extremely frail and limited. Mankind can travel to other planets, communicate at the speed of light across the world, plan colonies in space, and yet cannot develop workable solutions for understanding his own neighbours. It appears that the so-called 'progress' of science and technology, with its promise of creating a utopian world, does not, after all, provide all the answers.

Compared to the millions of years it has taken for the earth to evolve, man's appearance is minuscule indeed. Yet, we are reaching a crossroad in history where humanity must make a choice—either to develop our spiritual understanding for the betterment of humankind or to ignore the lessons of history and eventually destroy all forms of life on this planet.

The solution resides in our ability to develop more effective communication relationships between nations as well as individuals, so that we can participate in the world economy with a fair and just attitude. However, the world economic market, as it is being managed today, operates in a win–lose environment, dividing nations into the haves and the have-nots. This environment is actually a lose–lose environment, because when one nation loses, everyone loses. We must develop a philosophy of win–win, so that every nation, and therefore every individual, receives a just share of the bounties of this universe. In the final analysis, we are simply gatherers of the planet's fruits and these bounties belong to everyone.

SECTION FOUR:
Organisations and institutions

15 Simulations for learning about communication

STEWART MARSHALL
University of Technology, Lae, Papua New Guinea

The study of communication

A new discipline?

In the 1970s there was an exponential growth in Communication Studies courses in Britain. Although interest in the study of communication had been growing steadily for more than a decade, it appears to have reached a 'critical mass' in the mid-1970s. Sheffield City Polytechnic offered the first degree in Communication Studies in 1974. This was soon followed by similar degrees in other polytechnics and universities. Communication Studies, many people maintained, had at least evolved into a respectable 'academic discipline'—but had it?

Interest in the study of communication was not restricted to the higher education sector. The mid-1970s also saw the introduction of secondary school courses in Communication Studies. At the same time, the Business and Technician Education Councils were insisting on the inclusion of Communication Studies in their certificate and diploma courses in further education. The term 'Communication Studies' was soon to be seen in the prospectus of virtually every tertiary and higher education institution in Britain.

This phenomenon was not unique to Britain—the same was happening elsewhere in the world. But does this proliferation of courses mean that we do, in fact, have a new 'academic discipline'? What is meant by 'Communication Studies' seems to vary enormously from one institution to another. And, very often, much variation can be found between courses within a single institution. For example, some courses concentrate on the academic study of verbal communication; some concentrate on the analysis of mass media; while others seek to inculcate specific communication skills.

So a cursory examination of Communication Studies courses does not seem to reveal the existence of a new academic discipline. Historically, the differences which exist between courses seem to have arisen as a result of the circumstances which spawned them. In some cases, Communication Studies courses were the result of academic staff from various backgrounds joining together to investigate and teach this common problem area. Other courses arose in response to employer needs and were thus unashamedly functional. And, according to some cynics, some courses were developed in order to utilise otherwise redundant staff in a period of rationalisation in tertiary education. Given this variety in motivations and origins, there is little wonder that so much variety exists in the courses on offer.

It is possible to draw a distinction between those courses which are primarily concerned with the academic/theoretical study of communication and those which are concerned with developing students' practical communication skills. As a means of categorising courses, it may well be that we should really regard this theory–practice distinction as a continuum rather than a dichotomy, in which case the distinction can be seen as defining the extremes.

Let us now consider each of these types of course in greater detail.

Academic courses in communication

What does (and what should) the academic study of communication concentrate on? Many degree programmes follow the lead provided in Williams (1962) and put the emphasis on mass media. Programmes of this sort are labelled variously as 'Communication', 'Media' or 'Cultural' Studies. But even with the subject-matter limited in this way, there are at least three different perspectives one can adopt, depending on whether one takes a 'holistic' view of the media or concentrates on the 'content' or on the 'audience'.

Theorists who adopt a holistic view and emphasise the relationship between society and the media might draw on the disciplines of politics, economics, sociology, history or philosophy to explain this relationship. Thus, within this group one finds different schools of analysis, e.g. 'political-economic media theory' and 'Cultural Studies'. The Cultural Studies school of analysis, to a great extent identified with the Centre for

Contemporary Cultural Studies in Birmingham, draws on the traditions of historical and literary analysis. It is worth special mention as it has been particularly influential in determining the content and approach of Communication Studies in Britain. Even in programmes of study which do not concentrate on mass media, it would be unusual to find Cultural Studies unrepresented.

Cultural Studies also offers an approach to the second perspective on the media, namely the study of the content. For the analysts in this school, the meaning of any media text is interpreted in terms of its social and cultural context. Another important influence in the study of content is the Glasgow Media Group. This group, with its background in empirical sociology, sought to analyse British television news using rigorous quantitative methods combined with interpretations of 'cultural meanings' (Glasgow Media Group, 1977; 1980).

The third perspective, focusing on the audience, is very much dominated by the empirical sciences. Both psychology and sociology play important roles in describing and explaining audience choice, preference and behaviour. Theories and explanations offered from this perspective are very often antithetical to those of the first.

One can see from this brief examination that it is by no means easy to determine what should be included in a Communication Studies course even when it concentrates on the mass media. We find that the three (to some extent, incompatible) perspectives give rise to several different approaches depending on the disciplines used for analysis.

It is, of course, by no means self-evident that a Communication Studies course should concentrate on the study of mass media anyway. Even Williams's views of what should be included in Communication Studies changed (see Williams, 1974). Some Communication Studies courses concentrate on interpersonal and verbal communication. And within these areas one finds many approaches based on different disciplines. Little wonder then, that some confusion exists as to what the academic study of communication entails.

Even within a single degree course there are often competing paradigms for the study of communication. At Sheffield City Polytechnic, for example, one can discern four approaches based on linguistics, psychology, empirical sociology, and Cultural Studies. Given the different underlying methodologies and fundamental concepts, it is difficult to believe that it is possible to combine these approaches to create a new discipline concerned with the study of communication.

Does this mean that Communication Studies is, in fact, a 'ragbag' of many disciplines? And if so, does this multi-disciplinarity create any problems? Blumler (1977) suggests that students may be faced with learning so many varieties of conceptual thinking that they are never actually able to use them critically.

There is now a recognition of the value of an interdisciplinary approach to common concerns and problems. But this takes time and demands patience for both students and teachers. Scott (1980: 29) argued that 'it is still necessary to offer an adequate amount of core work in the disciplines before synthesizing rather than tackle the problems and let the necessary theory emerge "on the run"'. But at some point, synthesis is surely necessary. How are we to achieve this?

Certain areas of study can be identified as ones in which such a synthesis could take place, e.g. 'communication between groups'. Such an area can then be used as a common theme in the discipline strands of the course. Unfortunately, this approach can easily become a multi-disciplinary approach rather than an interdisciplinary one, the two major protagonists in this example being psychology and sociology. It is all too easy for such thematic areas to become battle grounds with each discipline fighting to control the territory. Indeed, this phenomenon is itself one that students should study as a means of learning about communication between groups.

So, the question remains: 'what teaching strategies are we to use to facilitate the interdisciplinary study of communication?' Let us now consider those courses at the practical end of the spectrum.

Communication skills training in professional education

For many years, there has been concern about the effectiveness of tertiary education in training students for their future professions. This concern is not particularly with deficiencies in subject knowledge. Instead, the concern is with personal motivation, professional commitment, flexibility and creativity in problem-solving, interpersonal and communication skills (CBI, 1976). For example, the Finniston (1980) Report identified most of these qualities and skills as being those required by British employers but found lacking in engineering graduates.

Of course, the problem is not unique to Britain—the same concerns are expressed, for example, In Australia (Webb, 1986), Belgium (Van den Berghe, 1983), the Solomon Islands (Ayyar, 1986), the United States (Albright & Albright, 1981) and elsewhere (Wearne, 1984).

Clearly, degree and diploma courses should include the development of these non-cognitive attitudes and skills among their objectives. In Britain, at diploma and certificate level, the Technician Education Council affirmed this, insisting on the inclusion of such objectives in science and engineering courses. Similarly, the Business Education Council identified communication (broadly conceived) as one of the four central themes required in business education. Consequently, we find that science, engineering and business courses often include the teaching of communication and related skills as part of the curriculum.

What is taught varies considerably (Hills *et al.*, 1979), but one can identify four general areas that are seen as important: receiver skills, including study skills, information retrieval, note-taking; presentation skills, including oral, written and visual presentation skills; skills in communicating person to person, including interviewing and being interviewed; and skills in working in groups, including participating in and leading groups, running meetings.

Unfortunately, many communication skills courses do not seem to have met with much success. Part of the problem experienced by teachers of Communication Studies may well be the teaching method—the attempt to teach communication starting from a theoretical perspective. Lectures may enable engineering students to answer exam questions about the process of communication, but are unlikely to improve their communicative ability. Similarly, a lecture on the psychology of needs may be of theoretical interest to a few business students, but will do little to improve their personal motivation. For many students such lectures do little to improve skills and are seen either as unwelcome additions to already full timetables or as entertainment.

Clearly, practice is required to improve skills. But practical communication skills work can also be unwelcome among students. It must be made relevant, otherwise students lack the interest and motivation required to achieve the desired objectives. The practical work must also be realistic, otherwise students will fail to recognise its importance.

Commenting on 'communication skills in engineering', Gray (1981) suggests that there is no need for a discrete course in communication at all. He suggests that the required communication skills can be taught 'between the lines' in the professional courses. There is merit in this suggestion, providing we can identify appropriate situations to be used for the development of the desired communication skills. This integration of the cognitive and non-cognitive aspects of engineering education would then ensure that students correctly perceive the importance of both aspects in the development of professional competence.

However, 'skill development is more effective if it follows or accompanies acquisition of knowledge and awareness about process' (Irwin, 1981: 4). Theoretical knowledge and principles are also required to enable the 'transfer' of the learning that has taken place, i.e. for the student to be able to apply the acquired skills in new situations. But to avoid the problems mentioned earlier, the communication theory required for these purposes needs to be introduced in the context of relevant and interesting practical work. The cognitive and non-cognitive aspects of communication studies need to be integrated in a meaningful way.

Thus, in order to develop the desired attitudes and skills, special teaching methods and strategies are required. This remains true whether or not we adopt Gray's suggestion. So what teaching methods can be used?

Towards a solution

Our brief survey of communication studies has revealed two questions about teaching: what teaching strategies can we use to facilitate the synthesis of the different academic disciplines which contribute to the understanding of the communication process? What teaching methods can we use to develop the desired communication skills and to teach the necessary theory? What we require are methods and strategies which can integrate different theoretical approaches to problems; combine theory and practice; interest and motivate students; and which are relevant and realistic. In all these respects, 'simulations' have an important role to play.

Simulations for learning about communication

The benefits in using simulations

There are many benefits to be gained by using simulations to investigate communication and improve communication skills. Simulations are dynamic representations of real situations (Gibbs, 1974; Bloomer, 1973; Percival & Ellington, 1980). Thus, by judicious choice of problem situations, simulations can readily be seen by students to be realistic and relevant. Of course, the communication processes which occur within simulations are real (Jones, 1980), and these are very often the objects of our study.

Problems do not present themselves in neat discipline packages. Thus, simulations (being based on such problems) are obvious candidates for integrating disciplines. It is perhaps this feature which enables simulations to cultivate in students realistic (as contrasted with idealistic) attitudes to problems (Garvey, 1971).

Finally, in so far as simulations are student-centred and active learning exercises, students perceive them as enjoyable and are motivated by them (Marshall, 1982; Marshall & Williams, 1986). Let us consider a few examples of using simulations to teach aspects of communication.

Examples of simulations for communication

It is important in any study of communication to investigate the complex relations between communication and culture. One cross-cultural simulation which can be used as a prelude to theoretical considerations or as a demonstration of them is CULTURE CONTACT. This shows students the 'need for flexibility in perception' and leads to a clearer understanding of the 'concept of cultural relativism' (Rockler, 1977).

Equally important is the study of 'mediated communication'. As we have seen, there are many approaches to the study of mass communication, but all can be related at some level to appropriate media simulations. Onc method which can be used is to set the students the task of creating a text for the media, as in FRONT PAGE and RADIO COVINGHAM.

Video-recordings can be used to good effect in creating the context and for stimulating communication in a simulation. A particularly interesting example of this type of use is CALL YOURSELF A MANAGER. Participants are shown short video-recorded scenes (often only a few seconds long), each depicting a different type of management problem.

> In most episodes what is being said is directed at the viewer who, imagining himself or herself as the person being addressed, has to respond to the issues presented. Thus the viewer is placed in a situation much like the one he or she faces at work: face-to-face with the boss or a subordinate, at a selection interview, dealing with a trade union official, and so on (Schofield, 1982: 23).

Also in the area of relational or interpersonal communication, Irwin (1981) uses the WESTERNPORT COMMUNICATION SIMULATION to 'generate interaction and argumentation'. In this simulation, students have to produce a plan for the future development of the Westernport Bay region. The argumentation, analysis and presentation involved in the simulation reinforce, summarise and integrate the material covered in a course on reasoning and argumentation and an earlier course on interpersonal communication.

By using science-based simulations to provide the content of a communication skills course for engineering or science students, it is possible to overcome the problems of relevance and motivation noted earlier. Many of the simulations given in Ellington *et al.* (1981) are suitable for adaptation and use in this way. The rationale is illustrated by Marshall *et al.* (1982) in two examples. In one example, PROTEINS AS HUMAN FOOD, the simulation provides the basis for an exercise on communication and decision-making in groups. In the other, THE ALTERNATIVE ENERGY PROGRAMME, a simulation about alternative energy is used as the focal point of a whole course in communication skills. The latter, which is outlined below, has been used successfully at Sheffield City Polytechnic since 1979 with, on average, 200 engineering and science students per year.

Outline of THE ALTERNATIVE ENERGY PROGRAMME

In this simulation, students work in groups to decide how to meet the energy requirements of the hypothetical island of Elaskay. Whilst they are involved in the task, the students also complete various exercises designed to provide them with the communication and technical skills they need to complete it satisfactorily. It is through these supplementary exercises (see also Marshall & Williams, 1986) that most of the theories and principles of communication are taught.

The communication aims of the course are to encourage organised literature searching, to introduce (and guide students through) some of the difficulties faced by groups in solving problems and making decisions, and to encourage the effective presentation of those decisions to other people through report writing and public speaking.

The course is suitable for upper secondary and first-year degree and diploma students taking engineering or science. It is designed to run for ten sessions (2 hours each) as outlined below:

1. *Introduction to the Communication Studies course.* In this first session, the lecturer explains the Communication Studies course to the class. The students then work in pairs and in small groups to complete an introductory exercise. In this exercise, the students in

each group list and evaluate alternative sources of energy, and also reflect on their group's performance in tackling the task. The session ends with an outline of the rest of the course.

2. *Introduction to the Library*. The students are given a briefing sheet asking them to produce an annotated list of materials on one source of alternative energy. They are then given an introductory tour of the library before completing the exercise.
3. *Preparation for a group talk*. After a brief lecture on using 'brain patterns' (Buzan, 1974), the class is divided into groups and asked to devise a brain pattern on 'oral presentation'. In the second half of the session, the groups are told to prepare a 10-minute talk on alternative energy.
4. *Giving the group talk on alternative energy*. In this session, the groups give and evaluate their talks.
5. *Writing a report on alternative energy*. The students are given a lecture on problem-solving with specific reference to report writing. The groups are then asked to write a report (using the same brief as for the group talk) following the set guidelines.
6. *Principles and practices in decision-making*. After a brief lecture on the importance of creativity and effective utilisation of resources in group work, the students are asked to complete an exercise on decision-making. In the second part of the session, the published case study POWER FOR ELASKAY is introduced, and time given for the students to read some of the preparatory material.
7. *Alternative sources of energy on Elaskay*. At this point in the course, the technical material from POWER FOR ELASKAY is used to provide information about using alternative energy on the island of Elaskay. The class is divided into five groups, and each group is provided with data relating to one of the following sources of energy: solar, wind, tidal, hydroelectric, and peat. Using these data to complete the worksheets provided in the published package, each group is able to calculate the technical and economic feasibility of using its respective source. Each group is then asked to produce a list of about five advantages and disadvantages in using its respective source of energy.
8. *Devising the rolling programme for Elaskay*. The class is divided into teams of 'consultants' such that each team contains at least one 'expert' on each of the five sources of energy. Each team is then asked to devise a rolling programme to meet the island's electricity requirements over the next 50 years. In designing this programme, the teams utilise the information gathered from the

previous sessions and from the material contained in the published package.

9. *Preparation of the oral presentation*. Each team prepares a short (10-minute) presentation of its rolling programme for the islanders of Elaskay. The lecturer guides the teams through the stages of preparation.
10. *Presentation and discussion of the rolling programme*. Each team presents and defends its rolling programme to the 'islanders' (the remaining students). After all the teams have presented their programmes, each one is evaluated using a prepared evaluation checklist.

Getting the most out of simulations

Whether one uses a simulation to illustrate a particular communication phenomenon or to train a skill, the object of the exercise is for the students to 'learn by experiencing'. But 'discovery favours a prepared mind' and so, to be effective, simulations need careful introduction.

It is also useful for students to reflect on the nature of the communication processes in which they are involved during or immediately after the running of a simulation. A device that can be used for this purpose is the 'Communication Studies (or Simulation) Log Report' (see Marshall, 1981b).

What the student actually experiences and learns in a simulation may not always be apparent to the facilitator and may be considerably different to what was intended. It is essential, therefore, to allow adequate time for a 'debriefing session' in which experiences are discussed, learning points clarified, and generalisations made.

Simulations are appropriate both for the kinds of communication material to be taught and the students being given that material. With care and attention by an effective facilitator, they can provide excellent vehicles for synthesis and integration of theories and practices in communication teaching.

16 Business games: From business schools to business firms

JAMES M. FREEMAN
University of Manchester Institute of Science and Technology, U.K.
and
PHILIPPE DUMAS
University of Toulon, France

Business games = Simulation + Communication

In the twin fields of business education and business training, the term 'simulation' has become largely synonymous with 'business gaming', a specific form of simulation modelled increasingly on real-life business situations. This chapter is devoted to an appraisal of business gaming and its particular contribution to the communication process in the classroom and the training department. We draw on our considerable experience with running business games in college and industry to highlight the emerging rules and conditions for successful implementation of this innovative pedagogic technique. Compared to non-gaming simulations, business games possess an additional (and special) dimension which, as we show, alters the traditional structure of associated communication.

The development of business games

Business games are a special kind of educational simulation (Cunningham, 1984) which emerged in the late 1950s. A business game typically attempts to duplicate selected components of a real-life business situation so that students or trainees involved in 'playing the game' (often in competition with one another) learn more about the situation that has been modelled. Some early examples of business games are not dissimilar to MONOPOLY in style and presentation but unlike MONOPOLY, where ludic activity amongst players is the main goal, business games are essentially concerned with communicating information, changing attitudes and facilitating skills practice.

The first business games were developed in university business schools, with the results of players' decisions, e.g. consequences on market shares, inventories, accounting statements, etc., processed by hand. A consequence of this manual processing was that games were difficult to implement and, of necessity, based on simplistic models. This in turn created heavy demands on teaching staff and meant that output was often not worth the effort that produced it. The introduction of computers began slowly to change all this though it must be admitted that early computerised games were as simplistic and idealistic as the manual prototypes they first translated.

Dissemination of business games has largely followed the revolutionary developments in microcomputing. It has followed three directions: refinements to models; commonplace utilisation; and specialisation of products. For instance, faster data processing and increased user friendliness have made possible the development of sophisticated business models, including hundreds of operations and producing admissible representations of the real world. Lower hardware costs have made microcomputers affordable by almost every school and small business: this has permitted the development of a large software market and prices of standard software have now begun to fall dramatically. Simultaneously, some experienced users have become more specialised in their demands which are now being met by much more precisely targeted software products.

Computerised simulations are amongst the most advanced educational aids currently available. They are particularly appropriate for dealing with problems requiring rational quantitative decision-making; in comparison, rival video simulations are more responsive to situations where there is a need for emotional, interpersonal and intuitive decision-making.

Communication

The view of simulation as a vehicle or catalyst for free interdisciplinary communication is now widely accepted. Business games, because of their competitive nature, build on this link, by formally allowing for interactions between participants. The effect of this is that a channel of communication not normally available in the learning environment can be fully opened, offering considerable benefits to teachers and taught alike.

Simulation gaming alters the normal classroom paradigm of sender-centred communication, in which knowledge is dispensed 'in a linear fashion' from the teacher (sender) to passive receivers (students). With the kind of experiential learning that takes place using business games, communication is changed to being primarily receiver-centred (Lederman, 1984). The effect of this is that the role of teachers is altered from being that of an expert to that of facilitator. Students, on the other hand, are able directly to influence the manner in which the learning process is conducted with the result that, in one sense at least, their education becomes much more democratic.

Business games in business schools

Objectives of business gaming

Business games are used for the achievement of three objectives:

— the acquisition and comprehension of new knowledge
— the application of new knowledge
— attitudinal change (Orbach, 1977).

These objectives are common to both business schools and firms. However, while the first objective is predominant in the academic environment, the second holds sway in business firms.

The acquisition and comprehension of new knowledge

In education, the broad aim of business games is to communicate management principles and business skills (not necessarily ethics) in areas such as marketing, production, stock control and labour relations. In this mode, students acquire knowledge and discover concepts and principles by exploiting the game as an active learning aid (active learning here referring to the learning that takes place when the content or data to be learned are acted out by the student before it is assimilated (Adams, 1973)).

Research findings in recent years seem to suggest that most simulation games are no more effective for imparting detailed factual information than alternative media such as case studies or lectures. Where they do seem to have an advantage, however, is in helping the assimilation of abstract concepts and the understanding of complex interrelationships. At a different level, evidence is beginning to accumulate that knowledge obtained through simulation games is retained longer than from other sources (Pierfy, 1977).

The application of new knowledge

For business games to meet this objective, it is necessary that the concepts on which the new knowledge is based are first thoroughly assimilated. The role of games, in this context, is effectively one of clarification and consolidation. This type of simulation gaming is more prevalent in training circles and is discussed at length on pp. 207–12.

Attitudinal change

Games have been found to be an especially effective means of creating empathy amongst learners for the situations being modelled. Attitude change appears to be much more likely with simulations and games than with other traditional methods.

The three components of attitude are knowledge, affect and predisposition—knowledge about some object, feelings towards it, and a willingness or unwillingness to act on the basis of the previous knowledge and feelings (Orbach, 1977). For learners to experience an attitudinal change, it is believed they must be provided with new knowledge in an atmosphere that is conducive to the expression and discharge of feelings. Such an atmosphere is thought to be generated under highly participative conditions. Business games that involve some degree of role-play are thought to have an even greater potential for changing attitudes.

Practical implications of simulation gaming

Simulation games require a significant investment in time and energy by teachers. In their role as administrator or animator, they need to play the activity once or twice at least before running it in class; they need to develop an instinct for the model and an understanding of its internal structuring. This can represent many hours of single-minded effort.

Conducting the activity can be exhausting, since the animator has to adopt the role of consultant to teams, in addition to that of educator. The animator has to process data, analyse it and prepare for successive decision rounds. The total work and personal involvement required by a simulation game is far greater than the equivalent preparation of a traditional class lecture and is unlikely to decrease in the foreseeable future.

Simulation gaming is sometimes discouraged by the school bureaucracy, who view it as complicating administrative tasks, disrupting timetables and making heavy demands on such resources as computers and class space. Such prejudice, where it exists, is beginning to lessen as authorities come to realise the increased value of gaming pedagogy, which has grown rapidly in power and sophistication.

Scheduling of business games

In business schools, game events have been integrated into courses in one of two ways: total immersion in the game; and class format.

Total immersion in the game (uninterrupted or continuous game time)

In this mode, the normal timetabling of classes is suspended and uninterrupted game play takes place over a period lasting for as little as one day or maybe as long as a week. This approach has the advantage, by breaking class routine, of fostering new relationships among students as well as between students and staff. In France, the first week of a course is often conducted in this way, providing students with a short period of sensitisation (see pp. 206–7 on Induction Training.) In Quebec, the last week of the course is more likely to be devoted to gaming. This arrangement can be regarded as a period of training *in vitro* (see pp. 207–12 on Skills Training) and is usually followed by a student project (Dumas, 1984).

Class format (interrupted or discrete game time)

This mode seems to be in more common use and has the advantage of not upsetting delicate class schedulings, since it normally takes place during tutorial sessions and may last for as long as a semester at the rate of 2 hours per week. Though some of the benefits (i.e. deep involvement of players in the simulation, renewal of interpersonal relationships, etc.) of gaming are lost in this mode, there are compensations in the form of a deeper study of related concepts, for instance in marketing, personnel management and finance.

Business games in firms

Business games are used at all levels of staff training (Tansey & Unwin, 1969). In particular, they have been found to be suitable for induction (pre-service), skills (transition) and refresher (in-service) training (Tansey, 1971). With both induction and refresher training the emphasis is on the provision of new knowledge and the achievement of attitudinal change.

Skills training, by contrast, has much more to do with applying existing knowledge.

Induction training

Induction training is concerned with introducing recently recruited staff to their work-place and their new job. Traditionally, it is supported by the use of employee handbooks and relies heavily on lecture and/or discussion sessions (Warren, 1975). A key objective of induction is to provide new employees with a formal opportunity for meeting existing staff in the organisation, including their manager (or supervisor) and peers and subordinates. More generally, the induction programme enables staff to acquaint themselves with the detail of their conditions of employment and, most importantly, to become familiar with the physical surroundings at work.

During the induction period, staff need to be told, as far as possible, what is expected from them in their work. Following on from this, it is desirable they have an appreciation of the standards against which their future job performance is judged. New staff also need to be aware of any plans for later training to help them understand their intended role in the organisation.

Induction is a vital part of the 'orientation' of new recruits—that is, the process by which recruits acquire a commitment to the organisation. Successful orientation requires a degree of attitudinal change on the part of recruits that is unlikely to be fully realised in a short induction programme. Nevertheless, the importance of induction training in promoting the orientation of new staff—at least in the early part of their employment—is now well recognised.

Business games are usually played towards the beginning of the induction programme. The advantage with this scheduling is that it accelerates the process of new staff getting to know each other. At the same time, the motivating qualities characteristic of simulation games can be fully exploited. An initial high motivation among trainees often continues for the rest of the induction programme and has favourable implications for the orientation of trainees in general.

Business games provide staff new to a business with a 'laboratory' experience, analogous to that undergone by scientific and technical staff in their initial on-the-job training. In this respect, such activities can yield the administrator many useful insights into participants' strengths and weaknesses, for example, and into players' analytical and decision-making skills. In the case of team-based games, an assessment can also be made of participants' co-operativeness, social skills and leadership potential.

Evidence is beginning to accumulate that game performance, in carefully controlled situations, can be predictive of future job performance. Indeed, business games are already finding modest application in staff-selection procedures. It is likely this trend will become more pronounced and that games will be used increasingly in the assessment of new staff and prospective recruits.

Skills training

Skills training is concerned with training people for the skills needed in productive work (Stokes, 1966). It has both knowledge and practice components. The manner in which these are integrated varies considerably according to type of skill. The traditional structure by which management skills are acquired is one in which knowledge (education) precedes practice (on-the-job experience), but with non-management skills—engineering skills, for instance—arrangements may be quite different: practical sessions in the workshop often take place concurrently with classroom instruction and indeed, for some applications, may well precede it.

Where trainees already possess an appropriate management education, the overriding objective of management training is to bridge the gap between the existing knowledge base and appropriate purposeful behaviour. The fact that much management training is conducted off the job militates against this and helps to create an impression of training as cognitive learning, divorced from real skills practice.

Management skills and business games

With skills training, business games are used to help bridge the gap between textbook learning and the operational circumstances that hold in real life. They afford a means of practising tools and techniques learned elsewhere (Shubik, 1975), and furthermore increase the probability of transferring experience between classroom and job. Gaming gives the benefit of 'direct experience' in the presence of skilled instructors.

Numerous studies have been undertaken to help understand and classify the skills required by management. Research by Mintzberg (1973) has led to the identification of eight definitive skills: peer skills; leadership skills; conflict-resolution skills; information-processing skills; skills in decision-making under ambiguity; resource-allocation skills; entrepreneurial skills; and skills of introspection. These are briefly described below, as is the specific contribution of management games to related training.

Communication forms a backdrop to all the skills listed, significantly so in the case of peer, leadership and conflict-resolution skills, less directly with the rest. Criticisms levelled at management often have their basis in poor communication. The need for good communication in management training is therefore paramount and should never be neglected.

Peer skills deal with the manager's ability to enter into and effectively maintain peer relationships. A number of skills can be included here. The manager must know how to develop implicit contacts with other parties to serve mutual needs. The manager must know how to build up and maintain an extensive network of contacts to bring him/her favours and information, and how to communicate with equals on a formal and informal basis.

Team-based simulation games are a well-established vehicle for developing social skills. Resulting from their interaction with other team members, players come to appreciate the reality of their interdependence and the need for mutual support. Individual abilities developed through the medium of play include those of bargaining, persuading, competing, co-operating, listening to others, issuing and accepting commands (Tansey, 1971).

Leadership skills focus on the manager's ability to deal with staff for which he/she is responsible—to motivate and train them, provide help, deal with problems of authority and dependence, and so on.

Here, too, team-based simulation games are supportive, creating an environment in which leadership skills can be nurtured, tried and observed. At an administrative level, such activities provide trainees with useful experience in the setting of business objectives as well as in related organisation and planning. Simulation games, and especially business games, lend themselves easily to the delegation of responsibility, so generating conditions for leaders to experiment at winning over the co-operation of their members and, on the basis of team performance, carrying out any necessary counselling and appraisal.

Many simulation games conspicuously make no demand of teams to be formally structured but even with these, natural leaders sometimes emerge, offering rich insights into subordinate–leader relationships and leadership styles (Vroom & Yetton, 1973). Where teams need to be organised hierarchically, leaders are usually elected by other team members but may sometimes be nominated by the game administrator. The latter arrangement has the advantage that chosen individuals can be given the opportunity to practise (be tested for) taught (inherent) leadership skills (Ferguson, 1971).

Conflict-resolution skills include the interpersonal skill of mediating between conflicting individuals and the decisional skill of handling disturbances.

Management games, like the early war games on which they are based (Loveluck, 1983) are rooted in disturbance and conflict—albeit in a commercial or social context. Competitive games accentuate this element of conflict. Significantly, non-competitive (conjectural) simulations, too, often model disturbances that occur in real life (e.g. SLICK by BP) as well as complex problems (in industrial relations, for instance) where there rarely appears any possible solution.

Business games and other simulations not directly linked with business contexts enable trainees to experience, in a controlled, harmless environment, problems that feature directly or indirectly in the underlying models. They provide a valuable medium for participant discussion—a framework within which opposing views can be reconciled and consensus agreement built.

Information-processing skills mean that managers should know how to build information networks, find sources of information and extract what they need, validate information, assimilate it, and build effective mental models. They should also learn how to disseminate information, express their ideas effectively, and speak formally as representatives of organisations.

Business information (interpreted, in this context, as knowledge of potential use to a decision-maker) comes in many different forms: for example, it may be obtained orally or through written reports; it can be categorised as quantitative or non-quantitative. In one form or another, simulation games make use of most types of information, but are especially well suited to dealing in quantitative information. (Given that many information systems are now highly automated, computer-based games are especially attractive in this respect.) In the past is was felt—with some justification—that games laid too much stress on the importance of quantitative data (Greenlaw *et al.*, 1962) but the situation is now less serious thanks to developments such as that of the 'in-basket exercise' and the realisation that feedback, obtained at the end of most modern activities, is often of a qualitative nature. Indeed the debriefing session offers considerable scope for the exchange of non-quantitative information—whether as informal oral communication by team members, formal presentation by team representatives or written responses (based on questionnaires or otherwise).

Whatever the format of the information being dealt with, players generally recognise very quickly from play which items are of interest and relevance. They learn to cross-check results and look out for possible relationships. Games stimulate the development of analytical skills (experience gained in piloting many new games points to a significant aptitude by participants for identifying inconsistencies and minor shortfalls with prototype packages.) Often by virtue of the mistakes that they make, trainees become adept at handling ambiguous and unreliable information.

Skills in decision-making under ambiguity are important because the unstructured situation is highly characteristic of management decision-making. The manager must decide when a decision must be made; diagnose the situation and plan an approach to it; search for solutions and evaluate the consequences; and select an alternative. Furthermore, the manager does not handle decisions one at a time; he/she juggles a host of them, dealing with each of them intermittently, all the while attempting to develop some integration among them.

A common weakness of managers confronted with the need to make a decision is to grab at the first possible solution that presents itself (Baehler, 1980). More generally, there are problems in dealing with uncertainty either because outcomes are probabilistic (risky) or indeterminate as a result of a lack of knowledge. The particular value of business games in this area is in terms of encouraging trainees to approach decision-making scientifically. Through their involvement in game exercises, participants learn to distinguish between those situations which dictate the need for a decision and those where the case for a decision is not sustainable. The quantitative character of many games also encourages the consequences of alternative decisions to be evaluated numerically. This, in turn, allows the application of objective criteria for choosing between the options available.

More broadly, games offer an ideal means for building and practising strategies. At the same time, their use in the formulation and testing of hypotheses is not to be underestimated.

Resource-allocation skills are used when managers are required to choose among competing resource demands. They must decide how to allocate their own time, determine what work their subordinates must do and in what formal structure they must work, and pass judgements, sometimes very quickly, on projects that require organisational resources. Where a business game closely approximates real-life circumstances, the manner in which resources are handled provides another pointer to the trainees' relative sophistication for resource allocation.

Entrepreneurial skills involve the search for problems and opportunities, and the controlled implementation of change in organisations.

Some management practitioners view problem-finding as more important than problem-solving (Baehler, 1980). Skills in finding problems cannot be developed merely by analysing problems discovered by someone else. Entrepreneurial skills must be acquired first-hand. Entrepreneurial skills require an understanding of the business, an awareness of matters that affect the business and an ability to extrapolate from limited data.

More and more, business games are used as a catalyst for new ideas, as a means of releasing the imagination and inventiveness of participants. Historically, they have been criticised for actually stifling entrepreneurial skills: this may have been so with some of the simple highly structured games that appeared early on. In comparison, many modern business games may be so complex that their designers cannot always anticipate the effects of every permutation of strategies that might be played. And of course, the relatively unstructured games that are still fashionable on many courses are, by their very nature, unrestrictive.

Skills of introspection are related to the manager's understanding of his/her job. A manager should be sensitive to his/her impact on the organisation: he/she should be able to learn by introspection.

The practical purpose of the debriefing session is to give trainees the chance to conduct a self-examination, based on their game performance. Self-appraisal, which usually goes hand in hand with assessment by the instructor(s), can be thought, at one extreme, as being 'game-centred' and, at the other, 'student-centred'. (In the latter case, attention is focused on the attributes of the players, displayed during play, rather than the outward manifestations of the model; with game-centred appraisal—which impacts more on the information-processing skills considered earlier—the emphasis is reversed.)

Applied successfully, student-centred appraisal lays the ground for the kinds of insight necessary for personal growth. The awareness gained by game participants from a period of self-examination leads on naturally to their development of self-expectations. And in striving to realise these expectations, trainees become more purposeful and self-directed.

Where the achievement in self-direction is able to transcend the immediate business game situation, simulation gaming might well be judged to have delivered its ultimate benefit.

Refresher training

Many organisations run regular refresher courses to help employees adapt to changes resulting from new legislation, technological advancement, improvements in housekeeping, etc. Indeed, refresher training is common and indispensable in all forward-looking concerns.

Formerly, a problem with using business games in refresher training was the considerable time taken for games to be developed. Given the enormous number of games now available, this is no longer a difficulty. Existing packages can be quickly customised to meet the latest needs (this is particularly true of computerised games). As a result, games are now able to compete with alternative methods for refresher training far more effectively.

Sometimes, refresher training is used as a substitute for remedial training. Remedial training is needed when skills have become rusty, or were poorly acquired in the first place. Giving remedial training to older employees is not always easy: they may show resentment at being told how to do their job and suspect the training is a way of showing them up. Incorporating remedial training in 'refresher' training avoids spotlighting poor performers and deters other workers from picking up bad habits (Sayles & Strauss, 1981).

One of the most relevant functions of business games used in refresher (and remedial) training is in terms of making employees more aware of the work of colleagues in other departments. With the increased specialism demanded by modern employment practices, the possibility of alienation among employees—of their losing touch with activities that affect them elsewhere—has become very real. Of all the methods that exist for dealing with this, simulation gaming is probably pre-eminent.

The way in which those with different expertise are brought together is often critical. Business games represent a disarming and entertaining means of channelling the views of those from related disciplines towards a common goal. Play is frequently of a democratic nature and simulation games, in general, are rightly admired for their levelling qualities. The success of remedial training can crucially depend on the discretion with which that training is carried out: business games are increasingly well placed to meet this requirement.

Conclusion

Business games were born in business schools in response to a need for new communication channels within the classroom. As simulation gaming has become more widespread so teachers have acquired a greater proficiency in the use of this sophisticated resource, enabling them to operate sessions with increasing effectiveness.

In business firms, business games have been adapted for a wider range of applications. They are now used to support induction and skills training as well as refresher training. Their success in helping to develop managerial skills—with particular relation to peer, leadership, conflict-resolution, information-processing, decision-making, resource-allocation, entrepreneurial and introspective skills—is no longer doubted. The achievements noted for business games in industry are more and more influencing the manner in which simulation gaming is conducted in business schools. The early development of business games from business schools to business firms may therefore be viewed as going full-circle and we watch with interest and excitement the growing interaction between the two worlds of business and academia.

The cross-fertilisation here is due in no small measure to the intrinsic richness of the simulation gaming tool. The power of business games to represent the complexity of real life, to communicate knowledge and to influence attitudes and behaviour will all help to consolidate the position of simulation gaming as a major pedagogic instrument for many years to come.

17 Understanding organisational communication processes: The use of simulation techniques

ALAN COOTE
The Polytechnic of Wales, U.K.
and
LAURIE McMAHON
King's Fund College, London, U.K.

Introduction

In this chapter we argue that communicating perspectives of communication processes within organisations is likely to be best achieved through non-traditional teaching techniques. This is particularly so with managers who have become socialised into accepting only orthodox views about communication and rejecting more radical approaches. We suggest that managerial performance is hampered by this artificial restriction of perceptions and that in helping managers develop, it is crucial that they at least become aware of the competing paradigms that can be used to explain communication processes in organisations. Finally, we show how simulation techniques can help the management developer communicate about organisational communication! A hierarchy of simulations is described, moving from those which deal with simple message transmission to those which concentrate upon communicating as the idiomatic currency of power bargaining.

Dominant paradigms in organisation theory

The starting point of our argument is a belief that the performance of managers can be improved by broadening their understanding of the communication process within organisations. This involves an appreciation, if not an acceptance, of two distinct paradigms that relate to alternative, and to some extent competing, views of organisational behaviour. These in turn lead to very different perspectives of communication processes which we would suggest influence managers in their attempts to fashion communication processes in organisations.

There is a growing body of literature which serves to contrast the orthodox view of organisations with a more radical power-based approach to understanding organisational life (see, for example, Bacharach & Lawler, 1980; 1981; Pfeffer, 1981; McMahon *et al.*, 1983). These two somewhat contradictory paradigms can be summarised as follows:

The rational paradigm

This is an orthodox view of organisations. Here the organisation is seen as a social machine which has as its very *raison d'être* the achievement of specific goals. Managers at the top of the organisation make decisions about goals and then work towards structuring, resourcing, controlling and co-ordinating the components of the organisation to try and ensure that these goals are achieved. This is a highly *dirigiste* view, one that has a great deal of general acceptance. It is grounded in a web of functionalist and systems theories as well as decades of normative thinking about the role of managers. It should be noted that the legitimacy of this approach is accentuated by the *language* which is used to describe and support it. Terms like 'authority', 'rationality', 'efficiency', 'effectiveness' are the 'positive' conceptual threads from which this approach is woven.

The micro-political paradigm

This is the view which challenges the orthodox approach. Organisations here are seen as being made up of competing groups and individuals who negotiate for advantage. Organisational goals are simply umbrellas under which such bargaining can occur, so that what organisations actually *do* is the outcome of bargaining processes rather than the achievement (or, more likely, non-achievement) of senior managers' optimal objectives. This view of organisation has as its roots conflict sociology coupled with political and behavioural perspectives. It carries with it its own language, and notions such as 'power', 'conflict', 'coalitions' and 'tactics' are the strands running through it.

Implications for understanding communication

These antithetical views of organisations foster two equally distinct approaches to understanding and then managing organisational communication processes.

In the first instance the rational paradigm casts a neutral light upon communication processes. This has a number of dimensions. Taking an overtly functionalist viewpoint, communication systems are seen as analogous with the nervous system in living organisms; the means by which senior managers are informed about what goes on at the periphery of organisations and also the mechanism by which instructions about appropriate responsive action can be transmitted. On another level, communications may also be seen as a way of enabling the elements of complex organisations to co-ordinate their activity effectively. Extending this idea, communication may be used in what is tantamount to a psychotherapeutic sense where 'communicating' denotes being open about motives and feelings within organisations. Allied to this, one can also find communications being used in a public relations sense, to describe the degree to which organisational leaders relate to staff at the periphery. So using the rational paradigm one could argue that 'better' communications (i.e. openness and clear transmission of reports and instructions) result in such things as improved co-ordination, more responsive decision-making and indeed better-quality decisions being made by senior managers. It also suggests that if junior staff are kept well informed by bosses, then they will be more highly motivated.

The micro-political paradigm, on the other hand, suggests something rather different. Here 'communicating' becomes the idiomatic currency of political bargaining. The very acts of collecting data and transmitting information are therefore viewed as political; as the means, or at least one of the means, by which individuals or groups secure advantage in complex negotiations. The creation and maintenance of formal communication systems, rather than being seen as routes to efficient managerial co-ordination, are perceived as tactics by which the most powerful groups in an organisation are able to control the communication process and thereby institutionalise their advantage over time. Using the micro-political paradigm, there can be no such thing as better organisational communication. 'Better' can only be judged by individuals or groups in that it helps them secure the best bargaining advantage.

It can be argued that both the rational and more radical paradigms are highly prescriptive for managers. In the former, managerial attention is focused upon clarity and accurate transmission of data, on the one hand, and being open about feelings and disclosing motives, on the other. In the latter, managerial attention is focused on determining what advantage there may be in certain acts of communication, and how partial or accentuated messages can be used in a selective way to produce desired outcomes. So, as we suggested earlier, the antithetical paradigms produce quite polar extremes in inferred managerial behaviour.

The problem

We have found that practising managers on development courses have a great deal of difficulty coping with the ambiguity of the mixed messages emanating from the two paradigms. The rational or orthodox view seems to be easily accepted and understood (at least as a prescription for behaviour), whereas the more radical micro-political perspectives are either rejected completely or marginalised. Indeed, there appears to be a strongly espoused desire to favour the rational perspective and to see other perspectives as somehow abhorrent; as a sign of organisational sickness. However, some managers will accept that micro-political activity occurs in their organisations or departments. This recognition seems to be related to the managers' depth of experience, but such an acceptance is seldom translated into prescriptive terms. Thus the *description* of organisations as contexts in which micro-political activity occurs is acceptable (at least to an extent), while the prescriptions that flow from it pose difficulties. There seem to be at least two possible explanations for the discomfort felt by our managers in considering, much less accepting, the more radical views.

First, rational approaches are comfortable, tidy and logical. They contrast markedly with the micro-political approaches which appear to suggest a lack of order and control bounding on anarchy. Cherished beliefs are by definition strongly held, and the feeling that micro-political approaches will affect trusting and 'civilised' relationships and jeopardise efforts to create open and honest communications within organisations is, not surprisingly, common. As Torrington & Weightman (1985: 81) observe:

> The idea of behaving politically is one that managers do not readily accept for themselves. This is partly because of the immediate association of the word 'political' with national and local government but also because the word carries connotations of insincerity and deviousness and managers disparage those qualities in their colleagues (not themselves being guilty of such behaviour) and deplore the extent to which they detract from the main tasks of the organisation in which they are employed.

The second and related problem is associated with the difficulty of accepting and incorporating new information if this conflicts with existing beliefs. It appears that practitioners experiencing cognitive dissonance (Festinger 1957) edit out the challenging information provided by the non-orthodox paradigm. Thus, the conflict about what a person intellectually knows and what he empirically experiences is overcome by ignoring or minimising the more challenging, less comfortable micro-political approach.

We are not necessarily implying that the micro-political approach provides the panacea for improving managerial performance but rather that there are considerable benefits accruing from an appreciation of both models. Thus, we feel that it is important that managers appreciate the strength of the more orthodox paradigm in their assumptive worlds and the degree to which this limits approaches to managing communications within organisations, in terms of both structure and process. They need to understand alternative perspectives and to realise that a concern about communications may be more than worrying about the accurate transmission of data, and might well be an essential part of developing a strategy to produce desired outcomes.

The challenge for management developers is therefore to communicate the less orthodox views in such a way that they are not rejected out of hand and to overcome the barriers which prevent a reasoned analysis and judgement of uncomfortable ideas.

Communication and simulation

Simulation techniques can go a long way towards overcoming the problem of helping managers to view organisational communication problems in a different light, towards broadening perspectives, and helping managers appreciate the pervasiveness of the rational approach in their assumptive worlds.

We suggest that to enable managers to experience the theoretical ideas in practice produces not only improved learning but also means that they are confronted with behaviour, very often their own, which cannot be explained through the rational paradigm. We have argued previously (Coote & McMahon, 1984; 1985) that this contradiction is a powerful tool in helping managers confront seemingly unacceptable ideas.

So having discussed the two paradigms which can help in understanding the communication process in organisations, we have gone on to suggest that simulation is perhaps the only way of helping managers explore and understand them. It is now possible to consider how different types of simulation may be effectively used by trainers and developers. Each example given below simulates selected aspects of real business environments.

To those familiar with the field it will be obvious that there is a whole range of simulations which can be helpful. Some, specifically designed to address issues of communication in organisations, are complex in structure (like the WESTPORT COMMUNICATION SIMULATION, described by Irwin, 1981) but where possible, we have used simulations which are more simple in structure and often abstract in nature. For us this has the advantage of avoiding constant comparison between the metaphor of the simulation and the manager's real world, because we have found that if the simulated organisation is too concrete, it provides an easy way out for the manager who argues that since his/her company, for example, is not structured this way, or does not deal in manufacturing, the ideas contained in the simulation cannot apply to him/her.

The simulations that we use can be presented in the form of a progressive hierarchy (see Figure 17.1) moving from those which deal with simple message transmission through those which further explain the rational perspective, and on to those towards the top of the hierarchy which illustrate micro-political perspectives and also demonstrate the behaviours which might be employed if communications within organisations are seen from this position.

Simple message transmission

We start with a simulation which is most often used to explore the issues in simple message transmission. This is a version of WHISPERS based on Bartlett's (1932) study of rumour and further discussed by Bond

HIERARCHICAL LEVELS	*SIMULATIONS IN THE HIERARCHY*	*KEY LEARNING POINTS*
Power bargaining applied	DIPLOMACY ↑	The importance of process on outcomes *using* communication skills. Underlying informal deals within formal communication processes.
	PRIMITIVE POLITICS ↑	Witholding information for 'political' advantage. Controlling communication channels and developing 'communication' languages as a tactic. Co-operation versus the 'will to win'.
Power bargaining as a concept	THE COLOUR GAME ↑	How partisan interests influence tactics and coalition formulation. Hidden agendas. The importance of non-verbal communication.
The influence of organisational structures	COMMUNICATIONS IN A HIERARCHY ↑	Managing the communication system for maximum co-ordination. Relationships between communication and organisational design.
Simple message transmission	BACK TO BACK ↑ WHISPERS	Communication 'channels'. The influence of feedback. Formal versus informal communications. Selective perception and retention of information.

FIGURE 17.1 *Progressive hierarchy of selected simulations relevant to understanding aspects of the communication process*

(1986); it is usually used to help managers experience how unwritten communication can be distorted in transition through selective perception and retention of information. Typically a written message is read by the first in a chain of managers who in turn whisper to each other their understanding of the message. Inevitably the message becomes badly distorted. It is invariably good fun to play and demonstrates adequately the 'dangers' of relying on informal communications, even if there is no intention to distort meanings. It also provides a good basis for exploring that aspect of communications theory which deals with selective perception, in that an individual's current concerns and/or past experience will act as a perceptual filter.

A second simulation which can be used to explore message transmission is designed to show how the use of different channels influences effective communication and also the importance of providing adequate feedback. Here a complex shape is given to a member of the group who is asked to describe the shape (without using any supporting 'channels' or allowing the group to ask any questions) so that the rest of the group are able to reproduce the character. Again this has high levels of intrinsic enjoyment and the point is demonstrated extremely well if, when using an equally complex shape, the possibility of communication feedback is allowed (in that the group can ask questions and receive answers) when typically the success rate is extremely high. A variation of this activity is THE BACK TO BACK GAME described by Jaques (1981).

The influence of organisational structure

In neither WHISPERS nor THE BACK TO BACK GAME is the communication process significantly influenced by the imposition of a formal organisational structure. The next simulation in our hierarchy introduces this dimension, making explicit, through direct experience, the problem of managing communications better. COMMUNICATIONS IN A HIERARCHY involves a large group being broken into three sub-groups —the planners, the administrators, and the executers. The object is for the executers to build a Lego model within a given time, using information received from the administrators who are acting on instructions from the planners. The three groups are physically separate and communication channels are controlled by the simulation directors. Thus the planners may communicate with the administrators by using diagrams only and the administrators may only send their messages to the executers using the written word.

The simulation usually produces high levels of frustration and the task rarely gets completed properly. Some mirth may be generated by allowing the planners to see, at the end of the simulation, what has actually been produced, despite the best-laid plans of the participants! The learning messages usually derived from the simulation are rich and complex (concerned as they are with organisational design, attitudes and behaviours) but have very direct implications for the structure of communication that enables effective co-ordination to occur.

Power bargaining as a concept

The simulations outlined above are well received, not simply because they are fun and the learning points clear, but we would argue because they are drawn from a theoretical perspective that conforms with most managers' assumptive worlds. Illustrating aspects of communication within largely 'rational' contexts may help individuals appreciate the technical aspects of communication better but does little to increase their range of understanding about organisational communication in general.

The power of simulations in this respect is illustrated when we add to our hierarchy simulations which allow for the existence of power bargaining in organisational settings and demonstrate the importance of interpersonal communications in the bargaining process.

The first of these is THE COLOUR GAME which can be used to demonstrate the inadequacy of rational models of decision-making and communication in explaining behaviour when there are powerful partisan interests negotiating for advantage (see Coote & McMahon, 1984). THE COLOUR GAME has been described more fully elsewhere (Jaques, 1981) but, in brief, it involves a group of up to ten managers trying to come to a decision about the new colour of (in our version) an organisation's trucks and vans; participants are briefed to have a range of preferences (for example: 'You must argue for blue; you will not compromise on any other colour'). The preferences are sufficiently diverse to prevent any easy agreement about colour. The differences of interest produce heated discussion in which communication skills are used to secure advantage over other group members. Also evident is the use of fabricated rationales that support and legitimise each individual's preference as well as the creation of temporary alliances formed and dissolved using subtle (and often non-verbal) means of communication.

The impact of the simulation is usually considerable, with participants and observers beginning to understand the difference between communicating as an integrative co-ordinating function, and as a competitive, negotiating function. THE COLOUR GAME also shows up *dissimilarities* with the 'real' world. For example, when asked about this, our managers normally identify the longer-term and often covert nature of negotiations, the fact that negotiations over many issues are occurring at the same time and the fact that a great deal of effort often goes into the development of relatively permanent, sometimes institutional, coalitions. THE COLOUR GAME invariably highlights managers' perceptions of these points.

Power bargaining applied

Having taken our managers to a stage where they (usually) begin to accept that there might be something in micro-politics, the next step is to use a simulation which concentrates more directly on bargaining and communication processes. Here we have found that PRIMITIVE POLITICS (see Laver, 1979) is ideal. This excellent simulation is simple in structure but deals with complex issues. Players begin with resources (cash) and the simulation proceeds with each player being required to expend some resources to stay alive. Thus each player contributes the same amount to a central kitty. The total in the kitty is matched by 'Nature' pound for pound. Players then bid (any amount) for the central kitty, placing their bids on the table. The player with the highest bid receives the entire kitty and the next round commences with the creation of a new kitty.

The fascination and relevance of this simulation for us is that playing invariably involves deals, negotiations and bargaining. It throws into sharp focus facets of organisational communication processes such as the withholding of information, attempts to control or formalise communication channels and the development and use of appropriate 'languages' with which to communicate. Most important, the simulation illustrates one of the fundamental problems in organisational (and political) life, namely the communication behaviours of partisans caught between the advantages of co-operation and the will to 'win'.

The next stage in the application of the power-bargaining perspective is to free up the constraints on negotiations imposed by the structure of the previous two simulations. We have tried to develop our own organisationally based simulation to provide us with an appropriate learning vehicle, but have come to the conclusion that we were trying to invent an inferior wheel. We have now fallen back on the proprietary board game DIPLOMACY to explore the more complex aspects of micro-political communications.

Many people will be familiar with the simulation; it is based loosely on wars between states in pre-World War I Europe. In order to play, participants (often in teams) have to form alliances to attack or defend others' positions. It involves unstructured periods of negotiation between teams of players, during which real or bogus deals are struck, followed by regular, formal 'accounting sessions' in which the products of the deals are recorded by moves on a board.

We like to allow DIPLOMACY to run throughout a course (say over a 3- or 4-day residential workshop), enabling the dealing to go on in a completely unstructured way between other formal sessions and holding accounting sessions first thing in the morning and last thing in thc afternoon. (A great deal of negotiating occurs during the evening).

It is an exciting simulation, producing for most participants moments of glory and of failure. Inexperienced gamers might heed a word of warning that the passions it arouses, especially when played in teams, are surprisingly strong.

The learning points drawn from the simulation depend to some extent on the imagination of the group. The principal ideas are that what organisations do is an outcome of a bargaining process and that, to some extent, success in bargaining depends upon the participants' ability to *use* communication skills. It also shows how informal deals, whether honoured or reneged upon, are a vital aspect of what appear to be formal organisational processes.

Having reached this stage, managers rarely, if ever, continue to reject outright the micro-political perspectives. The debate that follows the simulations usually centres on when one view rather than another is more illuminating and useful and on some of the ethical problems that may be involved. (For a discussion of the ethical issues related to the use of power-bargaining models see McMahon *et al.*, 1983).

Depending on the nature of the course we are running we will either use case material as a vehicle to explain these issues, or focus on the communication systems in the managers' own organisations to help build a bridge between the theoretical concepts employed in the simulations and the managerial practice of their 'real' world.

Conclusion

In summary, we have described the theoretical approaches in which we feel the whole issue of organisational communications can be grounded, and the problems this poses both for managers and those who seek to develop them. We have gone on to describe how simulation techniques provide a powerful tool in helping resolve these problems.

It is clear from what we have described that it is not our intention to use the simulations to teach communication skills. This is partly because we would not regard ourselves as expert in this respect, but more significant is that we feel it patronises our managers. We would suggest that even the most junior manager has a well-developed repertoire of interpersonal communication skills that are successfully utilised in other aspects of his/her life. As we stated in the introduction, we feel that managers are inhibited in the use of their communication skills not by incompetence but by their limited perceptions about organisations in general and about the use to which communication processes may be put in particular.

Simulation techniques have provided for us a way of helping managers widen their perspectives so that they can use their communication skills with greater effect in the micro-political systems in which they work.

18 Simulation and communication in women's networks: Power and corporate culture

BARBARA B. STERN
Rutgers University, NJ, U.S.A.

Corporate life involves a daily reality in which men and women interact and communicate to achieve the rewards of power, often defined as an ability to set and achieve goals (Korda, 1976). Since the framework of corporate interactions generally referred to as 'organisational culture' is predominantly male-orientated, women need special assistance in interpreting and communicating power in a business context. Communication, often considered as social interaction through messages (Lundberg, 1939), can be examined by means of simulation, defined as representations of reality. Likewise, simulation techniques can be studied as communication processes. Each field can contribute to an enhanced understanding of organisational culture by women, currently a minority in corporate management: within the United States, no more than 5–10% of executive positions are held by women, despite their presence as 50% of the labour force (Stern, 1985).

The masculine nature of the corporation has been so thoroughly assumed that very little attention has been paid to gender issues in organisational culture (Deal & Kennedy, 1982; Kanter, 1977). Yet men and women approach each other in the work-place carrying the baggage of deeply embedded symbolic gender-dominated images of the other sex (Mitroff, 1983). As a result, according to Kanter (1977: 159), 'Male–female communication is sometimes cross-cultural communication'.

The formation of corporate women's network groups represents a conscious effort by women to master the business and social communication skills essential to enjoy power (Kleiman, 1980; Stern, 1981; Welch, 1981). This effort embodies the social creativity of a minority group determined to reject former acquiescence to the inferior corporate status formerly accepted and move into the majority, i.e. masculine, power mode (Tajfel, 1981). Women's networks provide an information base, support system, and training ground where simulation game techniques can be used to coach women in the communication processes necessary for exercising power. A network can consciously use such techniques, structured into regularly scheduled courses for members, to help women communicate beyond the confines of their own feminine culture outward to the larger corporate milieu.

This chapter explores the connection between women's networks and simulation exercises as communication aids enhancing gender relations in business. Simulation games teach many types of group communication: network members can participate in management games, role-plays, scenarios, and executive exercises (Guetzkow *et al.*, 1972; Thierauf & Klekamp, 1975) in a formalised setting. Male–female communication is helped by network-sponsored activities which represent realistic office situations, cultivate insight into others' viewpoints, and develop empathy for others. Network-based simulations can help bridge the male–female cultural gap in communication by enabling women to 'try on' male reality. In so doing, the 'otherness' of gender can be demystified, and women can more easily gain access to their fair share of corporate rewards.

Women's networks

Women's networks are working towards development of both instrumental and expressive leadership skills. Task-driven and socio-emotional leadership are equally necessary to direct the goal-orientated actions of any group (Stoner, 1978), but women especially need to learn the highly valued task-directed team leadership often considered a male prerogative. American corporations are ambivalent in terms of commitment to special training specifically designed to develop leadership skills for women *qua* women (McLane, 1980). Many corporations adopt the viewpoint that all individuals should be treated alike, and that singling out women for special training is reverse prejudice. Thus, women's networks often need to assume the role of unofficial 'helpers' for executive women.

Women's networks have arisen within American corporations, professions, and geographical areas. Corporations such as Equitable Life Assurance Company, professions such as law (Women's Bar Association), industries such as communications (Women in Communication), and entire geographical areas (Florida Women's Network) have generated business and professional women's networks. Women's networks also exist in other countries: France is home to Les Femmes Chefs d'Entreprise, a group of entrepreneurial women. These groups share the unifying characteristic of formal association by women who want to move ahead professionally.

Most of these formal structured networks offer their members courses, activities, and events which can be adapted to include simulation exercises and communication courses led by a network member or an outside consultant. From my experience, most networks have regularly scheduled sessions, usually once a month. This structure in itself can be thought of as a simulation of corporate reality, especially *vis-à-vis* the looser unstructured feminine reality of domestic family life. While these networks may or may not limit the actual number of members, they frequently require objective qualifications for membership: career achievement demonstrated by rank, salary, and/or certification in a profession. Access and referral systems of the networks with structure and membership criteria tend to work well. The 'who do you know' route to advancement is also as much a simulation of reality as formal structure and membership qualifications, and most successful women learn that making the right contacts—a process itself called 'networking'—is necessary for corporate success.

A major reason, in fact, why women are banding together in networks and engaging in executive simulation exercises is that they want to learn about the patterns of social control much more familiar to those men who have been long at home in teamed hierarchical structures (Korda, 1976; Cunningham with Schumer, 1984). Until about a decade ago, women entering business situations were hampered by a tradition of powerlessness: women's history is marked by infrequent and isolated examples who achieved power on the non-domestic stage (Bullough 1974). There have been so very few women executives that viable role models barely exist. Almost every woman in Hennig & Jardim's (1976) study of high-level managers gained access to power through the secretarial route: hardly a relevant model for the newly minted generation of women business school graduates (Greene, 1982; Stern, 1985).

Networks where women combine to create viable managerial models are often separatist peer groups, and thus 'safe houses' for the power exercises employed. The safety factor cannot be overestimated: power is still viewed by most corporate men as legitimate for men only, or, at best for the few 'masculine women' who must be allowed access to power because government guidelines mandate that there should be equal employment opportunities for both sexes. Network group formation by career-orientated women has often engendered misunderstanding: male corporate managers are bewildered by women who feel obliged to organise. The predominantly male business world often judges networks as silly, unnecessary, or threatening. Even pro-female male executives see little value in women banding together, since many men have not grasped the significance of a work-force in which the workers are women, and the leaders men (Stern, 1985).

In fact, gender stereotypes dominant in the American cultural norm (Rosenkrantz *et al*., 1968) embody a fixed concept of different 'places' for men and women: women's in the home, men's in the external world (Richmond-Abbott, 1979). Different qualities adhere to each role and its appropriate place: women are expected to be nurturant, sympathetic, maternal, tender caretakers of people; men are expected to be strong, aggressive, paternal, powerful leaders. This bundle of socialised differences is visibly manifested in the impedimenta of civilisation: toys, clothing, games, books, media images, religious and family dogma, educational institutions (Richmond-Abbott, 1979), and even the structure and usage of language itself (Lakoff, 1975).

Dominant masculine modes of social interaction within the corporation can be understood by women if they are able to practise 'trying on' various roles in simulation games. And the games can serve as realistic representations of intergroup communication situations between men and women, often gender-bound by their view of each other as alien species. While both men and women need sensitisation to each other's cultural frameworks, women's networks are more readily available as change agents because they have been more or less consciously formed to help members achieve professional goals necessitating a restructuring of outlook from the domestic to the institutional.

Modes of power

Three kinds of organisational power are significant in corporate life, all of which can be fostered by a network's encouragement of critical communication skills: power of authority, power of expertise, and power of charisma. The network as a stage for simulation and communication functions as a support group, educational forum, meeting place and training ground.

Power of authority

The power of authority is the legitimate power of bestowing rewards and punishments which accrues to leaders of organisations. The problem is that not very many women at this time fit into this role. There are few legitimised female authority symbols as yet: even the designation 'Chief Executive Officer', with the obvious military connotations of the word 'Officer', is a very male-orientated term. Basic verbal and non-verbal communication cues are lacking for women who aspire to legitimate authority positions.

Power signs are the cultural cues signalling a person's mantle of authority. In our society, these signs are often material: stretch limousines, corporate jets, corner offices with windows, membership in prestigious clubs. But signs of authority can be found in communication as well: a habitual tone of command, use of declarative statements, and avoidance of 'filler' phrases.

On both verbal and non-verbal levels, women betray insecurity in the face of male power modes. It is, in fact, unlikely that women's power signs will ever be thick cigars or sleek Lear Jets, but they have not yet invented convincing ones of their own. Interestingly, some women in power seem to have adopted exaggeratedly feminised near-parodic symbols of authority: Mary Kay's pink Cadillac, Leona Helmsley's lavish jewels, Estée Lauder's fragile blue colour scheme. When such consciously feminised signals have not been invented, women in power have tended to cloak themselves in androgynous or even male-modelled neutrality: business suit and bow-tied shirt, leather attaché case, sterile office decor, all pointedly and non-stereotypically feminine. Women's communication styles are even more gender-stereotyped: many women habitually phrase declarative sentences as questions (Lakoff, 1975), allow their voices to sound whispery, sprinkle their discourse with non-essential interjections, and defer to men in dual gender communication groups (Kramarae, 1981).

One reason for women's difficulty in communicating authority is the lack of role models: women aspirants to corporate power have no one to emulate. They need networks for direction, for support, for specific career gameswomanship (Harragan, 1977; Pogrebin, 1975; Stern, 1981). These networks in effect set the group up as a training mentor, for the group itself becomes the source of composite power skills. A network can provide supportive and non-threatening simulation experiences within which women can learn how to communicate essential leadership skills. The use of management simulations specifically dealing with executive women and their subordinates can function as effective network exercises.

A programme utilising one such activity, WOMAN EXECUTIVE/ MALE SECRETARY, (Stern, 1986) has been successful in the consultative training process for several networks (Stern, 1979; 1980). This simulation deals with executive and secretarial office roles, and enables female executives to try on various peer–subordinate–superior relationships. The game concerns appropriate executive actions towards a female secretary who is given an opportunity to advance to administrative assistant; instead of being overjoyed by the suggested promotion, she quits. The sexually charged office reveals men and women doomed to miscommunication by reliance on gender stereotypes. Sexism in job interviews can be dealt with in this game, since a male executive is blamed for hiring the ungrateful secretary who puts personal whim ahead of male-identified 'proper' career commitment.

Power of expertise

A second kind of power, the power of expertise, is both theoretically and actually open to women. This is power accruing to the source of specific and valuable *ad hoc* knowledge which varies in importance situationally, such as the bag of skills possessed by the corporate counsel or director of management information systems. The 'ideology of professionalism' normally unites professionals in a community of interest, but those employed by corporations tend to be exceptions: they must serve the interests of their corporate masters, not the collectivity of colleagues (Johnson, 1972). Experts within a corporation know what others must find out at that moment, and they are paid highly and accorded great respect because of this knowledge. The problem is that even though the pay is impressive, and the jobs frequently allocated to women, these positions can be dead ends. They are 'gilded handcuffs', a trap which isolates those who are often answerable neither to the ethical code of their professional colleagues nor the corporate code of their managerial peers. One such position is corporate counsel: an in-house lawyer, particularly one below the rank of general counsel, who rarely rises to upper management, since the expert is viewed both as a person dubiously loyal to the corporation over the profession, and lacking in solid managerial skills as well.

The power of expertise has, by and large, meant a nice job, a nice office, and a nice gold watch after 25 years' service for the skilled employee who is rewarded and then retired. But this limited exercise of power is not the way to the top for men or women. While the distinction between line and staff applies unisexually, women have far less knowledge about the limitations of power of expertise within the corporate structure. Expert women often feel blocked from 'real' power, because they have failed to understand that the limitations are built into the position, not the individual occupying the role.

Networks can help their corporate expert members in very specific ways: they represent a secure place to discuss the situation openly, share information, and examine power–lifestyle tradeoffs. Networks enable 'collusive intimacies and backstage relaxation' for women who can benefit from sharing of information to realign themselves with the male power teams (Goffman, 1959: 206). Networks serve as a communication forum: a business and social arena where war stories can be swapped safely on an informal basis. Additionally, networks can function in a more formalised way by providing structured activities for assessing career goals and lifestyle choices. One significant point is that the expert role is not inherently undesirable as long as the expert understands that she is trading off one set of values for another.

The VALUES AUCTION GAME is useful in helping network members assess their goals and personal tradeoff choices (Stern, 1979). In this game, the network members are given a sum of money, often $10,000, to use in bidding for values on the auction block. There are 20 personal and career value statements up for bids: some examples are 'freedom to take the risks necessary for my career'; 'opportunities to take the limelight and be a company star'; and 'a work environment where I am left in peace'. The members bid for ownership of the values, and after the auction share perceptions about the necessary tradeoffs. The balance between personal and career commitments is explored, and the game enables ambivalence about life and work roles to surface by openly encouraging articulation of desired lifestyles. It also hones competitive skills, for the women have to compete against each other with limited funds to 'buy' their desired lifestyle.

Power of charisma

While women themselves can basically make the decision about accepting the role of expert or rejecting it and aiming beyond, there is a third kind of organisational power on which women rarely have the deciding vote: the power of charisma. Charismatic power is the trait that envelops the dynamic, forceful, magnetic individual perceived as a leader of others (Zaleznik & Kets de Vries, 1975). It is the aura of projected confidence, and has little to do with either legitimacy or expertise. Because it is so vague and compelling a force for both good and evil, charisma is often ignored as a basis for organisational power.

A serious problem for women is that charismatic power is nearly always defined as a male trait: the self-sufficient 'maximum man' (Zaleznik & Kets de Vries, 1975). There is no corporate analogue for women, since charismatic power in women is invariably associated with sexuality—good looks, physical beauty, bodily allure—and associated with the bedroom, not the boardroom.

These sexual stereotypes are reinforced by the media, for advertisements often portray women as 'stereotypic images of sex object or housewife and mother' (Richmond-Abbott, 1979). In advertisements, women are frequently reduced to child-like creatures, 'saved from seriousness' by benevolent protective men (Goffman, 1979). Even when women are shown in business attire and situations, they wear these roles like dress-up costumes, since the predominant media image of women is non-serious. Disappointingly, female images in the media in this decade have not reflected much progress towards portrayal of women as dignified human beings with multi-faceted personal identity (Caballero & Solomon, 1984).

Women who possess charismatic qualities have almost no means for communicating this dynamism or even transmuting it into a legitimate corporate asset. The same traits that are positively valued in charismatic men—ambition, forcefulness, persuasiveness, and narcissistic intensity—have long been associated with the most highly disruptive negative traits in women—abrasiveness, bitchiness, flirtatiousness, and exaggerated and paralysing self-love.

The woman who aspires to a leadership role out of inner desire to exert her force of personality is probably at this time doomed to failure in a corporate environment. She will almost certainly be viewed as a threat to the organisation: many women who have charisma have had to neutralise this force in order to function in a non-distracting team-approved manner. The charismatic woman, defined as one motivated by personal conviction to act out success-orientated behaviour, lives in the midst of dangers. She feels capable of managing entire corporations, yet is restrained by the need to avoid inspiring fear in either the men around her *or* their wives.

Women's networks can be extremely important here, in that they can provide explicit reinforcement for changing negative stereotypical perceptions of female traits. The open and shared examination of these stereotypes makes public societal prejudices, and reassures individual women that their actions are not necessarily causes of negative feminine images. The function of networks in airing information about women's role perceptions and opening lines of communication through simulation games is an important one in conquering prejudice.

Networks can go even further in enabling women to acquire at least one essential tool for non-sexual charisma: communication skills such as public speaking, effective negotiation, and leadership strategies. Networks cannot undo centuries of learned cultural values in one fell swoop, but they can provide women with acceptably non-sexualised tools of charisma—communication techniques—that in time may change the perception of this kind of power as sexually based.

Exercises which train women in the basic skill of effective public speaking are useful activities for women's networks intent on nurturing responsible uses of magnetic personal qualities. The development of confidence in public speaking, group presentations, and business negotiations can help women overcome barriers to the achievement or expression of charismatic force. Very basic network activities such as formal five-minute introductions by each woman, conducted as THE CELEBRITY INTRODUCTION GAME, can be used routinely at little or no cost to build communication skills. The use of tape-recorders (Stern, 1979) in these introductions is a simple method of showing network members a 'charismatic spectrum' of personality communication by means of vocal tone, mood, word choice, pacing, and so on.

Conclusion

The continued growth of women's networks both in the United States and abroad now seems assured: the number of American networks has risen from less than 1,500 in 1979 to over 5,000 in recent years. The International Alliance, a network of networks, functions as a central forum for almost 30 professional women's networks in the United States and one in Europe. Similarly, the National Women's Forum in the United States has 15 American chapters, and five chapters world-wide (Callahan, 1986). Many networks with secure power bases are beginning outreach courses for other women in earlier career stages: the New York chapter of the Women's Forum, an elite group of top-level female executives, has begun a course to help female high school students achieve success. Increasingly sophisticated communication strategies are also promoting world-wide contacts: the use of computer networking enables women with access to PCs and modems to reach each other via electronic bulletin boards. Simulation techniques seem likely to be useful communication aids for women's networks now reaching out to women all over the world. The growth, consolidation of power, outreach and technological innovativeness shown by networks since 1982 bodes well for enhanced group communication and improved gender relations on a global basis in the future.

These networks, which show advancing technological as well as organisational skills, still hold in common their function as quasi-classrooms for teaching leadership through communication and simulations. Meetings continue to be one of the safe places where women can examine the predominantly male reality governing corporate culture. The existence of a place where one can try on roles as 'the other' in order to see what makes the opposite half tick is an important prologue to increasingly positive gender communication and interaction throughout the world.

While current networks may act deliberately and self-consciously in their sponsorship of role-plays, simulations, game concepts, and other communication exercises, they represent a natural setting at this time for corporate women who want to break loose from their damaging isolation by meeting and working with other strivers like themselves. Although instant demolition of the barriers causing miscommunication is unrealistic, perhaps the greatest accomplishment for networks will be removing the stigma of 'otherness' which appears to be the real barrier to power that corporate women face.

19 Policy formation through simulation and communication

JAN KLABBERS
State University at Utrecht, The Netherlands
and
JEFF HEARN
University of Bradford, U.K.

Structures of social system

Social systems are based on interactions between individual members of the society. Through increasing interrelations, social systems evolve into complex collective structures. The building blocks of these collective structures have been labelled 'double-interacts'. They are a sequence of contingent response patterns in which 'an action by actor A evokes a specific response from actor B, which is then responded to by actor A' (Weick, 1979). On the basis of double-interacts very complicated structures can be aggregated 'without the necessity of any single person knowing, understanding, or even visualizing that entire structure' (Weick, 1979). From experience it is plausible to assume that collective structures are sustainable despite friction between the components, i.e. the double-interacts.

However, sometimes they fall apart because the building blocks disintegrate. Sometimes frictions build up and diminish the (self-)steering capacities of social systems. If this happens, social systems are in trouble, and the question is how they can cope with it. Collective structures can be looked on from the inside and from the outside. When considered from the inside, the actors are to a certain extent capable of developing a self-referential mode and thus are able to produce guidelines for coping with undesirably changing conditions: they are capable of self-steering, even if they do not comprehend fully the entire structure of the social system of which they are a part.

When taking an outside position, a social system can be viewed as a reference system. An outside actor can perceive that system as a virtual object. An actor may also take a boundary position—i.e. a balance between a mode of participation (inside) and reflection (outside). This change of perspective resembles a helicopter journey. When the craft takes off, it is physically removed from the level of individual actors who are engaged in numerous double-interacts. We lose detail at the micro level but gain perspective at the level of patterns of double-interacts. Hovering from a distance, we become aware of the structure and boundaries of the collective structure that give shape to the social system. After landing, we again are an inside actor, involved in various double-interacts.

Collective structures, being surrounded by and coupled to other social systems, cannot operate by an inside or an outside mode alone. They have to alternate between an external and an internal position of steering and thus cross perspective boundaries (Bråten, 1984). We consider both the self-reference and the reference mode necessary conditions for collective structures that retain themselves under changing conditions. Self-reference reinforces organisational self-closure, while the reference mode essentially stresses symbolic representation. Both modes are necessary conditions for the self-steering of social systems.

So far social systems have been described as collective structures. They continue to exist for many different reasons as defined by those who maintain them. However, those who maintain a social system are found inside and outside it. Insiders participate in negotiated meanings: they 'transform the identity of themselves and of their network through a more or less shared understanding of both themselves and the world' (Bråten, 1984). Outsiders reflect upon the social system and the way it can be represented. Thus the collective structure becomes a meaning-processing system and by doing so it operates in and by itself.

Social systems as collective structures are based upon double-interacts as their building blocks. Furthermore, acts are the carriers of communication between the actors. One action can contain various types of communication; in other words it can transfer different levels of meaning. Basically, social systems transform or reproduce themselves through communications, which percolate through the whole collective structure and in aggregated form constitute the ongoing policy-formation process, in order to be able to cope with changing circumstances. To understand the way a policy formation process through communications may develop, it seems reasonable to view policy formation as the result of reciprocal interactions between various actors (or parties), such that a multi-actor model of policy formation is proposed (Klabbers, 1985).

Against this background we present some powerful methods that have the potential to highlight communication processes in social systems in the context of policy-formation and negotiation processes. These methods, by making participants aware of their mutual actions, simulate basic features of past, present or future social systems. One illustration deals with simulation of processes in which the participants develop a short-term perspective. The other stresses a more middle- or even long-term view.

Communication and simulation in short-term policy formation

In this section we focus on communication processes in simulations of short-term (up to three years) policy-making and planning systems. To adapt Klabbers's (1985) taxonomy of forecasting and planning methods, we move here towards short-term 'horizons of forecasting' and 'more weakly defined systems', emphasising social and cultural norms rather than rigid technologies.

Incrementalism

The major framework for analysis of and prescription for short-term policy and planning is incrementalism (Lindblom 1965; Braybrooke & Lindblom 1963). Much literature on resource allocation, budgeting, planning and organisation theory relies on assumptions of gradual incremental development. Decision-making is serial, exploratory, moving from means to ends, and remedial. Informal communication is emphasised alongside (even over and above) formal channels. Information is 'disjointed' in form *and* content, and is accumulated rather than imposed, in the production of reactive decisions. Communication is multi-dimensional, multi-directional, and irreducible to a single level of interpretation. It is both expressive and instrumental, and reflexive as well as processing information and producing decisions.

Within the incrementalist approach, communication and simulation have a clear interactive relation: incrementalist systems may be simulated as systems of communication, and communication processes within incrementalism may be simulated specifically. Even in purportedly more comprehensive systems, incremental communication may be simulated. Part of this diversity of possible relations arises from the fact that incrementalism may refer to either descriptions of bounded rationality of planning or specifically designed prescriptions for 'more rational' decision-making, or both. Accordingly, incrementalist simulations in practical policy-making and in educational settings may be constructed for a variety of reasons—as descriptive models, as predictive instruments, and as prescriptive aids to decision-making. Within incrementalism, too simple a separation of informal communication processes and formal planning systems and procedures is not possible, as form and content interact dialectically.

Urban planning and policy-orientated incrementalism

The theorising of incrementalism in the 1950s and 1960s directly affected the development of simulations of incremental planning. These simulations focused on the modelling of urban and policy planning, policy development, and outcomes. Some reproduced the major economic and political dynamics of city development and large-scale land use, as in URBAN DYNAMICS, LUGS and WESTERNPORT COMMUNICATION SIMULATION. These simulate urban planning as either one element of policy-making in a complex pluralist process of urban interests and actors, or the outcome of pluralist dynamics, and thus as a *political* process (Glasson *et al.*, 1971).

These simulations closely relate to incremental simulations of urban dynamics for prediction and policy-making, sometimes constructed as aggregations of margin-dependent consumer or other decisions, as with retail gravity modelling (Cordey-Hayes, 1968). Communication is implicitly structured as diverse and *informed to differential levels of probability and uncertainty* rather than to absolute knowledge. More explicit modelling of *inherently uncertain* information and communication, and the consequent possibilities of planned intervention, were developed through Analysis of Interconnected Decision Areas (AIDA) techniques, and a variety of strategic choice simulations (Friend & Jessop, 1969). In these policy-orientated simulations, knowledge is uncertain in terms of the environment, related fields of choice, and values. Planning and the planner are accordingly reconceptualised as facilitators of communication within interactive networks, as in Power's (1971) reticulism and Friedman's (1969) action-planning, in which 'success will in large measure depend upon his skill in managing interpersonal relations'.

Social planning and organisational incrementalism

Uncertainty in communication and decision-making within planning systems may arise through both the content of planning and the immediate organisational environment. On the first count, the conditions for incrementalism are found *par excellence* in social planning of social services, health and welfare, where the objectives of plans are themselves uncertain. These objectives may be difficult to quantify, as the process of plan production and implementation is characterised by conflicts of interest, moral positions, and values. The SOCIAL SERVICES RESOURCE ALLOCATION GAME uses a modified role-play to simulate resource allocation in a social services department. In the simulation framework, plans arise incrementally from resource decisions, not vice versa. Communication is multi-channelled, multi-levelled, and subject to interpersonal and inter-role influence. The pluralist nature of the role-playing mirrors the qualitative subject-matter to produce an emotional and unpredictable decision process.

In such incremental simulations control over the limits of uncertainty is a common problem for game designers and co-ordinators (Boot & Reynolds, 1983; Hearn, 1983). In the SOCIAL SERVICES RESOURCE ALLOCATION GAME, this is handled by one sub-group, the 'System', which articulates those tangible and intangible factors and constraints embedded in the total system within which role-players operate.

Decrementalism

In recent years, planning and policy-making systems have faced further uncertainty from stringent financial constraints. In particular since the oil crisis of the early 1970s, public sector systems, and especially those of the welfare state, have been subject to a series of cutbacks, of both planned projections and service provision. These developments have considerably disrupted decision-making and communication processes in formal organisations, producing 'decrementalism'—the process of coping with small decreases rather than increases in planning. Decrementalism retains some of the communicative features of incrementalism: it is difficult to predict precise outcomes, and communication, which is reactive, is significant. However, decrementalism is not simply the mirror image of incrementalism: decision-making and communication are not necessarily serial and exploratory, and are certainly not remedial. They are characterised by a hybrid mixture of 'rational' and 'less rational' forms of communication—of 'rational talk' (or 'planning talk') *and* 'crisis talk' (Hearn & Roberts 1976; Hearn 1983). Simulations are ideally suited for reproducing the complexity of communicative patterns of such situations. Simulations can assist in focusing on the *form* of communication, as well as promoting evaluation of communication in systems facing disruption. Indeed the introduction of 'crisis' into simulations is itself an excellent way of learning about communication at various levels of interaction (Saunders, 1983). THE CUTS GAME simulates communication processes in a social services agency faced with demands for cuts in its budget. Difficult choices *between* projects and services are inevitably introduced. As in any rationing resource, limitations may engender uneasy competition between holders of unequal resources. THE CUTS GAME is a mixture of open-ended role-play, more formal gaming procedures, informal communication in 'negotiations', and committee decision-making. Negotiations are conducted 'in private', while final decision-making is completely public. Votes can be weighted to indicate how much a player is willing to risk reputation and influence. This adds a further dimension of political uncertainty into the proceedings, and hastens political processes that might normally develop over a series of meetings during 'no growth'. Under incremental growth there is a good chance that there may be no absolute losers, only winners and those left alone: with decrementalism there will be few absolute winners, some who maintain their position, while the rest are losers. With the prospect of cuts, anxiety may complicate communication and concertina group dynamics. Such processes are facilitated by the game's structure, not to mention the clock. As the deadline for decision is approached, activity is likely to grow more frantic, pointing to the crucial importance of ordering of agendas, in both committees and wider political arenas. To sum up, simulations are useful for understanding communication within short-term planning and policy-making. They may not only highlight the subtlety and reflexivity of such communication; but also assist in displaying more structural characteristics of communication, such as distortion, repression, class and gender domination.

Interactive simulation and middle-term policy formation

Interactive simulation fits in the taxonomy of policy-formation methods as developed by Klabbers (1985). From the point of view of systems theory an interactive simulation is defined as a system consisting of two sub-systems. One sub-system is related to the institutional aspects, the other to the collective structure of the actors (see Figure 19.1).

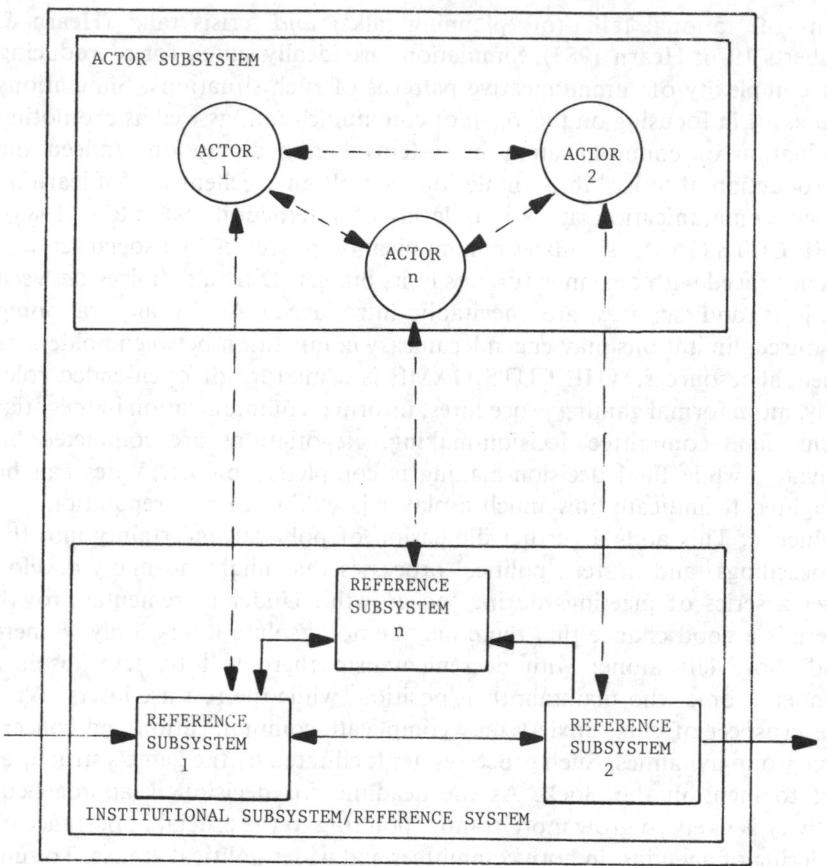

FIGURE 19.1 *Representation of interactive simulation of social system*

The institutional aspects refer to the physical properties of the policy-formation situation. These may be mathematically modelled as with a description of the dynamics of those physical or material aspects. Such a model provides most of the (time-series) data concerning the policy-formation situation. It allows the actors (policy-makers) to implement their decisions, and it feeds back the results or payoffs during the following time increment. During interactive simulation sessions the actors that constitute the actor sub-system are involved in negotiation processes, i.e. meaning-processing and communications, in order to establish a long-term policy and to adjust it according to the results of short-term policy decisions that have been implemented via the institutional sub-system. Thus interactive simulation reinforces a switching of perspective, from a reference mode to a self-reference mode of steering and vice versa. The actors are forced to ask themselves continuously: 'What do we have at hand?' With interactive simulation both modes are linked together and synchronised as the simulation evolves over time.

Interactive simulation integrates the following approaches:

1. *Systematic generation of an alternative 'path to the future'* (Harman, 1977). A system model adequate to describe the kind of knowledge of the desired future is constructed. When the model describes the recent past satisfactorily it is used to generate alternative futures. The Systems Dynamics Approach is a well-known example of this type.
2. *Collective opinion techniques*. Individual and collective rational and intuitive judgements are acted out over time in the presence of feedback from a system model (Gordon & Helmer, 1966; Gordon, 1974; Helmer, 1981).
3. *Normative search*. This approach deals with the question 'What is it that ought to happen?' (Gordon, 1977).
4. *Conflict and bargaining approach* (Elmore, 1978).
5. *Gaming* (Klabbers, 1985).

During simulations, initially a collective structure emerges that is based on the roles and rules that are activated by the actors. It is interesting to note that such simulations as DENTIST (DENTal health care Interactive Simulation Tool) (Klabbers *et al.*, 1980) and PERFORM (PERsonnel FORMation planning) (Klabbers, 1985) provide good opportunities for studying the switch from a self-reference mode of steering that is dominant during the negotiation rounds, to a reference mode after the consequences of plans and decisions that have been implemented have been fed back via the computerised processes. Actors notice the glimmer of the overall situation of which they are a part because they are confronted with the results of their collective action. However, because of the limited knowledge and the partial view of each actor, consequences repeatedly appear to be counterintuitive. This causes dissonance and frustration, but challenges the conception of reality of the actors as well. During subsequent rounds of negotiations, they communicate with each other to learn to understand the situation and the perspective of the other actors in order to be able to develop a long-term policy that is beneficial both for each actor individually and for all joint actors. However, after many DENTIST sessions these authors conclude that actors only look for a joint effort once it has become clear that there is no single clear winner. At the end of a simulation we have observed that occasionally actors try to tilt the game to collect a huge profit or maybe to satisfy their greed.

Summing up, communication via negotiations tends to limit the scope of actors to short-term incremental gains at the cost of long-term payoffs. Organisational self-closure lures individual actors or groups of players into strengthening their own position (local optimum) by weakening the overall situation of the social system (global optimum). Feedback of the consequences of the policies implemented and the mutual processing of its meaning via communications force the actors out of their internally orientated position (staring at one's navel) to take a boundary position or a reference mode of steering (a helicopter view). This switching of perspective, in combination with a preview of future consequences of current policies, does provide the actors with an opportunity to broaden their scope to a less incremental and more comprehensive view on a longer-time horizon.

Simulations, management and culture

Various types of simulation have been discussed as methods of inquiry, learning tools and vehicles for communication. We have highlighted features of communication and simulation against the background of policy formation. Let us now apply our knowledge and throw on the cloak of the consultant and enter the magic of the management culture. It will be self-evident that simulations can improve the communication capacities of organisations and the competence of managers as policy-makers. Eventually the whole spectacle of managing an organisation may be transformed, especially when simulations are used under operational conditions. We agree that professionals in the field of organisational science, like the operations research consultants (the 'high priests' of yesteryear with their signs and symbols related to Linear Programming and queuing methods) are being rapidly succeeded by a new generation of young 'wizards' brandishing their specific sign systems and symbols of information technology and software engineering. We are entering the bright new era of the information society, and many see a challenging mission ahead of them. Management simulations, coupled with optimisation and planning methods, like linear programming, data-base management, spread sheets, etc. are heralded as decision support systems and management support systems. And every manager who for the sake of his/her image has a microcomputer on his/her desk, had better listen to the new breed of sorcerers otherwise s/he runs the risk of losing constitutive power! What manager can neglect management and decision support systems when it is the convention that managers take responsibility, make decisions and, more generally, constitute the rules of the game called 'managing a company'? Don't they need all the support they can get to steer the enterprise through rough seas? Managers typically consider themselves the referees in such a game and they derive from it their (constitutive) power. Goodin (1978: 285) points out that such power depends on the conventions and rules of the 'game':

> appealing to a convention, one must necessarily be evoking a fiction, for a convention is by its very nature arbitrary. Some alternative might be more attractive (useful, amusing, stable, etc.) than others. But it is not truth that leads us to choose one over another. Once a convention is concluded, of course certain propositions can have derivative truth value within the context of the system of rules thereby established.

However, a big problem is rapidly emerging; the rules of the real-life game called 'management' are changing and managers older than 30 years of age do not understand one another's rituals and communication codes.

These rituals refer to conceptual schemata for 'coming to grips with complex sets of natural facts'. These schematising rituals form the basis of social construction of reality. But making legitimate social constructions of reality is a political question. As Goodin points out, the primary mechanism through which schematising rituals exert political influence is language itself. It will become apparent that the linguistic schemata and rituals that go with support systems, mentioned above, will have a powerful political impact. High-level computer languages, and concepts like 'relational data-base management', 'knowledge base', 'object-oriented language', 'process-oriented language', 'inference machine', decision support systems, and expert systems form the sophisticated language for constructing a brand new reality for management.

An era of new technology demands that the manager enters the company with the box containing the tiny microcomputer. Most managers are not yet aware of the long-term impact of the package they have bought. Via the schematising rituals that make those small machines run, the constitutive power of managers is gradually being tested, as conventions, rules and the social construction of reality shift. As most companies depend on computers for processing vast amounts of data, older managers especially may be caught in a social and technological trap. If they do not understand the schematising rituals related to computers and various kinds of support system, they may well lose their grip on the conventions and rules of the game and consequently lose their constitutive power. From this point of view simulations, like the ones discussed above on pp. 238–44, are worthwhile because participants, such as managers, can learn a lot about their actions in more or less hypothetical circumstances that are enactments of real management situations with the assistance of decision support systems. Through communications they are invited to test their reference and self-reference mode of steering and perhaps seek some improvement of competence. Managers and other potential users may become familiar with the linguistic schemata, and the social construction of reality in which support systems are embedded. Simulations, like DENTIST, PERFORM and many others, enable policy-makers and planners in a playful situation to become acquainted with the schematising rituals of consultancies of software houses, who as information analysts, system designers and software engineers constitute a new breed of young wizards. The playfulness of games and simulations, and thus the fun in playing a game, may indeed violate the sacred and consequently serious image of the general manager who gets down to business and epitomises Weber's work ethic. Therefore, to be less pretentious, we advise the use of simulations as initiation rites for middle and upper management to understand and problematise top management culture with its own rites and rules. The rites and rules that form the fabric of collective structures present themselves as enterprises, companies, multinationals, schools, governments (local, regional or national), hospitals, etc., that in turn make up society in its various capitalistic, patriarchal, state and socialist forms. Like many other rites and rituals before them, management cultures remain largely systems of communication between men, especially powerful men. Simulations are a particularly penetrating method of interrogating such communication systems.

20 The manipulation of information in urban planning and simulation

HUBERT LAW-YONE
Technion-Israel Institute of Technology

Introduction

The problem of communication and information control is crucial in the simulation of urban phenomena and yet existing models very rarely address it directly. The use of games to simulate the complexity of urban development has certainly added a new dimension to the technical and partial models that characterised much of early urban analysis. Nevertheless, it should be quite obvious to anyone acquainted with existing exercises that they are severely limited by lack of theory, particularly relating to the role of formal planning as agent of change and guidance. Planning, as we shall attempt to show, is intimately related to communication and control. Hence, the absence of an explicit role for planning in urban development is concomitant with the unstructured way in which communication is usually dealt with.

Meier (1962) has already suggested the fundamental nature of communication in urban development. Yet a formal model incorporating this insight has not been forthcoming. Long (1958) added a new perspective by proposing that the interplay of forces within the city be looked at as an 'ecology of games'. Simulation games of urban development have subsequently matured into a prolific field of study (see, for example, Nagelberg & Little, 1970; Monroe, 1972). Nevertheless, it seems fair to characterise the structural basis of communication in most of these activities, i.e. who communicates, what is communicated and how, and the relation of the parts to a larger social reality, as shaky at best. From the point of view of teaching and research it would seem that a major drawback common to most simulation games is an overly light-hearted and offhand treatment of the function of planning. Even specific games that intentionally relate to planning (e.g. Wynn, 1985) present only its professional or bureaucratic aspects. Urban planning is condensed into the actions of a role called 'planner' who is then pitted against several other roles in a struggle of wills for approving and carrying out various planning proposals. Obviously, the manner in which planning is incorporated into the game is contingent upon the way planning is theoretically explained. We shall see how different approaches lead to different types of simulation game, each having serious implications for the nature and structure of communication within them.

Conceptions of urban planning and communication structure

In order to incorporate urban planning into a simulation it is necessary to have a clear idea of what is meant by this elusive concept. The *technical* view of planning sees it as an attempt to integrate specialised knowledge in the drawing up of a physical plan in which land is allocated to various uses, transportation networks rationalised and services located. The *bureaucratic* view of planning sees it as part of local government administrative decision-making in which civil servants set rules and regulations for developers and the general public concerning the use of land and buildings. The *political* view of planning sees it as the intervention of the state in determining the spatial expression of class-based conflicts. It is viewed as part and parcel of local politics and as an important tool in the redistribution of resources among competing institutions.

The simulation of an urban system will obviously take different forms depending upon which aspect we wish to emphasise. Nevertheless, since there is some truth in each perspective, trying to construct a simulation game that contains the essential elements of all of them becomes a cardinal problem. Looked at in a wider perspective, there are three different approaches to defining urban planning, each having a specific implication for constructing the basic model on which a simulation game can be patterned. We shall examine these approaches in turn and analyse their respective implications. It will be seen that the key areas in which they can be seen to differ relate to the issues of communication and information control.

The *pluralist* approach looks at planning as simply one of many social institutions or activities of special interest groups. Decisions are made and resources distributed in society as a result of forces exercised by these groups and their *ad hoc* coalitions.

> Power is said to be distributed in a diffuse way so as to guarantee that no one group can dominate any particular segment of society. Different groupings of individuals align themselves in various combinations according to the issues. If a particular interest threatens to gain the upper hand, opposition groups will emerge to challenge the powerful group, and thus the equilibrium will be maintained (Kirk, 1980: 57).

Dunleavy (1980) identifies three central themes associated with this perspective. First, the polity is seen to have a poorly developed ideology and to be lacking a separate identity. It operates in an environment of strong external influence and is controlled by politicians mainly involved in achieving an electoral majority. Second, there is an assumption that public opinion is highly effective in bringing about changes in policy. Third, since it is those people with an interest in the outcome of a policy decision who become politically active, political activity then faithfully reflects the amalgam of interests in society. Furthermore, since the central polity is weak and plays no independent role, the political outcome will be a balance of forces reflecting the sum total of interests in the community.

This approach has perhaps an inherent appeal at least partly because of an implicit egalitarianism and apparent freedom of choice. It jibes well with free-market theories and the disjointed-incremental mode of planning. The key ideas that are essential for a model based on this approach are: *fairness* (in competition); *balance* (between different groups or classes) and *diversity* (i.e. many entities having legitimate claims on the market).

The second approach is often termed the *managerialist* approach. Several studies (such as Rex & Moore, 1967; Pahl, 1975) have put forward the view that the socio-spatial system is largely determined by the actions of 'urban managers' that play the role of social gate-keepers. These have been identified as housing department officials, estate agents, private landlords, social workers, planners and so on. These key decision-makers make their impact on the urban system by acting as mediators between the demands of the population and need for access to scarce resources resulting from a privatised economy. Managerialism is closely associated with *corporatism* which also sees a small number of hierarchically ordered, non-competitive units representing interests and recognised (if not created) by the state.

This approach has been faulted for lacking both theoretical substance as well as practical policy implications. Furthermore, by looking exclusively at the 'middle dogs' as autonomous arbiters of conflicting demands, the whole question of wider structural interests (rather than purely administrative ones) is neglected.

The third approach may be termed the *political economy* approach. It has its theoretical foundations in a neo-Marxist interpretation of urban phenomena (Castells, 1977; Harvey, 1973; Dear & Scott, 1981). Spatial phenomena are seen as part of social relations stemming from the prevailing mode of production. The capitalist system is based on an endemic conflict between opposing social classes inherent in the economic order. In modern societies, this conflict is mediated by the state which serves to perpetuate the system. This basic structure is reflected in various contradictions that repeatedly have to be faced. Urban planning is seen to be the tool of the state in its attempt to regulate the anarchy of the private market and to ensure the reproduction of the basic conditions for capitalism while minimising social disruptions. The manner in which the city develops, including its spatial aspects, then, reflects this three-way (state, capital and labour) interaction in the inherent contradictions.

The limitations of the present chapter do not permit a detailed analysis of the relative merits of these different approaches. What interests us are the conceptions of communication implied in each perspective since these are crucial to the practical problem of representation in a simulation model.

The structure of communication in the urban system

The various conceptions of the nature of urban planning have very different implications for constructing simulation models containing planning as an essential element. The key issues that have to be solved when trying to set up a gaming simulation are:

1. *Decision foci*: Who or what are the autonomous decision-makers (players)? What do they stand for and what is the theoretical basis for their determination?
2. *Communication structure*: What are the rules of interaction? What are the permitted (meaningful) actions? What are the interpretations to be placed on joint consequential actions?
3. *Information units*: What are the items of information? What do they represent and how to concretise the transactional units?

The definition of the players is crucial to the game. These roles are extracted out of a great many functions in reality and by concentrating on them we highlight what we consider to be the most powerful determinants of history. Obviously, a game proposing to simulate a city that is composed of several prospective, autonomous homeowners will differ in important respects from one involving government agents, landowners and finance institutions. Furthermore, the relative number of players assigned to each role also determines their (assumed) weight in swaying decisions. In short, we need a sound theoretical base for assuming that these are in fact the key roles and such is their relative importance.

The next consideration is how to represent the range of meaningful acts open to each player, how those messages which these acts represent are transmitted between each player and the defining of the contingent outcomes of several acts in terms of gains and losses between players. Again, this communication structure is a direct reflection of our theory of how the important decisions are in fact made in real life.

Finally, the outcomes have to be translated into transactions. The units of these transactions are highly significant indicators of what in our opinion are the most valued items in society. Thus, whether it is money, or prestige units or power units, they all make statements concerning our perspective of the real world. The more abstract these units are, the more difficult it also becomes to concretise them.

The various conceptions of urban development under planning have rather different implications for the form and content of simulation games. How the different approaches described above relate to the three key areas in their design are summarised in Table 20.1.

TABLE 20.1 *Approaches to planning and their implications*

Approaches	*Nature of decision foci*	*Nature of communications*	*Nature of information*
Pluralism	Large number, *ad hoc* coalitions	No special role, amorphous structure	No value on information except for organising coalitions
Managerialism	Small number, key roles 'mediators'	Hierarchical structure, top-down	Access to information highly controlled
Political economy	Capital, labour and state	Complex interactions	Multiple form, values to ideology

It is hence obvious that different approaches of incorporating planning into urban development call for different forms of simulation games. The traditional method of setting up players from anecdotal or circumstantial evidence, with communication being allowed to develop in a highly unstructured fashion, and with unconstrained access to information in play, is simply no longer adequate if we wish to simulate a more complex reality.

The reality that presented us with a challenge was urban development in Israel within its formal and informal planning systems.

The Israeli planning structure

The problem of defining the decision foci, i.e. the key players in the system, is a complex one. Although there is a formal statutory system of physical land-use planning based on a comprehensive law that was adapted with little change from the British colonial law, Israel has created a parallel system of pragmatic action-orientated planning by powerful quasi-governmental entrepreneurial bodies which often bypass the formal system. Thus, whereas if the formal process of urban planning were to be the only focus, it may have been sufficient to boil down the key players to Officialdom (the state) and the General Public (labour); if how things really get done is to be simulated then it becomes imperative to include the third sector of Entrepreneurs (capital).

The problem of communication structure and information exchange stands out as a key indicator of the effectiveness of the planning structure. A recent study (Alexander *et al.* 1983) showed that the communication pattern between the state and the public via the formal system was entirely different from that between the state and the entrepreneurial sector. Whereas the former was characterised by tightly controlled information both from the state and towards it, in the latter communication was relatively unconstrained and co-ordinated. One part of planning is concerned with an intricate structure of plan preparation, deposit, approval, appeals, issuance of permits, inspections, variances, payment of deposits and fees, and so on, all of which puts a premium on information especially concerning how the system operates.

The second, less visible part of planning has to do with internalised information exchange. Lawyers, agents and representatives of large companies not only have easy access to specialised information because of their position but also sit on planning committees and make the decisions. The exchange of information between these key figures and the political echelon takes place informally and is used to co-ordinate actions and to smoothen the implementation of large-scale projects. Furthermore, it was observed that much of the formal planning system's day-to-day operations was in what Roweis (1981) terms 'the pre-politics processing of political information'. This refers to a wide range of bureaucratic work in anticipation of, in response to or in order to forestall political disputes or confrontations. This preparing of the agenda ahead of time gives the state control of information and outcomes.

The communication pattern between the entrepreneurial sector and the public is very muted. This is in keeping with the interest of the former to remain in the background and let the state be proxy for planning. The information link to the public is thus pacifying in nature and almost entirely restricted to advertising and public relations.

To summarise, a close look at the Israeli planning structure shows a complex but patterned decision-making structure that cannot be accounted for by traditional simulation games based on a pluralist approach. The key feature of this structure is in the communication patterns between the foci representing the major interests in society.

Communication: Towards a simulation agenda

Wynn (1985) has already noted the apparent disparity between the 'decision-centred' paradigm and the 'political economy' paradigm in planning studies. Following Faludi (1980), he then proposes the case-study approach to constructing simulation games as a viable compromise. However, a close look at all seven simulations presented shows that, on the one hand, the definition of roles is very *ad hoc* and anecdotal, and that, on the other hand, communication in all the games is idealised, i.e. it is both unstructured and above board. Surely presenting reality, especially the Israeli case which can be surmised to be perhaps representative of many state-controlled economies, in such a simplistic fashion may not only be a poor simulation but also risks transmitting a dubious ideology?

The challenge, it seems, is in coming to grips with the elusive nature of communication and representing it in concrete form so that it can be a valid subject for analysis and change.

Drawing a distinction between instrumental and communicative action, the centrality of the latter for planning has been recognised. Forester (1980) has shown how the 'pragmatic norms of communication' (Habermas, 1970) may be violated at different levels. The norms of comprehensibility, sincerity, legitimacy and truth can be violated at the face-to-face level, the organisational level and at the political-economic level. These distortions of communication may be experienced, as proposed by Forester, in the following ways: at the face-to-face level by ambiguity, deceit, out-of-context meaning, and misinformation; at the organisational level by public exclusion via jargon, conflict of interests between organisation and client, unresponsiveness and professional dominance, withholding of information, obscuring of responsibility and misrepresentation of needs; at the political-economy level by mystification, misrepresentation of the public good, lack of accountability and the obscuring, withholding or misrepresentation of public policies. For example, how does one deal with the drop-out of the disenfranchised? How can the game be kept sufficiently interesting for those whose power has been negated and yet make the model realistic? If the only way to beat the system is to cheat, should this be allowed? To what extent is playing a simulation game a means of teaching someone to come to terms with a system (which may in his or her view be inherently immoral)?

Communication, or the 'shaping of attention', being a primary function of planning, the above distortions become a fundamental feature to be addressed in any simulation. However, our conception of communication includes both the controlled or distorted system and the co-ordinated and internalised system. The first would perhaps characterise the pattern between the state and the public (and to a certain extent between capital and the public); the second is, however, characteristic of the relations between the state and capital. This co-ordination and mutually supporting form of communication between these two powerful interests, which is to a large extent disguised crudely or subtly by ideology, also needs to be taken into account in order to capture the complexities of planned urban development. All the various forms of communication are present and operative simultaneously and together constitute the complex structure which gives the planned system its vitality.

To sum up, the prospective designer of a more stimulating simulation game faces three challenges. First, he/she needs to incorporate planning as a structural reality. Planning should be concretised as something more than simply preparing plans. It should be shown to represent the way in which urban land and spatial form are shaped by the clashing interests of major social forces. Second, he/she needs to make explicit and to formulate a theoretically sound method for determining the key roles of the simulation game. The identification of 'players', their range of decisions and their relative power have to be justified by confronting theory with reality. Third, he/she must represent communication as a key feature of structure and dynamics. The different forms of communication between the roles, including all types of information exchange, manipulation and distortion, have to be formalised. Information itself has to be recognised as a resource and has to be accepted as one of the key values involved in transactions.

Simulation gaming is an extremely powerful tool not only for the analysis of urban phenomena but also for comprehending and changing reality. It is our firm belief that if the essential qualities outlined above could be successfully incorporated into a simulation game this could lead to a more valid and stimulating direction for exposing not only the irrationalities of present urban land-use planning, but also the underlying contradictions of the social system we live in.

21 Media simulations

DANNY SAUNDERS
The Polytechnic of Wales, U.K.
TIM O'SULLIVAN
The Polytechnic of Wales, U.K.
and
DAVID CROOKALL
The Pennsylvania State University, U.S.A.

Media constitute a central component and focus for the study of communication and culture in industrial societies. In its broadest sense a 'medium' is a prerequisite for any form of communication; it may be understood as 'an intermediate agency that enables communication to take place. More specifically, a technological development that extends the channels, range or speed of communication' (O'Sullivan *et al.*, 1983). In recent times 'the media' have come to imply a specific collectivity of processes, forms and practices conventionally defined in terms of their dependence upon technologies and their consequent capacities to communicate with 'mass' audiences. Historically, such an emphasis has shifted and gained impetus, from press and publishing, to cinema and newsreels, radio and television broadcasting. The relations between 'the machines' and 'the mass' have been dominated by images of all-powerful manipulations of passive individuals—the effects tradition. Such themes, the products of a particular set of perspectives on relations between technology, culture and power, have also been evidenced in writing on other media, notably computers and their role within what has become popularly referred to as the 'communication revolution' (for further discussion of these themes see Williams, 1974; Hartley *et al.*, 1985).

Processes of mediation of what are commonly referred to as 'messages', 'meanings' or 'information' are seldom totally transparent in the context of media institutions or everyday interaction. Rarely are they unaffected by that process—by the medium. The relationships involved are constituted by acts of interpretation, distortion and misrepresentation, by selection and censure, as much as they are by 'perfect' or 'clean' communication. A certain kind of inherent simulation is thus fundamental to both consumers and producers of media output, given the nature of the relationships that bring them together. If simulation is no more than a projected version or schematic representation of some or all aspects of an event, process or structure taken to have relevance in 'the real world out there', then simulation is a process which is intimately a part of mass communication. Selected aspects of media production, media texts and media consumption provide fertile resources for the development of gaming and simulations.

At times such simulation can be at a literal, perceptual level—as with a two-dimensional television image that simulates a three-dimensional world of depth. At other times media simulations will be more vaguely identified, as when broadcasted texts attempt to exaggerate and explore aspects of our everyday lives—perhaps the very essence of soap opera, to take but one example. In each instance we identify machine-mediated communication through simulation. We also emphasise that the converse is also possible, in which simulations provide knowledge and experience about the mass media themselves. Such simulations familiarise participants with issues, problems, and processes that are associated with media institutions, media skills and media events.

In this chapter we suggest that simulations may be devised and carried out for two distinct pedagogic objectives. The first involves an applied or pragmatic aim of understanding certain key decision-making processes within media organisations. The second aims to analyse social interaction and interpersonal communication by recreating a situation based on media contexts.

Understanding media through simulations

One major objective of simulations which are based on media issues and organisations concerns the education and training of participants in areas and skills which they cannot directly experience or acquire. If they were placed in real media situations their actions might have catastrophic consequences, even if it were feasible to provide industrial and commercial placements for all interested students. Such ethical, legal and financial constraints make the simulation method a viable pedagogical alternative. As noted by Marshall (Chapter 15), the growth of Communication Studies has implied the need for many more students who are ignorant about the detailed operations of media organisations—but who want eventually to work within them—to gain some kind of relevant knowledge and experience at a more distanced level. Consequently, a popular tactic involves the design of an artificial situation that replicates and perhaps exaggerates a real-life dilemma, process or event within media contexts. Throughout the implementation of such simulations there is the desire to demonstrate media skills, and to illustrate theoretical debates about mass communication (for a discussion see Porat, 1987).

Two well-known examples are FRONT PAGE and RADIO COVINGHAM. In FRONT PAGE participants become sub-editors who have to decide what (already written) stories go on the front page of a daily newspaper. They do, however, compile the headlines, and there is a deadline that has to be respected. This could theoretically be played by one individual, but it is best completed by a group of people who represent a team of journalists. Consequently, much interpersonal communication takes place between players. In RADIO COVINGHAM the stage is that of radio broadcasting rather than newspaper editing, and again a group of participants has the task of working to a deadline on a media production: in this case a 10-minute programme of news, views and interviews.

More recently, CHOOSING THE NEWS has developed this theme of newspaper editing. Participants work in groups of two or three, and have to edit make-believe stories where paragraphs can be deleted and/or reorganised. They also have to select appropriate headlines from a list of possibilities already provided, and the same applies to photographs and captions that may accompany the edited stories. Although five stories are available, editorial teams may want to exclude one or more from the front page. Their editorial decisions will depend on their perceived roles which are prescribed at the beginning of the session: for example, there may be a commitment to journalistic integrity and the publication of the truth, come what may, or they may simply be committed to the boosting of sales for a large newspaper chain, and by whatever means possible. CHOOSING THE NEWS is a detailed and well-presented simulation package, but lacks the creative ‘sparkle’ of editorial work where, for example, headlines are made up rather than selected from a list, and stories are modified in many more ways than the simple deletion or rearrangement of selected paragraphs. There is also the very real danger of participants being overwhelmed by the sheer amount of information provided.

Still with the print media, THE SALE OF A NEWSPAPER involves groups of five or six players, who take on the roles of civil servants having to advise a government minister about which potential owner a paper, the

Daily Telegram, should be sold to. When such sales take place—as with *The Times* and the *Observer* in 1980—the British government has become increasingly involved. This is partly because of its general responsibility for national mass communication forms, and through the role of the Monopolies Commission which attempts to ensure balance and diversity of newspaper ownership in the United Kingdom. As the participants' instructions state:

> We are not trying to make the exercise like the real thing, nor discover how far you can initiate what you think is the behaviour of typical civil servants! Rather we want to face you with the issues about ownership of the media by asking you to choose between some concrete alternatives.

Whereas the first three simulations mostly address the skills and decisions of media production, the last tackles more topical, theoretical and political issues associated with mass communication in society—in this case, the macro issues of ownership and control.

Another simulation/game raises other important conceptual issues that are associated with the analysis of media texts. THE BRAND X GAME focuses on advertising as communication and asks participants to plan and produce a full-page advertisement that is suitable for a newspaper or magazine. The organisers' notes state that the emphasis of the game is on the proccss of advertising, but even so there is the obvious danger of this becoming an exercise in artwork rather than Communication Studies. Participants are asked to work in groups of four to seven, with one player being elected or appointed as campaign director. They have to decide on the product image, a brand namc, the packaging, the price and the target market. This is then followed by the drafting of the advertisement from a range of pre-supplied materials. After the deadline (of two hours) has passed, groups evaluate one another's final advertisements, but are then encouraged to consider more general issues of communication that are associated with media advertising.

This is a game that succeeds in merging experiential learning with the identification of academic concepts that are popular within media analysis (see Dyer, 1982). Important links can be made with such concepts as *anchorage* (where advertisement images tie down meanings for the reader of the text) and *intertextuality* (where advertisements refer to other advertising images and slogans that are presumed to be familiar to target audiences). Similarly, the experience of producing an advertisement emphasises the importance of *ideology* where the finished text plays on and uses the 'popular' assumptions of a particular society, and the dominant *stereotypes* within that society. Other concepts likely to be illustrated during debriefing are *interpollation* (where media products actually position the reader in a certain way so that they virtually become the image that the advertiser wants) and *mode of address* (where the language of advertising is analysed according to the style and content of an advertiser's approach to its reader—e.g. the excessive use of pronouns). All of these concepts can be introduced throughout debriefing, but with reference to the concrete productions that BRAND X GAME groups have created. Discussion will inevitably raise more theoretical issues about media and society, and the relations between mass communication and individual subjectivity.

With reference to television, by far the most impressive simulation is WHAT'S NEWS, which is designed to give college students a practical understanding of the ways in which television news is produced and constructed in the United States. The actual simulation involves three groups of participants which represent three television networks, and resembles a game format in that points can be won over a number of rounds; success is measured in terms of each group's ability to select newsworthy items from a wide range of alternatives, thereby increasing its national ratings through audience viewing. From this basis WHAT'S NEWS introduces roles and asks producers and reporters to prepare and present a broadcast based on their selection of news items. Additional decisions involve budgeting and allocation of camera crews to various geographical areas. The beauty of WHAT'S NEWS is that it combines simulation and game themes with detailed back-up based on *case studies* which provide factual illustration of newsworthiness. Consequently, participants can easily draw parallels between their simulation activity and real media dilemmas concerning choice of news items; thus the simulation is both highly relevant and factually accurate.

News is a central feature of media production, and news institutions have inspired a number of media simulations. The major problem with such simulations, including WHAT'S NEWS, is that the news items which participants have to edit are old, second-hand and out-of-date. NEWSIM has been designed to overcome this problem. This simulation is based on raw, unedited information which has not yet appeared in newspapers, radio or television. It involves tapping one of the real news sources, i.e. the press agencies' radio transmissions, which are used by media throughout the world. News items are thus obtained in the classroom at the very same time as they appear on teleprinters within the newspaper offices and broadcasting studios. Students then have the exciting task of comparing their own edited production with a 'professional' end product which deals with the same information. We should state, however, that NEWSIM requires special equipment in order to pick up RTTY (radioteletype) short-wave transmissions—this is likely to prove costly for most teachers and trainers.

Moving into the area of cinema production, THE FILM INDUSTRY asks participants to divide into two groups which can be labelled Production and Distribution. The former has to compile a plausible proposal for a new film that they want to make, while the latter has to decide on that proposal's feasibility as a plausible business venture. The simulation requires participants to attend a meeting, where detailed arguments develop between the two groups. If the proposal is accepted then contracts have to be drawn up and signed. One drawback in this simulation is that the Production group has a more interesting, exciting and demanding task—to produce something fairly sophisticated before the Distribution group meets. But it is an exciting and intriguing workshop for any student of media, or even the film fan. Participants have to decide on a film topic, the plot, the stars, the directors, and so forth. They also have to encounter elementary business concepts—such as production costs, potential sales, marketing, and the potential for later spinoffs. This is an exercise that ultimately asks participants to reconcile artistic and creative ideas with business values, and provides hours of debate based on enthusiastic research carried out beforehand. Consequently, it is not so much a simulation that asks people to learn the skills of film-making *per se*, although it undoubtedly develops knowledge about the intricate workings of the film industry.

All of the simulations/games mentioned so far provide vicarious experience about media institutions, production skills and mass communication issues. They are also all characterised by group discussion and activity, and involve a fair amount of group organisation and decision-making. It should be emphasised that an integral part of all such scenarios involves a basic concept in the study of communication—the concept of the *gatekeeper* (White, 1950). With gatekeeping certain information is let through while other material is either delayed or rejected. This is a simplistic interpretation of the editing process which fails to account for multiple keepers, rival news sources, and organisational constraints surrounding news agencies. None the less, gatekeeping can be viewed as synonymous with the process of filtering in information-flow models of communication, but with the addition of decision-making variables to the chemical analogy of 'a filter'.

Simulations clearly provide a relatively new and refreshing way of introducing media education to students who are also involved with television, radio, film and print production. Having said this, it is perhaps disappointing when so little mention is made of communication issues associated with group activity itself, and of the many conflicts, frustrations and rewards that can be experienced by people when teamed together for any production task.

The study of communication does after all involve other perspectives that extend and complement discussions of media—for example, culture, interaction and language. Emerging themes and interests focus on power relations, social skills, group conflict and decision-making—amongst many others. Fortunately, it is possible to use simulations within such a broad range of teaching, but again with the focus on media. This time, however, a media simulation is only a vehicle that allows participants to reach some other objective. It is here that a separate category of media simulations emerges: these generate *interaction* within make-believe media contexts, and have as their major objective the analysis of groupwork. Instead of emphasising media skills and products, we now wish to highlight the dynamics of social relations within organisational contexts.

Analysing interaction through media simulations

In our experience, most students who join a Communication Studies course are primarily interested in interaction, journalism, broadcasting and film production. The importance of interpersonal communication is emphasised, as well as the rapid development of technology associated with mass communication and media institutions.

It therefore becomes feasible to use the platform of media for the discussion of other aspects of communication, simply because students have experience of, and interests in, such productions as advertisements, soap operas and films. Katz & Lazarsfeld (1955) and Lewin (1947) first recognised the importance of everyday face-to-face interaction between audience members who, amongst other things, talk about their interpretations of information that was originally conveyed via mass communication. Media simulations now become much more of an active process that is dynamic and constantly changing: a media producer's idea of reality, and the eventual product based on the dramatisation of that idea, is not then taken as a verbatim report by an audience. Instead a media text will have a number of meanings or readings for a variety of audience members who are engaged within negotiation processes (Morley, 1980). There will not always be one simulation experience for all audiences exposed to the initial mediated material. Indeed some audiences will never see the information broadcast—at each stage in the chain the 'message' is open to reinterpretation, especially when opinion leaders are involved.

When discussing such social psychological issues as persuasion, role-play, and socialisation, all of which are integral topics within the analysis of interpersonal communication and social interaction, a wealth of examples can be selected from television, radio, cinema and newspaper contexts. Simulations and games that focus on media, but for the reason of analysing groups in action, thus prove popular in this respect.

One example is TAFFS PIT, which focuses on a crisis within a television soap-opera production about a small Welsh community. The programme has been a long-running success but is now declining in popularity because of the introduction of a new soap-opera called 'The Chalfonts'. Furthermore, two of the stars of the production have recently been involved in scandals, as revealed and amplified by various newspapers. The simulation exercise involves a boardroom meeting between five people associated with the serial: two central actors, the script writer, the director and the producer. The producer wants to sack the two central actors who have been attracting such bad publicity, and also seeks a new image for the programme.

It does not take much imagination to see parallels between 'Taffs Pit' and real television soap operas (e.g. *Coronation Street* in Britain and *Dynasty* in the United States). Assuming that soap operas really are as popular as the ratings suggest, the exercise allows for generalisation from previous television viewing experience. The major objectives of the simulation are not so much in asking students to consider the intricate politics associated with the production and marketing of a television programme —although this is a popular area for discussion in debriefing. Instead, the onus is on dramaturgy, persuasion, interpersonal conflict, and group decision-making. Aspects of body language and non-verbal communication are appraised by observers of the simulated boardroom meeting, and an audition session prior to the simulation asks participants to consider effective and influential acting skills that are then observed and assessed by the entire group. In this way perspectives on interpersonal communication are introduced and analysed through a simulated crisis within a media context.

It must be said, however, that TAFFS PIT can too easily degenerate into play-acting of the players' favourite soap-opera characters. It is worthwhile returning to Jones's (1974–5) concern about his own media simulations. Participants' instructions advise caution about play-acting within the prescribed roles. Instead players are asked to be themselves as much as possible in order to appreciate fully the objectives of the simulation, which are to introduce issues and dilemmas that confront media practitioners during their everyday business of meeting deadlines. If participants 'ham it up' by overdramatising a role, e.g. by imitating the behaviour of a famous media personality, there is little chance of achieving the original simulation objectives. Instead the situation becomes an exercise in theatre, rather than media.

Another media simulation moves towards the micro issues of interaction and social relations—in this case, the social psychology of interpersonal conflict, co-operation, and leadership. In THE WELSH COMMERCIAL TELEVISION STATION participants represent television departments within a media company that is faced with strong rivalry and financial cuts. The simulation is again of a boardroom meeting, but where the distribution of next year's spending among the drama, film, sport, news, wildlife, and comedy departments has to be decided. It is worth noting that with such a competitive simulation the danger of play-acting was superseded by the danger of some participants getting carried away with their role-play. Some students found the exercise disturbing in that they experienced too much involvement and identification with the roles that they, and others, were acting out. Indeed, for some of the time they appeared to have become the role, rather than to have played it. Over-involvement in media simulations is a common problem, simply because everyone has experience of, and opinions about, media programmes and programming.

The majority of our discussion has addressed the most popularly analysed media—newspapers, radio, television and cinema. We should also emphasise a relatively new variation on the theme of media: the advent of computers within the home, office or school (especially with reference to the development of computer games and word-processing facilities). Such communication is machine-mediated and the wide-scale marketing of identical hardware and software within technologically wealthy societies implies a sophisticated level of mass communication.

Accordingly, some discussion should address aspects of computer-based interaction within our overall review of media simulations. It is closely linked with the analysis of interaction through media simulations, but this time the focus is more on the individual's relations with the machine, rather than with other people through groupwork. The reader is referred to Versluis *et al.*'s review (Chapter 5), which examines computerised simulations in more detail.

Many computer simulations are concerned with business ventures, and rely on machine-mediated communication in order to develop knowledge about business skills and commercial organisations; this is often achieved through the widespread marketing of various computerised simulations. However, these are often designed for single-player use which prioritises the machine–operator relationship: as such they rapidly lose their appeal and are destined to follow the same faddish path as the video game (Saunders, 1987). Fortunately it is relatively easy to adapt such packages so that they can be used within intergroup contexts rather than in isolation—MANEDES is but one example of such adaptation.[1]

Conclusions

The concept of media has been discussed in a number of ways and with reference to a wide variety of contexts, ranging from the teaching of production skills through to the development of interpersonal communication within media contexts. It has been argued throughout that simulations and games prove invaluable when linked with media issues—partly because there is no other way by which experience can be gleaned about the 'real' media world, and also partly because the wealth of knowledge that we all have about mass communication provides endless fuel for debate within group contexts. Whilst McLuhan (1964) may have overstated the case when he wrote that the medium was the message, we might tentatively and clumsily suggest that simulation situates messages about media. With the growing interest about media production within schools and colleges—not to mention the rapidly expanding area of media production as a leisurely pursuit rather than an academic one—simulations have a promising future. As a final comment, the advent of interactive video will have exciting implications for the development of simulations which allow for communication between geographically dispersed participants by way of media networks. At the present moment no such simulation exists, but it can only be a matter of time before cable and satellite technology introduces such a new development in group interaction.

Note to Chapter 21

1. There are a great many published computerised simulations that give participants a grounding in business and management literacy. Some examples are: THE BUSINESS POLICY GAME; MANSYM IV; MODERN BUSINESS DECISIONS; PAINTOCO; SALES MANAGEMENT SIMULATION; STRAT-PLAN; and UNISIM. For discussions and further examples see Biggs (1986); Bryant & Corless (1986); Fritzsche (1987); Keys (1987); Teach (1987). Many such games, rather than asking a single person to make all the decisions, require a number of participants to work in teams, representing company

departments or competing companies. The result is that they have to interact and communicate within groups to reach decisions. Such games thus offer as much fascination for the social psychologist, the ethnomethodologist and other analysts, as they do for the teacher and student of business and management studies. Revealing ethnomethodological analyses of business-game participation are provided by Francis (1987); and Sharrock & Watson (1987).

SECTION FIVE: Discussion

22 Extending the range of experience

CATHY STEIN GREENBLAT
Rutgers University, NJ, U.S.A.

The heterogeneity of the volume

I should have known better. It required little imagination to foresee the extraordinary heterogeneity that would characterise the contributions that make up this volume. Thus I have no excuse for my failure to anticipate the difficulty of the enterprise to which I agreed: to write a concluding chapter in which I would try to note loose ends and to tie together the threads that ran through the chapters that comprise this volume. If you have read the full book, you can appreciate the enormity of the task. Even if you have thus far only sampled selections, it is likely that you have a taste of the whole and that you have seen the diversity of approaches and activities of the contributors, despite their common commitment to address the question of the relationship between communication and simulation.

For some, the relationship is quite straightforward. Richard D. Duke, for example, in Chapter 2, considers gaming/simulation a hybrid form of communication, a language. Echoing the thesis of his widely read volume, *Gaming: the Future's Language* (1974), Duke here describes the differences between more primitive and more sophisticated forms of communication. He also discusses some of the differences between communication in *dialogue* form, as in the lecture-discussion format, and in the *multilogue* form found in gaming/simulations, characterising the latter as follows:

> The [game] construct is all of one piece, and ... has no logical entry or exit point *per se*. This permits the individual to enter into the multilogue from his/her own frame of reference or point of perspective. It permits and encourages a tumbling, ongoing discussion among changing and unstable coalitions who come together as their ideas coincide,

> and quickly break away to form new conversational units. ... In reviewing this model it is important to differentiate between multilogue and many dialogues being conducted simultaneously. Multilogue is the organised simultaneous inquiry into some complex topic; contrast this with a cocktail party which is characterised by many simultaneous dialogues covering a broad array of disjointed subject-matter (Chapter 2).

For Hubert Law-Yone, too, simulation and communication cannot easily be separated into two distinct topics, for the primary concern of the simulation designer is modelling the intricate structure of communication of the social system of interest. In describing land-use planning simulations, for example, he tells us that 'conceptions of communication... are crucial to the practical problems of representation in a simulation model' (Chapter 20).

Most of the authors of the chapters in this volume come to this enterprise from one of two initial camps, and have more of a 'helpmate' perspective. Some began in the simulation field, using or designing simulations in some substantive area or areas. Others' earlier endeavours were in one or another of the branches of the communication field: teaching foreign languages and developing multilingual communication; fostering richer cross-cultural contacts; or training managers, counsellors, or students of communication. I find it striking that it is often difficult to ascertain whether a given author's original 'home' is in simulation or in communication. Rather, those engaged in simulation design or utilisation have learned much from those engaged in communication analysis, while those starting from the communication perspective have discovered the utility of simulations to accomplish their goals and are highly knowledgeable about them. Thus we find such compatible statements as:

> Against this background we present some powerful methods that have the potential to highlight communication processes in social systems in the context of policy-formation and negotiation processes. These methods, by making participants aware of their mutual actions, simulate basic features of past, present, or future social systems (Klabbers & Hearn, Chapter 19).

> But one of the most promising and increasingly popular techniques for encouraging communication in the [foreign language] classroom has proved to be that of simulation/gaming (Crookall *et al.*, Chapter 6).

> Simulation provides a relatively safe way to learn expert counselling

skills, without risk to people seeking counselling on real problems. Simulation also provides the opportunity for expanding counselling skills to new areas of expertise as a form of preparation for real-life situations. Communication and simulation are two fields with the same basic theme of preparing experts with maximum learning effectiveness and minimum danger to either the counsellor or the client (Pedersen & Pedersen, Chapter 11).

The questions, too, are convergent and from both vantage points we obtain at least preliminary answers to such questions as 'What *kind* of communication goes on within a simulation?' (e.g. Francis, Chapter 3; Sigman & Donellon, Chapter 4); 'What kind of *mis*communications may go on in a simulation?' (e.g. Ting-Toomey, Chapter 13); 'What kind of real-world communication can be improved by simulation practice?' (e.g. Crookall *et al*., Chapter 6; Stern, Chapter 18; Noesjirwan & Bruin, Chapter 12). A plethora of such questions are posed here; the answers and examples are tantalising and they pay testimony to the diversity of work that has been done in these fields.

The heterogeneity that characterises the volume's contents is also a function of the differences in the substantive foci of interest to the authors and the differences in the paradigmatic stances they take to these foci and to 'communication/simulation'. The fields include sociology, urban planning, foreign language teaching, counselling, political science, public policy, and many others, and the topics are approached from such perspectives as ethnomethodology, incrementalism, system dynamics, Marxism and positivism.

Finally, I must add that the volume is impressive for the heterogeneity of the contributors' geographic locale. Although the English-language literature in the simulation field is extensive, it is unfortunate that the bulk of it consists of either American-authored writings which largely contain references to work by other Americans, or British writings which largely contain references to other British work. There are exceptions, but they are few in number. This volume is thus also praiseworthy for bringing together scholars and scholarly work not only from the United States and the United Kingdom, but from Israel, the Netherlands, France, Papua New Guinea and Australia.

Indeed, it would be easy to spend the remaining pages simply paying homage to the quality of work done by the authors of the chapters in this volume and to the provocative ideas presented in the summaries presented herein. But I must do more than offer kudos. So let me first offer some

general observations and then a discussion of what I see to be the central theme or motif that runs through the volume.

Some general observations

The paucity of research data

First, I am struck by how little research data is presented in these pages. None of these chapters is a research report, and most of them contain little discussion of their authors' or other scholars' research findings. The reliance on anecdotal reports is problematic in the field of simulation, though the quantity of good empirical data has been increasing (see Bredemeier & Greenblat, 1981; and Wolfe, 1985, for reviews of the evaluation literature; see *Simulation and Games* and *Simulation/Games for Learning* for other research-based papers). The volume as a whole, then, suggests again to me the need for more research to back up our theories and to support our observations about processes and outcomes.

While the chapters contain few findings, they do contain a number of intriguing ideas on which interesting and important research enterprises could be based. I developed the following list of research ideas based on my reading of the chapters:

1. *What is the relationship between the emotional character of the simulation experience and short- and long-term learning?* In Chapter 7, Charles Petranek speculates that 'Whenever there is emotion, learning within a simulation leads to a lasting memory for participants years later'. Many of us who have run simulations can support the contention with anecdotes about students who have returned years later to tell us how well they remember their participation in STARPOWER, BAFA BAFA, BLOOD MONEY, or some other simulation in which they had a powerful emotional experience. We should ask, however, not simply whether they *remember* the experience, but whether the emotional component to the teaching led to long-lasting *learning*.

2. *Where the emotions involved in the learning experience are negative ones (e.g. frustration, anger, fear, threats to self-esteem), is there decreased or increased cognitive learning or attitude change?* (Again, one could add a question about the duration of the learning or change.) Some of the present authors (e.g. John Lobuts & Carol Pennewill, Chapter 14) worry about whether simulations teach too much competition, and whether they generate too much fear, anger and frustration in participants. Several other authors in this volume, however, suggest that these negative emotions may have important learning outcomes. For example, Dennis Sandole (Chapter 9), citing earlier research by Burton (1984), uses Festinger's (1962) notion of cognitive dissonance to argue for the effective role of discomfort in learning and attitude change. Thus, Sandole argues, simulation *may* play a role in facilitating the shift from competitive to co-operative processes. Competition in the simulation may lead to experiences which threaten or contradict self-esteem, and hence lead to dissonance. 'Simulation, therefore, may be relevant to generating, and to exploring the consequences of, dissonance', Sandole concludes, and I hope that he continues to undertake these exciting investigations.

In a similar vein, Jan Klabbers & Jeff Hearn (Chapter 19) argue that when actors in a simulation confront results that appear to be counter-intuitive, they experience dissonance and frustration, which ultimately lead to greater learning.

3. *How do differences in communicative style affect both what transpires during the simulation and individual learning outcomes?* Stella Ting-Toomey (Chapter 13), for example, tells us about communication barriers that arise because of stylistic and value differences when participants from low- and high-context cultures interact in simulations. I do not know of any studies of the impacts of such variations in communication style, however.

Ting-Toomey's list would provide a good starting point for this kind of investigation: how, for example, do simulation process and outcome differ depending upon communication differences in player groups in terms of such factors as: task focus in discussion versus socio-emotional, relationship, climate-building focus in group discussion; degree of directness (or indirectness) concerning intentions and motives in negotiation sessions; degree of self-disclosure concerning feelings and reactions during the debriefing session; confrontational versus conciliatory stance in conflict negotiation sessions; and reliance on verbal or non-verbal tactics in negotiations?

4. *How do simulation experiences alter communication skills?* For such research to be undertaken, the broad concept of 'communication skills' must be broken down to smaller component parts. Both Stewart Marshall (Chapter 15) and Anne and Paul Pedersen (Chapter 11) provide useful guidelines not only for the simulation designer but also for the researcher interested in measuring the impact of simulations in terms of improving communication skills. Marshall's list of skills that communication curricula attempt to impart to students includes the following: receiver skills, including study skills, information retrieval, note-taking; presentation skills, including oral, written, and visual presentation skills; interpersonal communication skills, including interviewing and being interviewed; and skills for working in groups, including participating in and leading groups and running meetings. Anne and Paul Pedersen, too, elaborate on the thesis that simulations are useful for strengthening counselling skills by talking of 'microskills' such as asking questions, paraphrasing, reflecting, interpreting, giving directions, and summarising. This conceptualisation could provide important guidelines to both simulation designers and researchers.

5. *What is the full range of communication skills that simulation participation may foster or expand?* This is, in some sense, a continuation of the previous question. I separate it to make clear that I am here calling not simply for more disaggregation of the large concepts or categories, but for attention to skills that teachers and trainers may not wish to foster but that may be fostered anyway. The 'claims' of simulation aficionados generally concern the creation of greater openness, trust, listening to others and so on. But we must recognise that participation in simulations also gives people safe practice in such communication strategies as bluffing, counter-bluffing, empty posturing, public speaking which relies on hyperbole and rhetoric masked as analysis, and so on. Any 'realistic' representation of the political world, for example, must have space for cheating, putting people off, or denying access. Greenblat & Gagnon (1981: 100) have argued that

> most games, because of the social realities of those who construct them, tend to support conventional, ameliorative, middle-class morality. The good aspects of a system are modeled to teach its virtues and its style. The bad aspects of a system are modeled in order to correct them, and it is known how they should be corrected.

These tendencies are then expanded by operators who also tend to be exponents of liberal morality. We cannot, however, afford to ignore the questions of what lesser-valued (by us, but not by everyone) skills participants develop through participation in simulations.

6. *In what ways does the utilisation of computers in simulations alter classroom communication patterns and dynamics?* In Chapter 5, Ed Versluis, Danny Saunders and David Crookall discuss student co-operation in the sharing of limited computer resources, but also mention instances in which limited access has led to greater hostility and instances in which full access has led to student isolation and fully independent actions. Where is the research into the conditions which foster co-operation versus competition for these scarce items and into the related questions raised in that article? As new computer-aided simulations are designed, it surely would be helpful to know how they might be employed to affect interpersonal dynamics in the ways these authors indicate they can. At this point we only seem to know that there is diversity, but not what the correlates and causes of this diversity are.

7. *How can simulation dynamics and outcomes be better understood by focusing upon different levels of involvement of different participants, and upon different levels of involvement of the same participants at different moments in time?* Several years ago, writing about gaming/simulations for teaching and training, I headed a section 'Unanswered questions'. A sub-section was entitled 'How can we understand the asymmetrical learning experiences of students who participate in the same game?'. In the first part, I urged that researchers focus on the different game roles that participants take, arguing that we should expect students in different structural positions to have different learnings. But I continued as follows:

> The problem of differential learning is compounded when we consider that the participant is really in three simultaneous roles: in addition to playing the simulated role, students are players in a game and students in a class. Those writing about games often ignore the latter two or assume that they are of no importance. Yet either of these may be dominant at any particular time and may seriously affect the learning that transpires. Add to this the effects of peer pressure, and the

> complications in understanding what is happening are magnified further. Teachers and researchers can ill afford to ignore the 'treble role' of players and must try to understand the factors contributing to dominance of one or the other at any given time (Greenblat 1981: 122).

I was thus delighted to find that David Francis's ethnomethodological analysis of game activities (Chapter 3) included attention to this issue. Speaking of the 'double-settinged' character of the simulation game, Francis points to the fact that at the same time as participants must enact their game role, they must pay attention to the organisational/educational context of the game—i.e. to whether they are players or organisers. This double-settingedness creates problems of interaction and communication for participants but, as Francis notes, we do not know the form that such problems take and how participants handle them. The important analytic work being done by Francis himself, but also by other ethnomethodologists in Manchester such as Watson & Sharrock (1987), makes me optimistic that this research will soon move forward.

The reliance on words

My second general observation is that I am struck by the reliance of the authors of these chapters on verbal communication. I have not done a count, but I know that there are very few diagrams in these pages. Graphics are not employed, either to capture the reader's attention or to display relationships more clearly. I would have expected that authors from two fields in which strictly verbal communication in the classroom (i.e. the lecture format or the 'talk-and-chalk' approach as it is called in Chapter 1 of this volume) is criticised, would be more imaginative in their utilisation of graphics in written communication. I believe that just as classroom presentations that contain various types of model (verbal, graphic, mathematical, simulation) are more engaging, so too written presentations, including graphics of various sorts, are both more engaging and more enlightening. At the very least, their inclusion presents a more diverse visual field to challenge the reader and keeps him/her alert. Tufte (1983) has convincingly argued that quantitative information can be much more powerfully communicated through the simultaneous presentation of words, numbers and pictures; surely much non-quantitative information is also more effectively communicated with the aid of graphics.

For those of you who read the last few pages wondering about the relevance of the picture of the two rabbits that appeared earlier in this chapter, the answer is that they are substantively irrelevant. But I hoped they would trigger your curiosity and engage you somewhat more in the prose in search of the explanation of their presence! They are thus relevant in a *process* sense and as examples of what is missing. I am sure that some of the material in the foregoing pages could have been interestingly presented in more imaginative form as well.

Thinking too positively?

I have now spent close to 20 years working in the simulation field. I would not have done so without a strong belief in the value of simulations as tools for understanding, whether in the laboratory or in the classroom. But this volume perhaps suffers from the overly positive tone that tends to be characteristic of published work in most fields. The contributors extol the virtues of simulation for a vast array of projects. We can be inspired by their successes and respectful of their talents of design and development of simulations and of programs for their use. But where are the reports of failure? of disappointment? of seriously troubling issues that press the intellectual and moral capacities of the contributors? I can recall none of the first two. Hubert Law-Yone (Chapter 20) offers the only example of the last that I noted, for it challenges us all to think in a much more complex way about simulation and communication:

> how does one deal with the drop-out of the disenfranchised? How can the game be kept sufficiently interesting for those whose power has been negated and yet make the model realistic? If the only way to beat the system is to cheat, should this be allowed? To what extent is playing a simulation game a means of teaching someone to come to terms with a system (which may in his or her view be inherently immoral)?

Similarly, I worry a bit about the tendency to treat 'communication' in a fully positive way. Here I am concerned not only about the failure noted above to address issues of learning less 'popular' communication skills such as bluffing and lying in such a way as not to be suspected. Rather, I think of the tacit assumption that it is always better to know more, to communicate more fully and openly. Self-disclosure and openness, however, may make it difficult to maintain interpersonal equilibria within social units such as families or work situations. Like it or not, the mythologies that allow some such arrangements to continue require combinations of concealment and openness. This is especially so because not all things that people have to communicate and share are positive; consider the following example from the marital realm:

> sharing feelings means sharing the negative as well as the positive, conflict as well as harmony, rejection as well as acceptance, boredom as well as interest. Since negative feelings, conflict, rejection, and boredom may be unwanted, ignorance may be bliss. A common prop to relationships is the assumption of agreement, and finding out it doesn't exist may bring problems. Thus many people, in urging more communication with their spouses, are really urging more positive communication, rather than full communication of both positive and negative. The conventional wisdom is that most disturbed marriages are afflicted with misunderstandings and misconceptions; what may be more dismaying in an intimate relationship is the existence of bitter *understandings*, when what is bitter is also true (Gagnon & Greenblat, 1978: 254–55).

The master theme

Beyond these general observations I must point to an overall message or theme that for me dominates the book: the enormous power of simulation/communication tools to expand the range of experience of participants. This appeared through all the pages, and I was struck many times by the way in which these tools and techniques permitted people to develop deeper self-knowledge, a more comprehensive set of events and people that make sense, and longer time horizons. I would like to conclude this chapter, then, with a re-emphasis on that message.

First, we see numerous examples of how simulations can permit us to understand ourselves, our capacities, responses, blind sides, and untapped talents. We can try new behaviours, shedding habits or styles we may have come to think of as immutable 'traits', and in so doing alter our behavioural repertoires. With this expanded set of behaviours, we may come to recognise ourselves as much more complex creatures than we had thought we were, and to accept ourselves as having multiple selves rather than one common core identity that is immutable across contexts if we are healthy (see Goffman, 1971; and Gergen, 1977 for the best discussions I know of concerning these topics.) Stuart Sigman & Anne Donnellon show us this in their analysis of simulations as discourse rehearsals (Chapter 4). The power of simulations for this purpose is perhaps most strongly expressed by Marvin Jensen (Chapter 10), when he speaks of how, by

> taking on contrary roles in a simulation, a person can experience type

> transcendence, and move towards greater respect for the complexity of self and others—a perspective which is essential to healthy communication;

and

> the individual can be different things depending on the demands of different interactions. An awareness of the multiple persons within each single body can be fostered through the simulation described in this chapter ... The goal of better communication is served when this and other simulations encourage increased respect for others arising out of deepened respect for self.

A second way in which simulations may expand the range of experiences of participants is through making formerly unacceptable ideas more comprehensible. Several chapters in this book clearly demonstrate how simulations may be helpful in leading people to a questioning of their assumptions—in much the same way that reading Thomas Kuhn's (1970) work often led to examinations of the reader's existing paradigms. For example, Alan Coote & Laurie McMahon (Chapter 17) indicate that their concern is not with the development of communication skills *per se*, but rather with widening the perspectives of managers about communications and organisations so that they can use their communications skills with greater effect in their own environments. They were concerned with the tendency of managers to accept the rational (positivist) view of management and to reject the micro-political perspective, with its emphasis on power, conflict, coalitions and tactics, as not being applicable to the business world. The authors took on the challenge of 'presenting these ideas in a way that they are not rejected out of hand, but are subjected to reasoned analysis and judgement, despite the fact that they initially appear uncomfortable'. Their successes should encourage many others with similar aims of making new or different ideas or paradigms more palatable, or of getting people to see old problems in a new light, to explore the utility of simulations.

Several chapters also document the ways in which people with different backgrounds, values or communication styles may be brought together and, through simulation tasks, develop greater understandings of one another. One of the most frustrating (but ultimately one of the most rewarding) developmental field tests I have ever done with a simulation was in Cameroon, West Africa, in early 1985. My fellow designers of CAPJEFOS (a simulation of village development) and I had arranged a field test at an agricultural training school in Kumba, about two hours from where we were working. A few days before the run was to take place, we drove to Kumba and carefully checked out the facilities, the arrangements for lunch, the number of students to be brought together for the exercise, and so on. It did not occur to us to ask about whether all the participants spoke English, the language in which the simulation materials were written! Hence we were dismayed when we began the day-long session and were immediately informed that half the participants were French speaking; most knew some English but they were not comfortable with it, and contended that they could understand neither us nor their simulation materials (such as role profiles).

Fortunately, two of us spoke some French. We were able to regain enough composure after the shock wore off to offer our introductory remarks and explanations in both languages, and to provide oral translations of the written materials. This slowed things down considerably, but at least we could proceed. The next problem was that participants needed to talk to one another to make the simulation operate. Several 'farmers', for example, were English-speaking but found that they had French-speaking 'spouses' with whom they needed to interact to make decisions. The 'traditional doctor' was French-speaking, and his services were needed by all. And many villagers found that the 'development agents', who offered the possibility of improvements in health and agriculture practices, sometimes did not speak their language, both literally and figuratively. They struggled to understand one another, however, and in most cases they succeeded.

By the time we stopped for lunch, we were exhausted and were concerned that the session was proceeding much more slowly than planned. Our spirits were revived, however, when we heard the exuberance of the regular faculty of the school. They exclaimed that this was the first time they had ever seen the two groups of students (the English-speaking and the French-speaking) interact with one another in anything but a superficial (and sometimes hostile) manner. Challenged by the simulation and by their desire to participate successfully in it, however, students had made the first attempt to overcome the barrier of language difference—an effort we were told continued beyond that day's enterprise.

Too often, members of different cultures have no opportunities to interact, or have encounters which are analysed only with those of 'one's own kind'. Bringing members of different groups together in the context of a simulation, however, presents a rich opportunity for first generating the typical misunderstandings and then for collective consideration of these differences—i.e. for understanding the misunderstandings. These chapters offer several examples of success in utilising simulations to motivate participants to overcome communication barriers between groups. For example, Stella Ting-Toomey's account, mentioned above, of the different behaviours that can be expected of low- and high-context culture members in the same simulation, is illuminating. In an unanalysed encounter, such differences increase the existing sense of difference and misunderstanding; when they emerge in a simulation and those divergent behaviours can be coupled with a discussion and analysis of the differences, however, greater understanding may result.

Similarly, I was intrigued by James Fernandes & Martin Noretsky's descriptions of the impediments to teaching the two disparate groups of hearing-impaired who come together at Gallaudet University (Chapter 8): those who learned American Sign Language from deaf parents, relatives and friends (and for whom English is therefore a second language), and those who learned English as their first language. Fernandes & Noretsky offer a fascinating account of the ways in which they have employed simulations to overcome communication barriers.

This utilisation of simulation can probably be seen most clearly in the contribution by Jenny Noesjirwan and Klaas Bruin (Chapter 12), reporting on their long-term project to employ simulations to reduce prejudice and discrimination. In their balanced discussion of the advantages and disadvantages, the possible pitfalls and the possible benefits of using simulations for both pedagogy and research on intergroup discrimination, they show us how

> By experiencing the differences of culture in an experimental, rather than abstract, setting, the participant has the opportunity to develop insights which can help facilitate communication processes in similar situations in real life later on ...

As a final example, I should point out that Anne and Paul Pedersen (Chapter 11) show how these increased understandings can be useful in improving professional encounters as well as personal ones. Their structured simulations, used with counsellors, manifest for participants not only their own assumptions (which they may not be aware of) but the ways in which different assumptions distort counselling communication across cultural boundaries.

There is another, more general sense, in which I think simulations can be employed to expand the range of experiences that make sense to participants. Like study abroad or internship or apprenticeship programmes, simulations may also serve to open doors, to take people figuratively to new places. Of course they do so less fully than the 'real thing'; spending a day in CAPJEFOS is not equivalent to spending six months in the Peace Corps in an African village, and engaging in underwater search and excavation activities in the MARY ROSE simulation described by Ed Versluis, Danny Saunders & David Crookall (in Chapter 5) is not the same as accompanying Jacques Cousteau on a voyage. Participating in one of the exciting media simulations described by Danny Saunders, Tim O'Sullivan & David Crookall (Chapter 21) may show the participants something about the power and control dimensions of the media world and may help them develop production skills, but the scale is much smaller and many elements of the real-life situation will naturally be omitted. And the long and rich history of the utilisation of business gaming described by James Freeman & Philippe Dumas (Chapter 16) gives us classic examples. In this chapter, we see how simulations in both conventional classrooms and in business training contexts can enhance the acquisition and comprehension of new knowledge and its application through placing participants in realistic settings, increasing the probability of transfer between classroom and job.

But these 'lesser' experiences are far less costly in time and money, can be made available to far more people, and, as the case studies suggest, the simulation experiences can elicit some of the same enthusiasms. As part of a larger learning programme, they also can be extremely effective. Several examples are offered in this volume, including Jan Klabbers & Jeff Hearn's report (Chapter 19) of their experiences with DENTIST and PERFORM, which leads them to say: 'we advise the use of simulations as initiation rites for middle and upper management to understand and problematise top management culture with its own rites and rules'. The advice is based on the authors' sense of these cultures largely as systems of communication between powerful men, and of simulations as particularly penetrating methods of interrogating such communication systems.

Barbara Stern, I am sure, would agree. And I believe she would also agree with my interpretation that Klabbers and Hearn are not using sexist language when they state that 'these are systems of communication between powerful *men*' (emphasis added). Rather this is a descriptive statement about male domination in the corporate world. Stern (Chapter 18) describes her creative utilisation of a range of simulations to help women break into that male domain, by introducing them to the norms present and the skills needed in the male corridors of power. Combining her understanding of the potential of corporate women's networks with the potential of simulations, she shows us how the latter can be used to help bridge the male–female cultural gap in communication by enabling women to try on and try out elements of the male world. The chapter is exciting in that it shows the wide range of communication problems that those not raised in the male culture or schooled in its symbolic structure may encounter. Stern shows us how simulations can help women learn such things as the patterns of social control that males tend to learn in teamed hierarchical structures beginning in childhood; modes of communicating authority (e.g. use of declarative statements, avoidance of 'filler' phrases, tones of command); and charisma-enhancing skills such as public speaking, effective negotiation, and leadership strategies. The network as quasi-classroom thus provides a way to extend the range of experience in the best of ways, serving as a place for the communication of information and as a site to practise utilising the new information and skills in safety.

This volume, then, has succeeded admirably in elucidating the many connections between communication and simulation, providing insights into the ways the two have been integrated in existing endeavours, and offering provocative challenges for those who wish to continue the effort to create one theme.

References

Note: Rather than having two separate reference lists (one for authors and one for games), a system which tends to require some awkward moving back and forth between the two, we decided to reference both authors and simulation/games together. That is, names of simulation/games appear in their respective alphabetic positions among authors' names in the single reference list below.

A-B-Z GAME, THE. Christiansen, K. 1977. See CHRISTIANSEN (1977).

ABELSON, R.P., ARONSON, E., MCGUIRE, W.J., NEWCOMB, T.M., ROSENBERG, M.J. & TANNENBAUM, P.H. (eds) 1968, *Theories of Cognitive Consistency: A Sourcebook*. Chicago: Rand McNally.

ADAMS, D.M. 1973, *Simulation Games: An Approach to Learning*. Worthington, OH: Charles A. Jones.

AGGER, R.E., GOLDSTEIN, M.N. & PEARL, S.A. 1961, Political cynicism: Measurement and meaning. *Journal of Politics*, 23, 3.

AID COMMITTEE GAME, THE. Thomas, O.G. & Clarke, M.F.C. 1970. Oxford: Oxfam.

AIRPORT CONTROVERSY. Jones, K. 1974–5. In K. JONES (1986).

ALBRIGHT, R.J. & ALBRIGHT, L.G. 1981, Developing professional qualities in engineering students. *Engineering Education*, April.

ALEXANDER, E.R., ALTERMAN, R. & LAW-YONE, H. 1983, *Evaluating Plan Implementation: The National Statutory Planning System in Israel*. Progress in Planning Series, Vol. 20, Part 2, Oxford: Pergamon.

ALGER, C.F. 1963, Use of the Inter-Nation simulation in undergraduate teaching. In GUETZKOW *et al*. (1963).

ALIBI. Anonymous. Undated. See CROOKALL (1979).

ALPHA CRISIS GAME, THE. Nesbitt, W. A. 1973. Albany, NY: University of the State of New York.

ALTERNATIVE ENERGY PROGRAMME, THE, Marshall, S. 1981. In MARSHALL (1981a).

ANDERSON, H. & RHODES, N.C. 1984, Immersion and other innovations in U.S. elementary schools. In SAVIGNON & BERNS (1984).

ANDERSON, R.J. 1987, The reality problem in games and simulations. In CROOKALL *et al.* (1987).

ANDERSON, R.J., HUGHES, J.A. & SHARROCK, W.W. 1985, *The Sociology Game*. London: Longman.

ARONSON, E. 1980, Persuasion via self-justification: Large commitments for small rewards. In Festinger (1980).

ARONSON, E. 1984, *The Social Animal* (4th edn). New York: Freeman.

ASHER, J. 1982, *Learning Another Language through Actions: The Complete Teacher's Guidebook* (2nd edn). Los Gatos, CA: Sky Oak Productions.

ASSASSIN. McLellan, V. 1985. See MCLELLAN (1985).

ASUNCION-LANDE, N.C. (ed.) 1978, *Ethical Perspectives and Critical Issues in Intercultural Communication*. Falls Church, VA: Speech Communication Association.

ATKINSON, J.M. & DREW, P. 1979, *Order in Court: The Organisation of Verbal Interaction in Judicial Settings*. London: Macmillan.

ATKINSON, J.M. & HERITAGE, J. (eds) 1984, *Structures of Social Action: Studies in Conversation Analysis*. Cambridge: Cambridge University Press.

AUNT SADIE'S GIFT. Ryberg, C. & Versluis, E. 1982. Ashland, OR: Southern Oregon State College.

AUSTIN, W.G. & WORCHEL, S. (eds) 1979, *The Social Psychology of Intergroup Relations*. Monterey, CA: Brooks/Cole.

AYYAR, K. 1986. Can engineers be managers? If not, what can be done? *Proceedings of the 1986 Engineering Conference*. Adelaide.

AZAR, E.E. & BURTON, J.W. (eds) 1986, *International Conflict Resolution: Theory and Practice*. Brighton, Sussex: Wheatsheaf; Boulder, CO: Lynne Reinner.

BACHARACH, S.B. & LAWLER, E.J. 1980, *Power and Politics in Organisations*. London: Jossey-Bass.

——1981, *Bargaining: Power, Tactics and Outcomes*. London: Jossey-Bass.

BACK TO BACK GAME, THE. Jaques, D. 1981. See JAQUES (1981).

BAEHLER, J.R. 1980, *The New Manager's Guide to Success*. New York: Praeger.

BAETENS BEARDSMORE, H. 1982, *Bilingualism: Basic Principles*. Clevedon, Avon: Multilingual Matters.

BAFA BAFA. Shirts, G.R. 1970. La Jolla, CA: Simile II.

BAGLEY, C. & VERMA, G. (eds) 1986, *Personality, Cognition, and Values: Cross-Cultural Perspectives of Childhood and Adolescence*. London: Macmillan.

BAKER, C. & COKELY, D. 1980, *American Sign Language: A Teacher's Resource Text on Grammar and Culture*. Silver Spring, MD: T.J. Publishers.

BALL, P., GILES, H. & HEWSTONE, M. 1984, Second language acquisition: The intergroup theory with catastrophic dimensions. In Tajfel (1984).

BANCROFT, W.J. 1978, The Lozanov method and its American adaptations. *Modern Language Journal*, 62, 4 : 167–75.

BAND, M. & FORGAS, J. 1984, Linking person perception to behavior intention across cultures: The role of cultural collectivism. *Journal of Cross-Cultural Psychology*, 15 : 337–53.

BANDURA, A., ROSS, D. & ROSS, S. 1963, Imitation of film-mediated aggressive models. *Journal of Abnormal and Social Psychology*, 66.

BANKS, M. (ed.) 1984, *Conflict in World Society: A New Perspective on International Relations*. Brighton, Sussex: Wheatsheaf; New York: St. Martin's Press.

BARROWS, J. & ZORN, J. 1983, Fifteen concise role-plays and how to use them. *English Teaching Forum*, 21, 1 : 23–27.

——1989, An adaptable role-play model for foreign language learning. In Crookall & Oxford (1989).

BARTH, F. 1966, *Models of Social Organization*. Royal Anthropological Institute, Occasional Paper, 23.

BARTLETT, F.C. 1932, *Remembering: A Study in Experimental Social Psychology*. Cambridge: Cambridge University Press.

BATESON, G. 1972, *Steps to an Ecology of Mind: Collected Essays in Anthropology, Psychiatry, and Epistemology*. San Francisco: Chandler; London: Granada (Paladin).

BELL, D. 1975, Simulation games: Three research paradigms. *Simulation & Games*, 6, 3.

BERGER, P.L. & LUCKMANN, T. 1966, *The Social Construction of Reality: A Treatise in the Sociology of Knowledge*. New York: Doubleday; Harmondsworth: Penguin.

BERLINSKI, D. 1976, *On Systems Analysis: An Essay Concerning the Limitations of some Mathematical Methods in the Social, Political and Biological Sciences*. Cambridge, MA: M.I.T. Press.

BERNARD, J. 1973, My four revolutions: An autobiographical history of the ASA. In HUBER (1973).

BERNE, E. 1961, *Transactional Analysis in Psychotherapy: A Systematic Individual and Social Psychiatry.* New York: Ballantine.

BEYSON, L. (ed.) 1948, *The Communication of Ideas*. New York: Harper & Brother.

BIGGS, W.D. Computerized business management simulations for tyros. In BURNS & KELLEY (1986).

BILLIG, M. 1976, *Social Psychology and Intergroup Relations*. London & New York: Academic Press.

——1982, *Ideology and Social Psychology*. Oxford: Basil Blackwell.

——1985, Prejudice, categorization and particularization: From a perceptual to a rhetorical approach. *European Journal of Social Psychology*, 15, 1.

BILLIG, M. & TAJFEL, H. 1973, Social categorization and similarity in intergroup behaviour. *European Journal of Social Psychology*, 3 : 27–52.

BIRDWHISTELL, R.L. 1970, *Kinesics and Context*. Philadelphia: University of Pennsylvania Press.

BLOOD MONEY. Greenblat, C.S. & Gagnon, J.H. 1978. See GREENBLAT & GAGNON (1978).

BLOOMER, J. 1973, What have simulation and gaming got to do with programmed learning and educational technology? *Programmed Learning and Educational Technology*, 10, 4.

BLUMLER, J. 1977, The emergence of communication studies. *Journal of Educational Television*, 3, 1.

BOND, M. & FORGAS, J. 1984. Linking person perception to behavior intention across cultures: The role of cultural collectivism. *Journal of Cross-Cultural Psychology*, 15, 337–53.

BOND, T. 1986, *Games for Social and Life Skills*. London: Hutchinson.

BOOT, G. & REYNOLDS, M. 1983, Issues of control in simulation and games. *Simulation/Games for Learning*, 13, 1.

BOUCHER, W.I. 1977, *The Study of the Future: An Agenda for Research*. Washington, DC: NSF.

BOWEN, J.D., MADSEN, H. & HILFERT, A. 1985, *TESOL Techniques and Procedures*. Rowley, MA: Newbury House.

BRAMMER, L. 1979, *The Helping Relationship*. Englewood Cliffs, NJ: Prentice-Hall.

BRAMMER, M. & SAWYER-LAUÇANNO, C. 1989. Simulation in business and commerce. In Crookall & Oxford (1989).

BRAND X GAME, THE. Scottish Film Council & Media Education Development Project. 1984. Glasgow: Scottish Film Council.

BRATEN, S. 1984, The third position: Beyond artificial and autopoietic reduction. *Kybernetes*, 13.

BRAYBROOKE, D. & LINDBLOM, C.E. 1963, *A Strategy for Decision*. New York: Free Press.

BRECHT, R.D., NOEL, R.C. & WILKENFELD, J. 1984, Computer simulation in the teaching of foreign language and international studies. *Foreign Language Annals*, 17, 6.

BREDEMEIER, M.E. & GREENBLAT, C.S. 1981, The educational effectiveness of simulation games: A synthesis of findings. *Simulation & Games*, 12, 3.

BREIN, M. & DAVID, K.H. 1971, Intercultural communication and the adjustment of the sojourner. *Psychological Bulletin*, 76, 2.

BRILHART, J.K. 1978, *Effective Group Discussion*. Dubuque, IA: William C. Brown.

BROWN, H.D. 1987, *Principles of Language Learning and Teaching* (2nd edn). Englewood Cliffs, NJ: Prentice-Hall.

BRUIN, K. 1986, Prejudices, discrimination and education. *School*, November (Dutch only).

BRUIN, K., DE HAAN, J., TEIJKEN, C. & VEEMAN, W. (eds) 1979, *How to Build a Simulation/Game*. Leeuwarden, Netherlands: Teacher Training Institute Ubbo Emmius.

BRUMFIT, C.J. & JOHNSON, K. (eds) 1979, *The Communicative Approach to Language Teaching*. Oxford: Oxford University Press.

BRUNER, J.S., JOLLY, A. & SYLVA, K. (eds) 1976, *Play: Its Role in Development and Education*. Harmondsworth: Penguin.

BRYANT, N. & CORLESS, H. 1986, The management of management games. *Simulation/Games for Learning*, 16, 3 : 99–112.

BUCCANEER BILLY'S BAD BARGAIN. Versluis, E. 1983. Ashland, OR: Southern Oregon State College.

BULLOUGH, V. 1974, *The Subordinate Sex: A History of Attitudes toward Women*, Baltimore, MD: Johns Hopkins University Press; Harmondsworth: Penguin.

BURGESS, J. 1986, Japan's education minister fired for remarks about World War II. *Washington Post*, 9 September.

BURNS, A.C. & KELLEY, L. (eds) 1986, *Developments in Business Simulation and Experiential Exercises*. Proceedings of the 13th Annual Conference of ABSEL. Stillwater: Oklahoma State University.

BURSK, E.C. & BLODGETT, T.B. (eds) 1971, *Developing Executive Leaders*. Cambridge, MA: Harvard University Press.

BURTON, J.W. 1969, *Conflict and Communication: The Use of Controlled Communication in International Relations*. London: Macmillan; New York: Free Press.

——1972, *World Society*. Cambridge & New York: Cambridge University Press.

——1979, *Deviance, Terrorism and War: The Process of Solving Unsolved Social and Political Problems*. Oxford: Martin Robertson; New York: St. Martin's Press.

——1984, *Global Conflict: The Domestic Sources of International Crisis*. Brighton, Sussex: Wheatsheaf; College Park, MD: University of Maryland, Center for International Development.

BUSINESS POLICY GAME, THE. Cotter, R.V. & Fritzsche, D.J. 1986. Englewood Cliffs, NJ: Prentice-Hall.

BUTTON, G. & LEE, J.R.E. (eds) 1987, *Talk and Social Organisation*. Clevedon, Avon: Multilingual Matters.

BUZAN, T. 1974, *Use Your Head*. London: BBC Publications.

BYRNE, D. & RIXON, S. 1979, *ELT Guide 1: Communication Games*. London: NFER & Nelson for the British Council.

CABALLERO, M. & SOLOMON, P. 1984, A longitudinal view of women's role portrayal in television advertising. *Journal of the Academy of Marketing Science*, 12:93–108.

CALL YOURSELF A MANAGER. Schofield, A. 1982. In SCHOFIELD (1982).

CALLAHAN, T. 1986, What's new in career networking. *New York Times*, 23 November.

CANALE, M. & SWAIN, M. 1980, Theoretical bases of communicative approaches to second language teaching and testing. *Applied Linguistics*, 1:1–47.

CANDLIN, C.N. (ed.) 1981, *The Communicative Teaching of English*. Essex: Longman.

CANNIE, J.C. 1979, *The Women's Guide to Management Success*. Englewood Cliffs, NJ: Prentice-Hall.

CAPJEFOS: THE VILLAGE DEVELOPMENT GAME. Greenblat, C. S. *et al*. 1986. See GREENBLAT (1987a).

CASTELLS, M. 1977, *The Urban Question: A Marxist Approach*. London: Edward Arnold.

CBI 1976, *Third Report from the Select Committee on Science and Technology*. London: HMSO. Quoted in *Education and Training*.

CELEBRITY INTRODUCTION GAME, THE. Stern, B. 1986. See STERN (1986).

CENTRE FOR CONTEMPORARY CULTURAL STUDIES 1982, *The Empire Strikes Back*. London: Hutchinson.

CHARADES. Unknown/anonymous. Undated. (Well-known parlour game.)

CHARON, J.M. 1979. *Symbolic Interactionism*. Englewood Cliffs, N.J.: Prentice-Hall.

CHASTAIN, K. 1976, *Developing Second Language Skills: Theory to Practice* (2nd edn). Chicago: Rand McNally.

CHEERY, C. 1957, *On Human Communication*. Cambridge, MA: M.I.T. Press.

CHEMICAL CONSTRUCTION COMPANY. Gottschalk, A. 1976. London: London Business School.

CHOOSING THE NEWS. Bethel & Simon—ILEA English Centre. 1985. London: Society for Education in Film and Television.

CHRISTIANSEN, K. 1977, *The A-B-Z Game*. Defiance: Defiance College.

CLARK, G. & DEAR, M. 1981, *Urbanisation and Urban Planning in Capitalist Society*. London & New York: Methuen.

CLARK, M. & HANSCOMBE, J. (eds) 1983, *On TESOL '82: Pacific Perspectives of Language Learning and Teaching*. Washington, DC: TESOL.

CLARK, R. & MCDONOUGH, J. 1982, *Imaginary Crimes: Materials for Simulation and Role-Playing*. Oxford: Pergamon.

CLARKE, A.C. 1983, Keynote address to the United Nations. Broadcast on the BBC World Service, 17 May.

CLARKE, M. 1978, *Simulations in the Study of International Relations*. Ormskirk, Lancs: G.W. & A. Hesketh.

CLAVEL, P., FORESTER, J. and GOLDSMITH, W.W. (eds) 1980, *Pergamon Policy Studies*. Oxford: Pergamon.

CLEMENT, R. 1980, Ethnicity, contact and communicative competence in a second language. In GILES *et al*. (1980).

COHEN, A. 1974, The Culver City Spanish immersion program: The first two years. *The Modern Language Journal*, 58 : 94–103.

COHEN, R. 1985, R. J. Reynolds: Blowing smoke, *Washington Post Parade*, 22 October.

COLEMAN, D.W. 1985, TERRI: A CALL lesson simulating conversational interaction. In CROOKALL (1985).

——1987, Computer-assisted language acquisition: Planting a SEED. In CROOKALL *et al*. (1987).

——1988, Conversational simulation in computer-assisted language learning: Potential and reality. In CROOKALL (1988b).

COLMAN, A. 1982, *Game Theory and Experimental Games: The Study of Strategic Interaction*. Oxford: Pergamon.

COLOUR GAME, THE. Jaques, D. 1981. See JAQUES (1981).

COMSTOCK, G. 1983, Media influences on aggression. In GOLDSTEIN & KRASNER (1983).

COOLEY, C.H. 1902, *Human Nature and the Social Order*. New York: Charles Scribner.

COON, A.M. 1957, Brainstorming: A creative problem-solving technique. *Journal of Communication*, 7, 3.

COOPERATION AND CONFLICT. Oppenheimer, J. & Winer, M. 1988. See OPPENHEIMER & WINER (1988).

COOTE, A., CROOKALL, D. & SAUNDERS, D. 1985, Some human and

machine aspects of computerized simulations. In VAN MENTS & HEARNDEN (1985).

COOTE, A. & MCMAHON, L. 1984, Challenging orthodoxy: The use of simulation/games in modifying the assumptive worlds of organizational policy makers. In JAQUES & TIPPER (1984).

——1985, Managers and reorganisation: Can simulation/gaming help old dogs learn new tricks. In VAN MENTS & HEARNDEN (1985).

COOTE, A., SAUNDERS, D., CROOKALL, D. & OXFORD, R. 1987. Management negotiated decisions simulation (MANEDES). *Training and Management Development Methods*, first issue.

CORDEY-HAYES, R. 1968, *Retail Location Models.* Centre for Environmental Studies Working Papers, 16.

CORNER, J. & HOWTHORN, J. (eds) 1985, *Communication Studies: An Introductory Reader* (2nd edn). London: Edward Arnold.

CRAIG, D. & MARTIN, A. (eds) 1986, *Gaming and Simulation for Capability*. Loughborough, Leics: SAGSET.

CRAIG, R.T. & TRACY, K. (eds) 1983, *Conversational Coherence*. Beverly Hills, CA: Sage.

CROOKALL, D. 1979, Variations on the theme of 'Alibi'. *Modern English Teacher*, 7, 1. (Reprinted in HOLDEN, 1983.)

——1983a, Picture Stories. *Modern English Teacher*, 10, 4.

——1983b, Voices out of the air: World Communications Year, international broadcasting and foreign language learning. *System*, 11, 3.

——(ed.) 1985, *Simulation Applications in L2 Education and Research*. Special issue of *System*, 13, 3.

——1986, *Simulation and Gaming in Foreign Language Education* (SAGSET Resource List no. 9). Loughborough, Leics: SAGSET.

——(ed.) 1988a, *Computerized Simulation in the Social Sciences*. Special issue of *Social Science Computer Review*, 6, 1.

——(ed.) 1988b, *Simulation and the New Technologies:Applications and Problems*. Special issue of *Simulation/Games for Learning*, 18, 1.

CROOKALL, D., COLEMAN, D. W. & OXFORD, R. 1989, Computer-mediated language learning environments. A research framework. In DUNKELL (1989).

CROOKALL, D., GREENBLAT, C.S., COOTE, A., KLABBERS, J.H.G. & WATSON, D.R. (eds) 1987, *Simulation-Gaming in the late 1980s*. Oxford: Pergamon.

CROOKALL, D., MARTIN, A., SAUNDERS, D. & COOTE, A. 1986, Human and computer involvement in simulation. *Simulation & Games*, 17, 3.

CROOKALL, D. & OXFORD, R. (eds) 1989, *Simulation/Games and the New Technologies: Applications and Problems*. New York: Newbury House/Harper & Row.

CROOKALL, D., OXFORD, R. & SAUNDERS, D. 1987, Towards a reconceptualization of simulation: From representation to reality. *Simulation/Games for Learning*, 17, 4 : 147–71.

CROOKALL, D., SAUNDERS, D. & COOTE, A. 1987, The SIMULATION DESIGN GAME: An activity for exploring the simulation design process. In FITZSIMONS & THATCHER (1987).

CROOKALL, D. & WILKENFELD, J. 1985, ICONS: Communications technologies and international relations. In CROOKALL (1985).

——1987, Information technology in the service of a world-wide multi-institutional simulation. In MOONEN & PLOMP (1987).

CROUCH, I. & OWEN, G. (eds) 1983, *Proceedings of the Seminar/Conference on Oral Traditions*. Las Cruces: New Mexico State University.

CULTURE CONTACT. Glazier, B. & Isber, C. 1969. Cambridge, MA: Abt Associates.

CULTURE GAME, THE. Freestone, C. & Noesjirwan, J. 1980. Melbourne: Kimbarra Press.

CUNNINGHAM, J.B. 1984, Assumptions underlying the use of different forms of simulations. *Simulations & Games*, 15, 2 : 213–34.

CUNNINGHAM, M. with SCUMER, F. 1984, *Powerplay: What Really Happened at Bendix*. New York: Simon & Schuster.

CUNNINGSWORTH, A. & HORNER, D. 1985, The role of simulations in the development of communication strategies. In CROOKALL (1985).

CURRAN, C.A. 1976, *Counselling-Learning in Second Languages*. Apple River, IL: Apple River Press.

CURRAN, J., GUREVITCH, M. & WOOLLACOTT, J. (eds) 1977, *Mass Communication and Society*. London: Edward Arnold/Open University Press.

CUTRONA, C. (ed.) 1985, The Elements of Good Practice in Dispute Resolution. *Proceedings of the 12th Annual Conference, Society of Professionals in Dispute Resolution* (SPIDR). Washington, DC.

CUTS GAME, THE. Hearn, J. & Hitch, P. J. 1977. See HEARN & HITCH (1977).

D'ARCY, J. 1969, The right of man to communicate. *EBU Review*, 118.

DE SAUSSURE, F. 1916, *Course in General Linguistics* (translated by R. Harris, 1983). London: Duckworth.

DEAL, T.E. & KENNEDY, A.A. 1982, *Corporate Cultures: The Roles and Rituals of Corporate Life*. Reading, MA: Addison-Wesley.

DEAR, M. & SCOTT, A.J. (eds) 1981, *Urbanisation and Urban Planning in Capitalist Society*. London: Methuen.

DEFLEUR, M.L. 1970, *Theories of Mass Communication*. New York: David McKay.

DENTIST. Klabbers, J., Van der Hijden, P. & Truin, G. J. 1980. See KLABBERS *et al.* (1980).

DENZIN, N.K. 1975. Play, games, interaction: The context of childhood socialization. *Sociological Quarterly*, 16, 458–79.

DEUTSCH, M. 1969, Conflicts: Productive and destructive. *Journal of Social Issues*, 25. Also in JANDT (1973).

——1973, *The Resolution of Conflict: Constructive and Destructive Processes*. New Haven, CT & London: Yale University Press.

——1980, Fifty years of conflict. In FESTINGER (1980).

——1987, A theoretical perspective on conflict and conflict resolution. In SANDOLE & SANDOLE-STAROSTE (1987).

DEVELOPMENT GAME, THE. Walford, R. 1969. London: Longman.

DIADORI, P. 1987, Simulation strategy and communicative approach in CALL. In CROOKALL *et al.* (1987).

DIPLOMACY. Calhamer, A. B. 1960/71. Baltimore, MD: Avalon Hill. Games Research Inc; London: Philmar Ltd.

DIRENZO, G.K. (ed.) 1977, *We, The People: American Character and Social Change*. London & Westport, CT: Greenwood Press.

DONNELLON, A., GRAY, B. & BOUGON, M.B. 1986, Communication, meaning, and organized action. *Administrative Science Quarterly*, 31 : 43–55.

DONNERSTEIN, E. & HALLAM, J. 1978, Facilitating effects of erotica on aggression against women. *Journal of Personality and Social Psychology*, 36. Cited by Morokoff (1983).

DRAWING A HOUSE. Pedersen, P. 1988. See PEDERSEN (1988).

DUCAN, S. 1972, Some notes on analyzing data on face-to-face interaction. In KEY (1972).

DUGAN, M.A. 1982, *Conflict Resolution*. Special issue of *Peace and Change: A Journal of Peace Research*, 8, 2–3.

DUKE, R.D. 1974, *Gaming: The Future's Language*. New York: Halsted Press.

DUMAS, P. 1984, *Simulations informatisées dans l'enseignement du marketing*. Co-operation Franco-Quebecoise.

DUNKEL, P. (ed.) 1989, *Computer-Assisted Language Learning and Testing, Research and Practice*, New York: Newbury House/Harper & Row.

DUNLEAVY, P. 1980. *Urban Political Analysis*. London: Macmillan.

DYER, G. 1982, *Advertising as Communication*. London: Methuen.

EGAN, G. 1986, *The Skilled Helper: A Systematic Approach to Effective Helping*. Monterey, CA: Brooks Cole.

EISER, J.R. 1980, *Cognitive Social Psychology: A Guidebook to Theory and Research*. Maidenhead, Berks: McGraw-Hill.

ELIZA. Weizenbaum, J. 1965. See WEIZENBAUM (1965).

ELLINGTON, H.I. & ADDINALL, E. 1978, Power for Elaskay—A learning package on alternative energy resources for use by science teachers. *School Science Review*.

——1981, *Games and Simulations in Science Education*. London: Kogan Page.

ELLIS, R. 1984, *Classroom Second Language Development*. Oxford: Pergamon.

ELMORE, R. 1978, Organizational models of social program implementation. *Public Policy*, 26, 2.

ERIKSON, F. 1972, Classroom discourse as improvisation: Relationships between academic task structure and social participation structure in lessons. In WILKINSON (1972).

ESTER, P. & LEEUW, F.L. (eds) 1981, *Energie als Maatschappelijk Probleem*. Assen: Van Gorcum.

EVANS, C., GAUDIN, J.-M. & RAVEAU, F. 1987, Testing advanced communicative competence through role-play. *British Journal of Language Teaching*, XXV, 2 : 109–11.

EXCAVATION OF OBJECT C-9. Versluis, E. 1984. Ashland, OR: Southern Oregon State College.

FALUDI, A. 1980, Towards a combined paradigm of planning theory? *Planning Outlook*, 22 : 2–80.

FENN, M. 1978, *Making it in Management: A Behavioral Approach for Women Executives*. Englewood Cliffs, NJ: Prentice-Hall.

FERGUSON, L.E. 1971, Better management of managers' careers. In BURSK & BLODGETT (1971).

FERNANDES, J. 1983a, On the tip of my thumb: Developing awareness of oral traditions among deaf college students. In CROUCH & OWEN (1983).

——1983b, Sign language and 'Picture Talk': An experiential learning approach. *Communication Education*, 32 : 197–202.

FERNANDES, J., ELLIS, G. & SINCLAIR, B. 1989, Learner training (learning how to learn). In CROOKALL & OXFORD (1989).

FERNANDES, J. & NORETSKY, M. 1984, Guided problem solving: An instructional approach to decision making in groups. Paper presented at the International Society for Individualized Instruction annual meeting, Atlanta, GA, 19 October.

FESTINGER, L. 1957, *A Theory of Cognitive Dissonance*. Evanston, IL: Row Peterson; Stanford, CA: Stanford University Press.

——1962, *A Theory of Cognitive Dissonance* (2nd edn). Evanston, IL: Row Peterson; Stanford, CA: Stanford University Press.

——(ed.) 1980, *Retrospections on Social Pyschology*. Oxford & New York: Oxford University Press.

FILLEY, A. 1974, *Interpersonal Conflict Resolution*. Glenview, IL: Scott Foresman.

FILM INDUSTRY, THE. Jenkins, T. & Stewart, D. 1986. Bracknell, Berks: The Media Centre.

FINNISTON, M. 1980, *Engineering Our Future*. Report of the Committee of Inquiry into the Engineering Profession. London: HMSO.

FINOCCHIARO, M. & BRUMFIT, C. 1983, *The Functional-Notional Approach: From Theory to Practice*. New York: Oxford University Press.

FISHER, D. 1982, *The Right to Communicate: A Status Report*. Paris: UNESCO.

FISKE, J. 1982, *Introduction to Communication Studies*. London: Methuen.

FITZSIMONS, A. & THATCHER, D. (eds) 1987, *Games and Simulations at Work*. Loughborough, Leics: SAGSET.

FLOOD, M.M. 1958, Some experimental games. *Management Science*, 5 : 5–26.

FOLGER, J.P. & POOLE, M.S. 1984, *Working Through Conflict: A Communication Perspective*. Glenview, IL & London: Scott Foresman.

FORESTER, J. 1980, Critical theory and planning practice. In CLAVEL *et al.* (1980).

FOSTER, L. & STOCKLEY, D. 1984, *Multiculturalism: The Changing Australian Paradigm*. Clevedon, Avon: Multilingual Matters.

FRANCIS, D.W. 1986, Some structures of negotiation talk. *Language in Society*. 17, 1.

——1987, The competent player: Some observations on game learning. In CROOKALL *et al.* (1987).

FRENCH, J.R.P. & RAVEN, B. 1977, The bases of social power. In Snow (1977).

FRIEDMAN, J. 1969, Notes on societal action. *Journal of the American Institute of Planners*, 35.

FRIEND, J. & JESSOP, N. 1969, *Local Government and Strategic Choice*. London: Tavistock.

FRIES, C.C. & FRIES, A.C. 1961, *Foundations for English Teaching*. Tokyo: Kenkyusha.

FRITZSCHE, D.J. 1987, The impact of microcomputers on business educational simulations. In WOLFE (1987).

FRONT PAGE. Jones, K. 1974. In K. JONES (1986)

FRUDE, N. 1983, *The Intimate Machine: Close Encounters with the New Computers*. London: Century.

GAMSON, W.A. 1984, *What's News?: A Game Simulation of TV News—Coordinator's Manual & Participant's Manual*. New York: Free Press; London: Collier Macmillan.

GAGNON, J.H. & GREENBLAT, C.S. 1978, *Life Designs: Individuals, Marriages and Families*. Glenview, IL: Scott Foresman.

GANNON, J.R. 1981, *Deaf Heritage: A Narrative History of Deaf America*. Washington, DC: National Association of the Deaf.

GARDNER, R.C. 1979, Social psychological aspects of second language acquisition. In GILES & ST CLAIR (1979).

——1981, Second language learning. In GARDNER & KALIN (1981).

——1982, Social factors in language retention. In LAMBERT & FREED (1982).

——1983, Learning another language: A true social psychological experiment. *Journal of Language and Social Psychology*, 2, 2–4.

——1985, *Social Psychological Aspects of Second Language Learning: The Role of Attitudes and Motivation*. London: Edward Arnold.

GARDNER, R.C. & KALIN, R. (eds) 1981, *A Canadian Social Psychology of Ethnic Relations*. Ontario: Methuen.

GARDNER, R.C. & LALONDE, P.N. 1989, Simulation-gaming and foreign language learning: Social psychological considerations. In CROOKALL & OXFORD (1989).

GARDNER, R.C., LALONDE, R.N., MOORCROFT, R. & EVERS, F.T. 1987, Second language attrition: The role of motivation and use. *Journal of Language and Social Psychology*, 6 : 1, 29–47.

GARDNER, R.C. & LAMBERT, W.E. 1957, Motivational variables in second language acquisition. *Canadian Journal of Psychology*, 13 : 266–72.

——1975, *Attitudes and Motivation in Second Language Learning*. Rowley, MA: Newbury House.

GARDNER, R.C., SMYTHE, P.C. & BRUNET, G.R. 1977, Intensive second language study: Effects on attitudes, motivation, and French achievement. *Language Learning*, 27 : 243–61.

GARDNER, R.C., SMYTHE, P.C. & CLEMENT, R. 1979, Intensive second language study in a bicultural milieu: An investigation of attitudes, motivation and language proficiency. *Language Learning*, 29 : 305–20.

GARFINKEL, H. 1967, *Studies in Ethnomethodology*. Englewood Cliffs, NJ: Prentice Hall.

——1986, *Studies of Work*. London: Routledge & Kegan Paul.

GARVEY, D.M. 1971, Simulation: A catalogue of judgements, findings, and hunches. In TANSEY (1971).

GATTEGNO, C. 1972, *Teaching Foreign Languages in Schools: The Silent Way* (2nd edn). New York: Educational Solutions.

GERGEN, K.J. 1977, The decline of character: Socialization and self-consistency. in DIRENZO (1977).

——1982, *Toward Transformation in Social Knowledge*. New York: Springer-Verlag.

GHETTO. Toll, D. 1969. New York: Western Publishing Company.

Gibbs, G.I. (ed.) 1974, *Handbook of Games and Simulations*. London: E. & F.N. Spon.

Giles, H. & Byrne, J.L. 1982, An intergroup approach to second language acquisition. *Journal of Multilingual and Multicultural Development*, 3, 1.

Giles, H. & St Clair, R. (eds) 1979, *Language and Social Psychology*. Oxford: Basil Blackwell.

Giles, H., Hewstone, M. & Ball, P. 1983, Language attitudes in multilingual settings: Prologue with priorities. *Journal of Multilingual and Multicultural Development*, 4, 2–3.

Giles, H., Robinson, W.P. & Smith, P.M. (eds) 1980. *Language: Social Psychological Perspectives*. Oxford: Pergamon.

Glasgow Media Group 1977, *Bad News*. London: Routledge & Kegan Paul.

——1980, *More Bad News*. London: Routledge & Kegan Paul.

Glasson, J., Minay, C. & Minett, J. 1971, Politics and planning: An educational game. *Oxford Working Papers in Planning Education and Research*, 6.

Goffman, E. 1959, *The Presentation of Self in Everyday Life*. Garden City, NY: Doubleday Anchor; Harmondsworth: Penguin.

——1971, *Relations in Public: Microstudies of the Public Order*. New York: Basic Books; Harmondsworth: Penguin.

——1972, *Encounters: Two Studies in the Sociology of Interaction*. Oxford: Basil Blackwell.

——1974, *Frame Analysis: An Essay on the Organization of Experience*. New York: Harper & Row; Harmondsworth: Penguin.

——1979, *Gender Advertisements*. Cambridge, MA: Harvard University Press; London: Macmillan.

Goldberg, S.B., Green, E.D. & Sander, F.E.A. (eds) 1985, *Dispute Resolution*. Boston, MA: Little, Brown.

Goldstein, A. & Krasner, L. (eds) 1983, *Prevention and Control of Aggression*. New York: Pergamon Press.

Goodenough, W. 1971, *Culture, Language and Society*. Reading, MA: Addison-Wesley Modular Publications, 7.

Goodin, R.E. 1978, Rites of rulers. *British Journal of Sociology*, 29, 3.

Gordon, T.J. 1974. The current methods of futures research. In A. Somit (ed.), *Political Science and the Study of the Future*. New York: Basic Books.

——1977, The nature of unforeseen developments. In Boucher (1977).

Gordon, T.J. & Helmer, O. 1966, Report on a long-range forecasting study. In Helmer (1966).

GOSHKO, J.M. 1986, Shultz warns on terrorism coverage. *Washington Post*, 10 July.

GRAIN DRAIN, THE. Wren, B. 1976. Oxford: OXFAM; London: Christian Aid; London: CAFOD.

GRAY, L. & WAITT, I. (eds) 1982, *Simulation in Management and Business Education*. London: Kogan Page.

GRAY, T.G.F. 1981, Communication skills in engineering. *Chartered Mechanical Engineer*.

GREENBLAT, C.S. 1975a, Basic concepts and linkages. In GREENBLAT & DUKE (1975).

——1975b, Teaching with simulation games: A review of claims and evidence. In GREENBLAT & DUKE (1975).

——1981, Group dynamics and game design: Some reflections. In GREENBLAT & DUKE (1981).

——1987a, CAPJEFOS: The Village Development Game. In CROOKALL *et al*. (1987).

——1987b, Communicating about simulation design: It's not only (sic) pedagogy. In CROOKALL *et al*. (1987).

——1987c, *Designing Games and Simulations: An Illustrated Handbook*. Newbury Park, CA; London: Sage.

GREENBLAT, C.S. & DUKE, R.D. 1975, *Gaming-Simulation: Rationale, Design, and Applications*. New York & London: Wiley (Halsted Press).

——1981, *Principles and Practices of Gaming-Simulation*. Beverly Hills, CA & London: Sage.

GREENBLAT, C.S. & GAGNON, J.H. 1978, *BLOOD MONEY: A Simulation of Hemophilia and Problems of Health Care Delivery*. Bethesda, MD: National Heart, Lung and Blood Institute.

——1981, Further explorations on the 'Multiple Reality' game. In GREENBLAT & DUKE (1981).

GREENE, G. 1982, The lasting changes brought by women workers. *Business Week*, 15 March: 59–63.

GREENFIELD, P. 1984, *Mind and Media: The Effects of Television, Computers and Video Games*. London: Fontana.

GREENLAW, P.S., HERRON, L.W. & RAWDON, R.H. 1962, *Business Simulation*. Englewood Cliffs, NJ: Prentice-Hall.

GUDYKUNST, W. (ed.) 1983, *Intercultural Communication Theory: Current Perspectives*. Beverly Hills, CA: Sage.

GUDYKUNST, W. & KIM, Y.Y. 1984, *Communication with Strangers*. Reading, MA: Addison-Wesley.

GUDYKUNST, W. & NISHIDA, T. 1986, The influence of cultural variability on perceptions of communication behavior associated with relationship terms. *Human Communication Research*, 13 : 147–66.

GUETZKOW, H., ALGER, C.F., BRODY, R.A., NOEL, R.C. & SNYDER, R.C. 1963, *Simulation in International Relations: Developments for Research and Teaching*. Englewood Cliffs, NJ: Prentice-Hall.

GUETZKOW, H., KOTLER, P., & SCHUTZ, R.L., 1972, *Simulation in Social and Administrative Science*. Englewood Cliffs, NJ: Prentice-Hall.

GUETZKOW, H. & VALDEZ, J.J. (eds) 1981, *Simulated International Processes: Theories and Research in Global Modeling*. Beverly Hills, CA & London: Sage Publications.

GUMPERZ, J.J. & HYMES, D. (eds) 1972, *Directions in Sociolinguistics: The Ethnography of Communication*. New York: Holt, Rinehart & Winston.

GUNS OR BUTTER. Nesbitt, W. A. 1972. Del Mar, CA: Simile II.

HABERMAS, J. 1970, *Toward a Rational Society*. Boston: Beacon Press.

HALL, A.S. & ALGIE, J. 1974, *A Management Game for the Social Services*. London: Bedford Square Press.

HALL, E.T. 1976, *Beyond Culture*. New York: Doubleday.

——1983, *The Dance of Life*. New York: Doubleday.

HALL, J. 1971, Decisions. *Psychology Today*, November.

HAMBURGER, H. 1979, *Games as Models of Social Phenomena*. San Francisco, CA & Reading, Berks: W.H. Freeman.

HANDEL, W. 1982, *Ethnomethodology: How People Make Sense*. Englewood Cliffs, NJ: Prentice-Hall.

HANEY, C., BANKS, C. & ZIMBARDO, P. 1973, Interpersonal dynamics in a simulated prison. *International Journal of Criminology and Penology*, 1 : 69–97.

HARE, G. & MCALEESE, R. 1985, LAG: Development of a training simulation. In CROOKALL (1985).

HARMAN, W.W. 1977, On normative forecasting. In BOUCHER (1977).

HARMS, L. S. & RICHSTAD, J. (eds) 1977, *Evolving Perspectives on the Right to Communicate*. Honolulu: University of Hawaii.

HARPER, S.N. 1985, Social psychological effects of simulation in foreign language learning. In CROOKALL (1985).

HARRAGAN, B.L. 1977, *Games Mother Never Taught You: Corporate Gamesmanship for Women*. New York: Warner Books.

HARRÉ, R. 1979, *Social Being: A Theory for Social Psychology*. Oxford: Basil Blackwell.

HARRÉ, R. & SECORD, P. 1972, *The Explanation of Social Behaviour*. Oxford: Basil Blackwell.

HARTLEY, J., O'SULLIVAN, T. & GOULDEN, H. 1985, *Making Sense of the Media*. London: Comedia.

HARVEY, D. 1973, *Social Justice and the City*. London: Edward Arnold.

HARVEY, J. 1974, The abilene paradox. *Organizational Dynamics*.

HARVEY, J. H., ICKES, W. & KIDD, R.F. (eds) 1981, *New Directions in Attribution Research*, Vol. 3. Hillsdale, NJ: Lawrence Erlbaum.

HASSEL, C.V. 1987, Terrorism and hostage negotiation. In SANDOLE & SANDOLE-STAROSTE (1987).

HAYAKAWA, S. I. 1973, Let's get the boredom out of the schools. *Washington Star*, 15 September.

HEALEY, P., MCDOUGAL, G. & THOMAS, M.J. (eds) 1982, *Planning Theory Prospects for the 1980s*. Oxford: Pergamon.

HEARN, J. 1983, Issues of control in simulation and gaming: a reconsideration. *Simulation/Games for Learning*, 13, 3.

HEARN, J. & HITCH, P. 1977, The Cuts Game. *SAGSET Journal*, 7, 1.

HEARN, J. & ROBERTS, I. 1976, Planning under difficulties: The move to decrementalism. In JONES (1976).

HELMER, O. (ed.) 1966, *Social Technology*, New York: Basic Books.

HELMER, O. 1981, Cross-impact analysis reassessed. *Futures*, 13, 5.

HENNIG, M. & JARDIM, A. 1976, *The Managerial Women*. New York: Anchor Press.

HERBERT, D. & STURTRIDGE, G. 1979, *ELT Guide 2: Simulations*. London: NFER & Nelson for the British Council.

HERITAGE, J. 1984, *Garfinkel and Ethnomethodology*. Cambridge: Polity Press.

HEWITT, J.P. 1979, *Self and Society: A Symbolic Interactionist Social Psychology*. Boston: Allyn & Bacon.

HEWSTONE, M. (ed.) 1983, *Attribution Theory: Social and Functional Extensions*. Oxford: Basil Blackwell.

HEWSTONE, M. 1985, Social psychology and intergroup relations: Cross-cultural perspectives. *Journal of Multilingual and Multicultural Development*, 6, 3–4.

HIGGINS, J. (ed.) 1986, *Computer Assisted Language Learning: A European View*. Special issue of *System*, 14, 2.

HIGGINS, J. & MORGENSTERN, D. 1989, Simulations on computers. In CROOKALL & OXFORD (1989).

HILLS, P. & GILBERT, J. (eds) 1977, *Aspects of Education Technology XI*. London: Kogan Page.

HILLS, P.J., GARDINER, P.F. & MCVEY, P.J. 1979, 'Communication skills' (results of a survey of books, material and courses in universities, polytechnics and Institutes of Higher Education in the United Kingdom). Guildford: University of Surrey.

HOFSTEDE, G. 1980, *Culture's Consequences: International Differences in Work-Related Values*. Beverly Hills, CA: Sage.

——1986, Cultural differences in teaching and learning. *International Journal of Intercultural Relations*, 10 : 301–20.

HOLDEN, S. (ed.) 1983, *Second Selections from* Modern English Teacher. Harlow, Essex: Longman.

HOLLINSHEAD, B. & YORKE, M. (eds) 1981, *Simulations and Games: The Real and the Ideal*. London: Kogan Page.

HOLMES, B., WHITTINGTON, I. & FLETCHER, S. 1982, Teacher's Notes (MARY ROSE). Aylesbury, Bucks: Ginn & Co.

HOLSTI, O.R., NORTH, R.C. & BRODY, R.A. (eds) 1968, Perception and action in the 1914 crisis. In SINGER (1968).

HORN, R.E. (ed.) 1977, *The Guide to Simulation/Games for Education and Training*. Lexington, MA: Information Resources.

HORN, R.E. & CLEAVES, A. (eds) 1980, *The Guide to Simulations/Games for Education and Training* (4th edn) Beverly Hills, CA & London: Sage.

HORNER, D. & MCGINLEY, K. 1989, Running simulations: Some practical considerations. In CROOKALL & OXFORD (1989).

HOROWITZ, D.L. 1970, Deterrence games: From academic casebook to military codebook. In SWINGLE (1970).

HOROWITZ, I. (ed.) 1963, *Power, Politics and People*. New York: Ballantine.

HORTON, D. & WOHL, R.R. 1956, Mass communication and parasocial interaction: Observations on intimacy at a distance. *Psychiatry*, 19 : 215–99.

HOTEL RECEPTIONIST. Maley, A. & Duff, A. 1982. In MALEY & DUFF (1982).

HOWATT, A.P.R. 1984, *A History of English Language Teaching*. Oxford: Oxford University Press.

HUBER, J. (ed.) 1973, *Changing Women in a Changing Society*. Chicago, IL: University of Chicago Press.

HUGHES-WIENER, G. 1986, The 'learning how to learn' approach to cross-cultural orientation. *International Journal of Intercultural Relations*, 10 : 485–505.

HUI, C. & TRIANDIS, H. 1986, Individualism-collectivism: A study of cross-cultural researchers. *Journal of Cross-Cultural Psychology*, 17 : 225–48.

HUMANUS. Shirts, G.R. 1971. La Jolla, CA: Simile II.

HUNGER ON SPACESHIP EARTH. Ciekot, J. & Sister Miriam-Therese. Undated. New York: American Friends Service Committee.

HUSBAND, C. 1982, *'Race' in Britain: Continuity and Change*. London: Hutchinson.

HUTCHINSON, T. & SAWYER-LAUÇANNO, C. 1989, Simulation in English for science and technology. In CROOKALL & OXFORD (1989).

HYMAN, I. 1978, Is hickory stick out of tune? *Today's Education*, 2. Cited by Goldstein in GOLDSTEIN & KRASNER (1983).

HYMES, D. 1974, *Foundations in Sociolinguistics: An Ethnographic Approach*. Philadelphia: University of Pennsylvania Press.

IACOCCA, L.A. 1979. Unpublished commencement address to the May graduation class, School of Government and Business Administration, George Washington University, Washington, DC.

——1986, *Iacocca*. New York, NY: Bantam Books.

ICONS. Wilkenfeld, J. & Brecht, R.C. Undated. Maryland, MD: University of Maryland. See CROOKALL & WILKENFELD (1987), NOEL (1979), NOEL *et al.* (1987), BRECHT *et al.* (1984), WILKENFELD (1983).

ICS. Goodman, F.L. *et al.* Undated. Ann Arbor: University of Michigan. See TAYLOR & GOODMAN (1987), WOLF (1987).

INTERACT II. Ruben, B. 1977. Wayne, NJ: Avery Publishing Group.

INTERACTIVE SYNECOLOGY. Jandt, F.E. 1973. See JANDT (1973).

IOR 1971, *Beyond Local Government Reform: Some Prospects for Evolution in Public Policy Networks*. London: Institute for Operational Research.

IRWIN, H. 1981, Integration of an extended communication simulation in a course for management students. *Simulation/Games for Learning*, 11, 1 : 3–11.

IVEY, A.E. 1983, *International Interviewing and Counseling*. Monterey, CA: Brooks Cole.

JANDT, F.E. (ed.) 1973, *Conflict Resolution through Communication*. New York & London: Harper & Row.

JANIS, I.L. 1968, Stages in the Decision-making Process. In ABELSON *et al.* (1968).

JANOVITZ, M. (ed.) 1966, *William I. Thomas on Organization and Social Personality: Selected Papers*. Chicago: University of Chicago Press.

JAQUES, D. 1981, Games for all seasons. *Simulation/Games for Learning*, 11, 4 : 147–56.

JAQUES, D. & TIPPER, E. (eds) 1984, *Learning for the Future with Games and Simulations*. Loughborough: SAGSET.

JERVIS, R. 1976, *Perception and Misperception in International Politics*. Princeton, NJ & Guildford, Surrey: Princeton University Press.

JOHNSON, K. 1982, *Communicative Syllabus Design and Methodology*. Oxford: Pergamon.

JOHNSON, T.E. 1972, *Professions and Power*. London: Macmillan.

JONES, G. 1986, Computer simulations in language teaching—the KINGDOM experiment. In HIGGINS (1986).

JONES, K. 1974–5, *Nine Graded Simulations*. London: ILEA. (Reprinted as Jones, 1986).

——1980, Communication, language and realists. In RACE & BROOK (1980).

——1982, *Simulations in Language Teaching*. Cambridge: Cambridge University Press.

——1985, *Designing Your Own Simulations*. London: Methuen.

——1986, *Graded Simulations*. London: Lingual House. (Reprint of Jones, 1974–5.)

——K. (ed.) 1976, *The Yearbook of Social Policy in Britain 1975*. London: Routledge & Kegan Paul.

JONES, L. 1983, *Eight Simulations for Upper Intermediate and More Advanced Students of English* (Participant's Book & Controller's Book). Cambridge: Cambridge University Press.

JORGENSEN, K. 1983, Understanding through communication. Paper given at the International Mass Media Institute's Fourth European Area Convention, Oslo, 1–3 July.

KANTER, R.M. 1977, *Men and Women of the Corporation*. New York: Basic Books.

KANTER, R.M. & STEIN, B.A. 1979, *Life in Organizations: Workplaces as People Experience Them*. New York: Basic Books.

KATZ, E. 1957. The two-step flow of communication. *Public Opinion*, 21 : 61–78.

KATZ, E. & LAZARSFELD, P.F. 1955, *Personal Influence: The Part Played by People in the Flow of Mass Communication*. New York: Free Press.

KATZ, P.A. (ed.) 1979, *Towards the Elimination of Racism*. Oxford: Pergamon.

KAY, A. 1984, Computer software. *Scientific American*, 251 : 53–59.

KEATS, J. 1819. Letter to George and Georgiana Keats, 14 February–3 May, 1819. Cited in TRIPP, R.T. 1970. *The International Thesaurus of Quotations*. Harmondsworth: Penguin.

KELLY, L.G. 1969, *25 Centuries of Language Teaching*. Rowley, MA: Newbury House.

KENDON, A. 1977, *Studies in the Behavior of Social Interaction*. Bloomington: University of Indiana Press.

KENT, R.C. & NIELSSON, G.P. (eds) 1980, *The Study and Teaching of International Relations: A Perspective on Mid-Career Education*. London: Frances Pinter; New York: Nichols.

KEY, M.R. 1972, *The Relationship of Verbal and Nonverbal Communication*. The Hague: Mouton.

KEYS, B. 1987, Total Enterprise Business Games. In WOLFE (1987).

KIM, Y.Y. 1988, *Communication and Cross-Cultural Adaptation: An Integrative Theory*. Clevedon, Avon: Multilingual Matters.

KING, M., NOVIK, L. & CITRENBAUM, C. 1983, *Irresistible Communication: Creative Skills for the Health Professional*. Philadelphia, PA: W.B. Saunders.

KIRK, G. 1980, *Urban Planning in a Capitalist Society*. London: Croom Helm.

KLABBERS, J. 1985, Instruments for planning and policy formation: Some methodological considerations. *Simulations & Games*, 16, 2.

KLABBERS, J., VAN DER HIJDEN, P. & TRUIN, G.J. 1980, Development of an interactive simulation game: A case study of DENTIST. *Simulations & Games*, 11, 1.

KLEIMAN, C. 1980, *Women's Networks*. New York: Lippincott & Crowell.

KLIPPEL, F. 1984, *Keep Talking: Communicative Fluency Activities for Language Teaching*. Cambridge: Cambridge University Press.

KOESTLER, A. 1964, *The Act of Creation*. London: Hutchinson.

——1967, *The Ghost in the Machine*. London: Hutchinson.

——1978, *Janus: A Summing Up*. London: Hutchinson.

KOHN, A. 1986, How to succeed without even vying. *Psychology Today*, 10, 9.

KOK, G.J. (ed.) 1979, *Vooroordeel en Discriminate*. Alphen aan de Rijn: Samson.

KOK, G.J. 1981, Attitudes en energiebewust gedrag. In ESTER & LEEUW (1981).

KOLB, D.A. 1984, *Experiential Learning: Experience as the Source of Learning and Development*. Englewood Cliffs, NJ: Prentice-Hall.

KOLB, W. 1944, A critical evaluation of Mead's 'I' and 'Me' concepts. In MANIS & MELTZER (1978).

KORDA, M. 1976, *Power: How to Get It, How to Use It*. New York: Ballantine Books.

KRAMARAE, C. 1981, *Women and Men Speaking: Frameworks for Analysis*. Rowley, MA: Newbury House.

KRASHEN, S.D. & TERRELL, T.D. 1983, *The Natural Approach: Language Acquisition in the Classroom*. Oxford: Pergamon.

KUHN, T.S. 1970, *The Structure of Scientific Revolutions* (2nd edn) Chicago & London: University of Chicago Press.

LABEL EXERCISE, THE. Pedersen, P. 1988. See PEDERSEN (1988).

LABOV, W. 1970, The study of language in its social context. *Studium General*, 23. (Reprinted in Labov, 1972.)

——1972, *Sociolinguistic Patterns*. Oxford: Basil Blackwell.

LAFORGE, P.G. 1983, *Counseling and Culture in Second Language Acquisition*. Oxford: Pergamon.

LAING, R.D. 1969, *Self and Others*. New York: Pantheon.

LAKOFF, R. 1975, *Language and Women's Place*. New York: Harper & Row.

LALONDE, R.N. & GARDNER, R.C. 1984, Investigating a causal model of second language acquisition: Where does personality fit? *Canadian Journal of Behavioural Science*, 16 : 224–37.

LAMB, M. 1982, *Factions and Fictions: Exercises for Role-Play*. Oxford: Pergamon.

LAMBERT, W.E. & FREED, B.F. (eds) 1982. *The Loss of Language Skills*. Rowley, MA: Newbury House.

LAMBERT, W.E. & TUCKER, G.R. 1972, *Bilingual Education of Children: The St Lambert Experiment*. Rowley, MA: Newbury House.

LAMBERT, W.E., TUCKER, G.R. & D'ANGLEJAN, A. 1973, Cognitive and attitudinal consequences of bilingual schooling: The St Lambert project through grade five. *Journal of Educational Psychology*, 65 : 141–59.

LARSEN-FREEMAN, D. 1986, *Techniques and Principles in Language Teaching*. Oxford: Oxford University Press.

LASSWELL, H.D. 1948, The structure and function of communication in society. In BEYSON (1948).

LAVER, M. 1979, *Playing Politics*. Harmondsworth: Penguin.

LAW-YONE, H. 1979, *MATA—An Israeli Planning Game*. Haifa: Technion, Center for Urban and Regional Studies.

——1984, SPACE—State Planning and Capital Expansion: A Marxist Game. Presented at the 15th International Conference of the International Simulation and Gaming Association, Elsinore, Denmark.

——1987, The production of SPACE: Experiments with a Marxist game. In CROOKALL *et al*. (1987).

LAWRENCE, E. 1982, Just plain common sense: The roots of racism. In CENTRE FOR CONTEMPORARY CULTURAL STUDIES (1982).

LEARNING GAME, THE. Ruben, B.D. & Budd, R.W. 1975; 1978. In RUBEN & BUDD (1975; 1978).

LEDERMAN, L.C. 1984, Debriefing. *Simulation & Games*, 15, 4 : 415–31.

LEE, J.R.E. 1987, Prologue: Talking Organisation. In BUTTON & LEE (1987).

LEEDS-HURWITZ, W. 1985, The communication of everyday life. Unpublished manuscript. University of Wisconsin at Parkside.

LEFLEY, H. & PEDERSEN, P. (eds) 1986, *Cross Cultural Training for Mental Health Professionals*. Springfield, IL: Charles Thomas.

LEHMAN, R.S. 1977, *Computer Simulation and Modelling: An Introduction*. Hillsdale, NJ: Lawrence Erlbaum.

LEVINE, R.A. & CAMPBELL, D.T. 1972, *Ethnocentrism: Theories of Conflict, Ethnic Attitudes and Group Behaviour*. New York & London: Wiley.

LEWIN, K. 1947, Channels of group life. *Human Relations*, 1 : 143–53.

LINDBLOM, C.E. 1965, *The Intelligence of Democracy*. New York: Free Press.

LITTLEJOHN, A. 1989, The use of simulation as a testing device. In CROOKALL & OXFORD (1989).

LITTLEWOOD, W. 1981, *Communicative Language Teaching*. Cambridge: Cambridge University Press.

——1984, *Foreign and Second Language Learning: Language Acquisition Research and Its Implications for the Classroom*. Cambridge: Cambridge University Press.

LIVINSTONE, C. 1983, *Role Play in Language Learning*. Harlow, Essex: Longman.

LOBUTS, J. & PENNEWILL, C. 1984, The Nickel Auction. In X. CURRIE & Y. GENTRY (eds), *Proceedings of the 1984 ABSEL Conference*. Stillwater, OK: College of Business Administration, Oklahoma State University.

——1986, Risk-free decision-making. *Journal of Business Ethics*, 5.

LONERGAN, J. 1986, *Simulation and Gaming in English as a Foreign Language: A Resource List*. Loughborough, Leics: SAGSET.

LONG, M. 1983, Native speaker/non-speaker conversation in the second language classroom. In CLARK & HANSCOMBE (1983).

LONG, N.E. 1958, The local community as an ecology of games. *American Journal of Sociology*, November.

LOST ON THE MOON. Hall, J. 1971. See HALL (1971).

LOVELUCK, C. 1983, The construction, operation and evaluation of management games. In TAYLOR & LIPPITT (1983).

LOZANOV, G. 1978, *Suggestology and Outlines of Suggestopedia*. New York: Gordon and Breach.

LUCE, L.F. & SMITH, E.C. (eds) 1986, *Toward Internationalism: Readings in Cross-Cultural Communication* (2nd edn). Cambridge, MA: Newbury House (Harper & Row).

LUCE, R.D. & RAIFFA, H. 1957, *Games and Decisions: Introduction and Critical Theory*. New York: Wiley.

LUDLOW, R. & WHEELER, B. 1986, The use of business games in general management programmes. In CRAIG & MARTIN (1986).

LUGS. TAYLOR, J. 1977. See Taylor (1977).

LUNDBERG, G.A. 1939, *Foundations of Sociology*. New York: Macmillan.

LYMAN, S.M. & SCOTT, M.B. 1975, *The Drama of Social Reality*. Oxford & New York: Oxford University Press.

LYNCH, M. 1977, *It's Your Choice*. London: Edward Arnold.

MACBRIDE, S. *et al.* (eds) 1980, *Many Voices, One World: Towards a New More Just and More Efficient World Information and Communication Order*. Paris: UNESCO; London: Kogan Page; New York: Unipub.

MACEOIN, G., AHLQVIST, A. & HAODHA, D.O. (eds) 1987, *Third International Conference on Minority Languages*. Clevedon, Avon: Multilingual Matters.

MAKEDON, A. 1984, Playful gaming. *Simulation & Games*, 15, 1 : 25–64.

MALEY, A. 1984, 'I got religion!' Evangelism in language teaching. In SAVIGNON & BERNS (1984).

MALEY, A. & DUFF, A. 1982. *Drama Techniques in Language Learning* (2nd edn). Cambridge: Cambridge University Press.

MANEDES. Crookall, D., Coote, A. & Saunders, D. 1984. In Coote *et al.* (1985; 1987).

MANIS, J.G. & MELTZER, B.N. (eds) 1972. *Symbolic Interaction* (2nd edn). Boston: Allyn & Bacon.

——(eds) 1978, *Symbolic Interaction: A Reader in Social Psychology*. Boston: Allyn & Bacon.

MANSYM IV: A Dynamic Management Simulation with Decision Support System. Schellenberger, R. E. & Masters, L. A. 1986. New York: John Wiley.

MARSHALL, S. 1981a, Communication studies: An alternative programme. *International Journal of Electrical Engineering Education*, 18, 4.

——1981b, An integrated case study approach to teaching communication skills. In HOLLINSHEAD & YORKE (1981).

——1982. Relevance and motivation in communication studies courses for engineering students. *European Journal of Engineering Education*, 7.

MARSHALL, S., ELLINGTON, H., ADDINALL, E. & PERCIVAL, F. 1982, Developing communication skills using simulation/gaming techniques. *Simulation/Games for Learning*, 12, 2.

MARSHALL, S. & WILLIAMS, N. 1986, *Exercises in Teaching Communication*. London: Kogan Page.

MARY ROSE. Holmes, B., Whittington, I. & Fletcher, S. 1982. Aylesbury, Bucks: Ginn & Co.

MASLEN, A. 1983, Newtown: A simulation game. *Simulation/Games for Learning*, 13 : 2.

MASLOW, A.H. 1964, *Religions, Values, and Peak-Experiences*. Columbus: Ohio State University Press.

MATA. Law-Yone, H. 1979. See LAW-YONE (1979).

MATHEIDESZ, M. 1987, RUNNING ERRANDS: A communication board game. *Simulation/Games for Learning*, 18, 1.

——1988, Self access language practice through CALL games. In CROOKALL (1988b).

MAUER, A. 1974, Corporate punishment. *American Psychologist*, 29. Cited by Goldstein in GOLDSTEIN & KRASNER (1983).

MAY, R. 1969, *Love and Will*. New York: Norton.

MCDERMOTT, R.P., GOSPODINOFF, K. & ARON, J. 1978, Criteria for an ethnographically adequate description of concerted activities and their contexts. *Semiotica*, 24, 4: 245–75.

MCGINLEY, K. 1985, ESP syllabus change and simulation. In CROOKALL (1985).

MCLANE, H.J. 1980, *Selecting, Developing, and Retaining Women Executives*. New York: Van Nostrand Reinhold.

MCLELLAN, V. 1985, The Assassins: Off Line. *Digital Review*, 2, 5: 15–18.

MCLUHAN, M. 1964, *Understanding Media*. New York: McGraw-Hill; London: Routledge & Kegan Paul.

MCMAHON, L., BARRETT, S. & HILL, M. 1983, *Power bargaining models in policy analysis ... What prescriptions for practitioners?* Occasional Paper, No. 2. Brussels: European Group of Public Administration.

MCQUAIL, D. & WINDAHL, S. 1981, *Communication Models for the Study of Mass Communication*. London: Longman.

MEAD, G.H. 1934a, *Mind, Self, and Society*. Chicago: University of Chicago Press.

——1934b Self as social object. In STONE & FARBERMAN (1981).

MEGARRY, J. (ed.) 1977, *Aspects of Simulation and Gaming*. London: Kogan Page.

MEGARRY, J., NISBET, S. & HOYLE, E. (eds) 1981, *Education of Minorities*. London: Kogan Page.

MEHAN, H. 1979, *Learning Lessons: Social Organisation in the Classroom*. Cambridge, MA: Harvard University Press.

MEIER, R.L. 1962, *A Communication Theory of Urban Growth*. Cambridge, MA: M.I.T. Press.

MELTZER, B. 1964, Mead's social psychology. In MANIS & MELTZER (1978).

MERTON, R.K. 1968, *Social Theory and Social Structure* (enlarged edn). New York: Free Press; London: Collier-Macmillan.

MIJN MAAT IS MIJN MAAT. De Groot, G. & Van der Zwaag, H. 1985. Leeuwarden: Teacher Training Institute Ubbo Emmius.

MILES, R.H. & RANDOLPH, W.A. 1979, *The Organization Game*. Glenview, IL: Scott, Foresman & Co.

MILGRAM, S. 1974, *Obedience to Authority*. London: Tavistock.

MILLS, C.W. 1963, Situated actions and vocabularies of motive. In HOROWITZ (1963).

MILNER, D. 1983, *Children and Race: Ten Years On*. London: Ward Lock Educational.

MINTZBERG, H. 1973, *The Nature of Managerial Work*. New York: Harper & Row.

MITROFF, I.I. 1983, *Stakeholders of the Organizational Mind: Toward a New View of Organizational Policy Making*. San Francisco: Jossey-Bass.

MODERN BUSINESS DECISIONS. Cotter, R. V. & Fritzsche, D.J. 1985. Englewood Cliffs, NJ: Prentice-Hall.

MONOPOLY. Darrow, C.W. 1935. Salem, MA: Parker Brothers.

MONROE, M.W. 1972, *Urban Games: Four Case Studies in Urban Development*. Berkeley: University of California Press.

MOONEN, J. & PLOMP, T. (eds) 1987, *Developments in Educational Software and Courseware*. Oxford: Pergamon.

MOORE, O.K. & ANDERSON, A.R. 1975, Some principles for the design and clarifying of educational environments. In GREENBLAT & DUKE (1975).

MORGENSTERN, D. 1987, Artifice versus real-world data: Six simulations. In CROOKALL *et al*. (1987).

MORGENTHAU, H.J. 1973, *Politics among Nations: The Struggle for Power and Peace*. New York: Knopf.

MORLEY, D. 1980, *The Nationwide Audience*. London: British Film Institute.

MOROKOFF, P. 1983, Toward the elimination of rape: A conceptualization of sexual aggression against women. In GOLDSTEIN & KRASNER (1983).

MORROW, L. 1984, *The Chief: A Memoir of Fathers and Sons*. New York: Random House.

MORTAL REMAINS. Versluis, E. 1985. Ashland, OR: Southern Oregon State College.

MOSCOVICI, S. 1976, *Social Influence and Social Change*. London: Academic Press.

MUNBY, J. 1978, *Communicative Syllabus Design*. Cambridge: Cambridge University Press.

NAGELBERG, M. & LITTLE, D. L. 1970, Bibliography of urban games. *Simulation & Games*, December 1970.

NATIONAL COMMISSION ON THE CAUSES AND PREVENTION OF VIOLENCE 1969, *To Establish Justice, To Insure Domestic Tranquillity*. Washington, DC: Government Printing Office. Cited by COMSTOCK (1983).

NATIONWIDE AUDIENCE, THE. Morley, D. 1980. See MORLEY (1980).

NETANYAHU, B. (ed.) 1986, *Terrorism: How the West Can Win*. New York: Farrar, Straus & Giroux.

NEWSIM. Crookall, D. 1985. See CROOKALL (1985).

NEWTOWN. Maslen, A. 1983. See MASLEN (1983).

NICKEL AUCTION, THE. Lobuts, J. & Pennewill, C. 1984. See LOBUTS & PENNEWILL (1984).

NOEL, R.C. 1979, The POLIS methodology for distributed political gaming via computer networks. In BRUIN *et al*. (1979).

NOEL, R.C., CROOKALL, D., WILKENFELD, J. & SCHAPIRA, L. 1987, Network gaming: A vehicle for intercultural communication. In CROOKALL *et al*. (1987).

NOESJIRWAN, J. 1978. A rule-based analysis of cultural differences in social behaviour: Indonesia and Australia. *International Journal of Psychology*, 13, 4.

NOESJIRWAN, J. & FREESTONE, C. 1979, The Culture Game: A simulation of culture shock. *Simulation & Games*, 10, 2.

O'SULLIVAN, T., HARTLEY, J., SAUNDERS, D. & FISKE, J. 1983, *Key Concepts in Communication*. London: Methuen.

OBERG, K. 1960, Culture shock: Adjustment to new cultural environments. *Practical Anthropology*, 7, 2.

OIL THREAT TO RADLEIGH. Lynch, M. 1977. In LYNCH (1977).

OKABE, R. 1983, Cultural assumptions of East and West: Japan and the United States. In GUDYKUNST (1983).

OMAGGIO, A.C. 1979, *Games and Simulations in the Foreign Language Classroom*. Arlington, VA: Center for Applied Linguistics & ERIC Clearinghouse on Languages and Linguistics.

——1986. *Teaching Language in Context: Proficiency-Oriented Instruction*. Boston: Heinle & Heinle.

OPPENHEIMER, J. & WINER, M. 1988, Using and creating a simulation authoring system: COOPERATION AND CONFLICT. In CROOKALL (1988a).

ORBACH, E. 1977, Some theoretical considerations in the evaluation of instructional simulation games. *Simulation & Games*, 8, 3 : 341–60.

OUTSIDE EXPERT. Pedersen, P. 1988. See PEDERSEN (1988)

OXFORD, R. 1988, *Language Learning Strategies: What Every Teacher Should Know*. New York: Newbury House/Harper & Row.

PAHL, R.E. 1975, *Whose City?* London: Longman.

PAINTOCO: A COMPUTERIZED MARKETING SIMULATION. Galoway, J.C., Evans, J.R. & Berman, B. 1985. New York: Macmillan.

PAULSTON, C.B., BRITTON, D., BRUNETTI, B. & HOOVER, J. 1975, *Developing Communicative Competence: Roleplays in English as a Second Language*. Pittsburgh, PA: University of Pittsburgh Press.

PEARL, D., BOUTHILET, L. & LAZAR, J. 1982, *Television and Behavior: Ten Years of Scientific Justice and Implications for the Eighties*.

Vol. 1. Summary Report; Vol. 2. Technical Reviews. Washington, DC: Government Printing Office. Cited by COMSTOCK (1983).

PECK, M. 1978, *The Road Less Traveled: A New Psychology of Love, Traditional Values and Spiritual Growth*. New York: Simon & Schuster.

PEDERSEN, P. 1986, Developing interculturally skilled counselors: A prototype for training. In LEFLEY & PEDERSEN (1986).

——1988. *A Handbook for Developing Multicultural Awareness*. Washington, DC: American Association for Counseling and Development.

PEDERSEN, A. & PEDERSEN, P. 1985, Developing interculturally skilled communication: A seminar workbook. Unpublished workbook. Syracuse, NY: Syracuse University.

PENGUINS OF DEATH, THE. Ryberg, C. & Versluis, E. 1982. Ashland, OR: Southern Oregon State College.

PERCIVAL, F. 1977, The development and evaluation of a structured scientific communication exercise. In HILLS & GILBERT (1977).

PERCIVAL, F. & ELLINGTON, H.I. 1980, The place of case studies in the simulation/gaming field. In RACE & BROOK (1980).

PERFORM. Klabbers, J. 1985. See KLABBERS (1985).

PETERSON, C. & SELIGMAN, M.E.P. 1984, Causal explanations as a risk factor for depression: Theory and evidence. *Psychological Review*, 91, 3.

PETRANEK, C.F. 1981, Using written journals to assist students in understanding simulations. Paper presented at the International Simulation and Gaming Association (ISAGA) Conference, Haifa, Israel.

PFEFFER, J. 1981, *Power in Organisations*. London: Pitman.

PIAGET, J. 1926, *The Language and Thought of the Child*. New York: Harcourt Brace & World.

PICTURE STORIES. Crookall, D. 1983. See Crookall (1983a).

PIERFY, D.A. 1977, Comparativc simulation game research: Stumbling blocks and stepping stones. *Simulation & Games*, 8, 2:255–68.

PILFOLD, D. (ed.) 1982, *Proceedings: 1982 Canadian Regional Business and Technical Communication Conference*. Kingston, Ontario: Queen's University Press.

PLEA BARGAINING. Katsh, E., Pipkin, R.M. & Katsh, B.S. Undated. Springfield, MA: Legal Studies Simulations.

POGREBIN, L.C. 1975, *Getting Yours*. New York: Avon Books.

POLITICS AND PLANNING. Glasson, J., Minay, C. & Minett, J. 1971. See GLASSON *et al*. (1971).

PORAT, I. 1987, Toward a theoretical framework of media simulation games. In CROOKALL *et al*. (1987).

PORTER LADOUSSE, G. 1987, *Role Play* (Resource Books for Teachers). Oxford: Oxford University Press.

POSTMAN, N. & WEINGARTNER, C. 1969, *Teaching as a Subversive Activity*. Harmondsworth: Penguin.

POWELL, C.P. 1969, Simulation: The anatomy of a fad. *Acta Politica*, April.

POWER FOR ELASKAY. Ellington, H.I. & Addinall, E. 1978. See ELLINGTON & ADDINALL (1978).

POWER, J. 1971. Planning: Magic and technique. In IOR (1971).

PRISONER'S DILEMMA. Invented or discovered (?) by Merrill M. Flood; name given by Albert W. Tucker. Undatable. See COLMAN (1982), EISER (1980), FLOOD (1958), HAMBURGER (1979), LUCE & RAIFFA (1957).

PROTEINS AS HUMAN FOOD. Percival, F. 1977. In PERCIVAL (1977).

PRUITT, D.G. 1987, Creative approaches to negotiation. In SANDOLE & SANDOLE-STAROSTE (1987).

RAABE, J. (ed.) 1980, *The Child and Play: Theoretical Approaches and Teaching Applications*. Paris: UNESCO.

RACE, P. & BROOK, D. (eds) 1980, *Simulation and Gaming for the 1980s*. London: Kogan Page.

RADIO COVINGHAM. Jones, K. 1974. In K. JONES (1986).

RAPOPORT, A. 1960, *Fights, Games, and Debates*. Ann Arbor: University of Michigan Press.

RAZ, H. 1985, Role-play in foreign language learning. In CROOKALL (1985).

REX, J. & MOORE, B. 1967, *Race, Community and Conflict*. Oxford: Oxford University Press.

RHYNE, R.F. 1975, Communicating holistic insights. In GREENBLAT & DUKE (1975).

RICHARDS, J.C. & RODGERS, T.S. 1986, *Approaches and Methods in Language Teaching: A Description and Analysis*. Cambridge: Cambridge University Press.

RICHARDSON, L.F. 1939, Generalized foreign politics: A study in group psychology. *British Journal of Psychology*, Monograph Supplements, 7, 23.

RICHMOND-ABBOTT, M. 1979, *The American Woman: Her Past, Her Present, Her Future*. New York: Holt, Rinehart, & Winston.

RINGER, R. 1978, *Looking Out for Number One*. New York: Faucet.

RIVERS, W.M. 1981, *Teaching Foreign Language Skills* (2nd edn). Chicago: University of Chicago Press.

——1983, *Communicating Naturally in a Second Language*. Cambridge: Cambridge University Press.

ROBINSON, J.A. 1966, Simulation and games. In ROSSI & BIDDLE (1966).

ROCKLER, M.J. 1977, Social studies. In HORN (1977).

ROGERS, C.R. 1961, *On Becoming a Person: A Therapist's View of Psychotherapy*. Boston: Houghton Mifflin.

ROGERS, R. 1986, *Six Role Plays*. Oxford: Basil Blackwell.

ROLE TRANSCENDENCE. Jensen, M. 1987. See Chapter 10 of this volume.

ROSENFELD, F.H. 1975, The educational effectiveness of simulation games: A synthesis of recent findings. In GREENBLAT & DUKE (1975).

ROSENKRANTZ, P.S., VOGEL, S.R., BEE, H., BROVERMAN, I.K. & BROVERMAN, D.M. 1968, Sex-role stereotypes and self-concepts in college students. *Journal of Consulting and Clinical Psychology*, 32 : 287–95.

ROSSI, P. & BIDDLE, B. (eds) 1966, *The New Media and Education*. Chicago: Aldine.

ROWEIS, S.T. 1981, Urban planning in early and late capitalist societies: Outline of a theoretical perspective. In DEAR & SCOTT (1981).

RUBEN, B.D. & BUDD, R.W. 1975, *Human Communication Handbook*, Vol. 1. Rochelle Park, NJ: Hayden.

——1978, *Human Communication Handbook*, Vol. 2. Rochelle Park, NJ: Hayden.

RUBEN, B.D. & LEDERMAN, L.C. 1989, Communication, culture, and language: The role of interactive simulations. In CROOKALL & OXFORD (1989).

RUBIN, A.M., PERSE, E.M. & POWELL, R.A. 1985, Loneliness, para-social interaction, and local television news viewing. *Human Communication Research*, 12, 2 : 155–80.

RYAN, E.B. & GILES, H. (eds) 1982, *Attitudes Towards Language Variation: Social and Applied Contexts*. London: Edward Arnold.

RYBERG, C.R. & VERSLUIS, E.B. 1987, Internal audiences in computer simulations. In CROOKALL *et al.* (1987).

SACKS, H. 1974, On the analysability of stories by children. In TURNER (1974).

SACKS, H., SCHEGLOFF, E. & JEFFERSON, G. 1974, A simplest systematics for the organization of turn-taking for conversation. *Language*, 50 : 696–735.

ST CLAIR, R. & GILES, H. (eds) 1980, *The Social and Psychological Contexts of Language*. Hillsdale, NJ: Erlbaum.

SALE OF A NEWSPAPER, THE. Open University 1982. Milton Keynes: Open University Press.

SALES MANAGEMENT SIMULATION. Day, R.L. & Dalrymple, D.J. 1985. New York: John Wiley.

SANDAY, P. 1981, The socio-cultural context of rape: A cross-cultural study. *Journal of Social Issues*, 37. Cited by MOROKOFF (1983).

SANDOLE, D.J.D. 1980a, Changing perceptions: An approach to teaching

international relations and its impact on the attitudes of mid-career students. In KENT & NIELSSON (1980).
——1980b. Economic conditions and conflict processes. In WHITELEY (1980).
——1983, Man, the state and war re-visited. Paper presented at the panel on Causes of War at the 6th Annual Scientific Meeting of the International Society of Political Psychology (ISPP), St Catherine's College, Oxford University, 19–22 July.
——1984, The subjectivity of theories and actions in world society. In BANKS (1984).
——1985, Training and teaching in a field whose 'time has come': A postgraduate program in conflict management. In CUTRONA (1985).
——1986, Traditional approaches to conflict management: Short-term gains vs. long-term costs. *Current Research on Peace and Violence*, IX: 3.
——1987, Conflict management: Elements of generic theory and process. In SANDOLE & SANDOLE-STAROSTE (1987).

SANDOLE, D.J.D. & SANDOLE-STAROSTE, I. (eds) 1987, *Conflict Management and Problem Solving: Interpersonal to International Applications*. London: Frances Pinter; New York: New York University Press.

SAUNDERS, D. 1983, Teaching communication studies by way of invested crisis within an artificial media situation. *Simulation/Games for Learning*, 13, 1 : 17–25.
——1986, Drama and simulation: A soap opera game that illustrates dramaturgical perspectives in communication studies. *Simulation & Games*, 17, 1 : 75–99.
——1987, More than a game. *Business Education*, 12, 12: 16–18.

SAUNDERS, D. & CROOKALL, D. 1985. Playing with a second language. *Simulation/Games for Learning*, 15 : 4

SAUNDERS, D. & JONES. K. 1986, *Simulation and Gaming in Human Relations Work: A Resource List*. Loughborough, Leics: SAGSET.

SAVIGNON, S. 1983, *Communicative Competence: Theory and Practice*. Reading, MA: Addison-Wesley.

SAVIGNON, S.J. & BERNS, M.S. (eds) 1984, *Initiatives in Communicative Language Teaching: A Book of Readings*. Reading, MA: Addison-Wesley.

SAVILLE-TROIKE, M. 1982, *The Ethnography of Communication: An Introduction*. Oxford: Basil Blackwell.

SAWYER-LAUÇANNO, C. 1987, Intercultural simulation. In CROOKALL *et al*. (1987).

SAYLES, L.R. & STRAUSS, G. 1981, *Managing Human Resources*. Englewood Cliffs, NJ: Prentice-Hall.

SCARCELLA, R. & CROOKALL, D. 1989, Simulation and second language acquisition. In CROOKALL & OXFORD (1989).

SCHEFLEN, A.E. 1968, Human communication: Behavioral programs and their integration in interaction. *Behavioural Science*, 13 : 44–55.

——1974, *How Behavior Means*. Garden City, NY: Doubleday Anchor.

SCHELLING, T.C. 1966, *Arms and Influence*. New Haven, CT: Yale University Press.

SCHOFIELD, A. 1982, Call yourself a manager?—A new approach to using simulation in management training. In GRAY & WAITT (1982).

SCHUTZ, A. 1967, *The Phenomenology of the Social World*. Evanston, IL: Northwestern University Press; London: Heinemann.

SCHUTZ, A. & LUCKMANN, T. 1973, *The Structures of the Life World*. Evanston, IL: Northwestern University Press.

SCOTT, W. 1980, Origins and problems of Communications Studies in the UK. *Communication Studies Bulletin*, 6.

SELIGER, H.W. & LONG, M.H. (eds) 1983, *Classroom Oriented Research in Second Language Acquisition*. Rowley, MA: Newbury House.

SHAFFER, P. 1974, *Equus*. New York: Avon.

SHANNON, C. & WEAVER, W. 1949, *The Mathematical Theory of Communication*. Urbana: University of Illinois Press.

SHAPSON, S. & D'OYLEY, V. (eds) 1984, *Bilingual and Multicultural Education: Canadian Perspectives*. Clevedon, Avon: Multilingual Matters.

SHARROCK, W.W. 1974, On owning knowledge. In TURNER (1974).

SHARROCK, W.W. & ANDERSON, B. 1986, *The Ethnomethodologists*. Chichester: Ellis Horwood; London & New York: Tavistock.

——1987, Epilogue: The definition of alternatives: Some sources of confusion in interdisciplinary discussion. In BUTTON & LEE (1987).

SHARROCK, W.W. & WATSON, D.R. 1985, 'Reality construction' in L2 simulations. In CROOKALL (1985).

——1987, 'Power' and 'realism' in simulation and gaming: Some pedagogic and analytic observations. In CROOKALL *et al.* (1987).

SHERIF, M. 1966a, *Group Conflict and Co-operation: Their Social Psychology*. London: Routledge & Kegan Paul.

——1966b, *In Common Predicament: Social Psychology of Intergroup Conflict and Cooperation*. Boston: Houghton Mifflin.

SHERIF, M., HARVEY, O.J., WHITE, B.J., HOOD, W.R. & SHERIF, C.W. 1961, *Intergroup Conflict and Cooperation: The Robbers' Cave Experiment*. Norman: University of Oklahoma Press.

SHERIF, M. & SHERIF, C.W. 1953, *Groups in Harmony and Tension: An Integration of Studies in Intergroup Relations*. New York: Harper & Row.

——1965, Research on intergroup relations. In AUSTIN & WORCHEL (1979).

SHUBIK, M. 1975, *The Uses and Methods of Gaming*. New York: Elsevier.

SIGMAN, S.J. 1980, On communication rules from a social perspective. *Human Communication Research*, 7 : 37–51.

——1983, Some multiple constraints placed on conversational topics. In CRAIG & TRACY (1983).

——1984, Talk and interaction strategy in a task-oriented group. *Small Group Behavior*, 15, 1 : 33–51.

——1985, Some common mistakes students make when learning discourse analysis. *Communication Education*, 34, 2 : 119–27.

SILLARS, A.L. 1981, Attributions and interpersonal conflict resolution. In HARVEY *et al.* (1981).

SIMSOC. Gamson, W. A. 1966. New York: Free Press.

SIMULATION DESIGN GAME, THE. Crookall, D., Saunders, D. & Coote, A. 1986. In CROOKALL *et al.* (1987).

SINGER, J.D. (ed.) 1968, *Quantitative International Politics: Insights and Evidence*. New York: Free Press; London: Collier-Macmillan.

SITARAM, K.S. & COGDELL, R.T. 1976, *Foundations of Intercultural Communication*. Colombus, OH: Charles E. Merrill.

SKUTNABB-KANGAS T. 1984, *Bilingualism Or Not: The Education of Minorities*. Clevedon, Avon: Multilingual Matters.

SLICK, Blackwell, G.K. (no date) Based on a BP Game by M. Lynch.

SMITH, L.E. (ed.) 1981, *English for Cross-Cultural Communication*. London: Macmillan.

SNOW, B. 1977, *Psychological Foundations of Organizational Behavior*. Santa Monica, CA: Goodyear.

SNOW C.P. 1959, *The Two Cultures: And a Second Look*. Cambridge: Cambridge University Press.

SNYDER, M. & GANGESTAD, S. 1981, Hypothesis-testing processes. In HARVEY *et al.* (1981).

SOCIAL SERVICES RESOURCE ALLOCATION GAME. Hall, A. S. & Algie, J. 1974. In HALL & ALGIE (1974).

SPACE. 1984. Law-Yone, H. See LAW-YONE (1987).

STARPOWER. Shirts, G. 1969. La Jolla, CA: Simile II.

STERN, B.B. 1979, A new communications program for women. *Lamplighter* (American Society for Training and Development), 11, 4.

——1980, The secretarial condition: Role-play, Alpha Products. *Northeast Training News*, 1 : 19–20.

——1981, *Is Networking for You? A Working Woman's Guide to the Old Boy System*. Englewood Cliffs, NJ: Prentice-Hall.

——1985, Women in managerial roles: An innovative course for women marketing students. *Journal of Education for Business*, 61 : 128–31.

——1986, The games women play: Simulation and women's networks. *Women in Management Review*, 2, 3 : 154–65.

STERN, H.H. 1983, *Fundamental Concepts of Language Teaching*. Oxford: Oxford University Press.

STEVENS, F. 1985, Using simulations as research instruments. In CROOKALL (1985).

——1987, The use of simulations for the purposes of research. In CROOKALL *et al.* (1987).

STEVENSON, A. 1963, Address to the Center for the Study of Democratic Institutions. MGM Records: E 4329D.

STOHL, M. & LOPEZ, G.A. (eds) 1986, *Government Violence and Repression: An Agenda for Research*. Westport, CT: Greenwood Press.

STOKES, P. 1966, *Total Job Training*. American Management Association.

STONE, G.B. 1970, The play of little children. In STONE & FARBERMAN (1981).

STONE, G.P. & FARBERMAN, H.A. 1981, *Social Psychology through Symbolic Interaction*. New York: Wiley.

STONER, J.A.F. 1978, *Management*. Englewood Cliffs, NJ: Prentice-Hall.

STRAT-PLAN. Hinton, R.W. & Smith, D.C. 1985. Englewood Cliffs, NJ: Prentice-Hall.

STURTRIDGE, G. & HERBERT, D. 1979, *ELT Guide 2: Simulations*. London: NFER for the British Council.

SUMAH. Eden, T. & Last, J. 1982. Brighton: Brighton Polytechnic.

SURVIVAL GAME. James, L. *et al*. 1982. London: Community Service Volunteers.

SWAIN, M. & LAPKIN, S. 1982, *Evaluating Bilingual Education: A Canadian Case Study*. Clevedon, Avon: Multilingual Matters.

SWINGLE, P. (ed.) 1970, *The Structure of Conflict*. London: Academic Press.

TAFFS PIT. Saunders, D. 1986. See SAUNDERS (1986).

TAFT, E. 1976, Coping with unfamiliar cultures. In WARREN (1976).

TAJFEL, H. 1978, *Differentiation between Social Groups: Studies in the Social Psychology of Intergroup Relations*. London: Academic Press.

——1981, *Human Groups and Social Categories: Studies in Social Psychology*. Cambridge: Cambridge University Press.

——1982, *The Social Psychology of Minorities*. London: Minority Rights Group.

——(ed.) 1982, *Social Identity and Intergroup Relations*. Cambridge: Cambridge University Press.

——(ed.) 1984, *The Social Dimension*. Cambridge: Cambridge University Press.

TAJFEL, H., FLAMENT, C., BILLIG, M.G. & BUNDY, R.P. 1971, Social categorization and intergroup behaviour. *European Journal of Social Psychology*, 1 : 149–78.

TANSEY, P.J. (ed.) 1971, *Educational Aspects of Simulation*. London: McGraw-Hill.

TANSEY, P.J. & UNWIN, D. 1969, *Simulation and Gaming in Education*. London: Methuen.

TAYLOR, B. & LIPPITT, G. (eds) 1983, *Management Development and Training Handbook* (2nd edn). New York: McGraw-Hill.

TAYLOR JR., E. & GOODMAN, F. 1987, Computer-mediated simulations: The global classroom. *Academic Computing*, Spring: 53–6.

TAYLOR, J. 1977, Instructional gaming procedures in planning education. In MEGARRY (1977).

TEACH, R. 1987, Desirable characteristics and attributes of a business simulation. In CROOKALL *et al.* (1987).

TERRI. Coleman, D. W. 1985. See COLEMAN (1985).

THATCHER, D. 1986, Promoting learning through games and simulations. In VAN MENTS (1986).

THATCHER, D. & ROBINSON, J. 1985, *An Introduction to Simulations and Games in Education*. Fareham, Hants: Solent Simulations.

THIERAUF, R.J. & KLEKAMP, R.C. 1975, *Decision Making through Operations Research*. New York: Wiley.

THOMAS, W.I. 1951, The four wishes and the definitions of the situation. In JANOWITZ (1966).

TING-TOOMEY, S. 1985, Toward a theory of conflict and culture. *International and Intercultural Communication Annual*, 9 : 71–86.

——1987, A comparative analysis of the communicative dimensions of love, self-disclosure maintenance, ambivalence, and conflict in three cultures: France, Japan, and the United States. Paper presented at the meeting of the International Communication Association, Montreal, Canada, May.

TORRINGTON, D. & WEIGHTMAN, J. 1985, *The Business of Management*. London: Prentice-Hall.

TRIANDIS, H. 1986, Collectivism vs. individualism. In BAGLEY & VERMA (1986).

TRUTH STATEMENT, THE. Pedersen, P. 1988. See PEDERSEN (1988).

TUCKER, G.R., HAMAYAN, E. & GENESEE, F.H. 1976, Affective, cognitive, and social factors in second language acquisition. *Canadian Modern Language Review*, 32 : 214–26.

TUFTE, E.R. 1983, *The Visual Display of Quantitative Information*. Cheshire, CO: Graphics Press.

TURNER, J.C. & GILES, H. (eds) 1981, *Intergroup Behaviour*. Oxford: Basil Blackwell.

TURNER, R. (ed.) 1974, *Ethnomethodology*. Harmondsworth: Penguin.

TURNER, R. 1976, The real self: From institution to impulse. *American Journal of Sociology*, 81 : 989–1016.

TURNER, R.H. 1975, Is there a quest for identity? *Sociological Quarterly*, 16 : 148–61.

TWENTY QUESTIONS. Probably BBC. Undated. (Well-known BBC radio game.)

TWITCHIN, J. & DEMUTH, C. 1985. *Multi-Cultural Education* (2nd edn). London: British Broadcasting Corporation.

UNISIM. Unilever plc. 1986. West Yorks: Unisim Sales.

UR, P. 1981, *Discussions that Work: Task-centred Fluency Practice*. Cambridge: Cambridge University Press.

URBAN DYNAMICS. Callahan, L., Caswell, D., McLellan, L., Mullen, R. & Savage, W. 1970. Institute of Higher Education Research and Services, University of Alabama.

VALDES, J.M. (ed.) 1986, *Culture Bound: Bridging the Cultural Gap in Language Teaching*. Cambridge: Cambridge University Press.

VAN DEN BERGHE, W. 1983, *General Education in University-Level Professional Studies*. Interim report for the University–Industry Action-Research and Evaluation Programme. Brussels: Industry–University Foundation.

VAN MENTS, M. 1983, *The Effective Use of Role-Play: A Handbook for Teachers and Trainers*. London: Kogan Page.

——(ed.) 1986, *Debriefing Simulation/Games*. (Special issue of *Simulation/Games for Learning*, 16, 4.

VAN MENTS, M. & HEARNDEN, K. (eds) 1985, *Effective Use of Games and Simulations*. Loughborough, Leics: SAGSET.

VANDENBERGE, P.L. 1978, *Race and Racism*. New York: John Wiley.

VERMA, G. & MODGIL, F. (eds) 1985, *Multi-Cultural Education: The Interminable Debate*. London: Falmer Press.

VOLKART, E.H. (ed.) 1951, *Social Behaviour and Personality: Contributions of W.I. Thomas to Theory and Social Research*. New York: Social Sciences Research Council.

VON BERTALANFFY, L. 1968, *General System Theory*. Harmondsworth: Penguin.

VROOM, V.H. & YETTON, P.W. 1973, *Leadership and Decision-Making*. Pittsburgh: University of Pittsburgh Press.

VYGOTSKY, L.S. 1956, *Selected Psychological Research*. Moscow: Izdatel'stvo Akademeii Pedagogicheskikh Nauk.

WALES, C.E. & STAGER, R.A. 1977, *The Guided Design Approach*. Englewood Cliffs, NJ: Educational Technology Publications.

WALSTER, E. & BERSCHEID, E. 1968, The effects of time on cognitive consistency. In ABELSON *et al.* (1968).

WARD, M.D. (ed.) 1985, *Theories, Models, and Simulations in International Relations: Essays in Honor of Harold Guetzkow*. Boulder, CO & London: Westview Press.

WARREN, M.R. 1975, *Training for Results*. Reading, MA: Addison-Wesley.

WARREN, N. (ed.) 1976, *Studies in Cross-Cultural Psychology*. London: Academic Press.

WATCYN-JONES, P. 1978, *Act English*. Harmondsworth: Penguin.

WATSON, D.R. & SHARROCK, W.W. 1987, Some social-interactional aspects of a business game. In CROOKALL *et al.* (1987).

——1989, The 'realities' of games and simulations: Some theoretical and analytical observations. In Crookall & Oxford (1989).

WATZLAWICK, P., BEAVIN, J.H. & JACKSON, D.D. 1967, *Pragmatics of Human Communication: A Study of Interaction Patterns, Pathologies, and Paradoxes*. New York: Norton.

WEARNE, S.H. 1984, Managerial Skills and Expertise Used by Samples of Engineers in Britain, Australia, Western Canada, Japan, the Netherlands, and Norway. Report No. TMR 152. Bradford: University of Bradford.

WEBB, A.J. 1986, Does the engineering discipline produce good managers? *Proceedings of the 1986 Engineering Conference*. Adelaide.

WEDGE, B. & SANDOLE, D.J.D. 1982, Conflict management: A new venture into professionalization. In DUGAN (1982).

WEICK, K. 1979, *The Social Psychology of Organizing*. London: Addison-Wesley.

WEICK, K.E. 1968, The panglossian world of self-justification. In ABELSON *et al.* (1968).

WEIZENBAUM, J. 1965, ELIZA—A computer program for the study of natural language communication between man and machine. *Communications of the Association for Computing Machinery*. 9, 1 : 36–45.

——1976, *Computer Power and Human Reason: From Judgement to Calculation*. San Francisco: Freeman; Harmondsworth: Penguin.

WELCH, M.S. 1981, *Networking: A Great New Way for Women to Get Ahead*. New York: Warner.

WELSH COMMERCIAL TELEVISION STATION, THE. Saunders, D. 1983. See SAUNDERS (1983).

WESTERNPORT COMMUNICATION SIMULATION. Irwin, H. 1981. See IRWIN (1981).

WHAT YOU SAID, FELT AND MEANT. Pedersen, P. 1988. See PEDERSEN (1988).

WHAT'S NEWS. Gamson, W.A. 1984. See GAMSON (1984).

WHISPERS. Traditional.

WHITE, D.M. 1950, The gatekeeper: A case study in the selection of news. *Journalism Quarterly*, 27 : 383–90.

WHITELEY, P. (ed.) 1980, *Models of Political Economy*. London & Beverly Hills, CA: Sage.

WHORF, B.L. 1956, *Language, Thought and Reality*. Cambridge, MA: M.I.T. Press.

WIDDOWSON, H.G. 1978, *Teaching Language as Communication*. Oxford: Oxford University Press.

——1983, *Language Purpose and Language Use*. Oxford: Oxford University Press.

WILKENFELD, J. 1983, Computer-assisted international studies. *Teaching Political Science*, 10, 4.

WILKINS, D.A, 1976, *Notional Syllabuses*. Oxford: Oxford University Press.

WILKINSON, L.C. (ed.) 1972, *Communicating in the Classroom*. New York: Academic Press.

——1982. *Communicating in the Classroom*. New York: Academic Press.

WILLIAMS, R. 1958, *Culture and Society*. Harmondsworth: Penguin.

——1962, *Communications*. Harmondsworth: Penguin.

——1974a, Communication as cultural science. *Journal of Communication*, 24, 3.

——1974b, *Television: Technology and Cultural Form*. London: Fontana.

——1981, *Culture*. London: Fontana.

WINE LAKE (The European Community: An Exercise in Decision Making). Clarke, M., May, J., Wallace, H. & Webb, C. 1978. London: University Association for Contemporary European Studies. (Also in CLARKE, 1978).

WOLF, C. 1987, ICS: Interactive Communication Simulation. In CROOKALL *et al*. (1987).

WOLFE, J. 1985, The teaching effectiveness of games in collegiate business courses: A 1973–83 update. *Simulation & Games*, 16, 3.

——(ed.) 1987, *A Practical Guide to Business Gaming*. Special issue of *Simulation & Games*, 18 : 1.

WYNN, M. 1985, *Planning Games: Case Study Simulations in Land Management and Development*. London: Spon (Chapman & Hall).

YELLOW RIVER KINGDOM. Anonymous. Undated. Cambridge: Acorn Computers. (Game provided on the 'Welcome Disc' accompanying the Acorn BBC Microcomputer; probably public domain.) See G. JONES (1986).

ZALEZNIK, A. & KETS DE VRIES, M.F.R. 1975, *Power and the Corporate Mind*. Boston: Houghton Mifflin.

ZIMBARDO, P.G. 1969, The human choice: Individuation, reason and order versus deindividuation, impulse and chaos. *Nebraska Symposium on Motivation*, 17 : 237–307.

Associations and periodicals

This volume is devoted to discussions of the connections between communication and simulation. Readers of this volume will not have too much difficulty in tracing materials in the field of communication. There are many associations (international, national, regional and specialised) which cater for many aspects of that field. There are also many journals which, collectively, deal with almost all aspects of it. We thought, therefore, that it would be useful to provide here a few sources related to simulation, as these are often more difficult to trace than those related to communication. There are four major simulation associations in the world. They publish their own newsletters and hold their own annual conferences. In addition, there are two major quarterly journals and an international newsletter devoted entirely to simulation/gaming.

Associations

ABSEL *Association for Business Simulation and Experiential Learning*. Information from: Dr Frank A. Dasse, Crummer Graduate School of Business, Rollins College, Winter Park, FL 32789, U.S.A. Annual conference usually in the spring.

ISAGA *International Simulation and Gaming Association*. Information from: ISAGA Secretary, Prof. Dr. Jan H.G. Klabbers, Faculty of Social Science, State University at Utrecht, Heidelberglaan 1, 3584 CS Utrecht, Netherlands. Annual conference in the summer; proceedings usually published by Pergamon Press (Headington Hill Hall, Oxford OX3 0BW, U.K.).

NASAGA *North American Simulation and Gaming Association*. Information from: National Game Center and Laboratory, University of North Carolina at Ashville, One University

Heights, Ashville, NC 28804–3299, U.S.A. Annual conference in the autumn.

SAGSET *Society for the Advancement of Games and Simulations in Education and Training*. Information from: The Secretary, SAGSET, Center for Extension Studies, University of Technology, Lougborough LE11 3TU, Leics, U.K. Annual conference in early September; proceedings always published. SAGSET also produces a series of useful resource lists.

Periodicals

Simulation & Games. This is the official journal of ABSEL, NASAGA, and ISAGA, and can be obtained either through membership of one of the above associations, or by direct subscription to Sage Publications (P.O. Box 5084, 2111 West Hillcrest Drive, Newbury Park, CA 91320, U.S.A; 29 Banner Street, London EC1Y 8QE, U.K.). The journal generally carries five or six longish articles, usually academic in style. It has book and game reviews, and contains an 'Informal Communications' section of news and notes from the three associations. The editor is Cathy Stein Greenblat, Dept of Sociology, Douglas College, Rutgers University, New Brunswick, NJ 08903, U.S.A.

Simulation/Games for Learning**.** This is the official journal of SAGSET, obtainable either as part of SAGSET membership or on a separate subscription basis (see SAGSET address above). The journal typically carries about four short to medium-length major articles per issue, generally of a fairly practical nature. It has very useful book and game reviews, and contains an abstract section based on ERIC/ChESS. The editor is Alan Coote, Dept of Management & Legal Studies, Polytechnic of Wales, Pontypridd, Mid Glam CF37 1DL, U.K.

ISAGA Newsletter. This is the official quarterly periodical of ISAGA. It can be obtained through membership of ISAGA (see address above). The newsletter generally runs to some 20 pages, containing news items, a couple of short articles, as well as book and game reviews. Parts of the newsletter are reproduced some months after publication in *Simulation & Games* (see above). The editor is David Crookall, 4901 Seminary Rd. Apt. 1122, Alexandria, VA 22311, U.S.A.

Contributors

KLAAS BRUIN, Stichting Lerarenopleiding, Ubbo Emmius, Postbus 1018, 8900 CA Leeuwarden, Netherlands.

ALAN COOTE, Dept of Management & Legal Studies, The Polytechnic of Wales, Pontypridd, Mid Glamorgan CF37 1DL, Wales, U.K.

DAVID CROOKALL, Dept. of Speech Communication, The Pennsylvania State University, University Park, PA 16802, U.S.A.

ANNE DONNELLON, Graduate School of Business Administration, Harvard University, Humphrey 35, Soldiers Field, Boston, MA 02163, U.S.A.

RICHARD D. DUKE, Multilogue, 321 Parklane, Ann Arbor, MI 48103, U.S.A.

PHILLIPPE DUMAS, Institut Universitaire de Technologie, Université de Toulon & du Var, Avenue de l'Université, 83130 La Garde, France.

JAMES J. FERNANDES, Gallaudet University Center on Deafness, University of Hawaii, Kapiolani Community College, 4303 Diamond Head Road, Honolulu, HI 96816, U.S.A.

DAVID FRANCIS, Dept of Social Science, Faculty of Humanities, Law and Social Science, Manchester Polytechnic, Cavendish Bldg, Cavendish St, Manchester M15 6BG, U.K.

JAMES M. FREEMAN, Dept of Management Sciences, University of Manchester Institute of Science & Technology, PO Box 88, Manchester M60 1QD, U.K.

CATHY S. GREENBLAT, Dept of Sociology, Rutgers University, New Brunswick, NJ 08903, U.S.A.

JEFF HEARN, School of Applied Social Studies, University of Bradford, Bradford, West Yorkshire BD7 1DP, U.K.

MARVIN D. JENSEN, Dept of Communication & Theatre Arts, University of Northern Iowa, Cedar Falls, IA 50614–0357, U.S.A.

JAN H. G. KLABBERS, Faculty of Social Sciences, State University at Utrecht, PO Box 80 140, 3508 TC Utrecht, Netherlands.

ROBERTA LAVINE, Dept of Spanish & Portuguese, College of Arts and Humanities, University of Maryland, College Park, MD 20742, U.S.A.

HUBERT LAW-YONE, Faculty of Architecture & Urban Planning, Technion-Israel Institute of Technology, Technion City, Haifa 32000, Israel.

JOHN F. LOBUTS, Dept of Management Science, School of Government & Business Administration, George Washington University, 2115 G St NW, Washington, DC 20052, U.S.A.

STEWART MARSHALL, Dept of Language & Communication Studies, University of Technology, Private Mail Bag, Lae, Papua New Guinea.

LAURIE MCMAHON, King's Fund College, 2 Palace Court, London W2 4HS, U.K.

JENNY NOESJIRWAN, Kuring-gai College of Advanced Education, PO Box 222, Eton Road, Lindfield, NSW 2070, Australia.

MARTIN NORETSKY, Dept of Communication Arts, Gallaudet College, Kendall Green, 800 Florida Av NE, Washington, DC 20002, U.S.A.

TIM O'SULLIVAN, Dept of Behaviour & Communication, Polytechnic of Wales, Pontypridd, Mid Glamorgan CF37 1DL, Wales, U.K.

REBECCA OXFORD, The Annenberg/CPB Project, 1111 16th St. N.W., Washington DC 20036, U.S.A.

ANNE B. PEDERSEN, Counseling & Guidance, School of Education, Syracuse University, 370 Huntington Hall, Syracuse, NY 13244–2340, U.S.A.

PAUL B. PEDERSEN, Counseling & Guidance, School of Education, Syracuse University, 370 Huntington Hall, Syracuse, NY 1244–2340, U.S.A.

CAROL L. PENNEWILL, Dept of Management Science, School of Government & Business Administration, George Washington University, Hall of Government, Rm 205, 710 21st St NW, Washington, DC 20052, U.S.A.

CHARLES F. PETRANEK, Dept of Sociology, University of Southern Indiana, 8600 University Blvd, Evansville, IN 47712, U.S.A.

DENNIS J. D. SANDOLE, Dept of Public Affairs, George Mason University, 4400 University Drive, Fairfax, VA 22030, U.S.A.

DANNY SAUNDERS, Dept of Behaviour & Communication, Polytechnic of Wales, Pontypridd, Mid Glamorgan CF37 1DL, Wales, U.K.

STUART J. SIGMAN, Dept of Communication, BA 220, State University of New York, Albany, NY 12222, U.S.A.

BARBARA B. STERN, Dept of Economics & Management Science, Kean College of New Jersey, Union, NJ 07083, U.S.A.

STELLA TING-TOOMEY, Dept of Communication, Arizona State University, Tempe, AZ 85287, U.S.A.

EDWARD B. VERSLUIS, Dept of English, Southern Oregon State College, Ashland, OR 97520, U.S.A.

Index

A-B-Z GAME 163
'Abilene Paradox' 178
Abstraction, in representation 13, 43–8
Action, instrumental/communicative 253–4
Advertising, as communication 259–60
Aggression 178–9, 180–1, 185
AIRPORT CONTROVERSY simulation 99
Alexander, E.R., Alterman, R. & Law-Yone, H. 252
Alger, C.F. 140n.
ALIBI simulation 99
ALPHA CRISIS GAME, THE 100
ALTERNATIVE ENERGY PROGRAMME, THE 198–200
American Sign Language (ASL) 118–19, 120, 121, 124, 281
Analysis of Interconnected Decison Areas (AIDA) techniques 239
Anger 178–9, 184
Aronson, E. 116, 131
Assimilation, of hearing-impaired 118–19
Attitudes
 –cultural 149–51, 153–4, 160–1, 162–6, 177, 180, 186, 281
 –managerial 222
 –shift in 127–39, 165, 203, 204, 205–6, 273
 –to language 120, 121
Attribution research 128, 131–2
Audience
 –internal 111
 –simulated 87–8
AUNT SADIE'S GIFT computer program 87–90
Authenticity, in simulation 103
Authority, power of 230–1, 283

BACK TO BACK GAME, THE 221
BAFA BAFA simulation 113–14, 115, 157–60, 171–2, 173, 273
Bandura, A. 180
Banks, M. 138
Bargaining, *see* negotiation
Bartlett, F.C. 219
Bateson, G. 142–3, 144–5
Bell, D. 167
Berger, P.L. & Luckmann, T. 22, 142
Berne, E. 144
Biculturalism 162
Billig, M. 10, 23, 130, 162
BLOOD MONEY simulation 273
Blumler, J. 194
Bond, T. 219–21
Brammer, L. 148
BRAND X GAME, THE 259–60
Braten, S. 237
Bruin, Klass xiv, 155–68, 271, 281
BUCCANEER BILLY'S BAD BARGAIN computer simulation 90
Burton, John 129–30, 131, 134, 135–6, 138, 140n., 273
Business
 –women in 226–35
 –*see also* management; organisation theory; skills
Business education, *see* education

Business negotiation game 56–67, 101
Button, G. & Lee, J.R.E. 27

CALL YOURSELF A MANAGER 197
CAPJEFOS simulation 29n., 279–80, 282
Categorisation 158–61, 165
CELEBRITY INTRODUCTION GAME, THE 234
CHARADES simulation 99
Charisma, power of 232–4, 283
Charon, 110
Cheery, C. 6–7
CHEMICAL CONSTRUCTION COMPANY simulation 56–67
CHOOSING THE NEWS simulation 259
Clarke, Arthur C. 8–9
Class, social, and planning 248, 250
Classroom
–jigsaw 116
–simulation in 92, 97–101, 205, 282
–social interaction 84, 275
–*see also* education
Codes 7, 156
Coding/decoding 41–2
Collectivism 170–1, 173, 175
COLOUR GAME, THE 222–3
Commentary, computer 88–9
Common sense, in simulation 59–61, 67, 150–1
Communication
–barriers to 10–11, 120, 121, 124, 160–1, 165, 178, 253–4, 273–4, 280–1
–in counselling 147, 149–50, 281
–definitions 6–7, 34–5, 177
–distortion 221, 271, 281
–as dynamic 7
–expansion 8
–group 121–5, 227, 258–62, 274
–importance of 5–6
–intercultural 102–4, 149–54, 155, 156–8, 197, 280
–as interdisciplinary 4, 19–27, 194, 202
–intergroup 169–76
–machine-mediated 86–90, 257, 264–5
–male-female 226–7, 229, 235, 282–3
–mediated 197
–multidisciplinary approach 193–4
–networks 103–4
–non-verbal 153, 174, 263, 276–7
–as reality 21–2
–of reality 43–5
–as representations 21
–as a right 3, 5, 9–10, 93
–as situation-specific 39–42
–as static 6–7
–student–teacher 103–4, 173
–styles 130, 230–1, 273–4, *see also* culture, low-context/high-context
–theory and practice 195–6, 198–200, 221
–in urban planning 247–55
–*see also* conflict resolution; gestalt communication; multilingualism; patterns, communication; skills, communication; transmission, communication as
Communication analysis 20
Communication/simulation, interdependency 3–5, 19, 22–3, 25–8, 104, 123–5, 238–9, 270
COMMUNICATIONS IN A HIERARCHY simulation 221–2
Communications Studies 5, 191–2
–academic courses 192–4, 198–9, 257–8, 262
–focus on media and culture 7
–simulations in 196–200
–and skills training 194–6
–view of simulation 23–4
Communications Studies Log Report 200
Competition
–in conflict resolution 129–31, 132, 139
–as destructive 178–87
–and discrimination 162
–in simulation 23, 201–2, 209, 273, 275

Complexity, communicating 43–6, 48–51, 52
Computer
–as catalyst for communication 83–5, 101, 102, 275
–as communication network 83, 104, 235
–as mass media 264–5
–as participant 86–90
–*see also* simulation, computerised
Comstock, G. 181
Concept report 45, 48
Conflict, interpersonal 141, 146, 174, 264, *see also* role conflict
Conflict resolution 23–4, 128, 243
–competitive/co-operative 129–31, 132, 139, 181, 274
–and use of simulation 132–9, 80, 184–6, 209
Conformity, pressure for 160–2, 182
Contact hypothesis 162–3
Content analysis, simulation texts 21
Context
–in language learning 98
–of social interaction 70–2, 80, 114, 161, 184, 276
Conversation analysis 55–6, 58, 71
Cooley, C.H. 114
Co-operation
–and competition 181, 184–5, 273, 275
–in conflict resolution 129–31, 132, 139
–and discrimination 162–3
Coote, Alan xiv, 214–25, 279
Corporatism, in planning 249
Counselling
–microskills 148–9, 154, 270–1, 274
–use of simulation in training 147, 150–4, 281
Creative Problem-Solving Sequence (CPSS) 122, 125
Crookall, David xiii, xv, 3–29, 82–90, 91–106, 256–66, 270–1, 275, 282
Cue
–cultural 230
–non-verbal 153, 174
Cultural Studies 192–3
Culture
–awareness of 149–54, 172
–and communication 99, 156–7, 197
–gaming/simulation approach 157–8
–low-context (LCC)/high-context (HCC) 169–76, 273–4, 281
–organisational 226, 235, 282–3
–*see also* communication, intercultural; meanings
CULTURE CONTACT simulation 157, 197
CULTURE GAME, THE 157, 167
Culture shock 156–8, 162, 167–8
Cunningsworth, A. & Horner, D. 99
CUTS GAME, THE 241
Cynicism, personal 134–5, 137–8, 140n.

D'Arcy, J. 3
Data, collection 55, 75–6
De Saussure, F. 21
Deaf
–education 119–21
–problems of communication 117–19
–use of simulations by 121–5, 281
Debriefing 12, 109, 172, 174, 210–11, 260, 274
–for counsellors 149, 153–4
–learning through 112, 114–15, 116, 121, 165, 200
–and reality 17–19
–and representation 18–19
Deceit 179, 184
Decision-making
–in media 257–62
–simulations used in 117, 122–5, 198–9, 210, 238–41, 245–6, 250–3
Decrementalism 240–1
DeFleur, M.L. 6
Denkin, N.K. 110
DENTIST simulation 243, 246, 282
Design, simulation 22, 48, 167, 270
–guided 122
Determinism, cultural 70, 72, 110

Deutsch, M. 23, 129–30, 132
DEVELOPMENT GAME, THE 29n.
Dialogue 43–5, 49, 269–70
Differentiation, social 162, 164
Dilemma counselling 86–7
DIPLOMACY board game 223–4
Discourse rehearsal, *see* rehearsal, simulation as
Discrimination 155, 160–2, 165–8, 281
Dissonance, cognitive 131–2, 157, 218
–in simulations 132–5, 137–9, 243, 273
Domination, cultural 160–1
Donnellon, Anne xiii, 69–81, 271, 278
Donnerstein, E. & Hallam, J. 181
Double bind 142, 145
'Double-interacts' 236–7
'Double-settingedness' 58–9, 276
Duke, Richard D. xiii, 11, 21, 33–52, 269–70
Dumas, Philippe xiv, 201–13, 282
Dunleavy, P. 249

Economy, political, in planning 249, 251, 253
Education
–business 191, 195, 201–13
–computerised simulation in 83–90
–for hearing impaired 119–21
–simulation in 12, 25, 117–26
–*see also* classroom
Egan, G. 148
Egocentrism 143–4, *see also* self
ELIZA computer program 86
Ellington, H. I. & Addinall, E. 198
Emotion, in simulations 114, 115, 273
Empathy 136, 144, 145, 148, 165, 174–5, 204, 227
English, as second language 118, 124, 281
Erickson, F. 72
Error cost, and use of simulation 13–14, 15, 98, 148, 157, 257–8
Ethics, and communication 224
Ethnocentricity 128
Ethnomethodology, and gaming/simulation 53–68, 71, 271, 276
EXCAVATION OF OBJECT C-9, THE, computer simulation 89–90
Expectation, in interaction 54, 71, 74, 110–11, 112–13, 156–7
Expert, outside 152–3
Expertise, power of 231–2

Facilitator 96, 122–3, 144, 150, 154, 200, 203, 204
Fact, and inference 151, 159–60
FALSE ALARMS, CASE OF THE 122–5
Faludi, A. 253
Feedback
–need for 6, 35, 52, 74, 114
–in simulation 152, 209–10, 221, 244
–written 122–5
Fernandes, James xiv, 117–26, 281
Festinger, Leon 131, 273
Filley, A. 184
FILM INDUSTRY, THE simulation 261
Finniston Report 194
Fisher, D. 5
FISHING TRIP 124
Folger, J.P. & Poole, M.S. 130
Forester, J. 253–4
Forms, communicative 39–43
Francis, David xiii, 53–68, 271, 276
Freeman, James xiv, 201–13, 282
Friedman, J. 239
FRONT PAGE simulation 197, 258
Frude, N. 86–7
Frustration 178, 184
Fujio, Masayuki 140n.
Futures, modelling 243

Gagnon, J. H. & Greenblat, C.S. 278
Gallaudet University, use of simulations 117, 120–6, 281
Game 13, 14–16, 23–4
–educational xii, 203
–as locally managed interactional order 54, 58–76
–in socialisation 110–11, 112

–team-based 207, 208–9, 224, 258–62
Gaming 14, 145, 243
–network 102
–theory 67
Gaming/simulation 33–52, 270
–business games 201–13, 282
in business schools 203–4
communication in 202–3
development 201–2
in firms 205–12
scheduling 205
and communication 36, 49–51, 52, 53–4, 67, 182–6
and conflict resolution 133–5
definition 33–4
evaluation 165–7
as language 37, 269
learning through 203–4
model in 48
players and organisers 63, 65–7, 275–6
and pulse 48–9
as reality 14–15, 46, 48–51, 54, 58, 61–3, 67, 167
and representation 15
as research tool 167–8
resistance to 165–6
as teaching competition 183–6, 273
see also ethnomethodology; prejudice
Gardner, R.C. & Lalonde, P.N. 97, 98
Garfinkel, H. 71
Gatekeeper 261, *see also* information, control
Gergen, K.J. 73
Gestalt communication
–in gaming/simulation 49–51, 167
–need for 36, 39, 42, 43–6
GHETTO simulation 115–16
Goffman, E. 15, 28n., 141–2, 144, 145–6
Goodin, R.E. 245
Goshko, J.M. 128
GRAIN DRAIN, THE 29n.
Grammar-translation method 94
Gray, T.G.F. 195–6
Greenblat, C. S. & Gagnon, J. H. 274–5
Greenblat, Cathy xv, 269–83
Greenfield, P. 85
Group
–judgements 160–1
–work in 122–5, 195, 198, 274
Guided Design, Center for, West Virginia University 122

Hall, E.T. 169–70
Handel, W. 71
Harms, L.S. & Richstad, J. 9
Harper, S.N. 98
Harvey, J. 178
Hayakawa, S. I. 183
Hearn, Jeff xv, 236–46, 270, 273, 282
Hennig, M. & Jardim, A. 228
Heuristics, need for 43–4, 51, 52, 167
Hofstede, G. 173
Holism, *see* gestalt communication
Holmes, B., Whittington, I. & Fletcher, S. 83–4
Horowitz, D.L. 23
HOTEL RECEPTIONIST simulation 99
House drawing task 153–4
HUMANUS simulation 116
Husband, C. 10

I, in socialisation 109–11, 112, 116
Iacocca, Lee 179, 186
ICONS (International Communication and Negotiation Simulation) 83, 89, 102–4, 106n.
ICS (Interactive Communication Simulations) 106n.
Identification 159
Identity management 58–65
Immersion teaching 95, 102, 205
Improvisation
–in interaction 71–2
–in simulation 59–64
Incrementalism 238–40, 241, 244, 249, 271
Individualism 170–3, 175
Induction, simulation in 205, 206–7, 282

Inference 159
  –and fact 151, 159–60
Information
  –business 203–4, 209–10, 218, 221, 223, 282
  –control of 247, 250, 252–4, 274, 283
  –and prejudice 159–60
Information theory 6–7, 21, 35
Ingroup/outgroup 128, 160–6
INTERACT II 185
Interaction, para-social 86–7
Interaction, social
  –as contingent 54, 70
  –counselling in 147–8
  –as locally orientated 54–5, 58–67, 71–2
  –patterns 34–5
  –as preprogrammed 69, 72
  –and simulation 20, 26, 165, 262–5
  –structures 69–72
  –studied through media 262–5
  see also context; culture, low-context/high-context; improvisation; negotiation
Interactionism, symbolic 109–16
  –and simulation 111–14
INTERACTIVE SYNECOLOGY simulation 132
Interpretation, in communication 7
Irwin, H. 196, 197–8
Israel, urban planning 252–3
Ivey, A. E. 148

Jandt, F.E. 129, 132
Janis, J.G. 138
Japan, as high-context culture 170–1, 174
Jaques, D. 221
Jargon, problem-specific language as 51, 52, 85
Jefferson, Gail 68n.
Jensen, Marvin xiv, 141–6, 278–9
Jones, K. 98, 100, 101, 263
Jones, L. 100
Jorgensen, K. 28
Journal writing 109, 112–13, 115–16

Kanter, R.M. 226
Katz, E. & Lazarfeld, P.F. 262
Kay, A. 82
Keats, J. 16
King, M., Novik, L. & Citrenbaum, C. 177
Kirk, G. 249
Klabbers, Jan xv, 236–46, 270, 273, 282
Koestler, A. xvi
Kohn, A. 182
Kok, G.J. 161
Kolb, W. 110
Kuhn, Thomas 128, 137–8, 279

Label exercise 151–2
Labov, W. 94
Laing, R.D. 142
Language
  –and communication 223, 245–6
  –and perception 121
  –problem-specific 51
  –simulation as 13, 21–2, 26
Language acquistion, and hearing impairment 118, 124
Language, foreign, right to learn 93
Language simulation 86–7
Language teaching
  –Audiolingual Method 94–5
  –communication in 91–2, 93–7, 270
  –communication through simulation 97–100, 101–4
    examples 100–1
  –Communicative Language Teaching Approach 95
  –Community Language Learning 95
  –Direct Method 94
  –Grammar-Translation method 94
  –immersion programmes 95
  –Natural Approach 95
  –Silent Way 96
  –Situational 94
  –Suggestopedia 95
  –Total Physical Response 95–6
Lasswell, H.D. 6
LaVine, Roberta xiii, 91–106, 270–1
Law-Yone, Hubert xv, 22, 247–55, 270, 277
Lawrence, E. 10

Learning
 –communication in 35
 –cross-cultural 169–76
 –differential 275–6
 –experiential xi, 171–2, 173, 183, 203, 259, 273, 278–9, 282–3
LEARNING GAME, THE 184–5
Lee, J. R. E. 16, 27
LeVine, R.A. & Campbell, D.T. 128
Lewin, K. 262
Lobuts, John xiv, 177–87, 273
Logical types, theory of 142
Long, M. 98
Long, N.E. 247
LOST ON THE MOON 184
LUGS simulation 239
Lundberg, G.A. 6

MacBride Report 6, 8, 10, 22
McLuhan, M. 7, 265
McMahon, L., Barrett, S. & Hill, M. 224
McMahon, Laurie xiv, 214–25, 279
Makedon, A. 145
Maley, A. 96
Management
 –and communication process 214–19, 221–4, 244–6
 –simulation in skills training 207–12, 231, 279, 282
Managerialism, in planning 249, 251
MANEDES computer simulation 84–5, 101, 265
Manis, J.G. & Melzer, B.N. 111
Mann, 138
Mapping 13, 45–8, 51, 177
Marshall, S., Ellington, H.I., Addinall, E. & Percival, F. 198
Marshall, Stewart xiv, 191–200, 257, 274
MARY ROSE computer simulation 83–4, 282
Maslow, A.H. 144
Materials, teaching 100–1
May, R. 144
Me, in socialisation 109–11, 112, 116
Mead, G.H. 109–11
Meanings
 –communication as exchange of 7, 21–2, 25, 151, 177, 242
 –and culture 151, 155, 156–8, 160, 237
 –in foreign language learning 95
 –in simulation 17
Media 7, 233
 –in Communication Studies courses 192–3
 –definition 256
 –effects 256–7
 –influence on competition 181–2
 –internationalisation 92–3
 –simulation in 21, 29n., 197, 256–66, 282
 –and study of interaction 262–5
 –training in 257–8, 261–2
Meier, R.L. 247
Meltzer, B. 109–11
Merton, Robert K. 128, 161
message 6–7, 8, 26, 35–6, 149, 151, 154, 226
 –exchange in gaming/simulation 49–51
 –mediation, *see* media
 –simulations 219–21
MICROLANGUAGE simulation 121
migration 93
MIJN MAAT IS MIJN MAAT 163–4
Milgram, S. 29n.
Mills, C.W. 111
Minorities, cultures 93
Mintzberg, H. 207
Model 13, 16, 21, 45–6, 48
Moore, O.K. & Anderson, A.R. 35–6
Morokoff, P. 180–1
Morrow, Lance 145
MORTAL REMAINS computer simulation 90
Motivation
 –in communication 35, 103, 195, 197–8, 281
 –in language-learning 96, 98, 105n.
 –in training 206
Multilingualism 91, 92–3, 104
Multilogue 33–4, 36, 46–51, 269–70

Negotiation
 –in classroom 84–5, 121

–in communication 7, 21–2, 25, 65, 69–70, 72, 73, 270
–in FL communication 102–3
–high/low-context cultures 170–1, 172, 173–4, 175–6, 274
–hostage 139
–in media communication 262–3
–in organisations 215–16, 222–4
–in policy formation 240–4
–in simulation 17, 169, 234
–in socialisation 111, 180, 182
–*see also* business negotiation game
Networks, women's 226, 227–32, 234–5, 282–3
NEWSIM simulation 260–1
NICKEL AUCTION, THE 184
Noesjirwan, J. & Freestone, C. 167
Noesjirwan, Jenny xiv, 155–68, 271, 281
Noretsky, Martin xiv, 117–26, 281

OIL THREAT TO RADLEIGH simulation 99
Opinion, collective 243
Oppenheimer, J. & Winer, M. 29n.
Organisation
–communication process in 214–25
–influence on communication 221–2
–*see also* culture, organisational
Organisation theory
–micro-political paradigm 215–18, 219, 223–5, 279
–rational paradigm 215, 217–18, 219, 222, 279
Osborn, Alex 122
O'Sullivan, T., Hartley, J., Saunders, D. & Fiske, J. 256
O'Sullivan, Tim xv, 256–66, 282
Other, generalised 109–11, 113, 116
Oxford, Rebecca xiii, 91–106, 270–1

Parnes, Sidney J. 122
Particularisation, social 161–2
Patterns
–communication 20, 22, 26, 102, 109, 176, 253
–culturally learnt 153–4, 185
Pearl, D., Bouthilet, L. & Lazar, J. 181
Peck, M. 177
Pederson, Anne and Paul xiv, 147–54, 271, 274, 281
Peers, pressure from 275–6
PENGUINS OF DEATH, THE, computer simulation 84
Pennewill, Carol xiv, 177–87, 273
Perception
–barriers to 43–5, 46, 178, 184, 225
–development of 143, 177
–distortion 178–9, 221
–and language 121
–and prejudice 158–60, 162
PERFORM simulation 243, 246, 282
Perspective, shift 237, 242–4
Petranek, Charles xiii, 273
Piaget, J. 143
PICTURE STORIES simulation 99
Pidgin Sign English (PSE) 120, 124
Planning
–and control 247
–in simulation 69, 72, 73–4, 239–40
–urban 239, 247–55
and communication structure 248–54, 270
Israel 252–3
simulations of 247–8, 253–5
technical/bureaucratic/political views 248
see also policy formation
PLATO computer program 86–7
Play
–in learning xii, 99, 109–16
–as rehearsal 14
–in socialisation 110–11
PLEA BARGAINING 112–13
Pluralism, in planning 248–9, 251, 253
Policy formation 237–8, 270
–middle-term perspective 241–4
–multi-actor model 238
–short-term 238–41
see also planning, urban
Postman, N. & Weingartner, C. xii

Power
–corporate 244–5
modes of 229–34
women's access to 226–9, 282–3
–and planning 248–9
–and prejudice 155, 156, 158
–and reading of texts 7, 21, 23
Power bargaining 222–4, *see also* negotiation
Power, J. 239
Prejudice 155, 158–62
–gaming/simulation approach 162–8, 281
Preparation, in socialisation 110, 112, 271
PRIMITIVE POLITICS 223
PRISONER'S DILEMMA 20, 133–5, 137–8, 184
PROBLEM SOLVING, GUIDED 122
Problem-finding 211
Problem-solving 130, 131, 135, 194
–simulations used in 117, 122–5, 198, 211
see also counselling
Program, for interaction 70–1, 72, 80n.
Projection, in interaction 73, 136
PROTEINS AS HUMAN FOOD 198
Pruitt, D.G. 130
Psychology, social experiments as simulations 18–19, 29n.
Pulse 48–9

RADIO COVINGHAM simulation 99, 197, 258
Reading, for fluency/accuracy 102
Realism, political 129, 134, 137
Reality
–and early socialisation 110, 111, 158–9
–testing, in socialisation 111
Reality strategies 177, 245
Realpolitik 129, 134
Reasoning, practical, and interaction 54
Receiver, role 35, 43, 149, 156, 195, 203, 274
Reference 237, 242–4, 246
Rehearsal
–discourse 69, 73–80
as event 73–4
as process 73–4
–simulation as 24, 26, 278
Relations, international, in simulation 102–4, 133–7
Research
–need for 272
–simulation in 12, 25, 167–8
–suggested topics 273–6
Rhyne, R.F. 36
Richmond-Abbott, M. 233
Rivers, W.M. 94
Robinson, James 139
Rogers, C.R. 144
Role
–conflict 141–3, 145–6, 174, 275–6
and simulation 143–5
–models 182, 230–1
–rehearsal 110
–reversal 163–4, 171
–transcendence 143–5, 278–9
ROLE TRANSCENDENCE simulation 143–5
Role-play 13, 15–16, 97, 110–11, 183, 235, 240–1
–in business games 204
–and conflict resolution 135–9
–in counsellor training 148
–in media simulations 263–4
see also play
Roweis, S.T. 253
Rules
–creation 70, 121
–in interaction 54, 78–9, 110–11, 113, 156, 161, 170, *see also* selection
–in model and simulation 13

Sacks, H. 60, 71
Sacks, H., Schegloff, E. & Jefferson, G. 71
SALE OF A NEWSPAPER, THE simulation 258–9
Sanday, P. 180–1
Sandole, Dennis J.D. xiv, 127–40, 273
Sapir-Whorf hypothesis 121

Saunders, Danny xiii, xv, 3–29, 82–90, 91–106, 256–66, 270–1, 275, 282
Saunders, Danny & Crookall, David 99
Scarcella, R., Crookall, D. & Ting-Toomey, S. 98
Scheflen, A.E. 70
Schelling, T.C. 24
Schemata, linguistic 245–6
Schofield, A. 197
Schutz, A. 143, 156
Schutz, A. & Luckmann, T. 54
Scott, W. 194
Search, normative 243
Selection, from behaviour repertoire 70, 73, 74–80
Selection, staff, simulation in 207
Self, in socialisation 109–11, 112–13, 142, 146
Self-communication 109, 111, 112–13, 115–16, 143
Self-knowledge 114–16, 165, 278
Self-reference 236–7, 241, 244, 246
Sequence, in language and communication 35–6, 37–9, 43–4, 48, 55, 71
Shaffer, Peter, *Equus* 141–2
Shannon, C. & Weaver, W. 6
Sharrock, W.W. & Anderson, B. 27
Sherif, M. 23, 29n., 168
Sherif, M. & Sherif, C.W. 164
Shultz, George 128
Sigman, Stuart xiii, 69–81, 271, 278
Sign language 121, *see also* American Sign Language; Pidgin Sign English
Sign systems 7, 21
Silent Way 96
Sillars, Alan 128, 131–2
SIMSOC simulation 112–13
Simulation
 –assembly 60–1
 –and communication skills 121–5, 196–200, 218–24, 226
 –computerised 82–90, 101, 102–4, 202, 212, 245–6, 264–5, 275
 –definition 33–4, 150
 –evaluation 277–83
 –interactive 241–4
 –as interdisciplinary 4, 11, 19–27, 197
 –intergroup 171–5
 –as language for learning 11–12, 183–6
 –as multi-disciplinary 4, 20, 23, 104
 –in policy formation 238–44
 –as reality 12, 15, 16–19, 21–2, 97, 99, 102, 105n., 113–16, 196
 –as representations 12–14, 15, 16, 18–19, 21, 150, 167, 196, *see also* games; role-play
 –as socially constructed 17
 –in women's networks 227–9, 231–2, 234–5
 see also communication/simulation; counselling; interactionism, symbolic; language teaching
Simulation/gaming, *see* gaming/simulation
Skills
 –business, simulation in 205, 207–12, 279
 –communication 274–5, 277
  in education 121–7, 194–200, 225
  for women 227–35
 –leadership 227, 231, 233–5, 283
 see also counselling, microskills
SLICK simulation 209
Snyder, Mark 128
Snyder, Mark & Gangestad, S. 128
Social learning theory 181
SOCIAL SERVICES RESOURCE ALLOCATION GAME 240
Socialisation 118–19, 153, 156, 158
 –and simulation 109, 111–14, 116
Speech, inner, *see* self-communication
Spontaneity
 –in communication 41–2, 112, 145
 –in socialisation 110–11
STARPOWER simulation 99, 164, 273
Stereotypes 162–3, 171, 229, 231, 233–4

Stern, Barbara xiv, 226–35, 271, 282–3
Stevenson, A. 141
Stone, G.B. 110
Strategies
–communicative 70–1, 98, 274–5
–in model and simulation 13
Stress, personal 141, 146, 180
Structures, collective 236–8, 241–3, 246
Style, social 80
SUMAH simulation 157
SURVIVAL GAME simulation 100
Symbols, use in gaming/simulation 13, 21, 51
System, social
–communication processes 238–44, 270
–structures 236–8, 241–2, 271
Systems Dynamics Approach 243

TAFFS PIT simulation 263
Tajfel, H. 10, 29n., 158
Teacher
–as facilitator 96, 122, 173–5, 203, 204
–role in language learning 96–8
Teaching, methodology 195–200
Technology
–communication 34–5, 244–5
expansion 8–9, 21, 92, 104
–as sequential 36
Telecommunications 104
TERRI simulation 100
Terrorism 127–9, 139
Text 7, 21, 257, 259, *see also* media
Thomas, W. I. 16, 28n.
Time, attitudes to 170–1, 174–5
Ting-Toomey, Stella xiv, 169–76, 271, 273–4, 281
Torrington, D. & Weightman, J. 218
Training
–refresher, simulation in 205, 212
–remedial 212
–simulation in 12, 25, 56–67, 117, 124–5, 132–3, 148–54, 168
business games 204, 205–7, 282
Transmission, communication as 6, 7, 21, 35, 39, 42–5, 218
–simulations 219–21
Truth statement 150–1
Tufte, E.R. 276
Turn-taking 98

Uncertainty, in simulation 239–41
United States, as low-context culture 170–1, 174
URBAN DYNAMICS simulation 239

Values, cultural 156, 166–7, 169–75, 182, 184, 234, 273
VALUES AUCTION GAME 232
Versluis, Edward xiii, 82–90, 264, 275, 282
Video, interactive 35, 265
Vygotsky, L.S. 143

Wales, C.E. & Stager, R.A. 122, 124
Walster, E. & Berscheid, E. 138
Wargames 23–4, 209
Watson, D.R. & Sharrock, W.W. 97, 276
Watzlawick, P., Beavin, J.H. & Jackson, D.D. 144
Weick, K. 236
Weizenbaum, J. 87
WELSH COMMERCIAL TELEVISION STATION, THE 264
WESTERNPORT COMMUNICATION SIMULATION 197–8, 219, 239
WHAT'S NEWS simulation 260
WHISPERS simulation 219–21
Williams, R. xi–xii, 192–3
WINE LAKE simulation 100
WOMAN EXECUTIVE/MALE SECRETARY simulation 231
Women, and corporate culture 226–35, 282–3
Wynn, M. 253

YELLOW RIVER KINGDOM simulation 100

Zero-sum strategies 24, 136
Zimbardo, P. G. 29n.